HOUSING *& the Democratic Ideal*

THE COLUMBIA HISTORY OF URBAN LIFE

KENNETH T. JACKSON, GENERAL EDITOR

THE COLUMBIA HISTORY OF URBAN LIFE

KENNETH T. JACKSON, GENERAL EDITOR

HOUSING & *the Democratic Ideal*

The Life and Thought of Charles Abrams

A. Scott Henderson

Columbia University Press

NEW YORK

Columbia University Press

Publishers Since 1893

New York   Chichester, West Sussex

Copyright © 2000 Columbia University Press

All rights reserved

Library of Congress Cataloging-in-Publication Data

Henderson, A. Scott.

Housing and the democratic ideal : the life and thought of

Charles Abrams / A. Scott Henderson.

p. cm.

Includes bibliographical references and index.

ISBN 0-231-11950-X (cl) — ISBN 0-231-11951-8 (pbk.)

1. Abrams, Charles, 1902–1970. 2. Housing policy—

United States—History—20th century.

3. Sociologists—United States—Biography. I. Title.

HD7293 .H464 2000

363.5'092—dc21

[B]   00-020693

Casebound editions of Columbia University Press books

are printed on permanent and durable acid-free paper.

Printed in the United States of America

c 10 9 8 7 6 5 4 3 2 1

p 10 9 8 7 6 5 4 3 2 1

To: M. H., R. H., and R. P.

Contents

Acknowledgments

I owe thanks to many people for helping me complete this book. During my initial investigations, Michael Ebner, Eugenie Birch, and Ken Jackson confirmed that no full-length study of Charles Abrams existed; I appreciate their encouragement of me to undertake such a project. Herbert Finch and Lorna Knight, archivists at Cornell University and curators of the Abrams papers, provided crucial assistance whenever I called upon them. Archivists and librarians at other institutions also provided significant help. These institutions include: the Archives of American Art, Buffalo State University, Clemson University, Columbia University, Columbia University Oral History Project, Erie County Public Library, Furman University, Georgetown University, John F. Kennedy Presidential Library, LaGuardia and Wagner Archives, Library of Congress, New School for Social Research, New-York Historical Society, New York Public Library, New York State Commission on Human Rights, Princeton University, Social Welfare History Archives, State Historical Society of Wisconsin, State University of New York at Buffalo, University of California at Berkeley, University of Pennsylvania, and Yale University.

Comments made by Ed Larson, Richard Harris, and Bob Bainbridge on chapters 2, 9, and 10, respectively, pushed me to revise my analyses of important topics. Insights from several anonymous readers were also helpful. Additional comments, assistance, and suggestions were given by Judy Bainbridge, Chris Blackwell, Tom Bolze, Jim Boylan, Susan Cahn, Fritz Casey-Leininger, Bob Catlin, Donald Critchlow, Brenda Custard, Lois Dean, Casey Dolgon, Steve Dyson, Bob Fairbanks, David Freund, Eric Fure-Slocum, David Gerber, Laurence Gerkens, Gary Gerstle, Ron Granieri, Charles Haar, Steve Halpern, James Harper, A. V. Huff, Aimee Kaplan, Michael Katz, Andy Kersten, Thomas Kessner, Robert Kolodny, Jackie Leavitt, Alan Lessoff, Chuck Lipp, Zane Miller, Ray Mohl, Paul Moreno, Rich Newman, Dave Nolan, David Perry, Paul Piccard, Robb Pruitt, David Schuyler, Joel Schwartz, David Shi, Terry Simpson, David Spear, Hans B. C. Spiegel, Tom Sugrue, Kristin Szylvian, Roy Talbert, Bernard Taper, Walter Thabit, Tadzui Trotsky, Alex von Hoffman, Ron Walters, and Marc Weiss.

Two individuals deserve special recognition. Gail Radford first suggested that I incorporate a state-building perspective into my analysis. Moreover, her enthusiasm and interest checked my many periods of self-doubt and frustration. Her scholarship continues to influence my thinking and writing. Mike Frisch provided detailed and insightful comments on every chapter. His immense knowledge of urban history and politics was an invaluable resource, without which my arguments would have been far less cogent. I am fortunate to have benefited from his mentorship and friendship, both during and after my formal academic training.

I greatly appreciate the assistance of Tim Rogers, who read the entire manuscript and offered valuable suggestions. I would also like to thank the editorial staff at Columbia University Press, especially Kate Wittenberg, Leslie Bialler, and James Burger, for their patience, advice, and skillful editing.

Special thanks go to the late Lloyd Rodwin, who graciously shared his memories of Abrams. Equally helpful were Abby and Judy Abrams. Time after time they clarified my understanding of their father and mother. Without their cooperation this book would not have been possible. I take full responsibility, however, for any and all errors of fact or interpretation.

Finally, I wish to thank my family. My parents always encouraged my interests, making numerous sacrifices in the process. My father, a wise and uncommonly decent man, did not live to see this book; nevertheless, he made characteristically constructive comments on an earlier draft. Perhaps the biggest debt I owe is to Richard. Only he knows how words alone will never adequately express my thanks.

HOUSING *& the Democratic Ideal*

Introduction

❖

INTELLECTUALS, HOUSING POLICIES, AND STATE EXPANSION

Public and Policy Intellectuals

Between the 1930s and the 1960s, Irving Howe, Alfred Kazin, Lewis Mumford, Charles Abrams, and others traversed the political and cultural landscape, presenting their observations in popular periodicals. With eloquent prose and colorful anecdotes, they discussed issues affecting millions of people. By doing so, they sparked national debates in which the well-read, if not formally educated, public could join. They also, to borrow the title from a recent book, illustrated the "power of public ideas," ideas defining the ends and means of "public action." Scholars and editorialists have lamented the disappearance of these individuals from American life, and their commentaries often emphasize an important point: "public intellectuals" could explain complex subjects to lay audiences.[1]

Among his peers, Charles Abrams was unmatched in this ability to communicate to the public. As a lawyer, college professor, urban reformer, author, lecturer, government official, and housing consultant, Abrams often had to discuss programs and policies with which even an

informed audience was unfamiliar. He eagerly responded to the challenge, filling the pages of *The Nation, Commentary, Survey Graphic, The
New Leader,* and the *New York Times* with lucid explanations of mortgage
financing, civil rights legislation, government policies, and urban renewal. If these issues had seemed arcane to most readers, Abrams' discussions made them understandable, even compelling. His studies of cities
and urban life became manifestos for almost two generations of students, scholars, and activists. Yet, when Abrams brought these sometimes
contentious topics into the public spotlight, he was able to distinguish
the fine line between polemic and persuasion.

Had Abrams simply remained a commentator or explicator of current issues, little would have distinguished his contributions from the
academic analyses of a Sidney Hook, or the more idiosyncratic exposi-
tions of an Irving Kristol. But unlike the majority of public intellectuals,
Abrams was also a policy intellectual—someone who actually developed
and administered government programs. This required both creativity
and political savvy, a combination Abrams advocated in a 1945 review of
Lewis Mumford's latest book: "Planning for city development must move
forward from the drafting of plans to include the drafting of statutes, to
the understanding not only of what the legislation means, but how to
secure its passage." While other public intellectuals engaged in literary
shuttle-diplomacy among various magazines (or lived in relative seclu-
sion writing books, as Mumford did for the last thirty years of his life),
Abrams crisscrossed the larger gulf separating the worlds of thought and
action. For him, action usually meant problem solving, something he
approached by linking his theoretical knowledge with lived experiences.
This was the key to his initial policymaking success, which underscored
his talents as a doer and a thinker. Given the drift toward think tanks
staffed by pundits with little if any hands-on experience, Abrams' ability
to move easily between analysis, advocacy, and the fray of politics was
indeed impressive.[2]

The contemporary press is awash in articles bemoaning the "self-
inflicted irrelevance of American academics" and the plummeting position of "professors" in opinion polls. Abrams' accomplishments speak to
this predicament as well. Despite a lack of formal education, he was an
intellectual in the Enlightenment sense of being an expert and a critic.
As an expert, he faced the uneasiness American society has historically
manifested toward intellectualism. Conversely, as a critic of housing,

banking, and urban renewal policies, his perspective provided him with social utility, at least in the minds of the public. Not everyone agreed with him; sometimes he had only a few adherents. His critiques, however, were connected to relevant issues. When they seemed otherwise, he persuaded readers and listeners to the contrary. His activities thus serve as a counterpoint to present-day intellectuals who have isolated themselves from general readers, or who have lost the ability to explain the salience of specific issues.[3]

Abrams' undertakings also addressed larger themes. He championed various policies because he assumed a democratic society was obliged to provide its citizens with equal rights and certain social provisions, such as affordable housing and municipal services. We would miss much, though, if we viewed Abrams only as an exemplar of twentieth-century political impulses. Rather than being an analog to the rise of the New Deal state, Abrams' career was the story of how a successful businessman became an influential scholar and policymaker whose *opposition* to certain aspects of centrist liberalism situated him to the *left* of the New Deal. This distinguishes him from other "New York Intellectuals," who, as Alexander Bloom has observed, "began as radicals, moved to liberalism, and sometimes ended up as conservatives."[4]

Abrams found himself on an ideologically divergent path primarily because he believed a "general welfare state" was slowly giving way to a "business welfare state." This involved a subtle but important distinction. During the 1930s, policymakers decided the most appropriate method for delivering social services was by giving subsidies and incentives to business interests, rather than by providing direct benefits to the public. Such an arrangement, according to Abrams, was undemocratic since it blurred the line between public and private power. Phrased differently, granting public power to private interests resulted, more often than not, in the "perversion" of social reform. Nowhere was this clearer than in policies sanctioning discrimination against African Americans. The Federal Housing Administration's (FHA) explicit support of racial segregation in its loan guarantee programs was only the most blatant example of how private sector discrimination was tolerated, even condoned, by public agencies. Abrams identified comparable outcomes in a range of other programs, including urban renewal. He also believed private sector abuses influenced the public sector to act in a correspondingly unethical manner, especially when dealing with the issue of race.

Though Abrams failed to convince contemporaries that his fears were justified, their reluctance to share his apprehension revealed crucial assumptions about policymaking, state expansion, and race.[5]

In order to assess the interaction between an individual (a public/policy intellectual) and the times in which he lived, the present study is necessarily biographical. In other respects, it is not a conventional narrative. To understand the process of state-building itself, the following pages examine the history of American social policy and the ways other scholars have analyzed the growth of government programs. A brief review of the recent literature indicates how Abrams' life relates to these broader issues.

The State as a Topic of Analysis

An expanding national government has been one of the signal characteristics of American history since 1900. Three intense periods of state-building (the Progressive Era, the New Deal, and the Great Society) created policies, programs, and agencies touching virtually every citizen. Proliferation of administrative regulations and new programs on the state level occurred as well. These developments dramatically altered the nature of intergovernmental coordination, the balance between public and private interests, and the relationship between individuals and government.

For decades historians have recognized the significance of these changes, but methodological inadequacies and shifting intellectual concerns limited their analyses. Traditional political history, periodized by presidential elections and constructed as top-down narratives, could not fully explain the complexity of modern state-building. Ascendant in the late 1960s, "new social history" minimized the role of the state, focusing instead on race, ethnicity, class, and gender. Even the emergence of "new political history" in the 1970s, which represented renewed interest in state expansion, provided few insights about policy outcomes, largely because of its emphasis on the cultural and socioeconomic dimensions of American political regimes. Historians therefore contributed relatively little to our initial understanding of why government programs emerged, prospered, or failed.[6]

Scholars in other disciplines, including political science, sociology, and public administration, filled this void. The work of Theda Skocpol and her colleagues in the 1980s was especially influential in generating new theoretical considerations pertaining to state-building. Her research resonated with the investigations of a small number of historians examining what they called the "organizational synthesis"—in short, the rise of bureaucracy (broadly embodied in corporations, "experts," and administrative structures) as the touchstone of contemporary social organization. Both the Skocpol group and "organizational" historians underscored the importance of internal influences on private and public decisionmaking. For Skocpol, this concern emerged as a polarization between "state-centered" and "society-centered" analyses. A state-centered approach emphasizes the role of administrators, policymakers, and institutional "capacities," while a "society-centered" approach stresses the importance of outside influences (political parties, court decisions, and social groups) on policymaking. Though this bifurcation was primarily a heuristic device, it reinvigorated interest in the growth of national states and their policies.[7]

Inspired by the scholarship Skocpol and various scholars had generated, a cross-section of historians turned their attention to similar issues beginning in the late 1980s. Among other topics, they examined the regulation of nuclear energy, welfare assistance for single mothers, social security, the interaction of private and public charity, and family-planning policy. But like their predecessors, these historians generally ignored the field of housing. Indeed, during the past four decades there have only been a few historical investigations of national or local housing policies.[8]

This inattention is unfortunate because housing policies were—and continue to be—significant government interventions. For example, subsidized housing projects have transformed many American cities, providing thousands of individuals with decent shelter while creating high-rise ghettos for thousands of others. Government lending and credit policies have also been critical forces. The Home Owners Loan Corporation acquired approximately one-fifth of the urban mortgage debt during the 1930s. Related programs presently insure countless numbers of private mortgage lenders against default. And, though most home owners prefer to think of their mortgage interest deduction as a right instead of a federal subsidy, this exemption amounts to more than $50 billion in lost revenues every year. Less well known but equally

important has been the establishment of a government-sponsored secondary mortgage market. It includes the Federal National Mortgage
Association ("Fannie Mae") and the Federal Home Loan Mortgage
Corporation ("Freddie Mac"), which were the largest servicers of corporate debt in the United States by the early 1990s. These programs, taken
together, have influenced the growth and reach of the federal government in ways that are still not clearly understood.[9]

State-Builders and Biography

This discussion returns us full circle to Abrams and the milieu of policy
intellectuals. Abrams' endeavors provide an ideal vantage for viewing
the relationship between housing policies and government expansion.
His career also allows us to investigate the assumptions associated with
state- and society-centered analyses. Following him through the historical thicket of administrative and legal battles from the 1930s onward
confirms the necessity of using both frameworks. In short, Abrams'
experiences in housing and antidiscrimination efforts—plus his critique of a "business welfare state"—demonstrate that policymaking was
a complex, highly contingent phenomenon. Government officials, partisan politics, intergovernmental conflicts, court decisions, interest
groups, and institutional "capacities" were all, at various points, determining factors.[10]

Abrams' journey also enables us to understand more clearly the content of state-building. It does so by revealing mid-twentieth-century
beliefs over how liberalism was supposed to work in a technical sense
(interest-group brokering); what liberal policies were obliged to accomplish (equality, but within a capitalist economic system); the mechanisms
decisionmakers used to effect policy goals (fiscal and monetary incentives); and why race became the most divisive aspect of American political discourse.

In trying to capture a historical figure from both a narrative and an
analytical perspective, limitations are apparent. First and foremost, this is
not a detailed account of every event in Abrams' life. I have omitted some
of his personal activities and even elements of his professional career. My
approach concentrates on those episodes illustrating his growth as a
thinker and policymaker. To this extent, what follows tends to have an

intellectual focus; nonetheless, I think readers familiar with Abrams primarily (or only) through his antidiscrimination crusades will be surprised by the breadth of his endeavors. Where necessary, details have been included to add texture and substance to the portrait of someone who was a very energetic, stimulating, and humorous individual. These sections also attempt to show how Abrams' temperament and personal characteristics either aided or hindered him in his undertakings.

Chronology presents other problems. For the most part, I have told a story defined by the boundaries of Abrams' life. Deviations, though, have been unavoidable because of the plethora of his activities, the complexity of issues he confronted, and the necessity of providing historical contexts to policy developments. Chapters are therefore grouped both sequentially and thematically. Chapters 1, 2, and 5 describe Abrams' immigration to America, his childhood in New York City, the evolution of his legal career, and his early scholarship. Chapters 3 and 4 examine Abrams' role in creating and helping run the New York City Housing Authority. This material helps us evaluate the influence of (and obstacles faced by) public officials as they tried to implement particular policies. Chapters 6 and 7 analyze Abrams' concept of a business welfare state and the conflicts that type of state engendered. Chapters 8, 9, and 10 focus on Abrams' involvement in antidiscrimination battles, international assistance programs, and urban renewal, respectively. They also link these specific topics to a broader discussion of state expansion. Finally, chapter 11 uses the last few years of Abrams' life to provide a coda to his accomplishments and to the arguments advanced in previous chapters. Of course, lives are not lived in neat little boxes—or in chapters with concise introductions and conclusions. Keeping this in mind, I did not ignore Abrams' inconsistencies or ambiguities, but have tried to identify and explain them.

Chapter One

IMMIGRATION AND COMMUNITY IN THE
EXPANDING METROPOLIS

The story of Charles Abrams begins with his birth in Tsarist Russia in 1902. Few records exist, however, to document his life there or his immigration to America. He never wrote an autobiography, and his oral memoir at Columbia University provides no details about his childhood or adolescence. Besides obituaries and entries in biographical reference works, the only extensive source of information concerning Abrams' early life is a two part "Profile" published by *The New Yorker* magazine in 1967. Written by a friend of Abrams, Bernard Taper, the article is insightful and highly engaging, but it is not a detailed account of Abrams' journey to America or a day-by-day narrative of his initial experiences in Williamsburg, Brooklyn.[1]

While our ability to re-create Abrams' upbringing and family life is circumscribed, we can nevertheless reconstruct the contexts in which they occurred. These contexts—immigration, urbanization, state expansion, and the creation of community life—are in no way incidental to Abrams' subsequent concerns. The processes shaping his own life were the very ones he would later analyze as one of the country's leading urbanists. Understanding the relationship between him and his early environment not only sheds light on the young—and mature—Abrams, it also helps us appreciate some of the fundamental forces at work during the early part of the twentieth century.

Coming to the United States

In 1900, the Abramses were among the thousands of Jews crowded into the slums and tenements of Vilna—then in Tsarist-controlled Poland, now in Lithuania. Like other Jews, Abrams' parents, Freda and Abraham, faced dim economic prospects. Freda was the daughter of a bookkeeper, a modestly remunerative occupation, though no evidence indicates her father was able to assist his son-in-law's growing family (there were four children: Joseph, Ralph, Charlie, and Esther). Abraham worked for a time on a communal farm, making him part of the tiny percentage of Jews who were agricultural laborers. These workers often supplemented their insubstantial incomes by peddling various items in a nearby city, an activity many of them, including Abraham, would pursue in America. By the latter half of the 1890s, overcrowding—a result of the residential restrictions placed on Jews—caused economic conditions to deteriorate further. Poverty increased dramatically, and the number of Jews dependent on charity or community assistance eventually reached 40 percent in many areas, with the figure probably higher for Vilna.[2]

Even those Jews who escaped poverty through steady employment received minimal wages and often faced intolerable work conditions. An 1892 petition to the Governor of the Vilna province complained about toiling regularly from 7:00 a.m. to 11:00 p.m. As discontent grew over this exploitation, so did the appeal of socialism. A number of Jewish socialist organizations merged in 1897 to form Der Bund, the "League of the Jewish Workingmen of Lithuania, Poland, and Russia," which held its first convention in Vilna that same year. The Bund inspired some Jews, like Sidney Hillman, to organize and educate Russian workers. Hillman would immigrate to the United States and become head of the Amalgamated Clothing Workers of America, where he would nurture a social-democratic strain within organized labor, and more broadly, within liberal Democratic politics. Years later, when Abrams entered the world of politics and policymaking, he would not do so by organizing the rank and file, as Hillman had, but by writing legislation on their behalf.

Ironically, in Russia the Bund might have affected the Abramses and other Jews in unintended ways. Because of its failure to make significant improvements in the lives of most workers, it underscored the misery and limits to reform in Russia, as well as the advantages of immigration.[3]

The Abramses' physical environment would have matched their economic status, combining elements of an industrializing urban center (overcrowding, unemployment, poor sanitation) with the traditionalism of Jews newly arrived from small villages (*shtetls*), where spiritual and communal solidarity were common. The tension between the *shtetl* and the city, between the sense of community found in villages and the anonymity of metropolitan life, was a challenge immigrants would confront again in urban America.[4]

This cultural antagonism paled in comparison to the discrimination and oppression Jews faced in Russia. By the end of the nineteenth century, more than a thousand laws and decrees regulated virtually every aspect of Jewish life. Even Vilna's population, usually divided along ethnic and linguistic lines, had "achieved a splendid unity in a deep and frank hatred of the Jews." Immigrant Jews would not soon forget the state-sanctioned discrimination that had limited their freedom of movement, their choice of jobs, and their ability to sustain religious and social traditions. These collective memories made American Jews generally supportive of civil rights struggles, and critical of any use of government power to perpetuate discrimination. Abrams would leave no doubt as to his own feelings about publicly sanctioned segregation: "It is when compulsion appears in any form that segregation becomes invidious, and when the segregation is in public institutions, practiced by public agencies, or with the use of public funds, the segregation is unlawful."[5]

In light of economic privation and ongoing persecution, Abraham Abrams decided to take his family to America. Many Jews decided to emigrate at this point because of the Kishinev massacre. Over a three- day period in 1903, mobs roamed the streets of Kishinev, the capital of Bessarabia, murdering 45 Jews and injuring nearly 600 more, all with the approval of local and regional authorities. This incident caused international outrage and triggered renewed efforts the following year to help Jews emigrate from Russia. The Abramses' decision to leave their native land in 1904 was therefore a logical, perhaps unavoidable step.[6]

Russian Jews commonly used several routes to reach European ports. Like the Abramses, emigrants leaving from northwestern or northern

Russia frequently traveled to Berlin, then to Bremen or another north-ern port for embarkation. Others made their way through Russia to Baltic ports such as Libau or Riga. Traveling to these ports presented its own set of hazards and obstacles. Since Russian law did not officially rec-ognize the right to emigrate, those seeking to leave Russia spent large sums purchasing passports and bribing border officials. Once on ship, emigrants usually traveled for six to twelve days in steerage with 800 to 1,000 others, though by 1900 some steamship lines offered an upgrad-ed steerage class providing improved sanitation and separate staterooms with six to eight berths. Even regular steerage rates, however, were expensive. Trips from Bremen to New York averaged $33.00–$36.00, and from Antwerp to New York, $29.00–$34.00, amounts poor families could raise only after selling all their possessions and using what little savings they had accumulated. Some individuals received financial assis-tance from the Baron de Hirsch fund, a philanthropic trust established to aid Jewish emigration, but despite this aid, many newcomers arrived in America virtually penniless.[7]

Immigrants entering New York harbor with the Abramses were part of a demographic revolution already underway. Between 1900 and 1910, more than nine million individuals came to America, nearly one-third the total number of immigrants who had arrived since 1820. Deviating from previous patterns, this wave of immigration, lasting from the early 1880s to the early 1920s, included a significant number of Southern and Eastern Europeans, which the press and policymakers referred to as "new immigrants." National and local commentators, agitated over the appearance and prospects of these groups (especially the more than one million Jews who arrived during the first decade of the twentieth century), feared the shiploads of "ignorant and brutalized peasantry" might diminish the "quality of American citizenship." While these nativist con-cerns proved unfounded, the influx of immigrants did have a significant impact on American cities, especially in the Northeast and Midwest. Immigrants fueled population growth, channeled urban development, and created new ethnic neighborhoods and communities.[8]

Despite being "greenhorns" themselves, the Abramses joined a large, well-established Jewish presence in New York City. East European Jews had initially settled in the older German neighborhoods of the Lower East Side, where they supplied a sweatshop labor force for the clothing industry. Many of the heaviest concentrations of Jews were in the Tenth

Ward, an area characterized by overcrowded tenements housing 524 people per acre by 1890, qualifying it as the most densely populated section of the city. Significant numbers of Jews also lived across the Bowery in the Sixth Ward and across Division Street in the Seventh Ward. By 1899, 72 percent of all Jewish immigrants entering America had given New York State as their destination, a statistic that would help give New York City a Jewish population of one million by 1910, the largest of any city in the world.[9]

Even as the U.S. Industrial Commission reported in 1901 that the "newly arrived Russian Jew is kept in the crowded East Side," both old and new immigrants were beginning to move to other areas throughout the metropolitan region. The opening of the Williamsburg Bridge in 1903, the extension of subway service to Brooklyn in 1906, and the completion of the Manhattan Bridge in 1909 linked downtown factories and markets to the communities of Brownsville, New Lots, and Williamsburg, making Brooklyn a potential home for both settled and "new immigrant" Jews. Describing as well as spurring its growth, the local press called Brooklyn a "Promised Land" for Jews and compared it to boom towns in the Old West. Between 1903 and 1904 the population of Brownsville increased from 40,000 to 60,000, causing contemporaries to assert "Judah" had "driven the Scot out" in this soon to be "greatest of Jewish cities." City life, symbolizing state oppression in Russia, could represent an entirely different constellation of meanings for immigrant Jews in America.[10]

The Dynamics of Metropolitan Growth

After a long journey across the Atlantic, and after going through the rigors of Ellis Island, the Abramses settled in the Williamsburg section of Brooklyn. Williamsburg, initially part of the town of Bushwick, was eclipsed by the shadow of its metropolitan neighbors during the first half of the nineteenth century. Its sleepy existence came to an end when it became part of Brooklyn in 1854. The area prospered economically, its population soared, and East European Jews quickly displaced Germans as the neighborhood's dominant group.[11]

The Abramses moved into a six-story building resembling Brooklyn's other 36,000 tenements. They managed to squeeze into a three-room apartment, but just barely. Abrams and his brother Ralph shared a tiny, windowless room whose sole bed was so narrow they had to sleep with their arms around each other to keep from falling off. The apartment had no heat or hot water, only a coal-burning cookstove. Each floor had a toilet, though there were no bathing facilities, a problem noted throughout New York City by the Tenement Committee of 1894. One of the Abramses' secular rituals was a weekly trip to the nearby public bathhouse, Bershadsky's Baths, which Abrams would later joke had probably inoculated him against the multitude of diseases his United Nations missions exposed him to. Whether tenement life represented upward or downward mobility for the Abramses cannot be determined. Whatever the case, Abrams certainly became acquainted with the kind of dilapidated housing most immigrants and the working poor occupied.[12]

While the Abramses' immediate neighborhood was Williamsburg, their larger world was Brooklyn. This suburban frontier represented as well as any American city the potential and the problems of immigration, industrialization, and urbanization. Initially settled in 1636, Brooklyn's proximity to New York City helped it become one of the nineteenth century's first commuter suburbs. Completion of the Brooklyn Bridge in 1883 contributed to additional demographic and economic growth, and by the 1890s Brooklyn had become a manufacturing and commercial center in its own right. Even before twentieth-century bridges made Manhattan more accessible, Brooklyn was a magnet for immigrants, largely because of its growing industries, relatively cheap housing, and plentiful economic opportunities. As early as 1890, it had 261,700 foreign-born residents, a number almost equal to the city's entire population three decades before.[13]

By 1900, Brooklyn's boosters marveled about the rate at which their borough was growing. During 1904, all previous building records had "gone to smash," with new construction totaling almost $46 million, 85 percent more than the previous year. New apartments and tenements accounted for a significant part of this increase, and their presence confirmed one of Brooklyn's many appellations: "borough of tenements." By the spring of 1904, over a thousand persons a week were crossing the Williamsburg Bridge, the so-called "Jews' Highway," in search of shelter in Brooklyn. Street widenings, drainage projects, extension of sewer and water service, bridge repairs, and tunnel excavations were other manifestations, albeit sometimes costly and inconvenient ones, of the area's vitality.[14]

Assessing these trends, the *Brooklyn Daily Eagle* confidently concluded the borough was going to be a "big town and a rich one." Underlying this sentiment was an assumption held by municipal officials throughout America. Growth, even largely unfocused growth, was seen as the best safeguard against economic downturns and social unrest. Admittedly, some reformers and planners—sensing the potential problems that uncontrolled development might present—introduced novel strategies to rationalize the expansion of late-nineteenth-century cities. But two of the most popular ideas, the "City Beautiful Movement," inspired by Chicago's Columbian Exposition in 1893, and "Garden City" planning, pioneered by the English visionary Ebenezer Howard, never received widespread support in the United States. As Abrams would accurately remark, the former was a "romantic concept" that "faded into history as speculation and the quest for profit became the dominant forces." In regard to the latter—and Howard's claim it would result in "a new hope, a new life, and a new civilization"—Abrams would provide an equally suitable epitaph: "A new hope there was, though a new life can hardly be ascribed to it, and a new civilization is still a long way off." The failure of these ideas to influence municipal leaders meant American cities remained relatively unplanned until after World War I.[15]

The same individuals who hailed metropolitan growth as a sign of ineluctable progress generally failed to note the conflicts and disruptions it caused. For instance, in 1903 construction of the Delancey Street approach to the Williamsburg Bridge left ten thousand people homeless; completion of the Manhattan Bridge would have a corresponding impact a few years later. In both cases, thousands of individuals were uprooted, and by reducing the supply of housing, such projects tended to inflate rents for remaining accommodations, an increase many tenants could not afford. Among contemporary observers, Abrams would be one of the first to stress the need to account for these factors in clearing slums and building low-income housing.[16]

If expansion created problems for Brooklyn's infrastructure, it also triggered conflicts among various racial groups. Unlike other large northern cities between 1900 and 1920, and in marked contrast to Harlem's rapid growth, Brooklyn possessed a relatively small African-American population. This, however, did not make whites any more tolerant of blacks. Residents of Fort Greene Place became "greatly perturbed" in 1894 when they learned Hiram B. Thomas, a college educated "colored" man, had purchased a home in their neighborhood. Fearing a decline in property values, they advised him to "remain out of Fort Greene Place, at least as a resident." A decade later, when three African-American families moved into apartments vacated by whites in East New York, a "race-riot" ensued, caused in part by the rumor that "black tots" had "mingled" with white children. The inability of Brooklyn's African Americans to live where they wished was a stark refutation of America's profession of equality. Abrams might not have been aware of this as a youth, but as an adult he described the effects of intolerance with precision: "The neighborhood is the most sensitive area of prejudice; once activated there, prejudice may take its toll in a mass exodus by the inhabitants or in a concerted effort by them to exclude the stereotyped group." He would spend much of his professional life grappling with this problem.[17]

Brooklyn's development during Abrams' childhood paralleled that of other major cities, and seemed to confirm Frederic Howe's observation that the city had become "the central feature in modern civilization, and to an ever increasing extent, the dominant one." Trying to understand this phenomenon, scholars created models to explain how and why cities grew. Perhaps no one contributed to this endeavor more than Robert Park, a sociologist at the University of Chicago, who concluded that cities were the result of natural processes; indeed, he felt urban growth most often resembled the spread of plant communities. This organic ("ecological") model tended to subordinate the sources of political and economic power to large, impersonal forces. Working against the grain of Park's ideas and prevailing assumptions in the nascent urban planning discipline, Abrams would insist on linking these broader forces with specific actions taken by municipal officials, developers, and entrepreneurs. For him, conscious calculations—not intangible processes—determined the size and location of industrial activities, the availability of housing, and the racial composition of neighborhoods.[18]

Creating Community

Upon settling in their new homes, immigrants had to find work. For some, such as the Romanian-born Marcus Ravage, obtaining employment was an arduous task full of frustration, humiliation, and self doubt.

For others, getting a job proved fairly easy, either because they possessed marketable skills, or because they had family and/or friends already in America. Lacking these abilities or connections, Abraham Abrams entered the humblest and least risky entrepreneurial activity: he became a street vendor. The life of "pushcart men," as vendors with mobile carts were often called, was neither easy nor lucrative. Working punishing hours and earning just enough to survive, they sold an assortment of goods and comestibles. At the time of Abraham's arrival, New York City was attempting to control the proliferation of the Brooklyn pushcart trade by confining it to a section underneath the Williamsburg Bridge. While there were spaces for only 300 vendors, the Bureau of Licenses continued to issue peddling permits as long as applicants could produce the four-dollar fee. By the time the Williamsburg market opened in the summer of 1904, more than 1,000 peddlers were competing for a third as many spaces, causing agitation and confusion.[19]

The pushcart fiasco illustrated how Progressive concerns (in this case, enforcement of sanitation ordinances) and the tenets of professional city management could have disruptive consequences unless decision-makers had a clear understanding of local institutions. A happy ending, though, was in store for the pushcart men. Continuing altercations and subsequent protests by the New York Peddlers' Benevolent Association brought an end to the new regulations; within a few weeks, pushcarts once again filled the streets and sidewalks. Still, a variety of anti-pushcart laws remained on the books, and perhaps fearing trouble from the police, Abraham rented a space in front of the building across the street from his apartment. On that spot, he sold herrings, pickles, and a few other items.[20]

With Abraham's steady but meager wages (probably no more than $12.00 to $15.00 dollars per week), the family's financial security remained precarious. Astounded by the wages skilled labor could command in America, immigrants were equally shocked by the cost of basic commodities. Periodic swings in the nation's economy often threatened the subsistence existence immigrants found so difficult to maintain even in good times. The depression of 1907–1908 was especially harsh, causing widespread suffering and deprivation, which self-help and charitable organizations could only partially ameliorate. For the first time in its history, United Hebrew Charities had to suspend its operations. During periods like this, according to *The New Yorker* article, Freda Abrams—a strong but proud woman—could not bear the shame of others finding out her family did not have enough money to eat adequately. She would cover pots of boiling water on the stove to create the illusion that she was preparing a substantial meal.[21]

Though the impact of early-twentieth-century depressions on eleemosynary institutions was severe, a variety of charitable organizations could and did aid immigrant Jews. Strong cultural traditions within the Jewish community, including self-help and mutual aid, were the impetus behind establishment of the New York-based Educational Alliance, United Hebrew Charities, the Hebrew Free Loan Society, and various institutions in Brooklyn, including the Jewish Hospital, the Brooklyn Hebrew Orphan Asylum, and the Hebrew Educational Society. Other organizations developed as well, including *Landsmanshafts*, groups of immigrants from the same town or region in Europe who joined together for social and economic purposes. The growth of these institutions—some transplanted from Europe, some developed in America—was further stimulated by America's dearth of direct benefits to the indigent. When available, public assistance was only "in proportion" to the degree that they poor were willing to help themselves. Abrams would be part of a political revolution in the 1930s liberalizing America's niggardly forms of public assistance, transforming what he called a "laissez-faire state" into a "general welfare state."[22]

Abraham Abrams might not have received economic aid or belonged to a *Landsmanshaft*, but Williamsburg was home to a large number of Polish, Russian, and Lithuanian Jews whose heritage of persecution and immigration provided the basis for friendships and mutual support. Granted, a shared past did not eliminate all divisions among immigrant Jews. Tensions existed between German and East European Jews, between Williamsburg Jews and Brownsville Jews, and between the tenets of Hassidism and Haskala. Nonetheless, knowledge of Yiddish allowed immigrant Jews to interact in the common culture of *Yiddishkeit*. Yiddish was also the language of the *Jewish Daily Forward*, a Brooklyn newspaper founded in 1897 that kept immigrants informed about current issues and offered advice on numerous topics, including traditionalism and assimilation.[23]

The creation of new communities did not prevent bigotry and discrimination from being a daily experience for many Jews. On June 5, 1904—the very year the Abramses came to America—a gang of twenty street toughs "savagely attacked men, women, and children," "smashed show windows," and destroyed property along Wallabout Street in Williamsburg, inflicting severe injuries on more than a dozen people. These and other incidents led Jewish leaders to form the Jewish Protection Association and to petition local authorities for greater assistance against anti-Semitic violence. In taking such actions, Williamsburg's Jewish immigrants realized America was not entirely unlike the world they had left, a world where being different could make one a target of hatred and violence. Fashioning identities in the New World was therefore sometimes as much a response to external factors as it was an expression of long-held cultural beliefs and practices.[24]

Poverty, discrimination, and ethnic fissures complicated the lives of immigrant Jews, but in the Abrams household familial bonds remained strong. The children, especially the three boys, were close and would remain so the rest of their lives. Probably because he was the youngest son, Abrams had a special relationship with his father. From the time he was a small child, he got into the habit of waking when Abraham returned home for the night. Sitting at the kitchen table, they would drink a pot of tea and discuss various subjects. Perhaps Abrams and his father spoke about the day's business transactions, the younger Abrams' day at school, current social and political issues, or life in Vilna. Whatever they discussed, Abrams, whose formal education would remain limited, believed much of his learning had come from these sessions. Summing up his feelings toward his father, he would remark: " 'There was something noble about everything he did.' " For Abrams, his father could even make selling pickled herrings a " 'courtly and humane transaction.' "[25]

Abrams contrasted his father's quiet dignity with his mother's dynamism. She was the guiding influence behind her children's goals and ambitions, urging them to " 'make something of themselves.' " That insistence, coupled with economic necessity, compelled the school-aged Abrams to hold a series of part-time jobs, a common situation among immigrant children. The first job he had was as a lookout in front of the tenement while his family surreptitiously wrapped herrings, pickles, and pickled onions to sell to their neighbors. With a characteristic pun, Abrams later described this activity as a " 'fragrant violation' " of Sunday work laws. By age nine, he was taking outside jobs, including a brief stint as a horseradish grinder. In high school he worked as a lamplighter for the Brooklyn Edison Company. At twilight he would put on a pair of roller skates, then zoom along Lafayette Avenue, Myrtle Avenue, and down to Fort Greene Park, lighting the neighborhood; at dawn, he would retrace his steps, extinguishing the lamps. Abrams soon quit that job and went to work in the Manhattan office of Western Union, where his salary increased from $4.00 to $12.00 a week. The trade-off was a grueling schedule. He worked an eight-hour shift, which started at 5:00 p.m. and ended around 2:00 a.m.[26]

The City as Text

Part-time jobs also functioned as Abrams' introduction to the modern city, to its diversity and cosmopolitanism, and to its slums and poverty. As Abrams traversed the streets of Brooklyn and commuted into the teeming heart of Manhattan, the rich, ever changing environment awakened and stimulated within him a remarkable visual perceptiveness that enabled him to analyze cities in a unique, almost intuitive way. The text for Abrams' knowledge about urban life was not books, museums, or lectures, but the city itself. In addition to its physical form, Abrams was also interested in its inhabitants. To make this point, he would often quote Socrates: "Fields and trees teach me nothing, but the people in a city do."[27]

While Abrams was learning about urban form out of necessity, two other individuals—who, like Abrams, never learned to drive automobiles—were wandering the streets of New York City. Lewis Mumford, one of the twentieth century's foremost authorities on the history of cities, had been taking walks around Manhattan since 1899. These outings introduced him to great educational institutions, such as the American Museum of Natural History and the Metropolitan Museum of Art. Above all else, Mumford's perambulations gave him the ability to "read buildings" like "so many pages in a book." The simile was appropriate since Mumford would achieve his greatest acclaim by writing lengthy studies of the world's cities.[28]

Another person who was viewing the city by foot was Robert Moses. Born into a wealthy family in 1888, Moses had grown up first in New Haven, then in an affluent neighborhood on East Forty-Sixth Street in New York City. As a student at Yale, Oxford, and Columbia, Moses spent summers in Europe, absorbing the architecture of its cities. He augmented his education by visiting New York's various neighborhoods and museums. The young Moses also took late afternoon walks through the six-mile-long Riverside Park—more wasteland than park—where he envisioned how he could make the entire stretch into a "wonderful scenic highway." Moses would build that highway and many more, forever transforming the city's landscape.[29]

Abrams certainly had more in common with Mumford than Moses. The two remained good friends for more than two decades, possessing a similar perspective on urban problems and often swapping books they had authored. The two also shared an animosity toward Moses. Mumford relentlessly criticized Moses' policies, frequently paying him backhanded compliments: " 'In the twentieth century, the influence of Robert Moses on the cities of America was greater than that of any other person.' " Abrams felt likewise. " 'In my opinion,' " he argued, " 'under present redevelopment laws, Macy's could condemn Gimbels—if Robert Moses gave the word,' " a remark intended as a jab at Moses as much as it was a criticism of the Housing Act of 1949.[30]

These affinities notwithstanding, the course Abrams steered would take him further and further from Mumford's moorings. Mumford knew how to communicate to a broad audience—as evidenced by his monthly "Sky Line" column in *The New Yorker*—but his writings regularly struck a tone of uninviting erudition. He would coin words (for example, "eotechnic"), yet they hardly had the colloquial resonance of Abrams' neologisms. Another way of describing their differences is in terms of Mumford's abilities as a policy intellectual. If "policy" refers to an active role in creating or implementing programs, and "intellectual" to critiquing certain initiatives, then Mumford ended up embracing the latter almost to the exclusion of the former.[31]

Moses offered a different set of contrasts. Like Abrams and Mumford, he had an idealistic streak; the "idealist," however, soon gave way to the "power broker." In this persona, he did not speak *to* but *at* the public, condemning any and all dissenting opinions. He quickly lost sight of what made cities decent and livable places, and thus moved from the "intellectual" to the "policy" end of the spectrum. In short, he would become more concerned with implementing policies than with their consequences. Abrams would find this approach unacceptable, protesting Moses' near obsession with superhighways and his support for projects such as Stuyvesant Town, which provided a significant amount of new housing, but at the cost of excluding African Americans. Moses, for Abrams and many others, came to represent the essence of undemocratic policymaking.[32]

Abrams' own career, though shorter than either Mumford's or Moses', would take a middle path between the two better known individuals. Similar to Mumford, Abrams worked from a set of first principles that defined ideal cities and communities. He was able, however, to go beyond this abstract stage—to convert mental blueprints into reality—because of his sense of timing and political strategy, something Mumford never possessed. Nor was Abrams as constrained by politics, or as concerned with power, as Moses. He used the distance of scholarship to evaluate various policies and their effects, unlike the typically unreflective Moses. Abrams himself was aware of these differences. In an unpublished review of Cleveland Rodgers' 1952 biography of Moses, he wrote: "The most important contributions of men like Moses are not as project-builders but as inspirers of the public-spirited and the young, the visionaries, the castle-builders, the frontier-breakers . . . the very men Moses did so much to impugn, frustrate, and discourage." Even Mumford, a modern-day stylite speaking truth from above, did comparatively little to inspire students or activists directly. Abrams, the genial seminar leader, author, and civil rights crusader, would fill this niche.[33]

Origins of a Reformer

If being an immigrant Jew, growing up in Brooklyn, and working in Manhattan during a period of frenetic urbanization affected Abrams' ideas about cities, one is prompted to ask if his physical environment also motivated him to become a social reformer. While his surroundings might have predisposed him to be an advocate for those without resources to defend themselves, the historical record does not suggest so simple or direct an equation. Admittedly, given subsequent standards of health and hygiene, the Abramses' tenement, coupled with their meager income, defined them as poor. Some friends and colleagues would argue these conditions had a lasting effect on Abrams. Echoing this belief, the New York Post eulogized that "construction of Williamsburg

Houses, near the site where [Abrams] himself had grown up, in a slum, was one of the major satisfactions of his life."[34]

Abrams himself offered another version of his childhood. He told Bernard Taper his personal experiences were not the primary reason he became a reformer; it was frustration over the irrationality of the nation's housing situation. Furthermore, he remembered life in Williamsburg as "endlessly stimulating," his family surrounded by a "warm circle of neighbors." Abrams even subsequently claimed he was unaware he had grown up in a slum until he provided the New York City Housing Authority with a legal definition for one.[35]

These interpretations are not necessarily irreconcilable. A combination of factors was probably responsible for Abrams' almost four-decade quest for better (and open) housing. His childhood was indeed relatively unscarred—giving him no immediate reason to become a social activist. Other individuals and groups, he later concluded, were *forced* to remain in slums, either because of poverty or discrimination. Such conditions were intolerable in a society based on the premise of equality. Since he could envision democratic alternatives to existing urban patterns, and since he felt he possessed the legal and political skills to help bring them about, Abrams eventually embraced the career of a reformer.

As a reformer, Abrams was neither judgmental nor moralistic. He assisted a wide range of people, intent on changing their circumstances, not their attitudes or beliefs. On a personal level, this generosity of spirit manifested itself in a variety of ways. Abrams would invite friends—and friends of friends—to stay at his house, occasionally for extended periods of time. He would also, according to Taper, aid them financially:

One friend, down on his luck after running through a small fortune, used to come into Abrams' office every week for money to keep him alive. The stipend always included an extra twenty dollars to bet on the races. Abrams never lectured his irresponsible friend or sought to reform him, believing that to this man being alive meant being able to gamble—that was the way he was.[36]

Even as a young man, Abrams mused over the other directions his life might have taken. In a letter to his sister in the mid-1930s, he wondered "what would have happened to all of us if Papa had not had the courage to leave for America thirty years ago." In answering his own question, he humorously opined: "Joe would have been milking cows, Ralph in the salt mines of Siberia for crap-shooting, and I would be some kind of rebel banished from the . . . government." The actual course of events for Abrams proved almost as exciting. By the end of his childhood, he had been a participant in some of the modern age's great transformations. He was a Polish Jew who had journeyed to the United States, a country whose cities both shaped and were shaped by immigrants. The new landscape of skyscrapers, factories, and tenement houses produced an array of emotional responses from those who worked and lived in them. Hope was possible because cities were growing at an unprecedented rate, offering seemingly limitless opportunities for geographic and social mobility. But despair often traveled in hope's wake: cities could be sites of enormous suffering and centers of racial and ethnic strife. Amid these conflicting fears and desires, and surrounded by the din of the expanding metropolis, Abrams realized communities could take many forms—and even flourish in the midst of profound poverty. These experiences and observations would remain with him for the rest of his life and, by degrees, influence his role both as a policymaker and an intellectual.[37]

Chapter Two

LAW, REAL ESTATE, AND PRAXIS

The decade of the 1920s was an important stage in Charlie Abrams' life. Like many Jewish immigrant families, the Abramses encouraged and supported intellectual ambitions. Nevertheless, economic necessity ruled out a traditional education for Abrams; instead, he attended night law school while clerking in a lawyer's office. This path to a legal career was becoming increasingly uncommon after World War I, but it was just the route some contemporaries insisted was a integral part of professional training. Abrams' life during this period also coincided with changing perceptions over the role of experts in public service. Social scientists were calling on intellectuals (broadly defined) to become more involved in policymaking and administrative reform. Abrams' background and aptitudes were consistent with the characteristics this new vanguard of civil servants would need to possess. On a related front, Abrams' involvement in Greenwich Village real estate gave him detailed knowledge about property transactions and finance, as well as lifetime economic security, freeing him for other pursuits. Finally, and no less important, the Village—especially its social tolerance—would become the kind of community Abrams extolled the rest of his life.

Education and *Tachlis*

Immigrant Jews took advantage of educational opportunities in America, especially since their admission to secondary schools and universities had been severely restricted throughout Russia. In New York City, public high schools and at least one tuition-free university, City College, allowed Jews to pursue their academic and vocational interests. Joseph Freeman, who became one of the founding editors of *Partisan Review*, described the social mobility he and other immigrants believed would result from education: "We would study hard, develop our minds, and through them rise to higher rungs of the American ladder whose top was in the clouds." The Yiddish concept of *tachlis* often informed and reinforced this utilitarian aspect of education. The term is somewhat ambiguous, in that it can refer to an individual's search for an adequate livelihood or to the goals one pursues. Financial concerns would initially define Abrams' *tachlis*; later, his professional activities redefined it and pointed him in the direction of social reform.[1]

Jewish children in Brooklyn could begin their education in one of the area's public institutions, or they could attend a *Heder*, a Hebrew elementary school. Desiring assimilation, increasing numbers of Jews enrolled in the former. By 1918, less than one-fourth of New York City's Jewish population was receiving any religious education at all. Reflecting this trend, Abrams attended Eastern District High School in Brooklyn, where his school work competed for time with the demands of home and part-time jobs. One of the subjects he excelled at was public speaking. School officials often called upon him to recite well-known orations for visiting parents or dignitaries. Abrams would retain this interest and skill throughout his life. As he later stated: "I don't mind hearing myself talk and don't mind if others listen."[2]

Attending a college outside New York City would have been problematic, even had Abrams' financial circumstances been different. Despite the relative openness of secondary schools, university study for Jews in America was limited by quotas and anti-Semitism. This was likely one reason Abrams spent his freshman year at the Polytechnic Institute of Brooklyn. Founded in 1899 with a focus on science and mathematics, it offered five general courses of study, each of which took four years to complete. Several considerations probably contributed to Abrams' brief stay. If he had decided to pursue an engineering degree, a few courses in that discipline might have convinced him his abilities lay elsewhere. Eager to make his own way in the world, he might have also felt four years was simply too long to prepare for a career; as it was, he would mislead university officials about his age to avoid waiting another year before entering law school. A final and perhaps overriding reason for leaving Brooklyn Polytechnic was his need to work full-time. Abrams later gave credence to this notion, indicating he had pursued a law degree via part-time study because it enabled him to "work during the day."[3]

Abrams ended up attending Brooklyn Law School, which was initially affiliated with St. Lawrence University (the latter was more than 300 miles away, but it could confer law degrees, a privilege granted by state legislation). The school was a typical part-time institution. It was located in a large urban area, it had a relatively high percentage of first- and second-generation immigrants, and it concentrated on preparing students for the bar exam. Less typical, it also enrolled some women and African Americans, establishing a reputation for social nonconformity. The school's openness, streamlined course offerings, and flexible schedules were appealing to others besides Abrams. By 1928 it was the largest law school in the country.[4]

Though Brooklyn Law School was popular among New York City's polyglot residents, the American Bar Association (ABA) was increasingly critical of such institutions, primarily because of the number of "new immigrants" (namely, Jews) who attended them. In order to undermine the viability of part-time schools, the ABA successfully lobbied for measures to reduce their enrollments (for instance, requiring applicants to possess an undergraduate degree). Had these "reforms" been implemented a few years earlier, Abrams might have been forever barred from entering the legal profession.[5]

Evolving Trends in Legal Education

In addition to changes in admissions standards, curricular innovations were also affecting legal education. American jurisprudence had long envisioned the law as a set of immutable concepts based on universal custom and self-evident postulates. Lawyers and judges, by interpreting these precepts in a "mechanical" fashion, were supposed to reach consistent and equitable conclusions. In the late nineteenth century, some jurists began to criticize the law's reliance on logic; they even questioned whether "neutral" interpretive principles existed in the first place. For these so-called legal "realists," the law had to be studied as it operated within a value-laden context of political and policy choices. Similarly, scholars like Roscoe Pound at Harvard Law School advocated a "sociological jurisprudence" that stressed the social consequences of judicial decisions, not just the precedents justifying them. Uniting the two groups was their emphasis on first-hand experience as a supplement to formal course work. In his 1921 study entitled *Training for the Public Profession of the Law*, Alfred Z. Reed recommended a combination of "theoretical instruction" and "some sort of practical activity pursued outside of the school." The young legal scholar Jerome Frank agreed. He argued that law schools should include the "methods of learning law by work in a lawyer's office." Abrams doubtless enjoyed and benefited from this pragmatic approach to instruction at Brooklyn Law School. Equally significant, the clerkships Abrams held during his studies helped inculcate within him the "art" of legal practice. They also illustrated that the law was not just an arid collection of precedents, but a means for achieving specific political and social objectives.[6]

Abrams' longest and most influential clerkship was between 1920 and 1923 with Arthur Garfield Hays. Born in Rochester, New York in 1881, Hays was the son of an affluent clothing manufacturer who had named him after a series of conservative American presidents. Moving with his family to New York City in 1893, Hays worked his way through Columbia Law School and eventually developed a lucrative practice representing corporate and show business interests. He devoted some of his energies to other causes to make "living a little easier" for those who were "perennial victims of persecution." "To press for some cause bigger than oneself," he subsequently remarked, was "not necessarily noble," but "just about the best fun" for people with his "disposition." Hays was also one of the American Civil Liberties Union's (ACLU) first counsels, taking on numerous cases, including the Scopes "monkey" trial with Clarence Darrow.[7]

Hays became a professional and personal mentor for Abrams during his clerkship. They remained friends afterward: Abrams sent copies of his publications to Hays and spent evenings playing chess at his nearby home on East Tenth Street. Initially awed by Hays and hoping to win his favor, Abrams imitated his limp and even learned to smoke a pipe in what he hoped was a similarly contemplative manner (cigar smoking finally won out, a habit Abrams would be unable to quit, despite several attempts). Hays took a quick liking to his young clerk and soon gave him substantive assignments, including preparation of a brief for an important free speech case. Abrams also provided assistance and suggestions on one of Hays' less celebrated undertakings, the Fuller-McGee bucket-shop case (a bucket-shop was a corrupt brokerage house). For Abrams, working on this case was a crash course in free-market economics. Learning how stocks were bought and sold, becoming familiar with the laws governing these trans-actions, and discovering how individuals evaded securities regulations cre-ated the basis for Abrams' encyclopedic knowledge of modern finance.[8]

Hays' support of civil liberties, and the public debate it often gener-ated, impressed Abrams greatly. In the spring of 1922, Hays went to Vintondale, a company town in the coal rich hills of Pennsylvania, where he planned to hold a free speech meeting. Attacked by the "coal and iron police," he was thrown into jail for a few hours, an episode he described as "nothing to write home about." Nevertheless, the incarcer-ation illuminated one of Hays' strongest convictions: individuals had to be willing to go to jail to protect their beliefs. Abrams was inspired by this dedication—and stirred by the passion, excitement, and even drama that swept through the office whenever Hays was involved in a civil lib-erties case. Hays engaged in legal crusades with a Puck-like mischie-vousness, admitting the "fight for civil liberties" was what gave "salt" to his professional work. Hays' protégé would later appreciate the need for some "salt" in his own career, though unlike his mentor, who viewed lit-igation primarily as an educative tool, Abrams conceived of it as a forum in which actual justice could be served.[9]

Clerking for Hays also influenced Abrams' evolving political views. Associating himself with "liberals" and "progressives," Hays thought the defining qualities of these groups were an "open mind toward any proposition" and the absence of "dogma" determining "whether or not things are advantageous, depending upon whether they are labeled . . . as conservative, capitalist, or communistic." Abrams' opinions were remarkably similar. He believed effectiveness, not partisan endorse-ments should be the litmus test for any given policy. And because Abrams possessed an "open mind," he (like Hays) defied conventional political categories. This flexibility would aid him in crafting policies acceptable to both Democrats and Republicans.[10]

In sum, Hays demonstrated characteristics Abrams could admire and emulate. He combined a successful private practice with social idealism, possessed keen legal knowledge tempered by the grit of experience, and gave uncompromising support to civil liberties without being a pious moralist. Put another way, Hays provided a model for the kind of career Abrams might pursue, the type of politics he might espouse, and the *tachlis* he might embrace. As Bernard Taper subsequently noted, the clerkship with Hays "probably did as much to determine the direction of his life as anything else that happened to him."[11]

Starting a Career and Marrying an "Artist's Artist"

After passing the New York State Bar Exam, Abrams, with money borrowed from Hays, opened his own office in 1923 at 271 Madison Avenue. He hired Bernard Botein as his clerk. A junior classmate from Brooklyn Law School, Botein would later become one of Abrams' partners and Chief Judge of the Appellate Division of the New York State Supreme Court. Abrams quickly prospered as a corporate and trial attorney in both state and federal courts. His clients included the League of Business and Professional Women, the Latin American Division of the Democratic National Campaign Committee, Ernst Gruening (editor of *The Nation*), and Daniel S. Reardon (president of U.S. Trucking). Within five years, Abrams was earning $25,000 annually, a figure two and one-half times higher than the average salary of Harvard Law School graduates. Here was a level of success most immigrants could only dream of.[12]

Abrams practiced law for the rest of his life, eventually moving his offices to 225 Broadway. He did not, however, rely on that profession for his primary means of support. Early investments (especially in real estate) permitted him to reduce his case load and use his legal talents to write legislation and advance civil rights. What could have been a relatively simple journey from rags to riches became a more complex story of how Abrams used financial independence to pursue a life devoted to reform.[13]

The demands of his legal work did not preclude Abrams from having an active social life. A quirky coincidence brought him together with his future wife, Ruth Davidson. They had both been attempting to call a mutual friend when the phone company accidentally connected the two of them instead. A conversation ensued, and they decided to meet for a date that same night. The two enjoyed each other's company, and after a short courtship, they were married on December 22, 1928.[14]

Slightly younger than Abrams, Ruth was driven by a desire for self-expression. She had taken dancing, piano, and riding lessons as a girl. Later, pursuing an interest in art, she submitted a portfolio of drawings to Cooper Union College; they were summarily and humiliatingly rejected. She then explored the possibility of a writing career, but that, too, proved disappointing. Political and volunteer work left her equally restless. Nothing, it seemed, could take the place of her first love—art. Years later she would describe the appeal of painting: "As to why I paint, it is as difficult to account for as to why I love. It is, at times, as painful, as frustrating, as it is rewarding. In giving birth to a child (I have two) there is no thought of the labor pains after the baby has arrived. The painting that arrives is much the same thing—something that astonishes."[15]

Ruth spent the early years of her marriage continuing to hone her skills as a painter and sculptor. In 1933, when her mother died suddenly, she traveled to Mexico in hopes of assuaging her grief. Once there, she sketched the local scenery and inhabitants. After three months, Abrams became concerned. He wrote Ruth asking her when she planned to return. Upon receiving the letter, Ruth apparently concluded that she could not have a full-fledged artistic career and fulfill her duties as a wife. She stayed in Mexico almost another month, agonizing over the choice confronting her. Ultimately, she decided to return to New York City, but only after promising herself another trip to Mexico.[16]

Ruth never returned. Instead, her time was consumed by the responsibilities of being a wife, then mother. Further artistic development was relegated to spare moments at inconvenient times. Divided loyalties like these were not easy for women in the 1930s, 1940s, and 1950s. Ruth concisely outlined the predicament: "Families resent mothers who are all absorbed in something else. They demand an audience, and they are bound to interrupt." Resentment could and did exist in both directions. Ruth's letters to friends sometimes revealed impatience over the time she spent hosting parties and taking care of frequent house guests, despite the importance of such gatherings and individuals to Abrams' career. Ruth's impatience was exacerbated by her determination to achieve certain artistic goals. In 1934, gathering up her paintings, she got into a taxi and went to various galleries in search of a willing exhibitor. The director of the American Contemporary Art Gallery, impressed by her pieces, agreed to show them. The exhibition, which included eighteen paintings and seven sculptures, was a success. "Altogether it is an unusually promising first show," the *New York Times* reported. Several years later, with a feminist sensibility rekindled by the works of Virginia Woolf, Ruth set up her own studio in order to work without interruption.[17]

Another obstacle Ruth faced, one she would never fully overcome, was lack of recognition from the art world itself. Admittedly, she had admirers. Lewis Mumford commented on one of her exhibitions: "I have been waiting for thirty years for woman, in all her bodily fullness, to come back into painting: have almost felt that her reappearance would mark the beginning of a new age, no longer victimized by the machine. And now, in your paintings, you announce her return!" This public support was matched by professional integrity. Ruth would study with leading contemporary artists, such as William Zorbach and Alexander Archipenko; she would be involved in the Art Students League and provide the inspiration for New York City's Artists Club; and, among others, she would count Willem de Kooning as a friend. But acknowledgment and approbation from the wider circle of modern artists never came. Ruth's correspondence indicates her awareness of these snubs:

About the art world, much seems to be happening, but very well it would appear, without me. There is another Whitney opening of contemporary work in which I am inconspicuous for my absence, as I was in the Museum of Modern [Art], previously. Out-of-town museum representatives are currying the N.Y. scene for sculpture and painting, but I've not run into any of them as yet. I hear it from afar, and people both likely and unlikely have managed to make themselves visible as eligible.

Fearing others might be similarly ignored, Ruth stipulated that funds from her estate be used to finance triennial exhibitions at the Grey Art Gallery in New York City for artists in mid-career who believed they had been unjustly overlooked.[18]

Ruth's artistic endeavors and Abrams' career as an urban reformer would have more in common than the two might have initially predicted. In struggling to forge an identity outside of family life, Ruth would encounter prejudice among artists and savants. " 'Come to think of it,' " she would recall, " 'it was worse than being a member of a minority group. If you were Black or Chinese or whatever in the art world, you were still accepted—if you were a man.' "Abrams' own work would focus on eliminating discrimination, especially racial prejudice. Not being accepted by one's peers was also something with which Abrams would be able to empathize. Late in life, he chided Ruth: "You are too prone to judge success as your own artists tend to judge them, which is a brutal way of being judged. I go through the same ordeal. One's own profession is cruel and jealous." There was validity to Abrams' assertion; his social critiques, political commentaries, and policy proposals often flew in the face of conventional thinking. But there was a significant difference between the consequences resulting from their iconoclasm. In Ruth's case, failure to conform to professional norms meant disappointment and frustration. For Abrams, rejecting strongly held ideas and practices brought respect, sometimes even praise.[19]

Greenwich Village and the Virtues of Heterogeneity

Abrams and Ruth moved into a Greenwich Village apartment shortly after they married. The Village had been a "rural hamlet" throughout the eighteenth century, but by the mid-1800s small manufacturing establishments began to appear, along with low-rise tenements for the area's Irish, German, Italian, and Jewish workers. As the twentieth century dawned, the Village was suffering from many of the era's urban problems: overcrowding, poor sanitation, and declining property values. These conditions were actually attractive to real estate speculators; they seized opportunities, sometimes risky ones, to purchase cheap properties, make improvements, then sell them for handsome profits. By the early 1920s, the Village was being hailed as an "investor's mecca" whose domestic "charm" and "quaint" buildings were ripe for restoration.[20]

Speculative interest was also fueled by the literary and artistic avant-garde congregating in the Village's bookstores, coffeehouses, and studio apartments. These individuals helped give the Village a well-deserved reputation as the country's most popular and self-conscious bohemian enclave. Not all observers, though, assumed the area's metamorphosis was positive. Writing in the 1930s, Caroline Ware warned of the Village's decline from a neighborhood to a "heterogeneous city" that "reflected or prompted social instability . . . on every hand."[21]

Unlike Ware, Abrams saw heterogeneity as a positive aspect of community growth. He believed "diversity" was why the Village continued to be "one of the most stable areas in the city." Views to the contrary manifested what Abrams called "city hatred," the belief urban development was "inhuman" and "threatening to the moral life of society." Abrams admitted the Village "hybrid of 1910" had become the "mongrel of the 1930s," but it was an "interesting mongrel" composed of "some wealth on Lower Fifth Avenue," "poverty on Bleecker Street," "bearded beatniks brushing with bigwigs," "browsers and bookkeepers," and "tearooms, speakeasies, [and] steakhouses." Heterogeneity thus eliminated some of the reasons for urban decline, such as boredom and the "sameness" of daily life. Rather than cause anomie, it provided opportunities to "escape loneliness." Abrams' advocacy of diversity presaged the ideas of another noted urbanist, Jane Jacobs, who stressed the necessity of mixed populations and land uses. "In our American cities," Jacobs would argue years after Abrams had sounded a similar tocsin, "we need all kinds of diversity, intricately mingled in mutual support."[22]

Endorsing diversity tapped into a broader cultural current subsequently described as the "cosmopolitan ideal." Those who shared this "ideal" thought exposure to novel situations produced social and intellectual growth. Abrams agreed: the urbanite's "cosmopolitanism" was a source of "strength," not "instability." To this extent, Abrams' journey from Williamsburg to the Village can be seen as more than just a process of relocation. The affinity he had felt for family and religious ties gradually gave way to the appeal of an entirely different community, one celebrating intimate *and* impersonal relationships. Moving from Brooklyn to Manhattan also illustrated upward mobility and assimilation for Abrams and other immigrant Jews. In describing his childhood in Brownsville (Brooklyn), Alfred Kazin noted: "We were the children of the immigrants who had camped at the city's back door. . . . 'New York' was what we put last on our address, but first in thinking of the others around us." Abrams himself never explicitly made this connection, but his lifelong characterization of cities as places where socioeconomic mobility was possible—even encouraged—resonated with his own experiences.[23]

Once settled in their new home, Abrams and Ruth took advantage of the Village's varied offerings. Ruth benefited from the fellowship and encouragement of like-minded individuals who supported artistic experimentation. The Village also put some much needed physical distance between Ruth and Abrams' family, who scorned her flouting of Jewish traditions. (The strong-willed Ruth gleefully coordinated the observance of various holidays, which included ham at Christmas.) A growing Village community of radical social critics gave Abrams the opportunity to debate timely issues. Gatherings at V. F. Calverton's Morton Street apartment provided one such forum. Calverton, founder of the influential journal *The Modern Monthly*, propounded an important strain of independent Marxism. His parties brought together a range of well-connected writers and commentators. Among them were Louis Adamic, John Chamberlain, Stuart Chase, Malcolm Cowley, Louis Hacker, Granville Hicks, Sidney Hook, Matthew Josephson, Sinclair Lewis, and Walter White. The core group, according to one observer, had "leftward pro-collectivist or economic planning leanings" and was "sharply, sarcastically critical of President Hoover and his 'rugged individualism.' " Though his presence at Calverton's soirees might have been awkward—Abrams, the successful capitalist sparring with open advocates of revolution—these interactions likely widened his political and intellectual horizons. They certainly gave a budding policy intellectual important contacts in the publishing world.[24]

The Village also offered Abrams and Ruth the chance to become involved in theater life. During the late 1920s and early 1930s, Abrams invested money in local productions, and at one point even bought the Gansevoort Theater. He and Ruth frequently went to opening night performances and to cast parties afterward. They became friends with George and Ira Gershwin (Abrams would often join Ira in his Friday night poker games), Oscar Levant, E. Y. "Yip" Harburg, and Zero Mostel. The accomplishments of these individuals inspired Abrams' desire to "write a great hit song," and could have been the reason why a friend described him as a "Gilbert who never found his Sullivan." The closest he came to fulfilling his musical ambition was when Ira Gershwin used some of his legalese in "Impeachment Proceeding," a song in *Of Thee I Sing*. That zany political spoof became the Gershwins' longest running Broadway show, and the first musical to receive a Pulitzer Prize.[25]

Related to Abrams' theatrical inclinations was his love of jokes and double entendres. Whether sitting at the piano, which he played by ear, or traveling in sparsely inhabited regions of Asia and Africa, he would never miss the chance to indulge in humorous word play. While most of his witticisms were at somebody else's expense, he sometimes poked fun at himself:

> I wish I were a jewfish
> The little fish I'd harry 'em
> And if the price of fish went up
> I'd buy the whole aquarium

Other rhymes seemed autobiographical:

> When a law clerk solves the problem of employment
> And keeps the hungry wolf from off his door
> Combines a wife and children with enjoyment
> T'will be a pleasure then to study law

But most of Abrams' jesting would center on his housing activities. Typically, he would rewrite the lyrics to a well-known song, then sing them to the intended audience. He composed a series of limericks (with a chorus based on "Farmer in the Dell") praising his fellow housing activists:

> A-housing we will go!
> A-housing we will go!
> Hi—ho-the derrior–
> The costs, they must be low"

In the late 1930s he wrote a jingle about the Housing Act of 1937. Its chorus mixed truth with poetry:

> We're the housing boys of the U.S.A.
> We're strong and adamant
> With capital subsidy swept away
> We've won the annual grant
> Our houses will be new and nifty
> Although we'll have to be quite thrifty
> It must be done below twelve-fifty
> We're the housing boys of the U.S.A.

Abrams satirized the same piece of legislation in "Dear Mr. President":

Here's to the Wagner-Steagall Act
It was tidy, neat, exact
Till some Senators from the South
Started shooting off their mouth

Another song, "Down a Few Quickies for Ickes," sarcastically lamented the Interior Secretary's elevated status:

He is Hiawatha's boy friend
He's a paleface not so coy friend
Of the parks and public spaces roundabout.
He takes care of bees and birdies
And can use no more bad "wordies"
'Cause he's now the nation's number one Boy Scout

Most of Abrams' targets were flattered by the attention and enjoyed his burlesques. After passage of the Housing Act of 1949, Abrams took charge of the entertainment for a victory celebration at the Mayflower Hotel in Washington, D.C. He wrote a number of lampoons and skits, which he performed himself. Among the evening's guests was the usually unflappable Republican Senator from Ohio, Robert Taft, who surprised everyone by loudly laughing at one of the songs. Years later, during a UN mission to Ghana, Abrams composed a short ditty with a show-tune beat: "I'm Ga-Ga About a Gha Girl and That Gha Girl's Ga-Ga Over Me." Even at the end of his life, Abrams' irreverent sense of humor persisted. In defining the term "city planning," he dryly observed: "City planning is as old as cities and might count among its earliest functionaries Cain, whose client was God, [and] God himself, who oversaw the creation of numerous towns and the destruction of some unsuccessful ones."[26]

Abrams' exuberance as a wordsmith revealed a quick and active intellect. It also indicated his love of life and people. Almost everyone who knew him commented on his intense and sincere sociability. It helped that he laughed infectiously at his own jokes and had a Jimmy Durante nose—instead of his name, he would often sign letters to Ruth with a comical sketch of a proboscis. To everyone, he was simply "Charlie." One of his close friends, Dwight Macdonald (the left-wing intellectual and founder of *Politics* magazine), probably spoke for many when he noted, "[I] can't think of him as 'Charles,' still less as 'Professor' or Commissioner,' and even 'Mr.' sounds too formal for a distinguished but undignified old party . . . who greeted female dinner guests 'Hiya, baby!' "[27]

Given their gregariousness, Abrams and Ruth frequently enjoyed the crowds and libertine atmosphere of Prohibition-era nightclubs (Ruth would capture the mood in her painting, *Fans at Minsky's Burlesque*). Abrams himself constantly needed to be "amid a wash of people." As he and Ruth moved to increasingly larger houses in the Village, having his own private study became an option. Laboring alone in peace and quiet, however, simply did not suit his temperament. Before long, he would migrate back to the living room, where he would find a corner to set up shop.[28]

The joy Abrams derived from being around people translated into appreciation for another element of Village life: tolerance. He associated this attribute with the "democratic tradition" of former Village residents, such as Thomas Paine, Mark Twain, and Emma Lazarus (coincidentally, the Abramses eventually lived in Lazarus' Village home). Tolerance, a "symbol of social integration," made the Village unique. Even Ware confirmed that "social tolerance," which included the "tolerance of friends and acquaintances as well as of strangers," was the area's primary feature. The Village's diversity, Abrams argued, was the equivalent to John Stuart Mill's definition of freedom: "pursuing our own good in our own way, so long as we do not attempt to deprive others of theirs." Social tolerance, according to Abrams, was the "mysterious formula for people living together without fear." Discovering how to replicate it was the "single great question [upon] which the unity of the earth" depended.[29]

The Profits and Pitfalls of Real Estate Speculation

If the Village helped shape Abrams' ideas, Abrams also helped shape the Village—literally. Speculation in and renovation of Village properties accelerated after World War I. As more and more buildings were restored, rents rose dramatically, posting a 140 percent increase in the 1920s. Some of Abrams' first clients were mortgage lenders involved in these activities. He therefore employed the services of a local appraiser,

Morris Strunsky. Strunsky was the younger brother of Anna Strunsky, a socialist married to the well-known reformer, William English Walling. (Both Anna and her husband were among the founders of the National Association for the Advancement of Colored People, an interesting coincidence considering Abrams' post-World War II antidiscrimination work.) Abrams, with Strunsky's enthusiastic advice and assistance, began to make his own real estate investments. Short on capital, he sometimes went to loan sharks and "shady mortgage discount operators" since banks were reluctant to underwrite Village speculators. He soon discovered that his money, thanks to Strunsky's "wild operations," was tied up in precarious deals. To regain his footing, he decided to "train" himself in the intricacies of real estate, which required taking out multiple mortgages and creating "fantastic financial structures." Against the odds, he somehow managed to survive. Friends and acquaintances attributed Abrams' success to his abilities as a "shrewd operator and a formidable negotiator." " 'Those Indians who sold Manhattan were lucky they didn't have to negotiate with Abrams,' " a real estate salesman remarked, adding, " 'I'll bet they'd never have got *him* to go as high as twenty-four dollars.' " Not surprisingly, Abrams' wealth rose with his reputation. Between the late 1920s and the mid-1930s, he bought and managed somewhere between 80 and 100 pieces of property. These investments were returning a 30 percent profit by 1942; this would provide a secure if not extravagant living for him and his family.[30]

Abrams subsequently characterized himself as " 'A reckless gambler for small stakes.' " Or, as he told Governor Averell Harriman: "Cautious was never a flattering word . . . and yet it fits me. I'm the most cautious of reckless youths and would never hesitate to march up to the cannon's mouth, after first making sure it wasn't loaded." On the surface, these comments suggest Abrams did not have a talent for self-analysis, given his frenetic speculation and zigzag pattern of career choices. But while his initial involvement in real estate was admittedly shaky, he responded by teaching himself how to avoid such situations in the future. Moreover, Abrams' decision to leave a lucrative law practice came after his investment income was sufficient to pad whatever salary cuts he might incur. The cannon, it turns out, was not loaded.[31]

In retrospect, Abrams' real estate activities would be framed by others as early attempts to renew or restore blighted areas. The *National Cyclopedia of American Biography* emphasized his "important role in preserving the character of the buildings and streets," while the *The New Yorker* described how his "ingenious conversions" turned "stables into studios" and "loft buildings into avant-garde shops." Though Abrams rarely discussed his personal finances, he did acknowledge the Village's transformation. In his opinion, the post World War I "real estate activity" made the Village thrive and preserved its "special configuration." This "activity" had been carried out by a "group of odd-ball investors" who coupled their "untutored creativity to their speculative urges." In restoring the Village, some had "borrowed at usurious rates on second, third, and fourth mortgages," a few "did well for a time," and still others "went for broke and made it." We do not know if Abrams meant to include himself among these "odd ball investors," but by placing their activities under the rubric of urban "rehabilitation," he implied they were motivated by public as well as private concerns.[32]

Abrams' real estate speculation did have some rough edges. A small community of African Americans lived on Clinton Street (also known as West Eighth Street), mostly in Clinton Court, a complex of eight houses built over the Minetta Creek and variously described as a "small slum" or a "number of small shacks." In the mid-1920s, Abrams and Arthur Garfield Hays decided to buy this property and develop it, which required razing part of Clinton Court. Abrams eventually owned the site's new establishments, the Eighth Street Playhouse (a movie theater) and the Village Barn, a theme-based cabaret located in the basement of the Playhouse. Abrams thought the new building (and subsequent additions) had improved the area by making Eighth Street a main thoroughfare and "one of the area's most walkable clusters." He failed to acknowledge, however, that demolition of Clinton Court forced its African-American occupants to move elsewhere. They were old residents and loyal Democrats, the ward boss protested, but Abrams and Hays apparently ignored his complaints.[33]

It would be easy to make either too much or too little of this incident. At the time, Abrams was a real estate speculator; to evaluate his actions retroactively on the basis of his subsequent career as a housing activist would be unfair. Mitigating circumstances could have existed as well. He might not have played a role in the eviction proceedings if his only responsibility was supplying capital; alternatively, these proceedings might have occurred prior to his involvement in the project. Or, using a sort of felicific calculus, he could have decided it was best for the neighborhood to tear down the "small slum." Whatever the case, evictions occurred, and Abrams was probably aware of the consequences. This episode, though, was unique. Once he turned his attention to housing reform and began to criticize the displacement of inner-city residents, he could do so without hypocrisy.

Property ownership did more than provide Abrams with a stable income. It forced him to develop expertise in property assessment, building codes, condemnation and eviction proceedings, mortgage financing, and tax policies. He came to understand how all these issues affected the development of cities and their inhabitants. This "worm's eye view" would channel his humanitarian and social concerns into areas he knew best: housing and urban planning.[34]

When Abrams did enter the public arena, his experiences thus differentiated him from some of his contemporaries. Lewis Mumford was primarily a scholar, not a practitioner. In Mumford's writings, the city increasingly became an ideal, and the forces shaping it often seemed abstract and uncontrollable. Robert Moses, who would be remembered best as New York City's building czar, had studied political science and public administration in America and Europe. Others, including Catherine Bauer and housing administrator Jacob Crane, followed a similar path.[35]

Abrams reversed the order of study and practice. He entered the world of policymaking only after he had seen how the law, real estate, finance, and government operated in everyday life. This is not to suggest Abrams suffered from an early if transient phase of anti-intellectualism. Nor is it to imply he consciously pursued a Dewey-esque course, acquiring knowledge only from experience. It does mean praxis—the actual implementation of an idea—provided Abrams with an intellectual scaffolding for theory. Emphasizing praxis sometimes limited the range and scope of his ideas, but it also gave him problem-solving insights his colleagues lacked.

"Reflective Practice" and the "Bones of History"

Contemporaries were troubled by the widening gap between professional and pragmatic knowledge, especially in regard to making and analyzing policy. Jerome Frank even believed one of the Depression's causes was the inability of lawyers to "comprehend the nature of business enterprise, to judge it critically, to advise their clients of its deficiencies and of the possibilities of its modification." "Among the best servants of the New Deal," Frank maintained, were "lawyers who . . . have arrived at some such wisdom." Abrams possessed this "wisdom," yet his future accomplishments were based on a more complicated dialectic than Frank's reasoning implied. Abrams combined his formal training with his personal experiences, self-consciously using each to assess the other. Scholars frequently describe this ability to reconcile the mismatch between theory and reality as "reflective practice." Because reflective practitioners are not dependent on "categories" of "established technique," they can "criticize the tacit understandings" structuring "specialized practice." In other words, they see framing and solving problems as an open-ended process where means and ends are not separate, but defined on the basis of each new encounter. Reflective practitioners ultimately use their technical knowledge and ongoing interactions to become more effective problem solvers.[36]

The typology of a reflective practitioner does not entirely describe Abrams' abilities, but it does help us understand how he approached certain problems. When working on a specific project, whether in the United States or overseas, Abrams often had to revise or reformulate established beliefs (including his own) about urban expansion, public finance, housing reform, legislative remedies, and social relations. He would then test these revised principles when faced with similar problems in the future. This flexibility and adaptability freed him from a narrow, strait-jacket approach to policymaking.[37]

Abrams' constant reframing of problems also made him critical of existing practices. For instance, he eventually championed the poor as potential home owners, castigated the FHA's racial policies, and condemned slum clearance as a primary method of housing reform. Whether he called them "myths," "fictions," or "sacred cows," he believed all assumptions were open to scrutiny. Moreover, he asserted that the necessary cycle of analysis was impossible to conduct from the vertiginous heights of ivory towers. "The more specialized these disciplines [associated with urban planning] have become," he complained, "the greater has been the tendency to withdraw from the unfolding theater of action that is urban life onto some veiled and isolated scene." In a mock, posthumous dialogue with Catherine Bauer, Abrams had Bauer's ghost echo his own views: "Yes, they [urbanists] simply dread

retracting a position they expressed a generation ago. Theories on policy are not as long as art—they are part of the bones of history. Their
value is assessable only against the facts of the times." In closing, Bauer's
ghost consoles Abrams, insisting he was among the few who "consistently contradicted" himself. Being able to distinguish between the "bones"
and "facts" certainly allowed Abrams to stimulate useful discussion and
debate. In the words of *House and Home* magazine, he was "one of the
wellsprings of new ideas which public housers pick up and rebroadcast
tirelessly across the nation."[38]

Many of Abrams' "new ideas" would combine his playful intellect with
insights into human behavior. He half-jokingly proposed the creation of
confessionals where individuals could boast about their accomplishments. He also coined the phrase "human nidology"—the study of
human habitats and the process of building them. Contemporary neglect of this topic meant zoo architects paid more attention to creating livable environments for animals than planners did for people. Connected
to this concern was Abrams' call for an "Urban Space Agency," with a
capitalization "comparable" to the National Aeronautics and Space
Administration (NASA). "Since the moon's land is presently unfit for settlement," Abrams would state only partially in jest, "at least a portion of
NASA's money might be diverted toward developing a few needed sections of our troubled planet." Perhaps the best publicity-catching idea
was his call for "trystoria" in America's urban areas, places whose encouragement of romantic liaisons might stem central city depopulation.[39]

Social Science and the Role of Intellectuals

In addition to real-world involvement, a larger intellectual context influenced Abrams' growth as a thinker. Even before his arrival in America,
the realist movement had stressed the use of "facts" in describing and
ultimately solving the so-called "social question" (a phrase referring to
the ills late-nineteenth-century America confronted). Similarly, in the
1920s and 1930s, academics, influenced by positivism and scientism,
attempted to apply the logical rigor of the scientific method to law and
the social sciences. Abrams himself supported scholarship as an integral
part of urban studies and eventually called for a "comparative science of
urbanization." He also echoed the utilitarian sentiments of social scien-

tists by subscribing to an instrumental, rather than philosophical or epistemological, view of the law. In his estimation, the public benefits of research would remain limited without some degree of applicability.[40]

Abrams' aptitudes and views were consonant with other developments as well. The emergence of modern social science in the 1890s had been marked by the recognition and study of interdependence—essentially the causal web linking social, political, and psychological phenomena. In some respects, urban studies was the examination of this interdependence within a specific physical unit, the city. Other trends—Progressive hopes for a neutral science of government, interest in public administration, and growing faith in expert advice—encouraged social scientists to assume positions as political confidants and policy advisers. No one promoted these new roles more than Charles Merriam, a University of Chicago political scientist. Merriam thought universities should be loci of research, data collection, and policymaking. Yet, despite his emphasis on expertise and experts, he remained committed to public accountability and democratic processes. His vision was not a Veblen-esque society run by technocrats but a rational one where trained administrators had limited functions. Merriam's views accurately described Abrams' own qualifications for public service. Trained in law, possessing an intricate knowledge of modern finance, and eager to use his energy to advance social reform, Abrams was ideally prepared to address complicated economic and political problems. Plus, he had an even more important quality: he could design programs and policies that actually worked. Averell Harriman, former Governor of New York, astutely described this unusual combination: " 'There's no one quite like Charlie Abrams. Some men are effective at rousing the public conscience. Others know how to get a practical job done. Abrams is one of the rare people who can do both things—he's a visionary who gets results.' "[41]

As a "visionary," Abrams could speak the language of ordinary people. He would write legislation and a legion of technical reports, but most individuals knew him through his editorials and articles in the popular press. Abrams himself downplayed his talents, simply attributing them to an ability to come up with some "gimmick," by which he meant a legal or financial mechanism to enact a certain reform or program. He colloquially referred to this process as "finagling," and it served him well in a number of capacities.[42]

Abrams and social scientists could take more active roles as policy-makers because the reach of public power was slowly expanding. The economic chaos generated by the Depression hastened this develop-ment nationally, though the general growth of government had been underway for several decades, especially on the state level. One of the clearest examples of the latter involved the struggle over housing reform in New York. But even as reform illustrated the rise of government agen-cies and administrators as important historical actors, it also under-scored the inability of policymakers to remain completely isolated from the tumult of politics, interest groups, and judicial decisions.

The man who had led a relatively carefree life during the late 1920s and early 1930s would plunge headlong into this ambiguous push-pull of policymaking. It would be a bruising experience, but his sense of humor still remained intact. As he looked back over his own journey, he would reflect:

I once was a promising lawyer
With causes and clients galore
'Twas then that I took up with housing
And now I ain't got them no more.[43]

Chapter Three

⋰⋱

FROM TENEMENT LAWS TO HOUSING AUTHORITIES
Social Provision and the New Deal State

On February 14, 1934, the *New York Times* reported that Mayor Fiorello LaGuardia had appointed five members to the recently established New York City Housing Authority (NYCHA). According to Langdon Post, NYCHA's first Chairman, "creation of the Municipal Housing Authority . . . was the most important legislation at Albany in the last seventy-five years." Abrams and two of his colleagues were the primary authors of that legislation. For Abrams, it was his initiation into the world of policymaking.[1]

The development of housing authorities did not occur in a political or historical vacuum. Reformers, municipal officials, and state legislators had been struggling against slums and substandard dwellings for more than half a century. Their efforts to reduce urban squalor had focused on mandating minimum standards for the multi-story apartment buildings known as tenement houses. This "restrictive legislation" represented a significant extension of police powers (the ability to take measures to secure the health, safety, welfare, and morals of the public), which itself marked an important stage in the expanding scope of state and municipal regulations.[2]

Having relied on restrictive legislation for decades, decisionmakers concluded that increased public intervention was necessary. City and state officials turned to Abrams and others to help establish "authorities," administrative agencies capable of building and running low-income housing projects. Authorities emerged as dominant mechanisms of social reform because larger changes had and were occurring in local, state, and national governance. These changes were connected to an array of interrogatives: What was the "state"? How were cities constrained from addressing social problems? What responsibilities did state governments have? How were local initiatives affected by federal policies? What role, if any, should the growing number of "experts" play? Even after Abrams scrutinized court cases and legislative history, there were few clear answers. One thing, however, seemed certain: neither slums nor the dearth of affordable housing could be "remedied by the ordinary operation of private enterprise." To understand why Abrams came to this conclusion requires a review of housing reform prior to the 1930s.[3]

Restrictive Legislation: Limitations and Alternatives

Before the emergence of a large national government, city officials looked primarily to state governments for assistance in solving municipal problems. Cities were relatively powerless to act on their own because they were considered legal creatures of states. While cities could pass and enforce ordinances covering purely local matters, state legislation was necessary to empower them to undertake more comprehensive tasks. What contemporaries usually meant by *the* state, then, was a *particular* state. In practice, this translated into legislative centralization and administrative decentralization. A growing number of city officials, sensing the limitations of such an arrangement, lobbied for extended police powers.[4]

This is exactly what happened in Abrams' home state of New York, where reformers slowly succeeded in augmenting sanctions against the most egregious examples of urban contagion. Tenement house laws enacted in 1867, 1884, 1895, and 1901 legitimized state and sometimes municipal use of police powers to regulate construction and management of private housing. Living standards did improve, though only twentieth-century legislation effectively outlawed construction of "dumbbell" tenements (commonly called "old law tenements" because they were the prevailing dwelling type prior to the "new" Tenement Law of 1901). Restrictive legislation could make these dark, poorly ventilated buildings safer, but not necessarily desirable, places to live.[5]

An additional, more significant drawback of restrictive legislation was its inability to increase the supply of affordable housing. Some contemporaries advocated "model tenements" to meet this objective. As a function of their voluntarily limited profits, these tenements charged relatively modest rents; on the other hand, their structural integrity remained fairly high since they conformed to and sometimes even exceeded building standards of the day. Enlightened capitalists were supposed to find this combination appealing. Public officials and some reformers certainly did. For municipal decisionmakers still wedded to Gilded Age notions of self-help and private charity, model tenements illustrated a method of channeling investment into social uplift without involving public funds. For reformers like Jacob Riis, they suggested a way of guiding the invisible hand of market capitalism toward worthy objectives without denying the "business of housing the poor" was "business." Investors, however, rarely found these arguments persuasive.[6]

Precisely what Abrams thought about restrictive legislation when he drafted the authorities law is uncertain. Several years later his views were unequivocal. "Legislation could prescribe what was not to be built in the future," he noted, "but it could not eradicate what had already been built in the past, was occupied, income producing, and vested." Prevailing attitudes also militated against significant change. In Abrams' opinion, "checking all popular pressure for reform was a climate in which any undue interference with property rights was viewed as repugnant to the democratic institution." Consequently, the "restrictive weapon in the government's power plant" was "largely outmoded." Abrams was equally unimpressed with housing initiatives that attempted to lower rents by reducing profits. Perhaps reflecting on his own experience as a real-estate entrepreneur, he remarked, "The limited-dividend scheme will remain inherently unsound so long as there is a gap between the market return on speculative enterprises and the return granted to the 'enlightened' investors." For this reason, profit-limiting enterprises had been, and would remain, mere "demonstrations."[7]

If restrictive legislation failed to produce new housing, contempo-

rarics pointed out another limitation: it was ineffective when enforcement mechanisms were unreliable or absent. Indeed, where the expansion of public power took the form of regulatory action, bureaucratic
independence and resources were essential for desired policy outcomes.
Recent scholars have described these characteristics as administrative
"autonomy" and "capacity," which are useful categories in helping us
understand the evolution of local governmental structures, including
the New York City Tenement House Department.[8]

Creation of the Tenement House Department had much to do with
the efforts of Lawrence Veiller, a former plan examiner in the New York
City Building Department who became Secretary to the New York
Tenement House Commission of 1900. The Commission's 1901 report
noted rampant code violations and lax enforcement of existing (restrictive) legislation. Veiller attributed these violations to a shortage of housing inspectors and the fragmentation of enforcement responsibilities
among the Health, Building, Fire, and Police Departments. To remedy
these problems, the Commission, including Veiller, supported and was
successful in establishing a separate New York City Tenement House
Department (1902) whose centralized authority and trained staff would
enforce state and municipal housing regulations.[9]

Reformers were continually disappointed by the new department's
performance. The Commissioner of the Department served at the pleas-
ure of the Mayor, and as a political appointee he was vulnerable to the
powerful New York City spoils system. This liability quickly surfaced when
Robert   DeForest,   the   Tenement   House   Department's   first
Commissioner, and Veiller (his deputy) were pressured to resign after the
return of a Tammany administration under the mayoralty of George B.
McClellan in 1904. Administrative ambiguities also weakened enforcement efforts. Officials, confused over vague and conflicting guidelines,
allowed certain cases to languish for three to four years until sending
them to the City Attorney, in whose office they could remain for equivalent amounts of time before action was taken. Abrams subsequently
acknowledged these weaknesses: "Government policing of real estate was
never successful. It was not adequate; it was not directed into the proper
channels; alone, it could effect no remedy . . . . Restrictive laws, particularly those for cheaper dwellings, were also hard to enforce."[10]

The Tenement House Department's ineffectiveness flowed primarily
from one source: insufficient funding. This led to cuts in personnel and

a high turnover rate among experienced inspectors. After peaking at 799 employees in 1910, the Department's staff declined to 438 in 1920, despite the increasing number of tenements that fell under their jurisdiction. These shortages prevented regular inspections, which left thousands of complaints unresolved. In 1930, the New York State Board of Housing provided a bleak assessment of the Department's performance, pointing out the previous decade of poor enforcement practices and budget shortfalls (appropriations had risen by only $25,000 between 1910 and 1926). Thus, while the Department might have had a degree of administrative autonomy, it was significantly undermined by a lack of institutional resources. Abrams would attempt to address this weakness by designing financially independent agencies, though they would be hindered by similar difficulties.[11]

Given the changes taking place on all levels of government, some of these blind spots were understandable. Yet it would take more than the historical lesson of the Tenement House Department for Abrams to develop a sophisticated understanding of how administrative capacities could be diminished by intergovernmental conflict and partisan politics. He held onto the characteristically Whiggish belief that the key shift from restrictive to constructive legislation had resulted primarily because "the government . . . [took over] the housing functions which private owners could no longer adequately perform." Later experiences would reveal a new set of challenges and contradictions ushered in by this transition.[12]

Before such a shift could occur, Abrams had to reconcile divergent attitudes toward public housing. Those of Lawrence Veiller and Edith Elmer Wood provided the starkest contrasts. Oddly enough, Veiller, a reformer with first-hand experience concerning the limits of restrictive legislation, was one of public housing's most voluble opponents. Veiller's views were not easy to deflect. He had founded the National Housing Association in 1910 and had written authoritative "model housing laws." He opposed both model tenements and municipal housing; for him, the former were idealistic and ineffective, while the latter would "at most . . . better the living conditions of a favored few, who had sufficient influence to secure apartments in them." He also feared municipal housing would compete with private builders, thus disrupting the salutary supply-and-demand equilibrium produced by an unrestrained private market.[13]

Conversely, one of the best known proponents of public housing was Edith Elmer Wood. Having assisted in clearing the alley slums of the nation's capital, Wood criticized reformers' single-minded focus on restrictive legislation. These kinds of policies might "forbid the bad house," but they did not "provide the good one." Building on the ideas of municipal reformer Frederick Howe and Romanian-born city planner Carol Aronovici, Wood supported housing initiatives requiring increased state involvement. She believed the market—with its profit imperatives—could never fully meet the demand for low-income housing. This failure meant municipalities would likely have to supply (and own) dwellings for the bottom third of the population. While Wood never completely spelled out the ramifications of her position, it would have entailed public housing on a massive scale.[14]

Wood and Veiller represented opposite poles of an important debate Abrams would join and ultimately influence. If, as Wood argued, industrial capitalism was incapable of meeting the housing needs of low-income citizens, then a drastic modification of laissez-faire principles was necessary. Alternatively, if Veiller's contention was valid—that tinkering with the laws of supply and demand would only worsen housing conditions—then state regulation, not municipal ownership was the appropriate course of action. Navigating between these viewpoints would require a solution sensitive to both capitalism's deficiencies and private market exigencies. Neither Wood nor Veiller realized it, but as Abrams (and others) soon grasped, public authorities might represent a viable compromise. Furthermore, authorities could be operated by cities, maintaining the locus of reform on the local level, where Abrams believed it belonged.

Economic Dislocation, Public Housing, and Urban Politics

Even after nationwide economic distress undermined faith in private-sector solutions, decisionmakers were slow to embrace public housing. In 1931 President Hoover convened a conference to study the problems of home building and home ownership; its recommendations reflected the prevailing anti-statist sentiments associated with housing debates. The primary responsibility for slum clearance, Ray Lyman Wilbur summarized, lay with "business men and the existing agencies for the

enforcement of building and housing laws." A year later, the editors of
Fortune called for similar cooperation between "private industry and
public control," though like the Hoover conference, they felt public
involvement should be limited to subsidizing urban land costs and
enforcing restrictive regulations.[15]

In contrast to these admonitions, atomized groups of housing reformers supported direct public intervention to clear slums and provide low-
income housing. This would require constructive, not restrictive legislation. Mary Simkhovitch, a graduate of Boston University and a long time
settlement worker, was instrumental in generating early support for such
legislation. Asked to give a talk in 1931 at New York City's Riverside
Church, Simkhovitch had an epiphany of sorts. "The cumulative impres-
sions of the housing picture," she explained, had convinced her of "the
necessity of government housing for persons unable to pay commercial
rents." Within a year, Simkhovitch had joined and become president of
the Public Housing Conference. Its secretary was Helen Alfred, another
settlement worker, who had run for the New Jersey State Legislature as a
Socialist in 1930. Simkhovitch and Alfred's initial objective was to establish a local housing agency. Their cause received support from Lewis
Mumford, the economist Stuart Chase, and Louis Pink, an attorney who
had briefly headed the New York State Board of Housing. Pink began
lobbying in 1932 for a city housing board to oversee the work of slum
clearance and model housing. Such a board, empowered to regulate
housing like a public utility, would have the authority to condemn and
clear land, replan streets, and construct low-cost dwellings. In 1933,
Pink, Alfred, and Columbia professor Joseph P. Chamberlain formulated a draft bill and had it introduced into the New York legislature, but it
died in the Assembly (the lower house).[16]

With efforts seemingly stalled at the state level, Simkhovitch traveled
to Washington, D.C. in early summer 1933, where she urged federal
administrators to include housing provisions in pending legislation. A
year earlier, Congress had passed the Emergency Relief and Construction
Act, which empowered the Reconstruction Finance Corporation to
"make loans to corporations, formed wholly for the purpose of providing
housing for families of low incomes." A year passed, but states were
unwilling or unable to create these corporations (hence the need reformers felt for additional activism). Simkhovitch and Edith Elmer Wood, who
joined her colleague in the nation's capital, were successful in persuad-

ing federal officials to link public works with municipal housing. In June the Public Works Administration (PWA) was authorized to provide federal grants to local housing agencies. Almost immediately, Governor Herbert Lehman (D) called a special legislative session to coordinate New York's response to the new programs. Lawmakers introduced several bills, but disagreement erupted over whether the proposed housing agencies would be under state or local control. When no compromise could be reached, the legislature adjourned without passing any of the bills.[17]

Though a New York City housing authority was not yet a reality, Abrams would interpret the events of preceding decades as an inevitable movement toward that end. Reflecting on the findings and ultimate failures of various commissions and committees, Abrams constructed a progressive view of history. Slum clearance had required restrictive legislation; its shortcomings had prompted creation of a Tenement House Department; the limits of that agency had led to further expansions of municipal power; and now, economic conditions necessitated assistance from the federal government. Abrams would cite these seemingly ineluctable transformations as background to—and justification for—many of his subsequent legal analyses and policy decisions.

Additional legislation had not yet been enacted by the fall of 1933 when New Yorkers were still debating how to tap newly appropriated federal funds. They were also in the midst of a hard-fought mayoral campaign. On September 1, 1932, New York City's flamboyant mayor, Jimmy Walker, had resigned after hearings conducted by Judge Samuel Seabury revealed corruption throughout his administration. Among those who supported Seabury's call for higher ethical standards was Langdon Post, a Harvard graduate and scion of a wealthy New York family. Post had been an anti-Tammany Assemblyman in the New York legislature, where he introduced several housing bills and a draft of the 1929 Multiple Dwellings Law. In 1932 Post lost his bid for reelection, which pushed him farther into the growing orbit of the "Fusion Movement," a coalition of independent Democrats, Republicans, intellectuals, reformers like Mary Simkhovitch, and prominent liberals such as Arthur Garfield Hays.[18]

Abrams met Post in 1933 and was attracted to him out of common concerns, including housing reform. He supported Post's bid for Manhattan borough president, first by helping him establish campaign headquarters above the Eighth Street Playhouse (which Abrams owned), then by stumping and writing speeches for him. Abrams became "intrigued with the whole business of politics," especially since his early efforts in the Post campaign intersected with what he would later call an "important change" in the "political climate." That change was the "rise of reform," a phenomenon characterized by the emergence of "do-gooders" in the sometimes rough world of urban politics and policymaking.[19]

Abrams' entry into politics and reform at this point was significant for other reasons. By the early 1930s, with economic recovery nowhere in sight, many of the issues policymakers had faced during the previous decades (restrictive versus constructive legislation, state versus local control, public versus private power, political versus administrative autonomy) required immediate answers. Abrams' legal training and his experiences in real estate and municipal finance provided him with insights into these problems. Moreover, his thinking was unfettered by traditional notions of federalism. The programs he and his colleagues designed would forge new links between cities and federal agencies, while severing others between municipalities and state governments. Had Abrams entered public service ten years earlier (during an era of Republican ascendancy) or ten years later (with the New Deal in retreat), his proposals might never have achieved tangible form. As it was, Abrams' own ideas coincided with and helped animate larger forces and trends.[20]

Unlike earlier attempts at municipal reform, Fusion politics stressed new programs in addition to honesty and thrift. This, in turn, reflected changes already occurring on the national level. Among reformers, academics, and New Deal policymakers, "efficiency" was coming to mean expansion of public services and benefits; thus defined, "efficiency" might require government expenditures to increase, not decrease. On the local level, Arthur Garfield Hays hinted at this evolving separation of "good" governance from low-cost government when he opined that New York City's chief executive needed to eschew the "self-righteousness" and "bungling ineptness of the merely good-government reformer," and instead embrace a comprehensive "program." Langdon Post, campaigning on the issues of a city highway and municipal housing authority, fit Hays' prescription for a candidate who supported both reform and increased public programs. As Post himself later asserted, "the interest in proper housing" was "inherent in good government."[21]

Fusionists and their supporters, including Abrams, endorsed Fiorello LaGuardia for New York City Mayor. LaGuardia, a former Republican Congressman who had been ousted during the 1932 Democratic landslide, did not hesitate to campaign for far-reaching programs: upgraded health services for the poor, reforms in the city's unemployment relief system, and municipal ownership of the subways were all part of his platform. These proposals also had an important but less immediate effect on Abrams' views. Though not actually apolitical, Fusionists believed politics could transcend partisan labels by embracing a set of clearly defined principles. This was the anvil upon which Abrams forged many of his political ideas, and it helps explain why he would always stress policies over candidates.[22]

In November 1933, LaGuardia won the mayoral election, yet in contrast to Roosevelt's sweeping victory a year earlier, his mandate was conditional. Chosen by a minority of voters, the new mayor's vision of expanded social programs was supported by elements within the middle- and upper-classes, but not by the city's poorest residents, many of whom lived in Democrat-controlled districts. These voters seemed more concerned about eliminating corruption than with redistributing wealth. LaGuardia, a pragmatist and master coalition builder, remained sensitive to this dynamic. He would slowly move rightward to the political center, while national politics, at least for a short period, moved in the opposite direction. This dimension of New York City politics—the clash between administrative goals and political realities—would help decide which housing policies succeeded and which failed.[23]

Public Housing Authorities

According to LaGuardia, "civic reconstruction" literally meant elimination of New York City's slums and construction of low-income dwellings in their place. A week before the election, LaGuardia released a five point housing program. It included support of a " 'municipal housing commission, composed of experts without regard to political affiliation' " to administer the city's slum clearance plan. A source of LaGuardia's ideas was likely the City Club, which had formed its own Slum Clearance Committee a month earlier to investigate the feasibility of a housing commission. Abrams was on this committee, as were tenement reformers, commercial builders, real estate brokers, and financial interests. At LaGuardia's urging, Abrams, along with Ira Robbins (a veteran of the settlement house movement) and Carl Stern (the general counsel for the State Board of Housing) began drafting housing legislation to be introduced in Albany should LaGuardia be elected. Ironically, the trio of reformers would create an entity whose eventual success endangered the mayor's own political survival.[24]

Abrams, Robbins, and Stern could have used a number of administrative structures as models for their legislation. Writing in a 1932 issue of *Architectural Review*, Arthur Holden, a New York City architect, had presented one of the more widely publicized alternatives to public authorities. "Both city officials and present property owners," Holden stated, understood "improvements" were "necessary before the desirability of property in the district [the Lower East Side]" could be "restored." Because neither individual owners nor the public (taxpayers) could afford to make these improvements, Holden thought the city should "grant to all owners within a given district the right to act together for their collective benefit and for the benefit of the city." This would require the "creation of a district authority to act in the capacity of trustee for the interest of all owners." In brief, owners within a given district would release their property to the authority (which Holden called an "equity trust"), and in return they would receive a "proportionate share" of the benefits derived from upgrading the area. Though Holden did not specify precisely how blighted areas would be cleared, his concept of equity trusts resembled the "improvement districts" real estate interests had been advocating for some time. In both cases, proponents wanted public powers to be transferred to incorporated private interests in return for their pledge to revitalize substandard neighborhoods. Missing from these private districts or authorities were any provisions for low-income housing. As Holden admitted, the "primary purpose of the Equity Trust is to increase the net earning power of the district as a whole." Such an objective might benefit the city through enhanced tax assessments, but the long held goal of reformers and progressive planners—construction of affordable housing—would remain unfulfilled.[25]

If the inability of equity trusts to provide low-income housing made them unsatisfactory to reformers, additional factors ruled out other options. States and cities had strict legal limitations on the money they could borrow and on the amount of taxes they could collect. These limitations blocked public intervention in a number of policy areas; they could also prevent states and municipalities from accepting or disbursing federal funds. One way to circumvent fiscal constraints was to create separate revenue districts, which, as their name implied, normally raised money through tax levies. Revenue districts, however, were generally confined to specific areas and failed to tap into adequate investment sources.[26]

Considerations like these pushed Abrams and his colleagues in the direction of public authorities. Authorities, an outgrowth of "special districts" (which had themselves originated in the late eighteenth century), became increasingly common between 1900 and 1920. Creating one for housing purposes, though, was *terra incognita*. Admittedly, a few states—Maryland, Michigan, New Jersey, Ohio, and Wisconsin—had already passed municipal housing laws by the end of 1933. This signaled dissatisfaction on a variety of fronts: inability to enforce restrictive legislation; discontent over private-sector strategies for ameliorating the Depression; and, in some instances, fear over potential social unrest caused by inadequate or nonexistent housing. These concerns indicated to lawmakers why change was necessary, but still left them puzzled over how to make it. Thus, even where states had authorized new public entities, none had actually materialized. As Abrams later remarked, "Nobody knew anything about housing, nobody knew whether public housing would be legal or illegal, nobody knew what kind of law to draw, whether land could be assembled for that purpose—it was all quite vague."[27]

In addition to investigating these legal questions, Abrams had to define an "insanitary" area, a euphemistic term denoting a slum. This task made him realize his boyhood neighborhood was technically one such area. His eventual definition encompassed older notions of structural and site deficiencies (overcrowding, excessive land coverage, lack of proper light, ventilation, and sanitary facilities), while also stressing the absence of an "adequate supply of decent, safe, and sanitary dwelling accommodations for persons of low income." Compared to tenement laws, Abrams' definition—emphasizing the quantity as well as the quality of dwellings—would significantly expand the purview of municipal power.[28]

The legislation's three drafters also believed they needed to insulate authorities from partisan politics. This especially concerned Abrams. In his estimation, New York City politics ran in fairly regular cycles. "The history of reform administrations in New York was not very good," he recalled. "They lasted for about one term, balanced the budget of the city, and then turned it over to Tammany for looting." Abrams therefore provided a number of safeguards against the policy inconsistencies these political cycles could produce. While an authority's five-member board would be appointed by a city's mayor, no more than one could be a city official. The members' five-year terms were staggered to ensure "some continuity" if a reform administration were "ousted." Members would receive no salaries, and their removal by a mayor could occur *only* after written charges had been presented and the individual had been given an opportunity to refute the accusations. Further enhancing the autonomy of authorities, initial chairmen were to be designated by mayors, but all subsequent ones were to be chosen by authority boards themselves. Finally, while cities had the power to dissolve their housing authorities, the final decision would be made after the local supreme court (New York's county courts) had conducted public hearings.[29]

The actual powers of authorities were significant, embodying the evolving concerns of urban planning professionals and those who supported increased public services. The twenty-five specific powers granted to authorities can be divided into five broad areas: data collection, public hearings, financing, project construction and operation, and property acquisition. Data collection involved not only investigating "living and housing conditions," but also making recommendations to city planning agencies and regional planning boards. Related to undertaking research and collecting data was the ability to convene public hearings, an activity for which authorities were given the power to issue subpoenas and receive testimony under oath. Authorities could borrow money, make and execute contracts, and invest their reserve funds in various securities. They could also raise capital by selling bonds to states, cities, and private parties. Though bond issues would be contingent upon the approval of local boards of estimate or governing bodies, they would still be less cumbersome and more autonomous than ordinary municipal bond issues, since the latter needed voter approval via referenda and were usually limited by debt ceilings. More central to carrying out their functions, authorities had the power to "construct, reconstruct, improve, alter or repair" municipal housing projects. This provision permitted the direct intervention in low-income housing markets never envisioned by tenement regulation.[30]

Crucial to supplying affordable housing was the final power granted to housing authorities: eminent domain. Abrams thought it was the most important component of housing legislation, though he realized he was traversing shaky legal ground. Historically, eminent domain was the power granted to sovereign governments to take private property for "public purposes." The phrase "public purposes" had been construed to mean those undertakings open to all people, not just a certain subset or class of individuals. Eminent domain could therefore be exercised to create a public park (admission was granted to everyone), but not necessarily to clear slums or construct housing projects (their clientele was limited to certain income groups). Abrams and his colleagues believed economic circumstances and changing judicial interpretations would subsequently uphold the use of eminent domain by housing authorities. If this were indeed the case, it would be an unprecedented expansion of public power based on general welfare objectives.[31]

In December 1933 Abrams, Robbins, and Stern completed their draft of the authorities law. Compared with existing legislation elsewhere, it was notable in two regards. First, unlike other states where public housing was under the direct supervision of state commissions/boards, or limited to the largest metropolises (in Wisconsin, only Milwaukee was eligible), all incorporated cities in New York were allowed to establish housing authorities. More significant, both the real property and the securities of New York's authorities were tax exempt; only Wisconsin's legislation contained a similar provision. This suggests Abrams and his colleagues were especially concerned with attracting institutional investors—exemptions would benefit them most—and with reducing the cost of borrowing money (tax-exempt municipal bonds normally pay lower interest rates than private sector ones). Empire State policymakers, including Abrams, likely felt these novel features were necessary because of the unique size and scope of New York's problems.[32]

As the bill's provisions became publicized, newspaper editors suggested a cautious approach. "If the opportunity is great," they remarked, "so are the risks and the dangers." LaGuardia was advised not to move "too fast" or promise "too much." Warning it was "dangerous to talk about rentals as low as $8 a room a month," commentators even suggested the "new municipal agency" should be restricted to slum clearance only. Nonetheless, Governor Lehman's support, worsening financial conditions, and the promise of federal aid contributed to the bill's

passage. "This bill will give to the cities of the State an opportunity to initiate a permanent program of rehousing," Lehman observed as he
signed the bill into law on January 31, 1934. Even Lehman, though, recommended a careful plan of attack. "Low cost housing and slum clearance through municipal housing authorities is a pioneering program,"
he asserted, one for which there was "relatively little experience to serve
as a guide."[33]

Hardly a cure-all, housing authorities seemed poised to resolve a
number of lingering issues associated with modern governance. They
gave municipal officials direct control over certain urban problems, a
power they had long desired. Legislators appeared willing to support
this arrangement since neither state nor city governments were responsible for an authority's financial obligations. Moreover, authorities were
given the power to construct and manage (not just regulate) housing.
That such housing would be open only to a small segment of the population helped dispel fears over "socialized" industries. So, too, the promise of federal funds, especially during a period of economic collapse,
substantially muted ideological protests. The additional ability to exercise eminent domain, though untested in the courts, suggested a broader shift from private to public power, a shift Abrams advocated. He and
others believed they had rescued social reform, or at least housing
reform, from the political cookie jar so often raided by elected politicians (with disastrous consequences). The possibility that nonelected
officials, such as Robert Moses, might use authorities for their own ques-
tionable purposes did not enter into his rose-colored thinking. It was not
the last time Abrams' naivete would get the better of his judgment.

Whether one saw them as essentially positive or negative, authorities
were part of the changing nature of governance. The long-standing dyad
of local and state government was quickly giving way to a triptych that
included the national government. Created by states, operating within
cities, but partially dependent on federal funds, authorities presented
policymakers with ambiguous and sometimes tricky administrative and
legal questions. Perhaps no one was better suited to answer these questions than Abrams. In doing so, he would help redefine the balance of
intergovernmental power.

Chapter Four

VISION AND REALITY
Implementing Policy on the Local Level

Initiating housing reform in the late nineteenth and early twentieth century had been complex and uncertain. Implementing public housing in the 1930s would be similarly challenging, especially for Abrams, who served almost four years as NYCHA's first general counsel. By the end of his tenure, NYCHA had emerged as the preeminent housing authority in the country, with three projects in various stages of completion (one being the largest such development in the United States). Thousands of families had been rehoused, and some of the city's worst tenements had been demolished.

Despite these successes, Abrams' work at NYCHA was frustrating. As an author of the authorities law, he thought decisionmakers would rely on his interpretation of that legislation. Events proved otherwise, and Abrams left NYCHA wondering whether his vision of public housing would ever materialize. This disappointment was related to the larger process of policy implementation; recent theorizing concerning agenda setting can help us understand why. One influential scholar, for example, has argued: "The separate streams of problems, policies, and politics come together at certain critical times. Solutions become joined to problems, and both of them are joined to favorable political forces." Such "couplings" are likely when "a policy window—an opportunity to push pet proposals or one's conceptions of problems—is open." "Couplings" had indeed occurred during the early 1930s. New administrative mechanisms, namely, public authorities, were the result. But once Abrams and Langdon Post began to use NYCHA to enforce tenement regulations, property owners demanded a curtailment of its powers. LaGuardia believed these critics could be placated without abandoning NYCHA's objectives, if only Abrams and Post would do so. Facing reelection in 1937, and demanding visible results from a program he had championed, the mayor eventually intervened directly into NYCHA's operations. This action ultimately led to Abrams' resignation and Post's dismissal.[1]

Even before local political forces limited Abrams and Post's autonomy, other factors complicated and impeded NYCHA's ability to build public housing. Disagreements over site selection for specific projects reflected broader debates over urban growth and blurred the already murky distinction between slum clearance and subsidized housing, delaying concerted action on both fronts. Even more significant, no one was quite sure what kind of relationship was supposed to exist between NYCHA and the national government. Were local authorities to construct or simply manage housing projects? If the former, what did municipalities need to do to qualify for federal funds? What strings would be attached? Questions like these underscored the continually shifting ground of intergovernmental relations and the dramatic reshaping of American federalism caused by New Deal social programs. They all also belied the notion of public officials creating and seamlessly implementing policy.[2]

The Housing Authorities Law and Contested Policy Objectives

Passed at the end of January 1934, the authorities law permitted communities throughout New York to create their own agencies for clearing slums and constructing low-income housing. New York City was one of the first to act. Consistent with his political sensibilities, LaGuardia's five appointees to NYCHA's board represented certain interest groups as

well as a general commitment to subsidized housing, LaGuardia chose
Mary Simkhovitch and Louis Pink, who embodied older reform currents
and important connections in Albany. The mayor also picked Reverend
E. Roberts Moore, administrative head of Catholic Charities in New York
City, and B. Charney Vladeck, a socialist, former alderman, and general
editor of the *Jewish Daily Forward*. For Chairman, LaGuardia appointed
Langdon Post, a fellow Fusionist whom the mayor had already selected
as Tenement House Commissioner. Among other appointees were the
architect Frederick L. Ackerman as technical director, Evans Clark as
economic adviser, and Abrams as general counsel. By the end of
February, with offices at Ten East Fortieth Street, NYCHA began functioning as the city's newest public agency.[3]

The authorities law provided few clues about where NYCHA's staff
should begin. Lawmakers had described the statute as an "act to promote the public health and safety by providing for the elimination of
unsanitary and dangerous housing conditions, to relieve congested
areas, and the construction and supervision of dwellings." Within this
mandate were the twin objectives of slum clearance and public housing.
An additional provision authorized NYCHA's use of eminent domain to
acquire non-slum property "necessary for the public use" and "included
in an approved project."[4]

Even with these directives, the statute was vague enough to sustain a
debate begun by reformers and policymakers in the early 1920s. Their
discussion focused on both the *sequence* and *location* of newly enacted
programs. Contemporaries argued about whether to clear slums first,
with construction of low-income housing to follow, or whether to build
housing on peripheral land, with slum clearance to occur only after
completion of these new dwellings. This debate revealed yet another set
of policy choices in addition to those clustering around restrictive versus
constructive legislation.[5]

Abrams believed slum clearance, low-cost housing, and peripheral
land development were *all* necessary to effect a true urban transformation. The order of these activities, though, was important. Peripheral
land was to be purchased and developed first. To this extent, Abrams
agreed with those who supported decentralization. Yet Abrams also
thought vacant land developments needed to supply low-income housing, something reformers often lost sight of when they envisioned ideal
communities. Low-income housing was crucial because it would provide

tenement residents with a place to live " 'so that they would not have to be thrown into the streets' " when " 'slum properties' " were demolished. As the population shifted to newer developments, demolitions in core areas could begin in earnest. Cleared slum sites could be used for a variety of commercial and residential purposes, including construction of additional low- and moderate-income housing. With ample dwellings located *throughout* a metropolitan area, densities and rents would remain fairly low. Abrams hoped this comprehensive strategy would lead to the rational and humane development of America's cities.[6]

Uniting a range of interests by eschewing either/or dichotomies, Abrams' vision was significant because he insisted public officials had to provide slum dwellers with alternative places to live, whether in their old neighborhoods or in new ones. The eventual drift of policy, however, was in another direction: at best, former slums would possess an amount of housing "equivalent" to the number of pre-clearance dwellings—but no more, and often fewer. The rest of the land would be used for higher priced housing or commercial developments. Abrams would label this a "perversion" of public policy because city officials were implementing only *one* aspect of municipal housing legislation (slum clearance). As he later explained in his many books and articles, "demolition alone intensifies the slum problem, drives the slum dwellers into other slums, increases overcrowding, booms slum values—only with provision of houses for the displaced tenantry can real slum clearance be effected." Without this provision, he thought it would be "more logical to follow English policy and prohibit slum elimination rather than require it."[7]

Blurring Administrative Authority

Other factors, along with disagreement over program priorities, influenced NYCHA's direction and activities. Contemporary scholars often use a "state-centered" analysis to examine and explain these phenomena. This approach stresses the ability of administrators, career government personnel, and "state structures" to influence policymaking and the expansion of government services. State-centered analyses therefore share much with trends in public administration. A "classical" model of policy implementation—one in which skilled, apolitical bureaucrats objectively carried out various functions—was long dominant. Several models eventually replaced this paradigm, but despite differences, they all viewed policymaking as a far more circular process than did the "classical" model. Like state-centered analyses, they assumed administrators can make substantial modifications to public policies.[8]

As administrators, Abrams and Harold Ickes did indeed possess a certain degree of power (Ickes, head of the PWA, determined which cities would receive federal funds for subsidized housing). Besides illustrating the influence of public officials, their actions also revealed the way intergovernmental disputes can affect policy outcomes. In short, Ickes' preference for centralized, nationally run programs conflicted with the desire of local decisionmakers to implement policy initiatives themselves.[9]

This mismatch between federal and local objectives was not yet apparent as Abrams and Post tried to determine the PWA's funding criteria. The PWA had been established on June 16, 1933 by the National Industrial Recovery Act (NIRA) and, out of an initial appropriation of $3.3 billion, it was authorized to spend $135 million for the "construction, reconstruction, alteration, or repair . . . of low-cost housing and slum-clearance projects." In January 1934, the PWA announced it had "earmarked" $25 million for the proposed New York City Housing Authority. LaGuardia took this to mean New York City would soon be eligible for millions of dollars in federal funding, though how this money could be spent, and what kinds of projects would result, was not clear.[10]

Uncertainty over specifics was due partially to the changing philosophy of the PWA's Housing Division. The Housing Division took over management of a limited dividend program previously initiated by the Reconstruction Finance Corporation (RFC). This program had authorized the federal government to make loans to corporations that agreed to construct low-income housing. Rents in these projects would remain low because investors agreed, in exchange for certain benefits, to limit their profits (hence the phrase "limited dividend"). Under PWA supervision, interest rates were lowered and loan periods extended. Nonetheless, just a few months later (November 1933), Ickes suggested the Housing Division's focus might change since America could not rely on limited dividend corporations to effect slum clearance or construction of low-income housing. The reason, according to Ickes, was simple: most commercial developers were unwilling to reduce or restrict their profits.[11]

Congress had also authorized the PWA to make grants and loans to "States, municipalities, or *other public bodies* [emphasis added]" for various undertakings, including low-income housing. Under these provisions, housing authorities (commonly accepted as "other public bodies") could receive grants for 30 percent, and loans for the remaining 70 percent of a project's cost. Moreover, Housing Division administrators had voiced approval of this approach early on, indicating federal intervention would occur *only* if local action was not forthcoming. It seemed reasonable, then, to conclude Ickes was going to rely primarily on housing authorities to carry out the task of urban reconstruction. But while efforts were already underway in several states (no housing authorities existed prior to the PWA's enactment), Ickes filed papers of incorporation for a *federal* housing corporation in October 1933. Such a move confirmed his intention to make the national government an equal partner in reshaping the metropolitan landscape.[12]

Thus, when NYCHA was being set up at the beginning of 1934, there were actually three distinct mechanisms for providing affordable dwellings: limited dividend corporations, housing authorities, and/or direct building by the PWA via its Housing Division. This array of alternatives proved illusory. The first option lasted only a few more weeks before the PWA abandoned it altogether. The second, while receiving the greatest publicity and support from reformers, was not the route Ickes ultimately preferred, despite previous remarks to the contrary. Rather, he would continually push for direct PWA construction, providing it with the lion's share of financial and administrative resources (although funds for his proposed federal housing corporation were never appropriated).[13]

Post, Abrams, and LaGuardia were unaware there would be two rather than three policy tracks, or that the surviving ones (housing authorities and the PWA) would be antagonistic. They initially believed federal officials would "go along" with whatever NYCHA proposed; instead, Abrams would watch as the status of authorities "sank with successive PWA bulletins from entrepreneur to co-venturer, from co-venturer to adviser, and from adviser to functionless entity." In light of these constraints, policy implementation would rarely be a straightforward matter of applying certain statutes to certain situations. Abrams would have to be ever mindful of his remarks to the New York Board of Real Estate: housing laws needed to "remain flexible to make room for changing times and conditions." Or, as the *New York Times* had cautioned NYCHA, its " 'reach of vision' " could not " 'too far exceed its grasp of realities.' "[14]

Intergovernmental Antagonism at High Tide: Williamsburg Houses

All of the problems associated with the initial relationship between federal and local authorities were illustrated in NYCHA's first attempt to construct low-income housing. On March 7, 1934, Post and Abrams traveled to Washington, D.C. They immediately received conflicting signals from the Housing Division. There seemed to be "no definite plan" for municipal housing authorities—yet the PWA listed specific criteria for receiving funds. "Concrete plans" had to be submitted; "some security" had to be given against government funds; and NYCHA had to acquire project sites before the PWA would make any loans. Abrams was shocked at these seemingly new stipulations. The PWA, he argued, was "taking the attitude of the banker in a private operation instead of viewing the authority as . . . interested in achieving the same social purpose as the government itself." Despite claiming Ickes' preconditions were impossible to satisfy, Abrams provided the Housing Division with eight proposals before returning to New York City. More sanguine than Abrams, Post was convinced NYCHA would have "many more things to do beyond the buying of land and erection of buildings"; it would actually manage the new communities it created.[15]

One such community was planned for Williamsburg, Brooklyn. With old law tenements comprising 51 percent of its housing stock, Williamsburg contained some of the city's worst slums; on the other hand, its land costs were relatively low, approximately $2.00 to $4.00 cheaper per square foot than for similar areas in Manhattan. These and other reasons inclined Abrams toward supporting Williamsburg as a model for the "initiation and construction of other [NYCHA] projects." The PWA approved the Williamsburg site, agreeing to purchase and assemble the land (in contradiction of its own guidelines), then convey title to NYCHA, which would build and operate housing for an anticipated 6,000 tenants. Transfer of the long-sought-after $25 million was, according to the PWA, imminent.[16]

In early summer (1934) Ickes decided to consolidate the Housing Division's control over slum clearance and housing. Virtually all aspects of project development were to be handled from Washington, with authorities given the limited role of leasing and renting buildings once they were completed. The leasing arrangement, Post would later state, was "unsatisfactory" and "could not by any stretch of the imagination be considered an adequate substitute for ownership." At the time, his actions were constrained by the implicit threat that noncompliance would mean a cancellation of federal funds. Post also discovered NYCHA and the PWA were *both* collecting option agreements from the 700 property owners on the Williamsburg site, a situation potentially harmful to NYCHA's authority. The title of a *Real Estate Record* article aptly summed up the tortuous path of policy implementation: "Confusion Attends the New York Housing Program." In late August, with Post and LaGuardia trying to free NYCHA from the PWA's administrative talons, Ickes complained New York had " 'taken an attitude different from that of any other city' " in wanting to construct low-income housing itself. Were he to make an exception for New York—and release the often promised but still undelivered PWA funds—other cities might feel discriminated against.[17]

LaGuardia and Post conferred with Ickes and Roosevelt in early September, after which Ickes was more flexible, though he remained recalcitrant about turning over the Williamsburg project entirely to local officials. A new agreement authorized the PWA to purchase the land, then lease it to NYCHA. In turn, NYCHA would provide public services, grant tax exemptions, build the project, and select its tenants. In all other areas, local and federal agencies were to maintain "joint supervision and control." On October 12, the PWA exercised its first options on the Williamsburg site.[18]

These agreements notwithstanding, Abrams believed the PWA was continuing to impede NYCHA's operations. From the fall of 1934 it took another three and a half years to build and fully occupy Williamsburg Houses. Delays were caused primarily by ongoing confusion and disagreements between the PWA and NYCHA. "Decisions and solutions," Abrams complained in 1935, could not be "made or found by remote control of the project." A year later he decried the still unresolved relationship between the PWA and Williamsburg Houses. Finally, in August of 1937, a lease was signed between the federal government and

NYCHA; the PWA, however, had already constructed the project by then, a violation of its earlier commitment to "joint supervision." As Post recalled, NYCHA had "something to say about the broad principles of site plan and design," but "the details, the specifications and the methods of construction were dictated entirely from Washington."[19]

Williamsburg Houses was a bittersweet victory for reformers. The PWA claimed it was the "greatest of all American low-rent housing projects," and even Post praised it as a "historical monument on the road to housing progress." But Post also acknowledged the project's defects, many of which he attributed to the PWA. Each of the 5,688 rooms had cost an average of $2,296, far higher than planners had originally hoped. In Post's estimation, lack of sufficient time to select tenants, postponed occupancy dates, "faulty construction," and "much bickering" were also the PWA's fault.[20]

Post's critique highlighted the problems Abrams had warned about from the very beginning, despite his general optimism over selection of the Williamsburg site. The project's 300 *additional* families actually increased the area's population density from 180 to 201 persons per acre. More problematic, *all* of the site's residents were forced to move before construction of the project began. While NYCHA attempted to "minimize the hardship" faced by these individuals, it could not guarantee them a place in Williamsburg Houses or affordable accommodations elsewhere. Uprooted tenants who did find new dwellings ended up paying higher median rents. Here was the cycle that eventually caused Abrams to oppose slum clearance unless additional low-income housing was built.[21]

Maneuvering Around Policy Obstacles: First Houses

Perhaps more important to Abrams than Williamsburg Houses, and equally illustrative of the difficulties involved in policy implementation, was the project known as First Houses. With PWA grants not forthcoming, New York City's newest agency had to rely on LaGuardia for funding, but he refused to cooperate, even though the authorities law authorized him to loan NYCHA up to $500,000. Abrams thought the mayor, with his gaze fixed on the next election, wanted to get the credit for building public housing. In what was perhaps an intended understatement, Abrams would remark: "The idea of the Housing Authority being autonomous, the idea of Langdon Post getting the publicity as its chairman, of Langdon Post building himself possibly as a rival of LaGuardia . . . annoyed LaGuardia." As a consequence, the mayor withheld municipal assistance. Hindsight allowed Abrams to reach this conclusion, since later developments did suggest LaGuardia belatedly realized he had released a political genie from its bottle by supporting NYCHA's creation.[22]

Seemingly at a financial dead end, Abrams and Post devised a method of raising revenue for NYCHA. Vacant tenements dotted the city's landscape, and during the Depression cadres of Works Progress Administration (WPA) employees had been put to work tearing them down. Some of the lumber and bricks from these structures were still in usable condition. Why not, Abrams and Post ruminated, sell them and keep the proceeds for NYCHA? NYCHA was soon in the reclamation business, "getting free labor from the WPA, making contracts with owners, and stimulating them to tear down their buildings." Almost two years after it was established, NYCHA was still operating "largely on sums derived from the proceeds of the sale of materials in buildings demolished under the Authority's program of clearance," a sum amounting to $149,982 out of $183,104 in revenues. By then, however, the New York City Comptroller had begun to question whether or not NYCHA's actions were legal. Sitting down to write a brief on the subject, Abrams grudgingly concluded the law was not on the Authority's side, so he met with NYCHA board members to apprise them of this fact. In a thick accent, B. Charney Vladeck—the "Russian Revolutionary" as Abrams called him—gave his opinion on the matter. "Do not give the money," he said. "I do not care what is the legal situation here," Vladeck intoned, "nobody can criticize a corporation for taking money which doesn't belong to it, so long as it doesn't go into the purse of the officers." Abrams decided Vladeck's position made "good political sense, even if it didn't make legal sense"; NYCHA consequently "kept the money and refused to turn it over." As Authority officials more tactfully put it in a subsequent publicity brochure, "the bricks of the old tenements" were "being used to carry on the war" to abolish New York's slums."[23]

Eager to build an actual project, Post and Abrams began accepting property offers almost as soon as NYCHA was up and running. In March, a newspaper article described the real estate holdings of Vincent Astor, heir to a huge fortune and owner of several rundown tenements. Astor, embarrassed by the condition of his properties and eager to remove this blemish from his family's noblesse-oblige complexion, contacted Post and offered to sell his thirty-eight Lower East Side buildings for "a price well below assessed valuation." Though Astor lowered his asking price almost immediately, NYCHA had no funds to buy any property. A few unpleasant realities began to sink in for Abrams and Post.[24]

The following October (1934), a serendipitous event temporarily raised NYCHA's collective spirits. Post was walking through Central Park when he happened to notice a new zoo nearing completion; the zoo itself was one of Robert Moses' projects, and was being constructed with substantial grants from the Federal Emergency Relief Administration (FERA). Inspired, Post took the next flight to Washington, D.C., where he met with FERA's head administrator, Harry Hopkins. (Abrams himself would call Hopkins a "very interesting character," one who was a "complete contrast to Ickes" because he "wasn't held back by technical obstructions.") Arguing that homes for people were at least as important as those for monkeys, Post asked for $300,000 to cover materials and labor for a housing project. Hopkins, inspired by Post's enthusiasm, set aside the requested funds. There was only one catch: these monies could be not be used to purchase land. Post therefore had to persuade Astor to accept NYCHA bonds (in the amount of $189,000) instead of cash. He did, and First Houses—so-named because it was the first project NYCHA actually built—was the result.[25]

Completed in July of 1935 and dedicated by Eleanor Roosevelt, First Houses' combination of renovation and new construction was not only unorthodox, it should have disqualified NYCHA from receiving assistance from FERA. After NYCHA inspected Astor's tenements, it decided many of them would have to be razed. FERA, though, had restricted its funds for use on *rehabilitation* projects, not *new* housing. NYCHA got around this additional policy obstacle by using the site's old foundations for the new structures and by conforming to an identical design scheme, which made the new buildings appear to be rehabilitated versions of the old ones. Frederick Ackerman, NYCHA's chief architect, was responsible for these decisions. Yet, like other aspects of the project, Ackerman's involvement was ironic. He initially advocated large, self-contained developments since they created their own environments. His support of the much smaller First Houses was consistent with this position: he fully expected it to illustrate the liabilities of modest projects. That First Houses did *not* fail suggested how uncertain—even wrong—the theoretical underpinnings of housing policies could be.[26]

First Houses was eventually home to 120 families, a number whittled down from more than 4,000 applicants. With an average rental of $6.05 per room, or $18.00 per month, First Houses represented a notable savings for its first tenants, who had previously lived in inferior apartments for $21.00 per month. But if rentals were relatively low compared to other slum dwellings, they were still too high for many of the city's poorest citizens. This did not trouble Abrams. In his opinion, public housing's initial success depended on whether it could survive at all, not on how great a percentage of the population it could accommodate. Related to this concern, Abrams decided the only way to get additional money for public housing was to borrow it (in exchange for housing bonds) from large insurance companies and investment houses. These entrepreneurs, however, might be reluctant to invest if they felt tenants would be unable to pay their rent. Their apprehension provided another reason, in Abrams' view, to exclude the *Lumpenproletariat* from public housing. Such a precedent would be difficult to overcome, as Abrams himself would discover.[27]

Keeping the Policy Window Open: *NYCHA v. Muller*

Ickes' support of slum sites for housing projects had entangled the PWA in complex, protracted negotiations. Within any block, there could be forty to sixty different property owners, as well as encumbrances associated with deed restrictions and trust provisions. To hasten property acquisition and, even more important, to bring down inflated land prices, the PWA had been given the ability to exercise eminent domain—the state's right to take forcibly (but with compensation) private property for public use. The opportunity to exercise this power, though, was short-lived. On January 4, 1935, the United States District Court for the western district of Kentucky handed down its decision in *United States v. Certain Lands in the City of Louisville*. It ruled against the federal government's use of eminent domain in slum clearance and construction of low-rent housing. While some reformers welcomed the decision—they believed it would turn renewed attention to vacant land

sites—local and national policymakers were alarmed. The court's reasoning, by embracing a literal instead of broad conception of "public
use," potentially endangered public housing and, more generally, the
New Deal itself.[28]

This issue came into sharp focus almost immediately for NYCHA.
Virtually in the middle of Astor's tenements were two buildings owned
by Andrew Muller. NYCHA had offered Muller $34,000 for his property,
but he refused to take bonds in lieu of cash. Post next went to LaGuardia
and asked if the city would accept bonds in exchange for cash, which
NYCHA would then use to pay Muller. LaGuardia, disapproving of the
way Post had handled the entire matter, refused. With few options left,
Post paid a visit to his friend, Bernard M. Baruch, a former economic
adviser to President Wilson and doyen of New York's financial elite.
Baruch, much to Post's relief, agreed to purchase the requisite number
of bonds. When Post returned to Muller to close the transaction, he
learned the asking price had been raised to $45,000. NYCHA countered
with an offer of $36,000, but Muller remained adamant.[29]

Hoping to test the constitutionality of eminent domain and public
housing on the state level, Abrams pushed NYCHA to file a condemnation suit against Muller. LaGuardia and the city's attorney, Paul Windels,
opposed this action. Better, they thought, to hold off provoking such a
test case until NYCHA had greater institutional clout. More optimistic
about NYCHA's chances, and convinced a victory would provide the necessary precedent for other states (and for the federal government in its
appeal of *Louisville*), Abrams persuaded NYCHA's board to support condemnation proceedings. As expected, Muller responded by obtaining a
"show cause" order from the New York Supreme Court, an order requiring NYCHA to justify its actions.[30]

Abrams argued the case before the lower court in April 1934, and
submitted an influential brief in January 1936 to the Appeals Court
(New York's highest judicial forum). In both instances, Muller's attorneys insisted the authorities law was unconstitutional because it permitted eminent domain proceedings to take property from one individual
and transfer it to another. Another charge against NYCHA was that "the
removal of buildings constituting a menace to the community [was] a
subject for the exercise of police power but not eminent domain." In
other words, states and municipalities could only use an older form of
public intervention—police power—to clear slums. Finally, NYCHA's

adversaries maintained the authorities law was analogous to NIRA's eminent domain provision, which the *Louisville* decision had declared unconstitutional.[31]

[In response, Abrams constructed a masterful, eighty-page brief that was at once a legal, historical, and sociological survey of urban development and the dearth of affordable housing. It was also a comprehensive, even dramatic recapitulation of Abrams' evolving thought as a lawyer and an intellectual. He began by providing a description of the three-stage history of housing legislation in New York State, labeling the successive periods "purely restrictive," "limited dividend," and "constructive." Because these stages suggested a progressive increase in public activity, Abrams concluded it was "no longer correct . . . to hold that urban housing is a matter so completely private in nature as to exclude at all times all forms of public interference. . . . even judicial decisions must necessarily be construed with the modifications imperatively required by a transmuted physical and social background." In addition to reflecting the influence of legal realism, Abrams' thinking revealed his views on how to rationalize urban expansion. "Only by the use of eminent domain as a force in planning," Abrams averred, "can the slums be totally eliminated and municipal finances stabilized." This planning "force" was entirely legitimate since "streets, transportation facilities, parks and other public improvements" depended on its use.[32]

Abrams then spoke to the specific objections raised by Muller's attorneys. He quickly dispensed with the contention that the authorities law was similar to NIRA's eminent domain clause. The *Louisville* decision itself had confirmed the right of states to venture into areas prohibited to the federal government. "Nothing in the Fourteenth Amendment," the decision further affirmed, prevented "a state from exercising the power of eminent domain to carry into effect a public policy which . . . may be regarded as promotive of the public interest."[33]

Abrams' case required his persuasiveness on two other points: the nature of "public use," and whether that term encompassed public housing. Abrams tackled the first issue by eschewing a literal interpretation of "public use." In support, he relied on the "most recent writer on the subject," Philip Nichols. Nichols, according to Abrams, maintained that a "public use for which property may be taken by eminent domain" existed when such an action allowed the federal government or a state "to preserve the safety, health and comfort of the public, whether or not the individual members of the public may make use of the property so taken." This was the broad conception of "public use" Abrams and other New Deal-era policymakers supported. Yet, as Abrams pointed out, no precedents linked it to public housing. Unless this connection were made, NYCHA's ability to exercise eminent domain would be drastically circumscribed, if not prohibited altogether. Abrams, in a flash of insight, decided the best way to address this problem was indirectly. He realized New York courts had sanctioned eminent domain in certain circumstances, notably when public health and safety were involved. If these concerns could trigger eminent domain proceedings, it hardly took a leap in logic to suggest construction of public housing might do the same. Who, after all, would deny that slum clearance and adequate dwellings weren't related to public health and safety? Reviewing additional data, he concluded that "in light of the purposes which are thus classed as public, it is difficult to understand how public housing of the poorer classes . . . can be considered as private; especially in view of the fact that the health and welfare of the whole public is concerned." Abrams hoped these arguments would sufficiently connect public housing with a public use doctrine authorizing eminent domain proceedings.[34]

In his summation, Abrams warned about the consequences of an adverse decision: "The damage that would be done by the invalidation of these statutes is too great to be measured in terms of money," he remarked, adding that "such a result would leave to be performed by private enterprise what private enterprise cannot do." Then, in what must have been a troubling thought for Abrams, he noted: "It would place the greater portion of the people of our metropolitan cities in the unthinkable position of having to dwell in hovels which both the Legislature and the courts have continually condemned, and for which no other remedy has been found." More than closing remarks to a brief, these were the guiding signposts of Abrams' own thinking and professional development. Private action had not cleared slums or built affordable housing. Limited public activity (restrictive legislation) had also proved inadequate. Only direct public intervention, something Abrams believed in philosophically and was now using his skills as a lawyer to legitimize, could accomplish the tasks at hand. The currents of legal discourse and policy debate intersected with Abrams' own journey here on the judicial battleground.[35]

As Abrams had predicted, NYCHA, armed with his briefs, was victorious in both the lower court and the Appeals Court. Writing for the former, Judge Charles B. McLaughlin noted it was "difficult to conceive of a law . . . more for the public good than the one under discussion." The Appeals Court likewise asserted, "The modern city functions in the public interest as proprietor and operator of many activities formerly and in some instances still carried on by private enterprise." For these reasons, NYCHA's attempted taking of Muller's property was adjudged a "public use." This meant NYCHA was able to obtain Muller's buildings, and at a price $10,000 less than originally offered. On a larger scale, the *Muller* decision upheld the power of authorities to exercise eminent domain and condemnation proceedings, which was nothing less than judicial approval of state and municipal housing projects. Contemporaries were well aware of the case's significance, especially since the appellate ruling came only twelve days after the government had decided not to argue *Louisville* before the United States Supreme Court. Abrams was praised for his efforts and received numerous requests for copies of his brief, including one from Edith Elmer Wood. His participation in the *Muller* case, along with his role in drafting the authorities law, made him the era's leading legal expert on public housing.[36]

Interest Groups and Policy Implementation

One of NYCHA's first jobs had been to take inventory of all real property in New York City, a mammoth project requiring almost a year to complete, even with the assistance of 6,000 employees from the Civil Works Administration. This investigation revealed seventeen square miles of slums, more than half of which contained dwellings recommended for demolition by NYCHA's Committee on Long Range Program[s].[37]

While neither NYCHA nor the federal government could clear and rebuild even a fraction of these slums, a series of tragic conflagrations in the winter of 1934 refocused public attention on old law tenements, most of which remained unprotected against fire and other dangers. With 19,000 violations already on file at the Tenement House Department, Post thought legal action against property owners would involve a long and costly process. One of his chief assistants, however, reminded him that the Tenement House Department, like the Health

Department, had the ability to vacate unsafe or unfit buildings. This power, though, was rarely exercised, presumably because of the political consequences involved in a direct attack on private property. Post, apparently sensing public opinion would support drastic measures, decided to vacate a large number of old law tenements. By the end of February 1934, the Tenement Department had condemned nine apartment houses in Brooklyn and had begun proceedings against eight more in Manhattan. The Council of Real Estate Associations of Greater New York, fearing Post would terminate a moratorium on multiple-dwelling violations (which was set to expire in April), threatened to abandon their 67,000 tenements, leaving 670,000 families homeless. But property owners could not make good on their threat for two reasons. Since the Depression caused families to double-up in order to save money, New York City had a high vacancy rate, about 25 percent in old law tenements. Evictions during this kind of housing *surplus* would be less problematic than if they occurred during a housing *shortage*. Post also had the backing of LaGuardia, a mayor whose first several months in office were marked by a distinct and publicly professed lack of sympathy for slumlords. Finding little support for their position, many tenement owners complied with code requirements, and more than 20,000 buildings were equipped with "proper fire escapes and fire-retarded cellar ceilings."[38]

Abrams' role in Post's campaign against old law tenements included drafting amendments to strengthen the Multiple Dwellings Law. One of them, passed in 1935, redefined "owner" to include any party who had an interest in a piece of property. This made banks, which held substantial mortgages, equally responsible and criminally liable if injuries occurred to tenants in substandard buildings. Within a year, another series of amendments required toilets in every apartment and fireproofing of public halls. Abrams' efforts gave real teeth to Post's claim that the city was not going to compete with old law tenements but "get rid of them."[39]

The attempt to rid New York City of old law tenements (via strict code enforcement) yielded impressive results. In 1933, only 39 vacation orders had been issued; between 1934 and 1935, 1,286 were issued. By the end of 1938, more than 8,000 tenements, housing tens of thousands of families, had been vacated. This was not an entirely positive development, though. A year earlier settlement-house workers began to warn that the banks' decision to board up their tenements rather than make costly renovations ($3,000–$4,000 per building) was making affordable housing scarce. Property owners who did meet the new requirements aggravated an already critical situation by raising rents. Concurrently, the Tenement Department was conducting its first "cycle survey" in twenty-five years. By June 1936, this systematic inspection of all tenement houses had reached the Lower East Side, an area where most of the bank holdings were located. Waiting until December, the fiduciaries served approximately 4,000 dispossess notices, which put LaGuardia in a precarious position. He had supported Post's attack on old law tenements, even in the face of vocal opposition from property interests. But now the possibility of a real crisis loomed: tenant groups, angry over evictions and rising rents, were picketing banks and LaGuardia's office— threatening to fill court dockets with litigation—while landlords protested the Tenement Department's unyielding position. Attacked from both the political right and left, and with his reelection campaign on the horizon, LaGuardia sought a middle road. To find one, and perhaps shift institutional culpability, he asked NYCHA to hold hearings on the housing shortage. Abrams was appointed as counsel to the hearings, and it would be his responsibility to see that they ran smoothly—and produced tangible, politically acceptable results.[40]

The hearings, held in late December, elicited testimony from a wide variety of groups and individuals. Landlords argued against the expense of additional renovations, while tenants and housing reformers stressed the social and legal reasons justifying them. NYCHA officials ultimately placed tenant concerns above those of landlords. Their recommendations called for an expansion of the Vacancy Listing Bureau and modifications in the Emergency Relief Bureau, municipal assistance for residents of vacated tenements, compulsory demolition of abandoned buildings, and renovation of structures whose owners refused to make necessary improvements (with liens against the properties to recover costs). A moratorium on the Multiple Dwelling Law requirements was rejected, but NYCHA did recommend suspension of civil and criminal penalties against code violators in exchange for their compliance with the law. A final recommendation called for direct regulation of tenements through "emergency rent legislation," which would forbid "unreasonable, arbitrary and oppressive rent increases" for families with incomes under $1,500. A few months later, Abrams would assure

NYCHA that if rent controls were again imposed on New York City (they had been in effect from the end of World War I to 1929), such regulations would not "contravene . . . constitutional inhibitions."[41]

NYCHA's recommendations were supposed to produce a viable compromise. Just the opposite resulted. Landlords, especially banks, still feeling menaced by enforcement of the new tenement laws and horrified at the possibility of rent restrictions, eventually boarded up 25 percent of their properties. At the same time, the option NYCHA gave property owners of abandoning their buildings instead of repairing them incensed tenant groups. Most disturbing to the mayor, policy decisions now seemed to rest with NYCHA, not Gracie Mansion. LaGuardia was confined, as he had stated in December, to do nothing but enforce the existing law. While such a statement might have initially provided political cover, by the end of NYCHA's hearings it suggested impotence more than anything else. As a result, the policy window that had opened in 1934 began to close. LaGuardia now demanded that construction of public housing replace tenement reform as NYCHA's top concern (like all effective politicians, LaGuardia needed to make good on campaign promises).[42]

To effect this new priority, the mayor had to reassert control over NYCHA, which he did with little hesitation. Following the hearings, he warned Post not to interfere with the administration's efforts to formulate solutions to the housing shortage. The role of Nathan Straus, a former NYCHA board member, as Administrator of the newly created Federal Housing Authority, raised tensions further. Straus wanted to decentralize his agency, an objective with which Ickes was not sympathetic. Moreover, Ickes associated Straus ("a rich man's son" who "never had to fight his way through life") with the "starry-eyed" group in New York "who think they are experts on housing because they write about it and talk a lot about it." Ickes also feared Post would "run Straus," and that "a wild-eyed female by the name of Catherine Bauer" would be "close to the front." LaGuardia, no political novice himself, probably realized a substantial percentage of New York City's federal aid depended on a good relationship with the PWA's top official. If Ickes rebuffed Post, Straus, and their supporters, perhaps it was best that the mayor do likewise.[43]

LaGuardia's opportunities for targeting Post and Abrams increased after November 1937. Despite a potential nomination fight with Robert

Moses, and in contrast to his own doubts, LaGuardia won a resounding second term as mayor. Two weeks later, at the annual Conference of U.S. Mayors, Abrams was asked to give an explanation of federal housing legislation. Though LaGuardia was in attendance, Abrams did not defer to him; instead, he proceeded with a technical analysis himself. LaGuardia was incensed, not only because he thought Abrams had taken it upon himself to speak for the city (therefore usurping the mayor's role), but because he felt Abrams' speech was overly cautious and " 'legalistic.' " " 'I was sick and tired,' " LaGuardia fumed, " 'of the semi-colon type of speech which Abrams delivered . . . . It created doubts as to the meaning of the law regarding housing.' " The mayor added he was " 'also sick and tired of Mr. Abrams' constant looking for fly specks in the law which did nothing but hamper . . . . Any one [sic] connected with such an organization as the Housing Authority should build and not make obstructionist speeches.' "[44]

The following week, Nathan Straus planned to hold a conference for local housing authorities. Until the latter's responsibilities were clarified, Straus was going to postpone processing any new project applications. In LaGuardia's opinion, the conference and delay were both unnecessary. "All of the information available in that respect has been obtained," he wrote Helen Alfred, adding, "I want no more talk, no more discussion, no more palaver about housing." LaGuardia telegraphed Straus, telling him NYCHA would not attend any "star-gazing" conferences unless Straus was willing to discuss concrete proposals. Abrams, accusing the mayor of overstepping his authority, resigned from NYCHA on November 22, 1937. Two days later he attended the Straus conference in his capacity as general counsel for the American Federation of Housing Authorities.[45]

For Abrams, LaGuardia's actions threatened NYCHA's very existence. If the mayor could keep NYCHA's representatives from attending conferences, he could also "draw to himself full control over the Authority and its functioning, destroying [its] independence." Without autonomy, NYCHA would be thrown into the "caldron of politics where favoritism, impartial selection of tenants and free choice of sites" would depend on the "honesty or dishonesty of the then current City Administration." Abrams believed this would gut the authorities law, and transform NYCHA into a municipal minister without portfolio. LaGuardia retorted by claiming his actions were entirely justified and, according to the local press, by calling Abrams a "pettifogging lawyer." NYCHA board members, rushing into the fray, issued an eloquent appraisal of Abrams' achievements, concluding that he had helped "doom" New York City slums by marching in the "vanguard where monetary compensation is neither possible nor expected." The *New York Times* added its editorial support, commending Abrams on his accomplishments and decision to resign.[46]

While Post did not take Abrams' suggestion to step down, he did plan to comply with Straus' request to refrain from submitting any new project proposals until January 1, 1938. LaGuardia, again livid, fired Post and swore in his own personal secretary, Lester Stone, as the new interim Chairman. When reporters noted the illegality of the mayor's actions, LaGuardia responded that he would appoint an entirely new board if NYCHA did not approve Stone's appointment. Post subsequently commented on this arrogation of power, characterizing LaGuardia's actions as a "benevolent dictatorship." "Local housing authorities," he stated, "should have the greatest degree of independence consonant with the spirit of home rule and the need for municipal cooperation." Arthur Garfield Hays, perhaps with Abrams as ghostwriter, dashed off a letter to New York Governor Herbert Lehman, describing the matter as one of "special significance" since the authorities law was "used as a model in almost every other State." "If the Mayor's acts are sanctioned by the State," Hays warned, "the powers which he has assumed in this instance might be assumed in other cities." Despite additional criticism from editorialists and Mary Simkhovitch—plus the resignation of Evans Clark—LaGuardia remained unapologetic. A month after he resigned, Abrams publicly denounced the local administration's history of neglect toward NYCHA. In response, LaGuardia had forty-four code violations filed against Abrams' properties. The mayor would not only define New York City's housing policy, he would quash any criticisms of it.[47]

Though New York City was exceptional in some respects, its experiences were duplicated elsewhere. In Cincinnati, relations among city officials, Authority members, and the federal government were also problematic, with land assemblage, costs, tenanting, and relocation all contentious issues. In Philadelphia, the Housing Commission bitterly fought with Ickes over the issue of slum clearance; public housing was delayed by curtailment of federal funds and opposition from the city's mayor; and initial appointments to the Philadelphia Housing Authority cast a shadow over that agency's independence. In Baltimore, conflicts with federal officials impeded early reform efforts, and even when these issues were resolved, the real estate industry and its allies effectively blocked implementation of public housing from 1935–1937. Thus, while policy entrepreneurs on the national level might have seen housing programs as a crucial part of creating an urban, "progrowth coalition," the fractious and contested nature of constructing actual projects suggests that additional concerns were raised on both the federal and local level.[48]

Abrams' experiences at NYCHA also revealed much about policy implementation during the 1930s. The process of clearing slums and building low-income housing was highly contingent and plagued throughout by confusion and ambiguity. Furthermore, conflict and outright hostility often characterized the interactions between federal and local officials (PWA and NYCHA) and between different units of local government (NYCHA and City Hall). This friction prevented NYCHA from receiving necessary resources and prompted local officials like Post and Abrams to wonder what level of government was best suited to administer certain programs. These questions were themselves complicated by the new relationships among cities, states, and Washington, D.C. that made older models of governance poor guides for implementing policy.[49]

Noting the uncertainty of policy implementation does not minimize Abrams' contributions. Just as federal courts struck a fatal blow against the PWA's Housing Division by denying it the ability to clear slums or build housing, state courts could have done the same to local authorities, had it not been for Abrams' judicial victory. His success was not unambiguous, though. Like the sepulchral ghost of Lazarus, the issue of eminent domain would return more than once to haunt him. What good, for example, was slum clearance if it ignored the needs of the individuals it uprooted? Abrams only belatedly realized that misguided or unscrupulous policymakers might use the tools of social reform to achieve their own dubious ends.

Yet another issue Abrams confronted was the influence of external forces on policymaking. Recent analyses have emphasized the ability of agencies and administrators to remain relatively "insulated" from outside pressures. Clearly, NYCHA was not immune to these factors, whether they were court decisions, property interests, tenant concerns, ᴏɪ political machinations. If nothing else, LaGuardia's actions demonstrated how fragile an authority's independence could be. As Maxwell H. Tretter, one of the individuals who supervised NYCHA's legal affairs after Abrams left, realistically noted: "In every phase of its work the authority will need the active cooperation and support of the mayor and all other agencies and departments of the city." The political scientist Annette Baker Fox, reflecting on New York City's experience, would more bluntly observe, "A forceful municipal executive can continue to influence housing authority policy, even contrary to the spirit of the law which specifies the independence of the authority." Abrams himself stressed the need for local authorities to retain control over site selection, land assemblage, contracting, and tenanting if their "integrity" and "purpose" were to remain "unimpaired."[50]

Like the strands of a double-helix, Abrams' career and NYCHA's progress were linked at critical points. An opportunity had existed to expand social provisions in America's metropolises, and Abrams seized that chance, forging, shaping, defining, and defending slum clearance and public housing in New York City. Along the way, the accumulating weight of New Deal administrative machinery, the jammed typewriter keys of too many potential courses of action, and LaGuardia's hard-boiled political decisions altered the direction of housing policy. As this phase of reform ended, so did a period in Abrams' life—his role as a legal/policy expert for NYCHA. Men of derring-do now replaced "starry-eyed" reformers. LaGuardia appointed Alfred Rheinstein, a well-known and well-connected builder, as NYCHA's new Chairman. Abrams would continue serving as the American Federation of Housing Authorities' general counsel, but he would not return to NYCHA. He was content, it seemed, with having made an important, though temporary, contribution.[51]

Chapter Five

THE PRACTITIONER AS SCHOLAR
Urban Studies and the Conflict Between
"Land" and "Industry"

By the 1930s, Abrams had emerged as a socially concerned lawyer. He had been drawn deeply into policy implementation and had worked at the center of a newly established agency. While these events provided Abrams with the evolving identity of a housing expert, a temporary departure from public life in 1937 required him to reassess his future plans. Financially secure and not yet forty, he could have revitalized his law practice or expanded his real estate portfolio, but neither option was appealing. What he really wanted was to convey to others his experience-derived insights and expertise in housing. Teaching and scholarship would become the avenues through which he channeled and refined this interest.

The New School for Social Research

Not all institutions supported the kind of applied scholarship Abrams found stimulating. The New School for Social Research was one of the few that did. Unique among universities, the New School was both a pedagogical and an academic experiment. It was an ideal place for Abrams to combine his skills as an instructor with his experiences outside academia. The courses he devised and taught there became the basis for the emerging discipline of urban studies. The New School was also the crucible for Abrams' evolving ideas concerning social and economic conflict. His major publication during this period—*Revolution in Land* (1939)—revealed a capacity for scholarly work often lacking in his contemporaries.

The New School opened on October 1, 1919, having been organized the previous year by Charles Beard, John Dewey, Alvin Johnson, and James Harvey Robinson. Its mission, solidly grounded in Progressive assumptions, was to create a purposeful intellectual environment, one connecting the world of ideas with the world of action. A broad range of individuals was attracted to this philosophy. Lewis Mumford took classes under the economist Thorstein Veblen, then returned in 1924 to give a series of lectures, which were the basis for one of his first books. Mumford's mentor, the British planner Patrick Geddes, gave weekly talks at the New School during the summer of 1923, while Sidney Hook, an outspoken political theorist, joined the faculty a few years later.[1]

Abrams and Ruth, residents of Greenwich Village for most of their lives, were well aware of the New School's presence and growing influence. They also likely realized it represented "modernism," a term the school's most recent biographers define as "artistic creativity, social research, and democratic reform." Ruth, identifying herself as a "modern" artist and an independent woman, took several New School classes and eventually assumed the directorship of its art gallery. This academic milieu played an equally important role in Abrams' development. German reform economists, who formed a visible presence at the New School, consistently stressed the sociological applications of economic theory and questioned the efficacy of private-market solutions. Abrams' early writings, including *Revolution in Land*, reveal these influences.[2]

In many ways, Abrams' own life and thinking paralleled the growth of the New School. The product of night law school, Abrams sympathized with attempts to establish alternatives to full-time, day-oriented campuses. He was also attracted to the New School's acceptance and even cultivation of tolerance, as well as its use of history as a didactic medium. Finally, the school's integrated approach to solving social problems struck Abrams as promising. He himself would soon insist reformers of every stripe needed to be experts in a number of disciplines, not just specialists in a particular field.

Urban Studies

Abrams became affiliated with the New School while he was still NYCHA's general counsel. After making some initial overtures, he was appointed as a regular lecturer in 1935. His decision to join the New School faculty was not that of a career academic looking for a lifelong post; he likely saw himself as an urban-practitioner moving back and forth along a spectrum of teaching, scholarship, and experience. Abrams' biggest challenge was a curricular one: the New School did not have any urban studies courses, though it occasionally offered lectures on architecture and planning. Abrams, with no real formal education of his own, would have to start from scratch.[3]

A possible inspiration for his courses was the relatively new discipline of land economics. That field was largely a product of the scholarship and teaching of Richard T. Ely. Initially affiliated with Johns Hopkins University, Ely subsequently organized the economics department at the University of Wisconsin. Officials there, disturbed by Ely's advocacy of socialism and support of labor unions, charged him with unprofessional conduct in 1894. Largely acquitted of these charges, Ely learned the language of activists was not always the language of academics, much the same as Abrams later learned the language of reform was not the same as politics. Ely's imbroglio redirected his attention to the relatively obscure and less controversial study of land economics, which he initially called "Land Property and the Rent of Land." Land economics, as Ely defined it, was concerned not only with the use of land, but also with the social relations its acquisition and management created.[4]

Abrams might have looked to urban planning for ideas as well, but that profession was still in its infancy. The first separate, degree-granting program did not get off the ground until 1929 at Harvard. Courses there and elsewhere tended to be highly specialized, drawing on curricula found in landscape architecture, civil engineering, and structural design. Students studying to become city planners learned how to site sewers, streets, transportation arteries, and other elements of urban infrastructure, yet formal training rarely provided them with a larger vision of how and why cities functioned.[5]

Perhaps not surprising, Abrams used his own experiences in law, real estate, finance, and public housing to construct a unique curriculum. His first two courses were entitled "Contemporary Housing and Rehousing" and "Modern Problems in Real Estate." Their syllabi and lecture outlines reveal a comprehensive and provocative treatment of numerous issues. For the latter course, Abrams discussed "Land and Industry," "Taxation," "The Mortgage Structure," "Land and the City," "Land in Theory and in Fact," "Urban and Rural Tenancy," and "The Government and Real Estate." As these topics attest, Abrams did not design a course for would-be real estate brokers (regardless of what the title might have implied), but for those who wished a greater understanding of how land had affected urban expansion. He also covered a wide range of subjects—everything from construction to public finance—in his housing course. Eschewing a traditional academic approach, he brought in a variety of impressive guest speakers. Catherine Bauer described urban developments in Europe; Warren J. Vinton of the U.S. Housing Authority spoke on public housing, as did Colonel Horatio B. Hackett, former Director of the PWA's Housing Division; Miles Colean of the Federal Housing Administration (FHA) lectured on the relationship between housing and private enterprise; and veteran reformers Langdon Post and Edith Elmer Wood analyzed the "social aspects of housing." Other speakers included Nathan Straus and Leon Keyserling of the United States Housing Administration, and the well-known architect Clarence Stein. This was the connection between the theoretical and the actual, the combination of scholarship and praxis that the New School, modern social science, and individuals such as Abrams hoped to establish.[6]

The effort Abrams put into teaching was repaid by diverse and loyal students. A typical class at the New School included an engineer, a real estate agent, a salesman, a lawyer with the New York City Planning Commission, a newspaper reporter, a social worker, and a community house manager. Abrams immediately impressed students with the breadth of his knowledge and professional experiences. Beyond his intellectual qualifications was something more important: zeal for the issues he presented. As a colleague later remarked, "How could anyone not succumb to his enthusiasm?" Those who regarded themselves as

Abrams' "disciples" reacted similarly. "He would get us all fired up to do our very best for people through our work," one of Abrams' subsequent students at Columbia noted, adding "because we admired him so, his faith that we could make a difference on this planet gave each of us strength and determination." Many of Abrams' students "did make a difference." Lloyd Rodwin and John Dean produced seminal scholarship on housing and urbanization; Eric Carlson became director of the UN Center for Human Settlements in Nairobi; Lois Dean ended up in the Community Planning and Development Office of the United States Department of Housing and Urban Development; and Walter Thabit was Baltimore's Director of Planning and a founder of Planners for Equal Opportunity.[7]

Building on his initial courses, Abrams helped launch the New School's Institute for Urban Studies in 1939. Given the interdisciplinary nature of Abrams' teaching, the Institute was one of, if not the first, urban studies programs in America. By 1943, Abrams himself believed the Institute was offering "the most successful courses of their kind in the country." Other colleges and universities, he noted, were starting their own programs modeled on the Institute's success. Abrams added courses over the next few years. One was "Government and Private Enterprise in Housing and Other Social Areas"; its final lecture, "Where are We Heading in the Process of Government Expansion," sketched out Abrams' criticisms of American state-building. Abrams also tried to persuade the United States Housing Administration to develop curricula in universities throughout the country. He hoped these courses would educate the public about contemporary urban problems and, in turn, spark a nationwide housing movement.[8]

Visitors from abroad, usually invited to speak at Abrams' request, also praised the New School's urban studies program. Jacqueline Tyrwhitt, a British planning specialist, remembered that the "regular front bench" at her New School talks included Abrams, Mumford, Albert Mayer, Julian Whittlesey, Charles Asher, and Clarence Stein. Tyrwhitt was equally impressed with the after-class parties. Students and speakers alike would reconvene at Abrams' house, where drinks and conversation lasted until early morning. Guests were initially awed by the size of his house: a "party" floor with sixteen-foot ceilings contained a drawing room, dining room, and foyer spanning almost seventy feet. The walls were covered with Ruth's art work, an interesting contrast to the house's nineteenth-century exterior. Despite the dignitaries who frequently attended these parties, a casual atmosphere existed. Public officials chatted with New School students, while other guests representing "varied disciplines and non-disciplines" added to the eclecticism. Moreover, as students spoke with someone like New York State Rent Administrator Robert Weaver, the distinction between classroom assignments and actual problem solving blurred. At one such gathering, a young I. M. Pei brought along his first plans for a cylindrical building; he spread them out on the drawing room piano, then engaged Abrams and William Zeckendorf, one of New York City's most successful developers, in an animated conversation.[9]

These parties were another dimension to being a public/policy intellectual. As one contemporary commented, they provided opportunities to socialize with individuals "with whom one was currently working on some problem . . . and with whom one simply reached out into freewheeling interpretations or inspirations that arose in the genie-like atmosphere." A cycle of sorts had thus run its course. While V. F. Calverton's home had been a common haunt of Abrams and Ruth during the twilight of Prohibition, their house became a favored destination among artists, students, and policymakers from the late 1930s onward.[10]

Even after he stopped teaching there on a regular basis, Abrams gave the New School his help and support. In the 1960s, when the school faced a severe financial crisis and increasing criticism over its administration, Abrams came to its rescue. He contacted fifty friends and former trustees of the school and invited them to his house. Before the night was up, he had raised $72,950. The New School was able to turn the corner on its economic problems, and an eighty-eight year old Alvin Johnson told Abrams he had not only saved the school from an "immediate financial crisis," but from "a dust cloud of petty ideas and interests."[11]

The New School was Abrams' first university affiliation, but certainly not his only one. He taught on a regular basis at the Massachusetts Institute of Technology ("much more alive," Abrams observed, than Harvard), City College, the University of Pennsylvania, and Columbia University. He was also a visiting lecturer at the University of Chicago, Johns Hopkins University, New York University, the Pratt Institute, the University of Wisconsin, Yale University, and Exeter University. Asked once how he had learned to be a professor, Abrams gave a humorous, though entirely truthful, response: " 'By teaching courses and writing books.' "[12]

As these experiences demonstrated, Abrams was an effective and creative teacher. For three decades he counseled hundreds if not thousands of students on their academic and professional careers. He never hesitated to place his teaching responsibilities above other commitments—he even missed a Cabinet meeting with Governor Averell Harriman because he had to teach a class at MIT. He also pushed his students to apply what they were learning to real situations and problems. This, however, did not keep him from assigning unusual projects. He frequently asked students to plan Heaven and Hell; perhaps imagining the worst about their grades, students gravitated toward the latter.[13]

The "Eternal Dichotomy": Land and Industry

The increasing pull of ideas and the need to make sense of them apparently prompted Abrams to write *Revolution in Land*. This work was significant because it focused on the important but often neglected topic of land utilization. It was also significant because Abrams coupled an examination of secular (long-term) economic trends with a broad framework for historical change. As such, it was nothing less than an attempt to define fundamental social and political forces. Abrams' analysis, conceptualized in this manner, was not unlike other Depression-era studies seeking answers to contemporary problems; its conclusions, however, reflected an unconventional synthesis of knowledge and experience. None other than Lewis Mumford hailed it as the most insightful investigation of land economics since Henry George.[14]

Writing, as one commentator asserted, in a "semi-popular" style, Abrams articulated his primary theses in the first three chapters. Land and the things it produced had represented the basis for one kind of society. Employing arguments that the historian David Potter would develop several years later, Abrams contended that widespread availability of land had resulted in a correspondingly high rate of property ownership. This, in turn, meant a "dynamic and fluid system" had replaced "the stubborn rigidity of the British way of life." With large numbers of people possessing modest amounts of property, the ability to use land as a lever to exert class advantage was minimal. Even the one exception, the slave-owning South, had been vanquished.[15]

Opposed to land was "industry" and the relationships flowing from it. Unlike land, industry was typified by "strength" and "union"; "concentration" had been its trademark from the beginning of mechanized production. "Industrial prices fixed by agreement" and "industrial price movements controlled by controlling the volume of production," Abrams acidly remarked, "contrasted with agricultural prices fixed by the vagaries of an unpredictable market, agricultural prices that would be accepted whatever they were, and a volume of agricultural production determined by chance alone." As a consequence of these trends, industry gradually superseded land as the template of social organization in America. And, as Abrams noted, the results of this shift were not positive. By 1900, "the era of free competition was . . . definitely past in most industries." This happened despite legislation outlawing monopolies. "In many cases," Abrams observed, "coordination of price and production policies by informal understandings approaching the nature of the cartel is quite efficient as a substitute for legal merger." Call them what you would, economic consolidations—especially in the building material trade—had been "one of the principal causes of the shelter problem" since they "forced the rents in newly constructed houses far out of line with the wages that industry paid to its workers, who were therefore compelled to live in the slums of the great industrial centers."[16]

More striking than Abrams' comments about the struggle between land and industry was the relationship he described between industrialization and urbanization: "Industrialization created urbanization. It dictated most phases of land use. It placed land in and about the cities in a position where business rather than sentiment would inevitably dominate its development." Since urban growth was a product of entrepreneurial activity, the design of cities conformed to economic priorities. "In this steady but aimless unfolding," Abrams lamented to the point of hyperbole, "the pattern of our cities was not fashioned with any predetermined symmetry or form, but was, within planless and random limits, fixed by the forces of new investment." Like the countryside, the city was subject to "disorder" and "utter subordination to the market."[17]

But if metropolises had grown as a response to economic expansion, their size, significance, and financial resources were diminishing as industrial decentralization and attendant suburbanization occurred. Having derived most of their revenues from property taxes, cities faced enormous fiscal crises as land values dropped in conjunction with industrial flight. Furthermore, they had become hostages to corporate business interests because of their need to stem centrifugal tendencies. "The modern city," Abrams asserted, "might now be compared to a poor hotel keeper, who finds it advisable to make all sorts of concessions to his richest guests lest they move, bag and baggage, to his rival across the street."[18]

Abrams' contentions diverged significantly from those of Robert Park and his associates at the University of Chicago. The Chicago School was interested primarily in the process of urbanization, especially its relationship to industrialization and its impact on individual behavior. Researchers involved in these areas often believed the processes they were studying were immune from human intervention. Their studies thus resembled social anthropology and ethnology more than hard-edged social or political analyses. Abrams sharply disagreed with the Chicago School's conclusions. For him, urbanization and industrialization were not blind forces but inextricable elements of capitalist development.[19]

Admittedly, Abrams would have also been guilty of focusing on abstractions if he had discussed "land" and "industry" only as concepts. He attempted, though, to identify specific groups with each term. Generally, he linked wealthier individuals to industry, while connecting poorer ones to land. With regard to the former, Abrams observed that America's most affluent citizens no longer derived their wealth from real estate but from "personal property . . . money, bank balances, accounts, patents and other legal claims." Abrams was not suggesting a bank account was sufficient to propel one into the ranks of the economic elite. His apprehension over monopolies, "concentration[s] of ownership," and sizable amounts of wealth made it clear he associated "industry" with the directors and trustees of America's largest corporations. In making this connection, he was adding his voice to the concerns of others, like Adolf Berle and Gardiner Means, who had also examined trends in U.S. political economy. Berle and Means, in their landmark study, *The Modern Corporation and Private Property* (1932), concluded that the corporation had become "both a method of property tenure and a means of organizing economic life"; in short, "corporate enterprise" was replac-

ing "private enterprise." Even more distressing, corporations had
become "concentration[s] of economic power" able to compete on
equal terms with the modern state. While Berle and Means focused on
the *power* of corporations, Abrams had taken a different tack, charting
the *powerlessness* of everyone who stood in the way of these giant financial
institutions. Berle, Means, and Abrams agreed, however, on the inherently undemocratic nature of "corporate enterprise."[20]

Abrams believed tenant farmers and urban wage earners (as renters
and small home owners) corresponded to "land." The farmer's essential
plight was being caught in the squeeze of price "scissors." In short, factors outside the agriculturalist's control (like weather and tariffs) often
determined crop prices, while business interests "strictly" controlled the
cost of manufactured goods. This predicament was clearly illustrated
during the late nineteenth century, when low revenues and high costs
forced a large number of farmers into tenancy. Though the immediate
overlord of these newly beggared farmers was usually a local landowner,
Abrams, in good Populist fashion, saw their real oppressors as financiers
and industrial conglomerates. Urban wage earners fared no better.
According to Abrams, when industrialization reached high tide, "economic law dictated the behavior of capital in urban areas and laid down
the basic pattern of our cities." With "almost mathematical necessity,"
buildings conformed "as closely as possible to the norm of minimum
possible expense and maximum possible income from the accommodation so provided."[21]

All these developments had led to a "drift into tenancy." This "drift,"
however, had not been inevitable. What had "fixed tenancy as the permanent status of men and women in the cities" and "fastened farm tenancy and sharecropping upon the agricultural communities" was the
absence of adequate wages. By blaming capitalists for withholding the
"minimal essentials of decent life," Abrams suggested the "eternal
dichotomy" of land and industry possessed a strong component of class
conflict.[22]

Abrams' analysis of another "mechanism of enslavement" (monopolies were the first) made an important contribution to the growing literature on land economics by turning the arguments of Henry George on
their head. George, a labor activist and self-taught economist, was born
in Philadelphia in 1839. At the time of George's writings (the 1870s and
1880s), land was still a critical factor in manufacturing. Speculators,

after buying cheap real estate, watched its value rise in tandem with industrial and urban expansion. They then sold it for far more than their purchase price. George called this gain an "unearned increment" because owners had literally done nothing in order to make a profit. Conversely, inflated land prices not only raised production costs, they drove down wages as industrialists attempted to reduce expenses. Believing the unearned increment was the primary cause of economic inequality, George wanted all taxation shifted to a "single tax" on land. This tax would depress property values, which would discourage any and all private investment (after all, no one would buy real estate with exorbitant tax levies). Lacking any purchasers, land would revert to public ownership, under whose direction it could be utilized to promote the general welfare, or so George had argued.[23]

Casting doubt on George's assumptions, Abrams emphasized the declining significance of land. It was in "oversupply in almost every form," and in manufacturing, a "steadily decreasing amount of it [was] required to meet all needs." Abrams also thought tax increases on unimproved property would have effects contrary to George's predictions. He himself had seen how increased taxes caused real estate investors to "improve" their property—converting a warehouse into office space, for example—in hopes of generating additional income. These improvements placed upward pressure on the value of neighboring properties. As everyone's properties rose in value, so did their tax liabilities, providing an additional incentive for further development. Abrams thus concluded taxes were not a function of property values, but just the opposite: property values flowed from tax assessments. Though Abrams did not fully resolve this complex relationship between taxes and urban growth, he hoped his alternative perspective might prove useful to planners and public officials.[24]

For Abrams, property taxes were inequitable as well as unconducive to rational development. They were initiated, he argued, "at a time when the ownership of property was the surest test of ability to pay, and when the amount of property owned was a rough measure of income and hence of the just proportion of the tax burden." In the intervening decades, a far-reaching transformation—Abrams called it the "revolution in land"—had occurred. As land became an increasingly common possession, its ownership became a less reliable indication of financial status. This was part of the "revolution." The other was a concomitant shift from real property—as a form of wealth—to a range of "intangibles," which included cash, stocks, bonds, machinery, equipment, automobiles, boats, and other personal articles. These items characterized the "upper" economic strata, and they frequently escaped significant taxation (some intangibles were not taxed at all). In cities, where municipal officials were scrambling for additional revenues, and where "vast masses of other [potentially] taxable wealth" existed, real estate was the only commodity substantially taxed. Business interests and the "titans" who led them were therefore exempt from paying their fair share, despite having contributed to many of the country's urban problems.[25]

One reason the "obsolete method" of property taxes still existed was "convenience." Property taxes were "relatively easy to collect," "impossible to avoid by leaving the jurisdiction," and inescapable by "concealing the property." Abrams, however, was convinced other factors were also at play. "Tax policy has always been extremely sensitive to group political pressure," he opined, and once "land had lost its primacy" and "had been distributed among countless inarticulate little men . . . no protest could be even formulated in dignity and pride, let alone attain some measure of effectiveness." As long as society's most powerful and affluent groups remained relatively unharmed by property taxes (that is, as long as their intangibles were taxed at low or nonexistent rates), then it was the "small farmer and the owner of a modest home" who would feel most acutely the burden of this "unearned decrement," a clever phrase Abrams employed to subvert George's arguments.[26]

In suggesting why there had been no repeal or reform of property taxes, Abrams was touching on something he would later work out in greater detail. Groups throughout society possessed unequal amounts of power; to expect those with the least (like tenant farmers, wage earners, and small home owners) to have a marked influence on policymaking was foolhardy at best. The appeals of Carol Aronovici and other housing activists, which urged the masses to "wrest from an unfavorable economy" the means to "decent shelter," were therefore misplaced as long as the average citizen was relatively powerless. Only Catherine Bauer had revealed a fairly comprehensive grasp of the political dynamics necessary to effect socioeconomic change. Adequate shelter, she argued in her 1934 housing study, was not a "normal product" of capitalism. She asserted it could be achieved "only when there is an active demand on the part of workers and consumers which is *strong enough* to over-balance the weight of real estate and allied interests on the other side [emphasis added]." Even so, Bauer, like Aronovici, overestimated the power of workers and consumers. Abrams, on the other hand, continually stressed the political disadvantages handicapping these groups.[27]

In Abrams' estimation, only additional public intervention could establish a balance of power among various economic groups. Such intervention was necessary because general conditions were already grim. The home owner had become a "debtor to the gigantic new lending institutions"; farmers were "forced into insolvency," with many becoming tenants or sharecroppers; and the wage earner had, in many cases, been reduced to a "slum-dweller." Abrams admitted New Deal decisionmakers "recognized . . . that the farmer, the sharecropper, the slum-dweller, and the home owner were living people on whose behalf government had to intervene." But he also insisted that New Deal programs were inadequate to meet the needs of these constituencies. The various alphabet agencies illustrated no coherent policy or program, and the government's "lack of adequate coercive powers" forced it "to rely on inducement and the hope of securing voluntary cooperation rather than on legislative and administrative mandates."[28]

If existing reforms had not alleviated the inequities within American society, what solutions did Abrams himself propose? Unlike the policy suggestions put forward in his later writings, Abrams' recommendations in *Revolution* were brief and tentative. Some of them were even similar to programs he criticized. Additional public housing, stronger enforcement of antitrust laws, federal taxation of intangible property, and credit liberalization for housing construction all fit within the parameters of existing New Deal programs. Perhaps influenced by the ideas of Lewis Mumford, Abrams also called for regional land authorities. Modeled on other autonomous public bodies, they "would recognize . . . geographic and economic interrelations beside which the importance of state lines and local subdivisions" would dwindle "almost to the insignificance of administrative detail." In creating these programs, Abrams warned against the "undue and unbalanced concentration of power in the hands of federal agencies." To prevent this, local bodies would have to administer the "details of method and application of principles." Such a sentiment reflected Abrams' concern for the "checks and balances assuring the maintenance of . . . democratic institutions." It also represented his advice on how to avoid the kind of friction and confusion NYCHA and the PWA had generated.[29]

While these proposals required limited public interventions, others appeared to call for outright socialism. Nationalization of unimproved land (both rural and urban), acquisition of mutual life insurance companies by eminent domain, and placement of "savings and investment" under "social control" were just a few of Abrams' ideas. He then ventured out to the furthest point on his philosophical limb: when the "new day" of reform came, the "public authority" would have "to intervene, regardless of formal considerations and vested rights, to rectify injustice, to restrain oppression, legal or not . . . and to secure to all that measure of opportunity which . . . the present economic confusion necessarily frustrates."[30]

Probably influenced by the New School's decidedly liberal ethos, these suggestions were not ones Abrams would make again, and as such, they represented a temporary intellectual impasse. Like George's one-note analysis and one-note panacea, which were attempts to circumvent the implications of a frontal, comprehensive critique of capitalism, Abrams' recommendations seemingly left little in the way of alternative economic frameworks. Yet Abrams might have had something else in mind. The "surest safeguard against the ultimate displacement of the business system by some *other* arrangement," he maintained, was "a somewhat more equitable distribution of the goods and services produced by the activity of all [emphasis added]." Then, as an almost philosophical postscript, he observed that "no matter what form" public control took, "liberty" could be "preserved and the consequences of concentrated power avoided only by following the middle road: by giving way a little, by surrendering some of our illusions about automatic readjustment, indefinite expansion and self-activating unimplemented social justice, and by ending the concentration of power in the hands of those reasonable in fact only to themselves." Perhaps, given these remarks, Abrams' earlier proposals were meant to serve the strategic objective of showing conservatives what radical measures would really look like; by contrast, the "middle road" Abrams now hinted at in *Revolution*'s final pages would appear more attractive. Whatever the case, Abrams subsequently distanced himself from *Revolution*'s immoderate recommendations, adopting instead his own "middle road" suggestions for American state-building. In part, this process reflected the actual trajectory of New

Deal policies, many of which (especially those backed by organized labor) began with radical diagnoses of society's ills but then accepted modest prescriptions as treatment.[31]

Assessments of *Revolution in Land*

Abrams presented a novel, if sometimes bleak, vision in *Revolution*. The work itself was entirely consistent with his overall development and identity: a reflective practitioner connecting scholarship with social concern, somewhat on the model of the New School's founders, but coming to that meeting ground from the public and applied side. Devoid of any direct rejection of capitalism or consistent class analysis, *Revolution* fit most closely within the Progressive frame of mind. Furthermore, Abrams' emphasis on the evils associated with monopolistic competition echoed contemporary debates among New Dealers, such as Leon Henderson and Thurmond Arnold, over the correct balance between private and public power.[32]

But if his arguments struck familiar intellectual and ideological chords, they were not a call for a return to a mythical golden age, however much Abrams might have romanticized certain aspects of the past. Indeed, if Abrams' thinking had a utopian element—a rejection of "Machine Age" values—it was forward, not backward, looking. In this sense, Abrams likely found a kindred spirit in Lewis Mumford, who not only provided an "incisive and imaginative reaction" to the first draft of *Revolution*, but also remarked in his own study of cities a year earlier: "The problem is to coordinate, on the basis of more essential human values than the will-to-power and the will-to-profits, a host of social functions and processes that we have hitherto misused in the building of cities and polities." Despite differences between the two men, they shared this vision of a better, more humane society.[33]

While Abrams' motivations for writing *Revolution* were never entirely clear, he revealed one of them in a 1960 letter to Perry Prentice, editor of *House and Home* magazine: "I tried futilely in a now-forgotten book to refute the idea [of *Lebensraum*], but the tanks had already begun to roll when the book appeared. No one had ever calculated that you could put the whole population of the world in present-day Western Germany at 25 to the acre." Though Abrams was admittedly unsuccessful in getting this larger point across, *Revolution* illustrated one of his first attempts to use scholarship to unravel and defuse a contemporary dilemma.[34]

Abrams' first book also had its share of flaws. Broad generalizations, poor organization, a relatively sketchy treatment of agricultural conditions, the reification of "land" and "industry" to the point where those concepts sometimes lost much of their meaning, and ambiguous references to the role of the state weakened the work's analytical power. Reviewers raised these issues in their reactions to *Revolution*. Abrams might not have bitten off more than he could handle, Bertram M. Cross wrote, but there had been "too little chewing." Elsewhere, Karl Brandt called Abrams' discussion of rural developments "impressionistic," while B. H. Hibbard, a leading agricultural economist, found faults (albeit minor ones) in almost every section of the book. Much to Abrams' relief, there were supportive reviews as well. According to Joseph Milner, Abrams had sent "an extremely necessary warning to government," while Leo Grebler, a respected urban economist, described Abrams' efforts as a "real contribution to the literature on land and housing." These positive reviews notwithstanding, Abrams would make every effort to eschew easy generalizations and conceptual vagueness in his subsequent writings.[35]

With publication of *Revolution*, Abrams ended a busy and productive decade. In 1930, there had been little indication he would enter public life or produce important scholarship; by 1940, he had done both. The New School had been a significant influence on his intellectual growth, providing him the opportunity to combine theory with praxis and exposing him to internationally known scholars. For the rest of his life, Abrams would use teaching as both a sounding board for his evolving ideas and as a way to apply his experiences—and the talents of his students—to America's urban problems.

Chapter Six

⣿

FEDERAL HOUSING POLICIES
AND THE PROBLEM OF A
"BUSINESS WELFARE STATE"

World War II, Abrams told a friend in the spring of 1943, was "too big a show to be wasting time on inconsequentials." Hoping to see active duty, he sought a commission by soliciting letters of recommendation from highly placed government officials. Colonel John B. Marsh, however, informed him on June 22, 1943, that he would not receive a commission, primarily because of the "highly specialized need of officer personnel and the limited number of vacancies under 1943 procurement objectives." Middle-aged, married, and the father of two young daughters, Abrams was also passed over by the draft. His destiny, it seemed, did not lie in military service. Writing a fellow housing activist, he explained: "I am contemplating doing something constructive. But it is hard, mainly because you have to be really hungry to keep on pressing for a position." Without a "position," Abrams feared he would continue doing what he had always done—"writing, practicing law and otherwise being generally useless in a volatile world."[1]

Abrams was correct in predicting he would be more of an observer than an active participant in America's war effort. But he was by no means "useless." As a member of the National Committee on the

Housing Emergency, he helped outline wartime and postwar housing needs, condemning the government's unwillingness to transfer temporary housing to public agencies once the fighting ended. In New York City, he became actively involved in the City-Wide Citizens Committee on Harlem, authoring an important report on living conditions in the nation's fastest growing African-American ghetto. He also taught at the New School and pushed for additional federal appropriations for public housing. By the end of the war, he had been appointed Special Counsel to New York's Joint Legislative Committee on Housing and Multiple Dwellings, a committee regulating a significant portion of the state's housing.

Ironically, the very activities Abrams associated with his seeming irrelevancy, writing and practicing law, would allow him to make important intellectual contributions during the 1940s. Unsuccessful in his bid to become part of the "show," he began a comprehensive examination of New Deal and post-New Deal state-building. His analysis eventually coalesced around one issue: the dangers of what he described as a "business welfare state." This concern was in sharp contrast to his initial support of liberal policies. Admittedly, in 1939 he had expressed misgivings about the absence of a coherent philosophy behind the proliferation of public programs. At that point, though, he believed the "clash between the public and private interest [had been] won by the former."[2]

Abrams' views had changed by the mid-1940s, a shift made evident in his second book, *The Future of Housing* (1946), which was a selection of the Book-of-the-Month Club (a good illustration of his public intellectualism). This investigation—unlike other, relatively formulaic housing studies—combined legislative insights with powerful invectives against the evolving American state. While an advocate of free-market economics and a relatively strong central government, Abrams now became a vocal critic of the *type* of state capitalism and state-building policymakers were embracing. In short, he downplayed his short-lived New Deal optimism and extended the more pessimistic critique he had begun in *Revolution*. "National policy," he noted, "seems now to be directed not toward keeping private and public efforts separate, but toward subsidizing private effort, socializing its losses, and removing the elements of stake and risk which always lay at the root of free enterprise." Conflating private and public interests was, according to Abrams, undemocratic because it usually subordinated the latter to the former. It also inverted a common assumption: instead of states establishing particular policies, policies were creating a certain kind of state.[3]

Federal Housing Programs: Direct Versus Indirect Social Expenditures

The origins of Abrams' business welfare state lay in steps taken by lawmakers to assist the Depression-racked housing industry. Abrams worried that these initiatives, having been institutionalized by the New Deal, might become the blueprint for subsequent state expansion. The specific programs Abrams singled out for criticism were the Federal Home Loan Bank System, the Home Owners Loan Corporation, and the FHA.

Congress created the Federal Home Loan Bank System (FHLBS) and its governing body, the Federal Home Loan Bank Board (FHLBB), on July 27, 1932. Modeled on the Federal Reserve System, twelve Home Loan Banks were set up to supply credit to member institutions—mostly savings and loans—either by making loans against the security of their first mortgages, or by reducing their liquidity requirements (the amount of money a bank had to keep on hand). In addition to these functions, the FHLBB was authorized to charter new savings and loans, which were required to become members of the Federal Savings and Loan Insurance Corporation (FSLIC). Established by Congress in June 1934, the FSLIC sought a reduction in "hoarding" and protection of small savers by insuring deposits up to $5,000. Lawmakers hoped these measures would blunt the Depression's impact by encouraging mortgage lending and by restoring faith in the nation's financial institutions.[4]

More than a decade later, Abrams expressed concern over the FHLBS's operations. He argued that government credit had been and was continuing to be used to "sustain an inefficient mortgage structure" and to "justify exorbitant interest charges." Reviewing the FHLBS's development illustrates some of the reasons for Abrams' concerns. By the late 1930s, the nation's 9,662 savings and loans, most of which were local institutions, averaged a relatively modest $591,000 in assets; some thrifts had been capitalized with as little as $5,000-$10,000. At first skeptical of federal initiatives (despite support of national lobbying groups), thrift institutions eventually became strong supporters of the FHLBS and the FSLIC, primarily because these programs offered distinct advantages to smaller fiduciaries. As John H. Fahey, Chairman of the FHLBB, told the Temporary National Economic Committee (TNEC) in 1939, the "Federal name and Federal supervision" were "important factors" in influencing the growth of savings and loans during the 1930s. Fahey omitted telling the Committee about another "factor," the town-by-town canvassing conducted by the FHLBB to persuade businessmen and real estate brokers to charter new savings and loans.[5]

Abrams was not convinced the expansion of savings and loans stimulated by the conferral of federal "respectability" was necessarily positive. The FHLBS's policies, dominated by its desire to "get business," could easily make it a "protagonist of the lenders." Abrams (like others) also linked a financial institution's size with its ability to administer loans cheaply and efficiently. Servicing costs (the costs of initiating and administering a loan) incurred by small, undercapitalized institutions could be as much as 1.5 percent greater than those of larger institutions. "A lender having only about $600,000 to invest," the TNEC pointed out, "must of necessity have a greater per-dollar cost in handling small items and spreading losses than would one having several hundred millions." And, as Abrams emphasized, higher servicing costs ultimately resulted in higher interest rates, which then inflated mortgage premiums. For example, raising interest rates from 4 percent to 5 percent to cover servicing costs would increase monthly mortgage payments by 5.4 percent.[6]

Worse still, nothing prevented these small, poorly run savings and loans from joining the FHLBS, a problem some lawmakers had foreseen. During debates over the Home Loan Bank Bill, Senators James Couzens (R-Michigan) and Clarence Dill (D-Washington) had both expressed concern over the FHLBS's minimal capital requirements. "All kinds of bucket shops and lending organizations," Couzens worried, would be formed to take advantage of the new programs. As Abrams later asserted, "a multitude of picayune companies with nominal capital" were given the opportunity to attain a "prime position in mortgage lending." Objections notwithstanding, liberal admission requirements were retained, and Fahey himself eventually admitted the FHLBS included "too many small institutions."[7]

In addition to the relatively undercapitalized position of the average savings and loan, Abrams also criticized the FHLBB's inability to set the interest rates of its member institutions. While Home Loan Banks might charge rates as low as 1 or 1.5 percent, member banks could re-loan this money (often in the form of home mortgages) at 6 or 7 percent. Even savings and loans with relatively high servicing costs could make handsome profits under these terms. Fahey confirmed some fiduciaries were guilty of this practice, though he contended they had to "meet the market," a tacit acknowledgment of the FHLBS's subordination to capitalist imperatives. He also conceded it was "doubtful" privately owned banking institutions would have accepted FHLBS interest rate ceilings in the first place. Such a conclusion seems valid. Warning against direct regulation of fiduciaries, savings and loan officials insisted the federal government should focus its energies on "labor and material monopolies, price fixing, and building-code rigidities." These concerns might explain why the only restriction lawmakers were able to enact, an amendment prohibiting FHLBS interest rates from exceeding the maximum established within a given state, was never strictly enforced.[8]

Abrams consequently identified two problems associated with the FHLBB's inability to regulate interest rates. As noted above, entrepreneurs with little capital or financial experience could establish thrift institutions, join the FHLBS, then use low-interest government loans to make profits of 3 to 4 percent, a relatively high return in the normally conservative banking industry. The second problem was subsidization of these profits by individual home owners, either through higher taxes or increased mortgage premiums. "The effect of all this," Abrams explained in characteristically blunt prose, "has been that the owner who subsidizes waste in home building now subsidizes it in mortgage financing as well."[9]

These and subsequent comments reveal the Populist and Progressive concerns informing Abrams' views. At the core of his critique was the Populist plea for cheap money. Yet, accomplishing this goal in home financing required the economies of scale possessed by large financial institutions, a tenet clearly rooted in Progressive notions of state-society interaction. That the two positions could be at odds with each other, especially if private institutions resisted regulation, was something Abrams never fully investigated.[10]

Abrams' final criticism of the FHLBS was its indirect promotion of speculation. The FHLBS, fulfilling the desires of the savings and loan industry, became a permanent, not temporary, part of the federal government's credit system. During World War II, with the economy growing at record rates, restrictions on new construction boosted the prices of existing homes, stimulating speculation in the process. Speculative home buying, however, was also fueled by the relatively low interest rates the FHLBS charged to its member banks. Given these circumstances, Abrams, having initially upbraided the FHLBS for failing to stem high-interest mortgage loans, now condemned it for supporting low-interest loans. Who, for instance, would want easy credit to encourage home buying, if the selling price of the homes so purchased was likely to drop as soon as wartime inflation abated? Yet instead of providing stability or a permanent "safeguard" against that sort of situation, the FHLBS was doing just the opposite. Abrams was positive it would protect no one except lenders—the FHLBS's real beneficiaries—should another collapse in real estate values occur. While this sentiment failed to acknowledge the direct assistance given to savers through deposit insurance, Abrams was correct in believing the FHLBS provided more security to lenders than to borrowers; though authorized to make loans directly to home owners, the FHLBB only approved three such transactions out of 41,580 applications. This provision was dropped altogether in 1933. Conversely, thrifts continued to benefit from publicly subsidized reserve banks, even during times of prosperity when these arrangements were theoretically unnecessary.[11]

Not designed to aid mortgages already in default or in danger of foreclosure, FHLBS's shortcomings were fairly apparent. Even Fahey reluctantly concluded the FHLBS had been "unable to contribute in any important way toward relief." To address this problem (there were almost 1,000 foreclosures a day by the middle of 1933), Roosevelt asked Congress on April 13, 1933 for "legislation to protect small home owners from foreclosure and to relieve them of a portion of the burden of excessive interest and principal payments incurred during the period of higher values and higher earning power." Congress responded by creating the Home Owners Loan Corporation (HOLC) on June 13, 1933.[12]

In Abrams' opinion, the HOLC, like the FHLBS, was another missed opportunity to provide direct aid or enact protections against subsequent economic downturns. Technically under FHLBS supervision, the HOLC's function was not to loan money (in this sense, "home owners" did not actually receive "loans"), but to purchase and refinance mortgages in default or foreclosure. In exchange for mortgages, the HOLC would give fiduciaries government bonds paying 4 percent interest (later reduced to 3 percent). Capitalized with $200 million from the

U.S. Treasury, the HOLC was authorized to issue $2 billion in bonds, an amount eventually increased to $4.75 billion. During a peak period in the spring of 1934, it processed over 35,000 loan applications per week and employed almost 21,000 people in 458 offices throughout the country. By the time lending operations ceased on June 12, 1936, the HOLC had made 1,021,587 loans, making it the owner of approximately one-fifth of the urban home mortgage debt in the United States.[13]

Contemporary policymakers and business leaders were quick to emphasize the benefits provided to home owners by the HOLC. The Roosevelt administration credited the HOLC with a "general restoration of morale," a reduction of foreclosure rates, and payment of almost $250 million in delinquent taxes to state and municipal governments. Subsequent scholars have generally agreed with these positive evaluations, asserting the HOLC was "important to history because it introduced, perfected, and proved in practice the feasibility of the long-term, self-amortizing mortgage." Indeed, with HOLC purchased mortgages refinanced at 5 percent interest over fifteen years, home ownership became economically feasible for those who had been unable to afford shorter mortgages at higher interest rates.[14]

Abrams' assessments of the HOLC were less favorable. He contended federal officials should have provided *direct* relief to home owners. The government, he thought, could have enacted a foreclosure moratorium or temporarily paid the taxes and interest on impaired mortgages, rather than incorporating these costs into HOLC mortgage premiums. These measures might have kept the government from buying up whole mortgages, especially if savings and loans had used FHLBS funds to refinance their mortgage portfolios at lower rates or to make loans directly to individuals. They might have also provided aid to the most penurious home owners (the unemployed), which the HOLC usually refused to help.[15]

Shifting his attention to administrative realities, Abrams identified three negative consequences associated with the HOLC's involvement in national mortgage markets. Like many of Herbert Hoover's initiatives and subsequent New Deal housing programs, the HOLC funneled relief indirectly to home owners by crafting legislation to aid mortgage lenders (mortgagees). As long as mortgagees could count on the federal government to intervene and buy their impaired securities at full value, they had no incentive to help home owners refinance or reduce their outstanding debts (creditors often do the latter because some repayment is better than none at all). For this reason, Abrams believed individual home owners should have been the recipients of HOLC loans. In taking this position, he implicitly identified himself with progressive elements within the 73rd Congress that had pushed for direct relief programs. Representative John J. Cochran (D-Missouri), arguing the FHLBS had been "nothing more than a sales agency for the building and loan agency," urged his colleagues to pass an amendment permitting the HOLC to make loans to home owners. Similarly, Senator Park Trammel (D-Florida), fearing the proposed HOLC legislation was "more in the interest of capital than for the ordinary everyday citizen," had insisted home owners were deserving of "equal generosity." Both Cochran and Trammel's amendments were defeated, and the final legislation—with no little irony—provided direct loans only to *mortgagees* if they refused to accept government bonds for their mortgages.[16]

Abrams found a second aspect of the HOLC problematic as well. In a significant deflationary period like the Depression, payrolls and real estate assessments usually drop precipitously, leaving home owners with mortgage payments incurred when property values and wages were higher. Abrams felt the HOLC should have reduced home owner indebtedness by refinancing mortgages for amounts closer to their deflated market values instead of their inflated mortgage values. Under this formulation, lending institutions would have suffered losses, but they would have received government-backed bonds in place of frozen mortgage loans, a tradeoff Abrams believed would have kept relief programs centered on modest home owners, not on business interests engaged in unrestrained speculation.[17]

Similar to his analysis of other federal programs, Abrams' opinions about mortgage financing contrasted sharply with the way policy developments had actually unfolded. The HOLC purchased home mortgages either close to their face value (the amount originally loaned), or at least above the prevailing market values for the property in question. In fact, the HOLC refinanced mortgages it purchased for only 7 percent less than their previous, admittedly inflated values. Thus, a $10,000 mortgage might be refinanced as if the initial amount had been $9,300, but that figure—$9,300—could still be significantly higher than the deflated value of the property. Such outcomes represented the conflicting objectives of reducing the borrower's indebtedness versus the need to combat unprecedented deflation. Ultimately, concerns over declining property values superseded those over mortgage debts, a change reflected in Roosevelt's contention that the HOLC had been an "important step toward the ending of *deflation* [emphasis added]," a statement at odds with his earlier remarks about the HOLC's objectives.[18]

The hardships imposed on home owners as a result of refinancing mortgages on the basis of inflated property values were offset in the short run by the HOLC's lower mortgage premiums (spreading amortization over a greater period of time reduced monthly payments). Nevertheless, lengthening repayment schedules granted less relief than a reduction of outstanding principal, since total interest costs over the life of a mortgage were frequently higher—the longer money is borrowed, the more interest one pays. Furthermore, policymakers often failed to acknowledge that Depression-era incomes were significantly lower than those of only a few years before. Home owners lucky enough to be employed were spending their deflated 1930s wages for inflated 1920s real estate. While the disparity between these figures is difficult to determine, a study made by the National Industrial Conference Board in 1936 of twenty-five manufacturing industries reported hourly earnings had decreased 23.7 percent and weekly earnings had decreased 49.1 percent between 1929 and 1933. Though hourly wages had returned to their 1929 levels by 1936, both weekly wages and employment rates remained lower, down 14.4 percent and 12.6 percent, respectively.[19]

According to Abrams, a final problem connected with HOLC policies was the pattern they set for government intervention. Because the HOLC was purchasing mortgages at full value, fiduciaries, even solvent ones, were given an incentive to encourage their mortgagors (borrowers) to seek HOLC assistance; in exchange for investments carrying some risk (mortgages), lenders could obtain risk-free securities (interest and principal on HOLC bonds were federally guaranteed) for their portfolios. The HOLC thus underwrote both distressed and healthy financial institutions. With this precedent in mind, speculators would have no reason to act prudently in the future, since they could depend on the government to bail them out in the event of another economic crisis. Abrams therefore concluded the HOLC provided neither long-time security for future home owners nor protection against the "old sequence of boom and collapse," a process many economists believed was caused largely by real estate speculation.[20]

A third program, the FHA, caused even greater concern for Abrams.
As we have seen, Abrams spent most of the 1930s fighting for low-
income public housing. By the early 1940s he was also advocating
increased housing opportunities for African-Americans and the "middle
income group." Why, then, did Abrams oppose the FHA so vehemently,
especially given its reputation for making America a nation of home
owners? The answer can be found in the FHA's origins and operations.[21]

In his May 14, 1934 message to Congress, Roosevelt had outlined the
necessity for additional housing legislation: "Many of our homes are in
decadent condition and not fit for human habitation . . . . new homes
now are needed to replace those not worth repairing." The proposed
legislation, however, was not comprehensive housing rehabilitation but,
as Roosevelt and Congressional leaders admitted, an attempt to "return
many of the unemployed to useful and gainful occupation" by stimulating the building trades. To meet this and other objectives, Congress
passed the National Housing Act (1934), which included establishment
of the FHA. In simplest terms, the FHA would provide mortgage insurance to fiduciaries; if a mortgagor defaulted, fiduciaries would receive
government bonds in place of the impaired mortgage. Borrowers were
supposed to benefit from liberalized financing terms (FHA mortgages
were fully amortized, usually written for twenty years, charged 5 percent
interest, and could cover 80 percent of appraisal value), though they
received no assistance from the FHA if they defaulted. Policymakers
hoped these actions would spark an immediate surge in home construction. Here was the same connection Abrams had noted in other
housing programs between indirect versus direct assistance on the one
hand and the merging of private and public interests on the other.[22]

Business and financial leaders immediately expressed strong support
for the National Housing Act and FHA mortgage insurance. Lewis H.
Brown, President of Johns-Manville Corporation, Wilson Compton,
General Manager of the National Lumber Manufacturers Association,
Henry Harriman, President of the U.S. Chamber of Commerce, William
H. Kingsley, Vice-President of Penn Mutual Life Insurance Company,
and Walter S. Schmidt, Chairman of the Mortgage Finance Committee
of the National Association of Real Estate Boards, endorsed the use of
public funds and guarantees to aid private sector construction and real
estate concerns. The legislation's only vocal critic was the savings and
loan industry. Morton Bodfish, an official of the U.S. Savings and Loan

League, was troubled by the provisions dealing with mortgage insurance and national mortgage associations, calling them the "fundamental beginning of the nationalization or socialization of the whole urban mortgage business in this country." Though his arguments were framed ostensibly by fears over state expansion, Bodfish was more worried the legislation might create additional competition in mortgage financing. Objections based on "socialization" rang conspicuously hollow in light of his support for expanded FHLBS and HOLC funding (in lieu of the FHA), which were two major state interventions, but ones beneficial to savings and loans.[23]

While Abrams later admitted the FHA had accomplished "much that was good" and "long needed," he also argued "another side to the ledger . . . had to be balanced against the credit side." The FHA's supporters claimed its policies had resulted in lower interest rates on home mortgages. Technically, this was true: maximum rates of 5 percent (subsequently lowered to 4.5 percent) and widespread elimination of second mortgages represented more favorable terms for home owners, especially in areas where credit was tight. During and after World War II, however, changed economic circumstances actually made these rates higher than those offered for other government securities or even for some uninsured mortgages. Abrams criticized these practices, arguing that interest rates remained inflated because the FHA limited the number of financial institutions qualified to offer federally insured mortgages. Within this "artificially restricted market," lowering rates was considered an "unethical" competitive tactic. The FHA, left unmodified, permitted lending institutions to collect too much interest; or, to use Abrams' more colorful language, "The FHA device . . . suggests that government power may, without great difficulty, be hammered into a shield to protect intact the very evils which it is the function of government to destroy."[24]

In a different but related vein, Abrams charged the FHA with foisting home ownership onto individuals financially unprepared or unable to assume such risks. "FHA was designed to encourage builders to build and lenders to lend," Abrams asserted. To achieve these objectives, it was also "driven to encourage families to own." The target of Abrams' criticism, government promotion of home ownership, had begun as early as 1918, when the U.S. Department of Labor (in cooperation with private businesses) launched a nationwide "Own Your Own Home" campaign to spur the economy and minimize domestic political protest. In 1921, the

Department of Commerce, under Hoover's leadership, created a Division of Building and Housing, which soon published a pamphlet entitled "How to Own Your Home," a so-called "handbook" for potential home owners. It stressed the virtues of owning over renting and was prefaced with Hoover's injunction, "He [the home owner] works harder outside his home; he spends his leisure more profitably, and he and his family live a finer life and enjoy more of the comforts and cultivating influences of our modern civilization." The Department of Commerce also supported the "Better Homes in America" movement in the 1920s, which endorsed home ownership and repair.[25]

These activities, coupled with deteriorating real estate values during the Depression, generated skepticism over unqualified endorsements of home ownership. Journalist Rose M. Stein, economist Stuart Chase, and Langdon Post all condemned the federal government's aggrandizement of home ownership. As Post trenchantly argued, it was "deliberately setting out to exploit the very human desire to own a home in order to stimulate the construction industry."[26]

Abrams significantly expanded Post's line of attack, criticizing the FHA for combining forces with local businesses to promote seemingly indiscriminate home buying. Substantial evidence lay behind Abrams' concerns. As early as the spring of 1935, the FHA was using 6,174 local "Better Housing Committees" to "acquaint property owners" with how they could utilize the National Housing Act. Concurrently, the FHA published a guide on how to conduct "Better Selling" meetings, gatherings where contractors, builders, architects, and bankers could be taught how to be "active salesmen." The National Housing Act was a "profit-producing 'sales tool' for realtors," C. C. McGehee, Deputy Administrator of the FHA, told a 1938 Realtors' Housing Conference. Elsewhere, the trade journal *American Builder* lauded the FHA's work, noting that "high administration officials" were "putting the final touches on a gigantic national home building drive under the joint leadership of the FHA, the United States Chamber of Commerce, and private building interests." As part of this "drive," the FHA circulated posters and "millions of pieces of literature encouraging home ownership"; loaned models of houses to real estate developers; promoted specific subdivisions in tandem with local banks and real estate firms; sponsored a "sales" movie for California real estate agents; and conducted radio programs featuring nationally known speakers discussing the importance of their homes (during air time donated to the FHA by General Electric). Thus, if Americans did value home ownership as a cultural ideal, it had been thoroughly reinforced, perhaps even exaggerated, by government and business salesmanship.[27]

Abrams might have been out of step with this campaign to promote single-family homes, but his attack on the FHA was not animated by a wholesale condemnation of home ownership. He was neither a nineteenth-century moralist concerned about profligacy among the working class nor a "modern moralist" who faulted mass culture for destroying traditional communities. With his interest in and study of political economy, he was primarily troubled by the federal government's promotion of private business interests and the failure of the FHA to emphasize the pitfalls as well as the advantages of home ownership. On this latter point, Abrams feared countless individuals had been persuaded to buy (or "modernize") homes because they erroneously assumed FHA mortgages and loans meant government protection against faulty construction or workmanship. Some first-time homeowners didn't even realize a mortgage, unlike rent payments, was really a loan requiring repayment even if one's dwelling were sold or abandoned. Finally, in contrast to the FHA's flood of positive "propaganda," Abrams noted the absence of any significant literature explaining the risks and responsibilities of home ownership. He tried to remedy this in a 1945 *McCall's Magazine* article, "Your Dream Home Foreclosed," but only then did he discover how entrenched the home-owning ideal had become. Instead of commenting on the substance of his argument, most letter-writers—having read only the article's title—wanted Abrams to send them plans for the so-called "dream home."[28]

Business Welfare Policies:
Summing the Whole from the Parts

Building on his specific criticisms of mortgage financing, banking structure, and interest rates, Abrams outlined the broader contours of a business welfare state. The new function of government, he feared, was to "underwrite private losses and insure private profits." If this were to become common in other policy areas, the "way would be paved for a remarkable innovation" in governance.[29]

Abrams often referred to this privileging of business interests over the general welfare as "socialism from the Right." Real estate and mortgage lending interests, he explained, wanted the government to "expand its activities further than starry-eyed reformers ever dreamed," just so long as these activities were "directed toward their own, not the public welfare." Indeed, "socializing" losses was a common leitmotif throughout federal housing policies: the FHLBS's low interest rates to relatively undercapitalized fiduciaries, the HOLC's purchase of impaired mortgages, and the FHA's mortgage insurance were just a few examples. Conservative publications like *Savings and Loans* confirmed and applauded this trend, believing government intervention was legitimate when it absorbed business losses but illegitimate when it reduced profits. While segments of the private sector thus adopted the "idiom of conservative business," Abrams argued they actually supported a "policy wholly repugnant" to private enterprise.[30]

Much to Abrams' consternation, low-income housing advocates were the ones accused of being sympathetic to socialism. He rejected this charge, telling Herbert Nelson, Executive Secretary of the National Association of Real Estate Boards, in 1947, "The difference between our viewpoints is that you fear socialism if the government intercedes in housing while I fear socialism if it doesn't." "I concern myself," he continued, "with the *kind* of intervention that will solve the housing problem, employ the greatest amount of private effort in the process . . . and desocialize housing ownership as soon as possible [emphasis added]."[31]

Despite these comments, Abrams did not think the issue was so much a choice between public and private housing, but whether government subsidies would benefit "the public or the private entrepreneur." Nelson himself addressed this point more directly when he testified before Congress in 1950. While still opposed to public housing, he denied programs like the HOLC were "socialistic," or that any "stigma" resulted from using *public* credit to sustain *private* enterprise. With seemingly unlimited praise, he called the FHA "the greatest piece of legislation for home ownership ever adopted by any government in any period anywhere." What Nelson lauded so unconditionally was the process Abrams had criticized so unrelentingly: the tendency of policymakers to provide direct assistance to business interests because this conveyed indirect benefits to the public.[32]

The most comprehensive statement Abrams made about business welfare policies remained unpublished. In a 1950 manuscript entitled

Democracy in Crisis, he took the New Deal and its legacy to task. Without denying that improvements in the overall economy indirectly served the general welfare by raising wages and employment, he felt alternative policies should have been devised during the 1930s to help the common man. Even if economic stimulation had been the central objective, the federal government should first have decided in what circumstances private enterprise no longer functioned. Where this was the case, the state should have intervened directly to restore production and distribution. Abrams believed a "mixed economy . . . weighted mainly toward private capitalism" might have evolved had policymakers distinguished between direct relief and economic stimulation, and between functional and nonfunctional segments of the private sector. Instead, as these distinctions became blurred, a "private enterprise economy *underpinned* and *subsidized* by government credit and power [emphasis added]" had emerged.[33]

Few contemporaries charted American political or economic history in these terms. James Burnham's *The Managerial Revolution* (1941), Friedrich Hayek's *The Road to Serfdom* (1944), and Ludwig von Mises' *Omnipotent Government* (1944) were conservative warnings against state expansion in general, though Burnham was more temperate than Hayek or von Mises. Admittedly, John T. Flynn's popular diatribe against "creeping" socialism, *The Road Ahead* (1949), lambasted the government's increased role in banking and credit, but it failed to acknowledge the widespread support this development had received from the business community.[34]

Abrams highlighted a different component of modern state-building. Debates over the federal government, he asserted, no longer concerned a laissez-faire versus a planned economy but *how* increased state powers would be used. Abrams' primary illustration of this contention—his concept of a business welfare state—certainly contained fault lines he failed to analyze fully. The savings and loan industry's initial criticisms of the FHA and the objections of mortgage bankers to the FHLBS indicated that there was neither monolithic support for (nor opposition to) government programs. These disagreements, however, confirmed rather than refuted the accuracy of Abrams' general critique. Business constituencies challenged state intervention when they believed it favored particular industries, not when it violated theories of limited government.[35]

Lobbies, in Abrams' estimation, were important in creating and sustaining a business welfare state. Granted, opening up the legislative and policymaking process to historically underrepresented segments of American society (like organized labor and farmers) had been one of the New Deal's chief accomplishments. This sort of "broker state" politics, though, also allowed others, especially real estate and financial interests, to influence both legislation and regulation.[36]

Noting the developing ties between "pressure groups" and policymakers, Abrams insisted a "growing number of lobbies" were attempting to "harness government and its power plant to their own interests," which inevitably resulted in an "increasing tendency on the part of the governmental proprietary agency to collaborate politically with its principal beneficiaries." Abrams' analysis prefigured concerns of political scientists who would lament the ability of various groups to "capture" agencies they were supposed to regulate. Abrams pointed to one such collaboration between the FHLBS and the U.S. Savings and Loan League. Established in 1893, the League was supposed to advance the interests of savings and loans and the "American home," which the association called "the safeguard of American liberties." By 1939, under the leadership of Morton Bodfish (described by Coleman Woodbury, Assistant Administrator of the National Housing Agency, as "one of the most powerful lobbyists in Washington"), the League represented approximately 4,000 institutions that held 80 percent of all savings and loan assets. Bodfish influenced the FHA's initial provisions, including a successful attempt to reduce reserve requirements for the insurance fund (this benefited savings and loans by increasing the amount of money they could loan). Bodfish's actions notwithstanding, the arrangement Abrams questioned was the League's support of legislation advantageous to the FHLBS in return for the FHLBS's continuation of policies assuring moderately high returns on construction and mortgage loans.[37]

Abrams was also concerned with the effect lobbies had on the average citizen. The League's "vast political strength," he argued, had easily overwhelmed the interests of home owners in the 1930s, a point all but conceded in a history of savings and loans written by Josephine Hedges Ewalt, a League official. The League had decided to offer FHA mortgages, Ewalt asserted, because its member institutions would then be able to dominate the lending of insured loans; this, in turn, would allow the League to "dictate the policies of the FHA." These hopes were partially fulfilled since the FHA accepted more than half of the League's suggested amendments in 1935. Moreover, cooperation between the two groups continued because a significant number of individuals from the real estate and banking industries held administrative posts in the FHA.[38]

Identifying what he thought was an even bigger problem, Abrams claimed the League was part of a "Real Estate Lobby." He described this entity as "one of the most important pressure groups in Washington." A key player in the real estate lobby was the National Association of Real Estate Boards (NAREB). Founded in 1908, NAREB represented approximately 1,100 real estate boards and 44,000 individuals by the end of the 1940s, making it the second largest trade organization in the United States. Headed for more than three decades by Herbert Nelson—who had helped draft the legislation for the FHLBS, HOLC, and the National Housing Act—NAREB established the Washington Realtors Committee in 1942 to forge personal links between its members in each state with their respective Congressional delegations. At the close of World War II, NAREB was spending more than $90,000 a year on lobbying and openly admitted to working with federal agencies on legislation before it was introduced in Congress.[39]

Abrams believed the real estate lobby's desire to create a business welfare state was illustrated by its inconsistent positions. For example, it depicted public housing and direct government lending as "socialist" schemes designed to strangle private enterprise. Yet, despite frequent lamentations against an activist federal government, the real estate lobby hardly desired a return to a competitive, free-market economy. As Abrams often noted with no little irony, it supported the FHLBS, the HOLC, various aspects of the FHA, and government-initiated slum clearance. Because of these contradictory stances, Abrams excoriated housing lobbies as nothing more than "private ventures" trying to "cash in on the public purse in the name of social reform." Nelson, equally critical of Abrams, described him as a "wealthy lawyer" who was a "philosopher and deep thinker," but one whose claims about the government's being able to do some things "cheaper" and more "efficiently" than private enterprise were heretical to democracy and capitalism.[40]

Combating Business Welfare Policies

Never at a loss to offer policy advice himself, Abrams consistently returned to a few main themes throughout the 1940s and 1950s. His recommendations were based on Adam Smith's injunction concerning public-private economic activity: among the duties of the state was "that of erecting and maintaining those public institutions and those public works . . . of such a nature that the profit could never repay the expense to any individual." Using this as his touchstone (and doubtless relishing the reaction from conservatives when he cited Smith to justify public expenditures), Abrams pushed for government initiation and operation of enterprises considered unprofitable by the private sector. In housing, this policy might create the "clearly demarcated" zones between "private and public enterprise" Abrams deemed crucial. Builders, without public assistance, could construct homes for upper-income groups, while the government could erect and coordinate housing for lower-income groups. Abrams, however, realized it would be impossible to prevent the federal government from using or encouraging private sector interests to effectuate public purposes—that development seemed too well established by the 1940s. He therefore advocated "rigid regulation" of industries when they were used for this purpose.[41]

As these views indicate, Abrams did not condemn capitalism outright but supported a more liberal version of the New Deal. Often described by adherents as a "mixed economy," it rejected ideological rigidity by embracing both free markets and state-run enterprises. Popular in Scandinavia, mixed economies allowed policymakers to choose between a wide range of options to achieve certain objectives. The resulting economic systems usually funneled social provisions directly to the public, not indirectly through business interests. This was the implicit distinction Abrams made between his definition of a "mixed" economy (in which citizens received direct assistance) and a "blurred" one (in which the private sector received many if not most state benefits).[42]

Even when attempts to continue or expand New Deal social policies were called "socialist" or "communist," Abrams stuck by his liberal guns, becoming more outspoken as he watched veterans scramble to find adequate shelter after World War II. He complained "American liberals" were "not daring enough to demand a complete program," while "conservatives" were "not conservative enough" to relinquish unnecessary public subsidies. Rejecting small-scale solutions, Abrams advocated use of public agencies to plan and initiate residential construction. "The housing problem," he maintained, "can only be met by recasting the role of the home builder, by replacing him with an entrepreneur large

enough and strong enough to rationalize building along twentieth-century lines." According to this arrangement, the private builder would act
upon the direction of a public agency to organize subcontractors,
acquire materials, and undertake actual construction. Determining the
location, timing, and size of developments would be a public—not private—function. To carry out this proposal, Abrams called not only for
local planning and housing agencies but federal ones as well. Such a program, though, did not require "permanent government intervention."
"In 10 or 20 years," Abrams pointed out, "public building could withdraw when its purpose [had] been fulfilled."[43]

Abrams also supported modifications in New Deal housing programs.
A proponent of home ownership for those who could afford it, he
thought the government should offer insurance to borrowers rather
than lenders, just the opposite of FHA policies. When defaults occurred
because of unemployment, illness, death, or "other temporary misfor-
tunes," the insurance fund would cover interest, taxes, and maintenance
for a maximum of three years, thereby preventing foreclosure.
Moreover, if the FHA continued insuring lenders, despite Abrams' view
to the contrary, then initial monthly premiums should exclude interest
payments; home owners could then accrue equity sooner. For returning
World War II veterans, Abrams suggested benefits be extended to
renters as well as buyers. In the area of public housing, he urged the
more conservative approach of "desocializing" ownership by "conveying
title or at least conferring the greatest measure of control and responsibility upon the tenants." One reason Abrams accused laissez-faire advocates of not being "conservative enough" was their opposition to this last
proposal.[44]

Reactions to Abrams' Business Welfare State

The public mostly ignored Abrams' policy recommendations and his
fears of a business welfare state. The "average citizen," Abrams noted as
an explanation, was not able "to distinguish the true substance of housing laws from the nobly worded but meaningless pronouncements of
their preambles." He also thought organizations fighting the real estate
lobby, like the National Public Housing Conference, were "hampered by
poverty and public apathy." While these comments were valid observa-

tions, they failed to go far enough. Abrams' critique fell on deaf ears primarily because it ran squarely against contemporary intellectual and political currents. True, concern over the influence of lobbying groups remained an element of political and popular discourse from the 1920s through the 1940s (as evidenced by the hearings held by the House Select Committee on Lobbying Activities in 1950). During that same period, however, commentators and decisionmakers increasingly described lobbying in relatively positive terms. According to this alternative line of reasoning, lobbies were a compensation for ineffective political parties because they provided a "dynamic force for the shaping of governmental policy." In sum, they represented a "healthy democratic development."[45]

These positive views of lobbying reinforced an emerging consensus among economists and political scientists who downplayed the negative potential of interest group liberalism. For John Kenneth Galbraith, the leading liberal economist of the era, private power was no longer regulated by competition between buyers and sellers but by different groups within society: laborers, farmers, capitalists, and consumers. Each group provided a check on the other through an ill-defined mechanism called "countervailing power." When a group lacked sufficient countervailing power, it was the responsibility of the state to intervene. What Galbraith failed to emphasize sufficiently, but what Abrams recognized as a missing element among home owners and the indigent (both groups would have been "consumers" in Galbraith's schema), was the need to be organized in order to provoke state intervention on one's behalf. Nonetheless, Galbraith's ideas helped persuade contemporaries that power and *access to power* had been successfully fragmented among various groups.[46]

Political scientists were no less willing to embrace this view. Beginning in the 1930s and 1940s, as both an explanation of and accommodation to the New Deal, political scientists moved away from the concept of a "public interest" or even a "state." Instead, they believed American society was composed of different groups whose competition was an essential safeguard to democratic governance. While a new generation of scholars would eventually question whether groups competed from positions of equality, or if lobbies necessarily produced publicly desirable outcomes, support of interest group liberalism combined with consensus interpretations of history to undermine the apparent threat—and sometimes even existence of—a business welfare state.[47]

Recent examinations of American state-building outline another reason Abrams' concerns had little impact. They argue the modern state is essentially the result of a struggle between two different visions of political economy. Alternately described as "regulatory" versus "compensatory" intervention, "social" versus "commercial" Keynesianism, or a "developmental" versus a "fiscalist" state, the debate that occurred during the 1930s and 1940s, contemporary scholars assert, was over direct versus indirect regulation of national markets. The most influential and contested element in these debates was the economic philosophy of the English economist John Maynard Keynes. Despite the range of Keynes' prescriptions, policymakers endorsed only his more conservative recommendations—fiscal and monetary mechanisms. This evolving preference clearly influenced New Deal housing policies. And, by producing political and economically acceptable results, it prompted officials to transform some *short-term* programs into *permanent* parts of the American state.[48]

In this context, Abrams' tirade against "socializing losses" and the use of private interests to achieve public purposes can be seen as protests against the *kind* of economic levers policymakers were manipulating. His support for direct state interventions in housing markets contrasted with "commercial" Keynesians, who called for the less radical policy of using residential construction to stimulate the economy and maintain high rates of consumption. As Leon Keyserling, Administrator of the National Housing Agency and later Chairman of the Council of Economic Advisors, told Abrams in 1945: "We must have reasonably high employment and reasonably full production in the postwar decade to avoid an economic catastrophe . . . . Housing is one of the most important items in achieving this relatively full economy."[49]

Ideologically closer to "social" Keynesians, Abrams thought the federal government's macroeconomic powers should be used to plan and initiate construction of actual housing, rather than encourage private building and home sales through insuring home mortgages and other indirect policies. "The words 'full employment,' " Abrams noted in 1944, "seem to have taken on a magical quality in recent months . . . . but little attention is being paid either to the method by which it can best be achieved or to the institutional modifications that may be involved if

we usher it in in the wrong way." Ultimately, though, Abrams was fighting on the wrong side of a "fiscal revolution"; those who *minimized* the
state's role in providing direct relief for society's poorest citizens eventually won the battle to define economic policy.[50]

For these reasons, neither the pubic nor policymakers followed
Abrams' critical lead. Most of the programs he criticized had already
become accepted fixtures of the newly expanded state, with powerful
public and private sector supporters. As early as 1943, Lewis H. Brown
of the Johns-Manville Corporation could praise federal housing policies
(which he helped draft) because they illustrated for him how the state
could "properly utilize private business agencies to achieve public goals."
Almost a decade later, Lawrence N. Bloomberg of the United States
Public Housing Administration (USPHA) confirmed the continuing
appeal of federal housing initiatives by confidently asserting the FHA
had been "completely accepted" as a part of the "free enterprise system."
Had Bloomberg been asked to document his statement, he could have
pointed to the enthusiastic use of federal credit and mortgage guarantees by postwar builders to construct suburban housing. Abrams' alternatives to business welfare policies thus appeared unlikely trajectories
for the post-New Deal state; his criticism of existing arrangements, however, clarified the path it did take.[51]

It was no coincidence that Abrams formulated his initial and most
comprehensive critique of the American state during the 1940s. Unable
to serve in the military, he possessed the time and opportunity to undertake a careful analysis of recent policy developments. Moreover, being
situated outside of formal institutions (with the exception of the New
School) seemed to give him the freedom to express a range of views
bound to generate controversy on both ends of the political spectrum.

Abrams' perspective also provides a counterpoint to subsequent
scholarship. The primary consequence of housing initiatives, historians
have argued, was to secure middle-class support for the New Deal by
effecting a "revolution in expanded credit." These mostly positive assessments overstate the degree of direct assistance given to individuals and
underemphasize the benefits provided to business interests. By suggesting that credit liberalization often helped fiduciaries without providing
similar assistance to ordinary citizens, and by showing how housing initiatives elicited business as well as middle-class support for the New Deal,
Abrams' critique offers a useful corrective.[52]

Whatever its impact, Abrams' thinking and writing did not occur against a static backdrop. Millions of people relocated to central cities in order to secure employment in the nation's wartime industrial plants. This included the "great migration" of approximately 700,000 African-Americans from the rural south to the urban north and Midwest. Their entry into cities like Chicago and New York swelled African-American ghettos and highlighted the need for additional low-income housing. Abrams was aware of these dynamics, though he did not appreciate the underlying issues they raised until he became involved in a legal struggle concerning New York's largest postwar redevelopment project. His participation in that controversy would reveal how the quotidian facts of race and racism could explode the angels-on-pinheads debate over the role of the state, as if hypothetical models of political economy rather than a complex social reality were at the base of policymaking.[53]

Chapter Seven

"THE WALLS OF STUYVESANT TOWN"
Urban Redevelopment and the Struggle Between
Public and Private Power

Frederick H. Ecker, chairman of Metropolitan Life Insurance Company,
announced in the spring of 1943 that Stuyvesant Town, a proposed New
York City housing development being financed by his company, would
not admit African Americans. In justifying this policy, Ecker noted with
certainty, " 'Negroes and whites don't mix. Perhaps they will in a hundred years. . . . If we brought them into this development, it would be to
the detriment of the city, too, because it would depress all the surrounding property.' " His comments generated a firestorm of protest
from a small group of civil rights supporters. Among their voices,
Abrams' was the loudest. But Stuyvesant Town was more than just a case
of discrimination, which was the rule, not the exception in housing. It
also represented a tangible manifestation of the trends Abrams identified with a business welfare state. In his estimation, the use of public subsidies and powers on behalf of Metropolitan illustrated nothing less than
state approval of discriminatory policies.[1]

To appreciate this conflict in concrete policy terms, and to understand why Abrams ended up playing a crucial role, we must again step
back, examining how and why Stuyvesant Town emerged, what it repre-

sented historically in terms of public/private financing of urban redevelopment, and why it raised ultimately inescapable issues. Such an analysis reveals yet another layer of policy discourse. In addition to debates over restrictive versus constructive legislation, decisionmakers in New York State also argued over the merits of providing public incentives to private parties for the purpose of stimulating slum clearance and construction of additional housing. The result of their legislative efforts was to grant significant benefits to financial and real estate interests without enacting corresponding safeguards against the misuse of these privileges. Abrams' views on this subject would be in direct opposition to those of Robert Moses, one of the most powerful individuals in New York City.

Enlisting Private Capital for Housing

While Abrams was finishing law school and clerking with Arthur Garfield Hays, a housing shortage plagued the Empire State, especially New York City. As a remedy, lawmakers tried to stimulate increased private investment in housing. Though life insurance companies held the largest pools of untapped capital, the state had prohibited them from investing in real estate, given the speculative and often risky nature of property transactions. In light of the post-World War I housing emergency, however, lawmakers almost passed a bill requiring insurance companies to invest at least 40 percent of their funds in mortgage loans. Instead, in 1922 lawmakers amended statutory restrictions so these institutions could voluntarily invest up to 10 percent of their assets in low-rent housing (defined as an average of $9 per room per month). Since this legislation resulted after extensive negotiations with the Metropolitan Life Insurance Company, the press dubbed it the "Metropolitan Bill." Shortly after the bill's passage, Metropolitan began construction of a large housing development in Long Island City, appropriately called Metropolitan Houses.[2]

New York State's Housing Law (1926), the first such legislation in the United States, was another attempt to induce private capital into low- and moderate-income housing. This statute created a State Board of Housing and authorized creation of both public and private limited dividend housing corporations, though none of the former was ever formed. Profits for limited dividend corporations could not exceed 6 percent, and their rents were subject to state regulation. In exchange for these restrictions, limited dividend corporations were exempt from state and municipal property taxes (though cities were not *required* to grant such exemptions), and their bonds, mortgages, and interest payments were free from state taxation. Lawmakers also granted the power of eminent domain to public limited dividend corporations; in future legislation, this distinction would be dropped, giving municipalities the right to exercise condemnation proceedings on behalf of a wide range of private corporations.[3]

Limited dividend housing remained limited in both profits and appeal (the one likely a function of the other) and never contributed significantly to New York's housing supply. Yet the emerging pattern markedly influenced subsequent policy innovations. By creating a variety of financial inducements, state and city officials had chosen to limit direct government participation in favor of policies emphasizing private sector involvement. Despite passage of the Municipal Housing Authorities Law in 1934, it was this pattern that would characterize New York's urban redevelopment laws, which again targeted life insurance companies as sources of capital.

Louis Pink, a friend of Abrams and member of the New York City Housing Authority, was one of the first individuals to highlight the augmented role life insurance companies might play. In his 1928 book, *The New Day in Housing*, he had listed the assets of the five largest insurance companies; he thought some of these funds could find a "safe and useful field for investment" in the "erection and management of workers' dwellings in all the great cities of the land." "Life insurance companies," he concluded, "could well afford to invest a few hundred million . . . to clean out the slums." Fulfilling Pink's hopes, a 1938 amendment to the New York State Insurance Law once again allowed insurance companies to enter the field of housing finance (the previous amendment authorizing such activity had expired). Insurance companies could now invest up to 10 percent of their assets in real property for the purpose of providing an "adequate supply of decent, safe and sanitary dwelling accommodations for persons of low and moderate income." Because this amendment did not authorize tax exemptions, only one major housing development—another project built by the Metropolitan Life Insurance Company—resulted. Parkchester, as the development was known, did little to increase low-income housing since it charged relatively high rents, a clear violation of limited dividend requirements.[4]

The failure of the 1938 amendment to attract private capital convinced Pink and others of the need for comprehensive programs, not temporary expedients. The groundwork for such programs had already been established by the so-called Housing Article to the New York constitution (1938), which authorized the creation of quasi-public redevelopment authorities. The experience of the 1920s and 1930s, however, had demonstrated the unwillingness of conservative financial institutions to invest in housing unless they could count on high profits and low risks. By the late 1930s, still wary of another economic downturn, fiduciaries—especially life insurance companies—held out for greater incentives and less regulation.[5]

Whether or not foot-dragging on the part of life insurance companies prompted Abrams' radical (albeit fleeting) 1939 suggestion that they be acquired via eminent domain is uncertain. More clear was his support of public housing authorities—not redevelopment corporations—as the agencies to coordinate planning and new construction on the local level. Abrams realized this was a minority viewpoint; he also understood public funds would be insufficient to finance most redevelopment undertakings. These concessions notwithstanding, Abrams continued to believe private sector participation should be strictly regulated when it occurred. This kind of relationship, one favoring public over private interests, had basically prevailed up until the late 1930s in New York. In Abrams' opinion, the balance quickly tipped in the other direction after the state legislature passed a series of redevelopment laws. The substance of these laws owed much to the political power of Robert Moses.[6]

By the outbreak of World War II, Moses had already been head of the New York State Park System, New York's Secretary of State, Chairman of the Triborough Bridge Authority, and a member of the New York City Planning Commission. As early as 1939 he had begun discussing possible redevelopment legislation with various life insurance companies. "Everything possible should be done," he later stated, "to encourage semi-public housing and the investment of funds of fiduciaries . . . in slum clearance." These negotiations helped shape the Nunan-Mitchell Bill, which the New York legislature passed in 1940, but which Governor Lehman vetoed, primarily because it contained "several" unspecified "defects." Losing no time, Moses arranged a meeting between Mayor

LaGuardia and life insurance executives, where the latter discussed their concerns and criticisms of the bill Lehman had vetoed. Believing "private capital" was fearful of entering an "unexplored and highly speculative" field, Moses used input from this meeting to influence subsequent legislation.[7]

The Urban Redevelopment Corporations Law, enacted on April 29, 1941, was the result. It was an "attempt to strike a balance," explained its author, Thomas C. Desmond (R-Bronx), "between privileges and inducements granted to private capital . . . and standards and restrictions necessary to insure that redevelopment projects" would be a "permanent benefit to the community." Tax exemptions were granted on improved land for ten years and the power of eminent domain was given to redevelopment corporations as long as 51 percent of an affected site's property owners consented to its exercise. Other provisions were less inviting to investors. Local planning commissions had to review and approve all redevelopment plans, and these plans had to contain options for relocating displaced tenants—a restriction likely responsible for the law's limited impact. The legislature passed a new statute in 1942, the Redevelopment Companies Law, which offered additional incentives for private investment. One company, New York Life Insurance, showed interest in building a project under this legislation, but backed out at the last minute; arrangements, it said, were just " 'too thin.' "[8]

Moses, frustrated and fearing redevelopment in New York City would have to rely primarily on public housing, contacted Frederick H. Ecker, chairman of Metropolitan Life. Ecker indicated the kinds of changes he wanted made to the Redevelopment Companies Law; what emerged was a set of amendments illustrating the state's eagerness to employ private capital in urban redevelopment. These amendments increased the period of tax exemption to twenty-five years, eliminated the need for tenant relocation provisions, significantly reduced the supervisory role of planning commissions, and, by payment of exempt taxes, allowed redevelopment corporations to ignore rent and dividend restrictions. The revised statute also defined condemnation for redevelopment purposes as a "superior public use." This novel legal phrase not only placed redevelopment above such ordinary public "uses" as playgrounds and schools, it left little ambiguity over the priority the state was willing to give private corporations in acquiring urban property.[9]

Greatly dismayed, Abrams urged Governor Thomas E. Dewey to veto the proposed revisions. "While tax exemption on public housing" was "warranted and essential," he did not believe the state should grant similar exemptions to insurance companies in order to "assure them of a handsome profit at taxpayers' expense." Dropping the requirement for relocation plans was even more problematic. "So long as there is no provision for rehousing the tenants displaced from the slum buildings," Abrams maintained, "no extensive slum rebuilding can ever be achieved by private enterprise." "Poor families" would be "driven from one slum to the other," pushing derelict property values ever upward. Thus, if "too many" developments were built under the amended legislation, Abrams thought the city would face a "disaster." Despite his attacks on this "vicious" policy, and despite Dewey's doubts about some of its provisions, the governor signed the amendments into law. "The immediate practical problem," Dewey stated, was "housing or no housing."[10]

"Suburb in the City": The Decision to Construct Stuyvesant Town

Many of Abrams' fears came to pass. In April 1943, LaGuardia announced Metropolitan Life Insurance Company would be the first fiduciary to construct a project (Stuyvesant Town) under the amended legislation. Stuyvesant Town's 35 thirteen-story buildings, located on a 72-acre tract on Manhattan's Lower East Side, would house 24,315 people. New York City would assemble land, condemn the site's buildings, evict residents from their homes, release public streets for incorporation within Stuyvesant Town, and grant lucrative tax exemptions to Metropolitan. The cost for such a development was estimated at $50 million, though that figure would eventually reach $90 million. Stuyvesant Town would cover much of the blighted "gas-house district"; "blight" was a term contemporaries used to described a combination of population loss and deteriorating buildings. Officials hoped Stuyvesant Town would address this problem by restoring the district to "economic respectability" and by bringing "back to the center of the city those most important elements of the functioning community, families with children." Perhaps this was why the *New York Times* tersely described the project as a "suburb in [the] city."[11]

Stuyvesant Town's size and overall design did not receive universal praise. The project's density of 397 persons per acre, *Architectural Record* pointed out, would be "well above average for Manhattan." Others raised concerns about the development's dearth of schools, nurseries, and libraries. New York City Councilman Stanley M. Isaacs criticized the whole undertaking, asserting it would create a " 'medieval walled city, privately owned, in the heart of New York.' " His comment would prove to be only a slight exaggeration.[12]

On May 19, 1943, Frederick Ecker, buttonholed by a newspaper reporter, admitted Stuyvesant Town would be for whites only. Coming just a day before the City Planning Commission was to vote on the project, this admission generated little opposition or protest. Consequently, the Commission approved Stuyvesant Town by a vote of 5–1. The lone negative vote was cast by Lawrence M. Orton, whose primary objection was the absence of a public school within the project's boundaries. After the Commission's vote, Councilmen Isaacs and Adam Clayton Powell Jr. (an African American) announced they would support a resolution to add a provision to Stuyvesant Town's contract forbidding racial or religious discrimination. Civic groups also mobilized to oppose Metropolitan's policy. New York City's oldest African-American paper, *New York Age*, accused the life insurance giant of knowing the "principles of good business" better than the "spirit and letter of the Constitution." Speaking to a different constituency, Loula Lasker, a long-time housing activist, told readers of the *New York Times*, "The right of any citizen, regardless of race, creed, or color, to share the benefits of public-aided projects has long been accepted in this state."[13]

The Board of Estimate convened on June 3 to decide whether to approve the city's contract with Stuyvesant Town. It listened to arguments from both sides during a sometimes heated three and a half hour meeting. Civil rights advocates believed the project would have a "public character" since it depended on tax exemptions and eminent domain. They therefore urged the Board to reject the contract until Metropolitan disavowed its discriminatory intentions. Moses, an unqualified supporter of Stuyvesant Town, described the benefits in question (tax exemption and eminent domain) as " 'minimum inducements' " to encourage slum clearance and the construction of new housing. Indeed, that very morning the *New York Times* had printed a long letter from Moses in which he anticipated the objections Abrams and others would raise: "Those who insist upon making projects of this kind a battleground for the vindication of social objectives, however desirable, and who persist in claiming that a private project is in fact a public project, obviously are looking for a political issue and not for results in the form of actual slum clearance." If Stuyvesant Town failed, Moses grimly concluded, there would be "no further proposals of this character."[14]

Apparently fearing Moses' predictions might come true, the Board of Estimate voted 11–5 to approve the project. "If one is convinced that private enterprise is on the way out and the future belongs to public enterprise," the *New York Times* editorialized two days later, "then the entrance of the big insurance companies into the housing field is an event of primary importance." Much of this "importance," the editors noted, was linked to the "huge battalions of cash" that had been "thrown in on the side of private enterprise." The less optimistic *Age* called the decision "a dangerous Fascist step and one which will help nullify the victory we will win over Hitler." Both papers, though, had separately identified two important points: the city had certainly provided enormous funding (without adequate restrictions) for "private enterprise," and in doing so, it relinquished responsibility to uphold basic civil rights.[15]

Racial Discrimination and Business Welfare Policies

Abrams' feelings toward Stuyvesant Town differed from those of Mumford and Moses. Mumford, in preparing a *New Yorker* piece on Stuyvesant Town, contacted Abrams, asking for any items he had written on the topic. Whatever Abrams' influence, the resulting article attacked Stuyvesant Town on planning and aesthetic grounds. Calling it "prefabricated blight" and a "caricature of urban rebuilding," Mumford, like housing activist Catherine Bauer, criticized the project for establishing a pattern of "greater congestion." He cautioned, however, against blaming the architects and planners "too severely." Instead, he pointed an accusatory finger at Moses: "Once the decision was made to house twenty-four thousand people on a site that should not be made to hold more than six thousand, all other faults followed almost automatically."[16]

Moses, in a heated *ad hominem* response, called Mumford a "paper planner" whose "wisecracks" bore "little resemblance to the truth." Especially irked by Mumford's comments about Stuyvesant Town's playgrounds, Moses lauded his own practical experience over Mumford's theorizing: "Having built and run more city and suburban playgrounds than almost anyone else around, and never having seen any designed or operated by Mr. Mumford, I don't know what all this mumbo-jumbo is about." As Moses would later characterize their differences, the choice was between "subsidized lamas in their remote mountain temples and those who must work in the marketplace."[17]

While Abrams told Bauer he was "not inhibited on the physical issues of Stuyvesant Town," he did not think Mumford had come off "first best" in his tangle with Moses. By discussing the development's architectural flaws (and imputing them to Moses), Abrams thought Mumford might have appeared insensitive to the "average guy's" plea for "houses" and not "monuments." Only a little reading between the lines was necessary to discern Abrams' concern that Moses might become a sort of hero among working-class New Yorkers who were less concerned with aesthetic niceties than with affordable shelter.[18]

Abrams' own attacks, which would develop over the next few years, were derived from practical experience in housing and the law. Ultimately, no one, not even Mumford in his spirited exchange with Moses, did more to publicize the problematic dimensions of Stuyvesant Town than Abrams. In speeches, newspaper editorials, *The Future of Housing*, and articles written for *The Nation*, *Commentary*, and *The New Republic*, he relentlessly attacked Stuyvesant Town's discriminatory practices. In 1947, when Abrams began a two-year stint as a housing reporter for the *New York Post*, he gained an even larger audience. True to the muckraker tradition, he criticized everything from high rents to "restricted communities," while reserving his sharpest barbs for Moses. With headlines leaving little to the imagination—"Robert Moses, the City's No. 1 Housing Bottleneck"—Abrams blasted the master builder for having a "throat-hold on the housing program" and for using Metropolitan instead of the city's housing authority to effect slum clearance. Moses, for the most part, ignored these attacks, but Mayor William O'Dwyer apparently offered Abrams a sinecure if he would resign from the *Post*. Abrams politely declined.[19]

The criticisms Abrams advanced in his speeches and articles, while illustrating his abilities as both a public and policy intellectual, were significant because they reflected arguments he employed in legislative and judicial attempts to prevent Metropolitan from discriminating. One of his first concerns was Stuyvesant Town's defects as a slum clearance project. The most obvious drawback, at least in terms of fiscal logic, was the amount the city would lose in tax exemptions versus land costs. As mentioned earlier, Stuyvesant Town received a twenty-five year exemption from paying taxes on the improved valuation of its site. This cost the city a total of $25 million. The land itself had been sold to Metropolitan by the city for $14 million. Millions of dollars could have been saved, Abrams argued, if city officials had given the land to Metropolitan as a gift, instead of providing a costly tax exemption.[20]

Abrams also feared Stuyvesant Town would set a dangerous precedent by uprooting residents without providing them comparably priced housing in other neighborhoods. Both LaGuardia and Moses tried to quell these fears. The mayor stated that low-income groups would be rehoused in one of the city's low-cost housing developments, while Moses simply said displaced residents would be accommodated elsewhere. Their assurances were necessary since approximately 3,000 families would be evicted. It was unlikely that many of the evictees would return to the completed project, since there was a large discrepancy between their previous rents (about $5 per room) and those Stuyvesant Town planned to charge (about $14 per room). This revealed one of the significant shortcomings of tax subsidies as a form of public policy: subsidies were usually high enough to attract private capital into housing, but not high enough to bring rents down sufficiently to meet the needs of low-income families.[21]

Residents uprooted by Stuyvesant Town did indeed face limited options. According to a study made by New York City's Community Service Society, a bare 3 percent could afford Stuyvesant Town's rents, and only 22 percent met the eligibility requirements for public housing. The remaining 75 percent were forced to move, usually into already overcrowded neighborhoods. This increased demand for affordable housing, Abrams noted, "pressed into service" hundreds of abandoned dwellings. "Slums ripe for the wrecking crew" were now "booming." The entire process was similar to the one Abrams had outlined in his 1943 letter to Governor Dewey. It was also a concrete example of how state assistance to private interests could hurt, not help, certain groups.[22]

More central to Abrams' critique was the failure of Stuyvesant Town to provide a vision of what post-World War II communities should be like. Abrams, like other planners and policymakers, viewed construction of new housing as an opportunity to clear slums and eliminate blight.

But for Abrams, the "largest building program" in history presented an additional opportunity for "recasting . . . communities in a democratic mold." With a "proper grasp of the facts" and a little imagination, "livable communities and the democratic way of life" were attainable. Establishing these communities required destruction of "barriers" standing "in the way of real racial harmony and understanding." This would entail not only abolition of the "old segregated patterns" perpetuated by the FHA and the HOLC, but also elimination of "segregated areas" that nullified the chance "to level out social differences."[23]

Abrams understood the difficulty of integrating *existing* communities; after all, segregated neighborhoods could not be "immediately broken up." Integrating *new* communities, though, was a different matter. This was why the "government housing program" encompassed "more than housing." It could be a "proving ground on which the practical validity of a great ideal" was "demonstrated," or more forbiddingly, the forum in which "any hope of ever again creating the environment necessary for a new interracial understanding" was "shattered." According to Abrams, public housing residents already possessed this "understanding": their interactions illustrated racial comity was possible within integrated settings. Abrams thus countered Ecker's justification for barring African Americans from Stuyvesant Town by asserting, "If the fear that 'Negroes and whites don't mix' is based on a myth, the projects where 'Negroes and whites do mix' represent an important frontier."[24]

Publicly subsidized developments like Stuyvesant Town, however, were ignoring this "important frontier." Instead, they were creating "Jim Crow" housing arrangements, something Abrams eventually labeled as the "Stuyvesant formula." "If carried to its logical conclusion," he argued, it would mean "selected 'respectable' families living in fenced off neighborhoods, while the 'undesirables,' poor or rich, are relegated to ghettos." Such a situation was especially intolerable to Abrams since it would all but destroy the ability of African Americans and other "undesirables" to escape from ghettos.[25]

Metropolitan's plans to build another development ("Riverton") gave credence to Abrams' fears. Riverton was actually little more than a transparent effort by Metropolitan to mount a separate-but-equal defense in the wake of public and legal pressure against its decision to discriminate. As with Stuyvesant Town, Moses said he "induced" Metropolitan to construct Riverton, which one business periodical described as an attempt to "convert a dormant area" into a "parklike residential unit." For its part, Metropolitan contended that housing developments had to be built " 'with due regards to the needs of the neighborhood.' " Riverton, located in Harlem, would be for African Americans, while Stuyvesant Town would be for whites. African Americans would therefore have " 'no room' " to claim they were being denied equal protection.[26]

Abrams denounced Riverton as another attempt to effect segregation in subsidized developments. Speaking to African Americans directly, he advised: "The issue to be determined by the Negro community resolves itself into whether it is more interested in the few projects that may be built (and it is likely that those will only be token projects), or whether it is more interested in establishing an accepted principle of equality in housing, etc." If the "Negro community" were "interested in the more fundamental principle," then it should condemn the project. Abrams' concerns highlighted a choice African Americans increasingly confronted. Was new, potentially equal housing worth the price of continued or increased segregation? This question could be especially divisive in cities like New York and Chicago, where severe housing shortages and racism had confined African Americans to inner-city neighborhoods. The political scientist James Q. Wilson would describe the two sides of this debate as a conflict between those who supported "status" goals (integration) versus those who supported "welfare" objectives (new facilities). Though Abrams never adopted this particular terminology, he maintained—at least during the Stuyvesant controversy—that the fight for "principle" was more important than short-term gains since no fixed racial precedents had yet emerged in urban redevelopment.[27]

Dependence on state assistance made Metropolitan's activities even more problematic. "The Stuyvesant Town formula . . . . would authorize the use of public moneys and public powers to establish ghetto patterns in our cities," Abrams remarked. This would eliminate the "hope of ever restoring the lost equality between races." To combat the Stuyvesant formula, Abrams tried to persuade the Marshall Field corporation to build a limited dividend housing project open to all races; the company tactfully refused. These developments frustrated and demoralized Abrams. He concluded that if the "blend of races, cultures, incomes, groups, ages, colors, religions, and types" could not be preserved, then the "democratic chaos of unplanned cities" would be "preferable to the undemocratic order of stratified communities." The model here was not the homogeneity of Stuyvesant Town, but the heterogeneity of Greenwich Village.[28]

Abrams' greatest anguish was caused by the inappropriate use of mechanisms he himself had helped legitimize as municipal tools (including eminent domain). Those who crafted New York's urban redevelopment legislation had disregarded the safeguards these mechanisms required, such as antidiscrimination clauses and relocation provisions. "We are faced with the dilemma," Abrams explained, "that the very social reforms in housing and city planning—zoning, slum clearance, and so on—which are thought to advance social progress lend themselves most easily to devices for achieving discrimination." Or as he more concisely put the matter, " 'Urban redevelopment' is but the latest of a succession of devices conceived originally to improve housing and neighborhoods, but which have been perverted to keep minorities 'in their place.' " Redevelopment, however, was different from previous "devices" and the "implications of its perversion" were "far more sinister." While "racial zoning ordinances and restrictive covenants aimed only to bar minorities from coming into certain areas," redevelopment authorized cities "to root them out of areas" where they *already* lived. Worse still, because slum clearance was a "recognized public purpose," the city could forcibly sell homes and property. This could turn redevelopment into "one of the most oppressive instruments for racial segregation and discrimination," as well as a "prelude to mass homelessness."[29]

In Abrams' estimation, slum clearance and urban redevelopment had been "perverted" by the same phenomenon: business welfare policies. He admittedly attributed some of the problems created in housing and redevelopment programs to administrative power and discretion. "A broad bill of rights, adequate enough for a laissez-faire society," he observed, was "too general for the more mixed economy or the social service state" where the "floating area of administrative discretion" could become the "area of unbridled tyranny." A "new set of very specific criteria" defining "official conduct and administration in the creation and operation of new neighborhoods" was necessary.[30]

More specifically, Abrams believed the unrestricted exercise of public power on behalf of private interests was what transformed social reforms into tools of oppression. "Freedom" had survived in America not only because of the separation of powers, but also because of the "separation of government from business." As public subsidies to particular industries began to chip away at this separation, beneficiaries expected the "same immunity from regulation they enjoyed before they drew upon the government purse and the government's powers." This raised an important question: "Where government funds or public powers are used for a private or quasi-private agency, shall the same principle of equality be applied as if the power or funds were used by public agencies?" While Abrams thought it should be answered in the affirmative, policymakers were commonly giving a contrary response. Abrams argued this was because the "primary concern of public administrators" was no longer "equality in the marketplace" or "experiments in racial harmony" but rather the "financial success of the joint venture [between government and business]." Administrators thus freed private developers to pursue policies of discrimination and segregation in the "name of social reform."[31]

For Abrams, then, the most threatening aspect of developments like Stuyvesant Town was the "liaison" between public and private interests. The concomitant separation of "public power from public responsibility" permitted the "private company" to become a "medium for depriving individuals of rights." Having suggested where the problem lay, Abrams made his own views clear: the conferral of public power and privileges was justified only when there was a "clear social purpose" and when private beneficiaries were just as accountable as public ones. Without this accountability, current policies represented nothing less than "democracy in crisis" since they allowed "private organizations" exercising "a government function" to operate outside constitutional "limits."[32]

Legislative and Judicial Remedies for Racial Exclusion

At the same time Abrams was publishing critiques of Stuyvesant Town, he was also directly involved in efforts to prevent what he called the city's "bartering of public power." As noted previously, City Councilmen Stanley M. Isaacs and Adam Clayton Powell Jr. announced their intention to introduce a resolution requiring a revision of Metropolitan's contract to forbid discrimination. Subsequently, Isaacs and Councilman Louis Cohen asked Abrams to help write an antidiscrimination ordinance. This sort of legal proscription had few if any precedents pertaining to private landlords. New York's Public Housing Law stated that "no person shall, because of race, color, creed or religion, be subjected to any discrimination" in *public* housing projects, but all three urban redevelopment laws had remained silent on the subject. Every attempt to classify housing as a civil right during the 1938 New York Constitutional Convention had failed, and while a 1946 issue of *American City* would counsel legislative draftsmen to pay "careful attention . . . to such factors as racial discrimination," few decisionmakers had or would follow this advice.[33]

The failure of past initiatives notwithstanding, Abrams hammered out a draft ordinance. Relatively brief, it prohibited any "previous or future redevelopment corporation" organized under the Redevelopment Companies Law from denying "directly or indirectly to any person, because of race, color, creed or religion, any of the dwelling accommodations in such property or projects." Two additional sections defined penalties for breaking the ordinance, which included fines and revocation of tax exemptions. In January 1944, Abrams presented his draft to the Citizens Housing Council (CHC). Though Isaacs found the draft acceptable (he and Abrams belonged to the CHC), at least one member was troubled by its contents. James Felt, a prominent New York City real estate broker, believed CHC's job was "primarily housing." When tax exemption and eminent domain were given to companies to "clear substandard areas," CHC's actions were to be guided "essentially by considerations concerning redevelopment rather than social factors." Like most realtors (and some policymakers), Felt wanted to keep discussions of housing free from the volatile topics of racism and segregation. Unwilling to sweep the issue of discrimination under the rug of polite silence, the majority of CHC's members voted to endorse Abrams' draft.[34]

A couple of weeks later during a public hearing before the City Council's Finance Committee, Abrams presented his draft. Its enactment, he noted, would be nothing more than an affirmation of the "principle of non-discrimination in all undertakings" where the public was "directly or indirectly involved." Furthermore, if the Stuyvesant Town precedent were ignored, it would "mark the beginning of a process of whittling down the safeguards and traditions . . . built up for equal rights under the law since the Nation was founded." Finally, taking a position sure to make supporters of privately financed urban redevelopment uneasy, Abrams stated: "But even if Mr. Ecker is right and the experiences of the New York City Housing Authority completely unjustified, and the presence of a few Negroes would affect the project, then I say the project must be subordinated to the greater principle." In a small but significant way, Abrams was challenging the City Council to reconcile its professed adherence to democratic principles with its legislative actions. The conflict this posed for the Council—enforcing basic civil rights at the cost of potentially stopping or impeding redevelopment— was not unique to New York City or urban reform. That very year the Swedish sociologist Gunnar Myrdal published an influential study of race relations, *The American Dilemma*, in which he described a central contradiction between the United States' democratic creed, with its promise of equality, and the way (white) Americans actually treated African Americans. Abrams felt the Council could help resolve this dilemma by deciding to place "principle" over Metropolitan's desire to discriminate.[35]

Also speaking at the public hearing was Moses, who was sure a dilemma would exist if the Council passed the ordinance. Proclaiming the " 'great era of public housing' " was " 'about over,' " Moses stressed the need for private capital. " 'The great insurance companies and the savings banks,' " he declared, " 'will have to supply the money, and they should not be discouraged from doing it because of legislation imposing on them the same controls that are imposed on public housing projects.' " Passage of the ordinance would only " 'add to the bad atmosphere and effectively stop any future housing developments by the insurance companies and the banks.' " Perhaps influenced by Moses' opposition, and fearful of Metropolitan's reaction if its tenant selection policy were rejected, the Council decided to amend Abrams' draft so only *future* projects would be affected. Isaacs, certain the Council would quash any other bill, hoped the revised ordinance appeared "all right" to Abrams. As it turned out, the Council debated no fewer than three antidiscrimination bills. On May 15, 1944, after a three-hour session during which it appeared all the bills would be defeated, the Council passed the revised version of Abrams' original ordinance. On June 8 the Board of Estimate gave its approval, and on July 5 LaGuardia signed it into law.[36]

In one sense, the ordinance was a disappointment to Abrams and others who had wanted to include Stuyvesant Town under its provisions. This failure would unite liberals in support of subsequent legislation and prompt Abrams to challenge Metropolitan's policies in court. Yet despite its shortcomings, the ordinance was the first time city or state legislation prevented discrimination in publicly assisted private housing. The ordinance and Abrams' role in crafting it were significant for two other reasons as well. First, it reflected Abrams' goal of bringing private interests under public regulation when they received public funds or benefited from the exercise of public powers. Congress would eventually enshrine this logic in Title VI of the 1964 Civil Rights Act, which prohibited discrimination by any "program or activity" receiving federal funds. Second, the ordinance illustrated how civil rights activists and African Americans would increasingly rely on statutory remedies in their fight for equal justice. Reliance on the law would have its own limitations, but it would also provide the early civil rights movement with tangible victories during a period when such triumphs were rare.[37]

    If local efforts to prevent Stuyvesant Town from discriminating failed, so did ones on the state level. Between 1944 and 1948, no fewer than fifteen antidiscrimination bills were introduced in the New York Assembly. Under the aggressive leadership of Louis Peck (D-Bronx) and Bernard Austin (D-Brooklyn), these bills attempted to establish "as a civil right" the "opportunity to purchase and lease real property without discrimination," or similarly, to prohibit "redevelopment corporations" from discriminating in "furnishing dwelling accommodations." The Assembly rejected all fifteen bills, which left the courts to clarify the legal questions posed by urban redevelopment.[38]

    Seeking judicial remedies, property owners and civil rights activists (the latter assisted by Abrams) brought three suits against Metropolitan. They raised important but legally ambiguous issues, namely the reach of the Fourteenth Amendment and the essential distinctions between public and private activity. Precedents and doctrines governing these issues were neither clear nor consistently applied by the courts. Initial decisions had asserted Fourteenth Amendment prohibitions pertained only to actions taken by public bodies or officials, though some jurists, following the reasoning of Justice Harlan's dissent in the *Civil Rights Cases* (1883), denied "any law or state action" needed to be at issue in order to invoke the Amendment's authority. Muddying the already turbid waters, political scientists and legal scholars were noting by the early 1920s the Supreme Court's failure to establish any "fundamental distinction" between "public" and "private" agencies. These ambiguities gave both sides in the Stuyvesant Town dispute some basis to hope for success.[39]

A group of property owners launched the first suit, *Murray v. LaGuardia*, in 1943. Expecting inadequate compensation for their holdings on the Stuyvesant site, they sought to enjoin construction. Even though their case reached the Appeals Court, they ultimately lost. In ruling against the plaintiffs in the lower trial court (called Supreme Courts in New York), Judge Benjamin F. Schreiber's arguments especially alarmed Abrams, since Schreiber cited the *Muller* case to support the city's use of eminent domain proceedings on behalf of Stuyvesant Town. Expansion of state power had led policymakers—and now judges—in directions Abrams never intended.[40]

In August 1944 (during the *Murray* appeal), the CHC and several other civic organizations initiated a second suit, *Pratt v. LaGuardia*. It attacked Metropolitan's policy of discrimination more directly, and while Abrams was not the plaintiffs' chief attorney, his designation "of counsel" indicates he provided important substantive and tactical advice. Because Stuyvesant Town benefited from tax exemptions, use of public property, and condemnation proceedings (all manifestations of "state action"), the plaintiffs argued that the equal protection clauses of the U.S. and New York constitutions could be invoked to prevent Metropolitan from discriminating. In making short work of the case, Judge Bernard Shientag dismissed the suit since no one had been actually discriminated against (construction of Stuyvesant Town had not yet begun). Both the Appellate Division—the first level of appeal in New York—and the Appeals Court affirmed Shientag's decision. Metropolitan had now won the first two rounds of litigation.[41]

The American Civil Liberties Union, the American Jewish Congress, and the National Association for the Advancement of Colored People (NAACP) launched the final suit against Metropolitan, *Dorsey v. Stuyvesant Town*, in late 1946. The suit was instigated on behalf of three African-American veterans: Joseph R. Dorsey, Monroe Dowling, and Calvin B. Harper. That *Dorsey* was filed at all was due largely to Abrams' efforts. It was he who contacted the ACLU and suggested the merits of filing another suit. Without any apparent hesitation, the ACLU accepted Abrams' services (which he provided *pro bono*), then solicited the City-Wide Citizens Committee on Harlem for potential plaintiffs. In constructing his arguments, Abrams would draw upon many of the developments he had observed in both state and federal housing programs. Squaring off against him was a worthy though unlikely opponent,

Samuel Seabury. One of the most distinguished members of New York City's legal and political circles, Seabury had spent most of his early career fighting for unpopular social causes and crusading against corruption in high places. Now, with silver hair to match his silver tongue, Seabury seemingly placed loyalty to his client (Metropolitan Life) above his own scruples.[42]

By the time *Dorsey* reached the New York County Supreme Court in mid-1947, Metropolitan admitted discriminating against African Americans by denying them admission into Stuyvesant Town. But Metropolitan also argued it was free, like any other private landlord, to select whichever tenants it desired, especially when the economic success of the development was (supposedly) at stake. No one denied *private* landlords possessed this right. Whether or not redevelopment projects were in fact private—or conversely, whether their creation and operation represented "state action"—was the issue. If the court decided the case involved the latter, Metropolitan and other developers could be prohibited from discriminating.[43]

In his brief, Abrams articulated why he believed Stuyvesant Town was a "public undertaking": it benefited from the powers of eminent domain and tax exemption. He would subsequently call these powers the "working tools of any government." A "salient" difference between totalitarian and democratic regimes was how autocracies subjected such "tools" to the "whim of a single dictator," while in a democracy "their arbitrary exercise was effectively checked." To ignore this distinction was, for Abrams, the first step toward undemocratic governance.[44]

Finding Abrams' brief unpersuasive, Judge Felix C. Benvenga ruled against the plaintiffs on July 28, 1947. Benvenga acknowledged slum clearance had a "public purpose," and that condemnation of private property was a "public use," but he did not think the resulting housing was in any way "public." He thought the "public purpose" ended once a blighted area was cleared and rebuilt. In making this assertion, Benvenga was implying Stuyvesant Town could and would have been built without public intervention, a proposition clearly at odds with the historical record; more than two decades of legislation, including the Redevelopment Companies Law, testified to the necessity of state and municipal incentives to persuade fiduciaries to engage in "public purposes." As Metropolitan's Vice-President George Gove had told a Congressional committee just a few months earlier, "We feel that unless the element of risk can be substantially reduced, it is not wise for us to go into housing. There are only certain conditions under which it is wise . . . to do so, and when those conditions prevail, we will and we have." Benvenga's response to Metropolitan's discriminatory policies also illustrated the potential limitations civil rights activists might face when seeking judicial redress. "It may well be," Benvenga admitted, "that . . . a policy of exclusion and discrimination on account of race, color, creed, or religion is not only undesirable but unwise." "But," he affirmed, "the wisdom of the policy is not for the courts."[45]

On December 11, 1948, more than a year later, the Appellate Division unanimously affirmed Benvenga's decision without issuing an opinion. The plaintiffs would have to take their case to the Appeals Court. By this point the suit had generated significant publicity, especially since every legislative attempt to prevent Metropolitan from discriminating had failed. Joining Abrams on appeal would be the rising young lawyer Thurgood Marshall, who represented the NAACP. All parties in the dispute assembled before the Appeals Court on April 11, 1949. Signifying the importance civil rights groups placed on the case, supporting briefs (*amicus curiae*) were filed by the Friendship House of Harlem, the Citizens Housing and Planning Council, the Town and Village Tenants Committee to End Discrimination in Stuyvesant Town, the Board of Home Missions, and the National Lawyers Guild. No such briefs were filed on behalf of Metropolitan or the city, which was also listed as a defendant in the suit. Many white and African-American activists hoped a decision favoring the plaintiffs would be a turning point in the crusade against discrimination.[46]

Both parties presented familiar arguments. Predictably, Metropolitan insisted its rental policy was not subject to public restrictions or regulations since Stuyvesant Town was "privately owned" and "engaged in constructing and operating a private project." Echoing this view, John P. McGrath, Corporation Counsel for New York City, maintained Stuyvesant Town had the "power by its private action to fix its own policies with respect to selection of its tenants without any governmental act, consent or approval." In other words, Metropolitan and the city sought to demonstrate a lack of "state action" by denying Stuyvesant Town was a "public undertaking."[47]

Metropolitan advanced another, more technical argument as well. It admitted the city had exercised its "power of condemnation" and "its power to close streets and exchange property." But it denied this made Stuyvesant Town subject to Fourteenth Amendment prohibitions. Phrased differently, Metropolitan did not believe these powers, including eminent domain, gave a "public character" to private projects as long as they were exercised *on behalf of* and not *by* the developments themselves. Though Metropolitan was factually correct—the city never actually gave Stuyvesant Town public powers—Abrams would question the validity of this distinction.[48]

The plaintiffs' arguments were based on the contention that "discrimination by private agencies" was "constitutionally forbidden when it is supported, participated in, effectuated, or made possible by state action." By including the relatively passive phrases "participated in" and "effectuated by," Abrams was trying to convince the court of its ability to invoke Fourteenth Amendment protections if public powers were exercised on behalf of private parties. He was also subtly suggesting the terms "public" and "private" no longer represented discrete, absolute categories but points along a continuum. The movement away from a laissez-faire to a general welfare state, and then to a business welfare state, had blurred the linguistic and judicial distinctions between "public" and "private." To argue whether Stuyvesant Town was entirely private or entirely public missed the point; instead, one had to determine whether there was *sufficient* public involvement to justify public restrictions. In answering this query, Abrams claimed Stuyvesant Town was close enough to the public end of the continuum—the "state action" pole—to warrant Fourteenth Amendment protections. By presenting this argument, Abrams was implicitly comparing Stuyvesant Town to two recent Supreme Court cases. In *Smith v. Allwright* (1944), the Court had defined political parties as state entities if they received legislative benefits or were subject to legislative controls. In a more closely analogous case, *Marsh v. Alabama* (1946), the Court had decided company towns were not exempt from Fourteenth Amendment strictures, even though they were privately owned. Abrams hoped that Stuyvesant Town, in many ways also a private town, might be covered by the reasoning advanced in *Marsh*.[49]

On July 19, 1949, Judge Bruce Bromley issued his decision. In his seventeen-page opinion, Bromley first outlined the evolution of slum clearance in New York, then reviewed the failure to introduce antidiscrimination clauses in the Housing Article, in any of the redevelopment laws, or in statutes themselves. Finding no prohibitions in New York State law (and thus no violation of the state's equal protection clause), Bromley focused on establishing whether *federal* equal protection clauses were operative. To do so, he would have to determine if "state action" had occurred. Taking a narrow view, he reasoned that "state action" could be substantiated only where the government had "consciously exerted its power in aid of discrimination," or where private individuals had "acted in a governmental capacity." Assured neither had occurred in the present matter, Bromley ruled that the "aid which the state had afforded to respondents [Metropolitan and the city] and the control to which they are subject are not sufficient to transmute their conduct into state action."[50]

Though Bromley suggested that he, like Abrams, viewed the public/private issue along a continuum, his emphasis on direct government involvement and the need for individuals to have acted in a "governmental capacity" revealed a relatively inflexible definition of "state action." Bromley's closing remarks hinted at some of the reasons for this position. He believed as the public and private sectors became more dependent on each other—as American society became more "entwined"—it might be difficult (perhaps even unwise) to hold America's "industrial and economic life" up to the standards the state itself operated under. This exchange of principle for expediency was exactly what Abrams had feared business welfare policies would foster.[51]

The decision was a bitter blow for Abrams, who had spent significant time and effort preparing and arguing the case. He vented his anger in the pages of various magazines, giving his own summary of the decision. "Private corporations," he fumed, "may now be lawfully handed the powers and funds of government and use them unhindered by constitutional restraint." The court's decision also represented an "ominous relaxation of democratic controls"; states and cities could now become "partners to discrimination and injustice." These remarks indicated Abrams' growing pessimism, and on June 5, 1950, his gloomy outlook proved justified. The Supreme Court denied the plaintiffs a writ of certiori; the decision of the New York Appeals Court would therefore stand. In a rare break from tradition, both William O. Douglas and Hugo Black publicly dissented from the majority's decision not to hear the case. Though the precise reasons for their dissents are unclear, a memo written by Douglas' clerk is suggestive. While a decision in favor of the plaintiffs might "discourage slum rehabilitation by large corporations," the clerk ("WMC") still thought Douglas should review the case and decide whether to take the "next step forward in expanding the concept of state action." The Court, however, declined to take that "next step," thereby temporarily halting an expansive interpretation of "state action."[52]

Despite the Supreme Court's decision, virtually all major law journals disagreed with the ruling of the Appeals Court. Closely paralleling Abrams' arguments, these journals described the decision as "too mechanical in its application of the constitutional provisions for equal protection" and an "unsound interpretation of the 'state action' doctrine as established by the federal courts." The broader implications were equally disturbing. "As long as the instant decision stands unreversed," the *University of Pennsylvania Law Review* predicted, "states will be able to avoid giving aid to Negro citizens, while simultaneously assisting the welfare of others."[53]

These views, as well as the decision itself, seemed to contradict the optimism articulated a few years later by a noted legal scholar. Morroe Berger, after surveying almost one hundred years of legal history, confidently concluded, "Law in our society is a formidable means for the elimination of group discrimination and for the establishment of conditions which discourage prejudicial attitudes." In "The Limits of the Law," a review of Berger's book, Abrams revealed how his own views concerning litigation had been tempered. "The right to equality is created not out of law or decree alone," he admonished readers, "but out of national rights, traditions, administrative rulings, legislative findings, executive pronouncements . . . and the whole combination of factors we call public policy." That there were ways to influence public policy outside the courtroom was evidenced by creation of the New York State Committee on Discrimination in Housing, an organization Abrams and others helped found as a response to the Stuyvesant Town dispute. This organization soon led to the formation on another antidiscrimination group, the National Committee Against Discrimination in Housing, which Abrams would be chosen to lead in 1961.[54]

Abrams' criticisms of Stuyvesant Town and his legal activities had other consequences as well. Abrams established himself as one of, if not the leading liberal critic of urban redevelopment. By basing his criticisms primarily on Metropolitan's discriminatory practices and Stuyvesant Town's quasi-public character, he added a white voice to an increasing number of African Americans who were challenging the racial dimensions of state and federal housing policies. His briefs and arguments illuminated the legal grounds these and other civil rights lawyers would use. Finally, Abrams' discussions of Stuyvesant Town in popular, mainstream publications confirmed his ability to explain complex legal and economic issues in terms general readers found understandable and compelling.

Equally significant was Abrams' association of Stuyvesant Town with the least palatable aspects of what he saw as a business welfare state. He correctly identified Stuyvesant Town as the culmination of a long series of policy decisions (legislative and constitutional amendments, the State Housing Law, and urban redevelopment legislation) that used tax exemptions and the exercise of eminent domain powers as enticements to encourage private capital to participate in pubic undertakings. But he was also one of the first individuals to call attention to the potential dangers of these inducements. "The subsidy is only a single aspect of housing policy," he argued, "yet the form it takes will influence more than the housing program alone . . . . The kind of economy in which we are to live may be influenced by the policy we devise for its dispensation."[55]

Never one to look back, Abrams' involvement in the Stuyvesant Town controversy presaged the direction toward which his professional and academic interests would soon turn. Even during the dispute, Abrams had begun assisting the NAACP in its efforts to overturn racially restrictive housing covenants. And while his persistent plea for open housing alienated him from fellow liberals who felt the topic of integrated housing was too inflammatory, it would be the cause to which he would devote much of the last twenty years of his life.

Chapter Eight

⠿

THE QUEST FOR OPEN HOUSING
Racial Discrimination and the Role of the State

"If Negroes are integrated with whites into self-contained communities without segregation," Abrams told readers of *The Nation* magazine in 1947, "initial tensions tend to subside, differences are reconciled, and cooperation develops—in short, an environment is created in which interracial harmony will be achieved." Few people shared these views. In an era when segregation was socially accepted in the North and legally prescribed in the South, when attempts to integrate neighborhoods often resulted in riots, and when popular attitudes insisted African Americans were inferior to whites, Abrams' vision of "interracial harmony" seemed utopian. Just as Wendell Phillips ("abolitionism's golden trumpet") had faced hostility when he agitated for the immediate emancipation of slaves, Abrams encountered resistance when he called for immediate social and legal equality for African Americans.[1]

But it would be inaccurate to characterize Abrams as a wild-eyed idealist fixated on soap-box oratory. From the 1940s through the 1960s, he fought for civil rights in legal, policy, and political arenas, all the while questioning what role, positive or negative, the state played. In these endeavors, he sometimes functioned as an independent policy expert.

This freed him from various institutional constraints, though it also created awkward situations as different reform coalitions vied for his intellectual and professional support. Serving as an elected or appointed official was an equally challenging task. As both the head of an influential state antidiscrimination agency and chairman of an important national advocacy group, Abrams became reacquainted with the lessons he had learned at the New York City Housing Authority. One of them was that policymaking is often a handmaiden to partisan politics.

Abrams' suggestions for fighting discrimination also presaged an approach to racial issues that one scholar has called a "social scientific . . . discourse focused on public policy." This perspective supposedly illustrated the isolation of so-called "New York intellectuals" from the real nature of African-American concerns. It is not, however, an apt description of Abrams—he was a dedicated participant in the day-to-day struggle for social justice. Admittedly, one aspect of his involvement focused on administrative and legislative reform, yet that was precisely what white and black activists were advocating. In historical terms, one might (albeit anachronistically) fault Abrams for not engaging African Americans in the policymaking process, but his proposals manifested an unusual (white) commitment to racial equality and integration.[2]

The Fight Against Racially Restrictive Covenants

Throughout the first half of the twentieth century, housing for African Americans was overpriced, substandard, and confined to racially segregated communities. Restrictive covenants—long-term deed restrictions on the use or sale of property—were the most common devices for sustaining segregation. Their use prevented African Americans from moving into areas where the most housing existed: white neighborhoods. Consequently, a kind of Malthusian racial specter emerged in many cities. As African-American population increased, their supply of housing decreased.[3]

Covenants, given their invidious nature, were among the first targets of Abrams' antidiscrimination efforts. Calling them a form of "legal racism" and "unthinkable in democratic America," Abrams blamed their spread on the "separate but equal" doctrine established in *Plessy v. Ferguson* (1896). The courts, though, were not the only culpable institu-

tions; Abrams singled out the real estate industry for some of his harshest criticisms. Real estate professionals, as well as their trade organization, NAREB, had been enthusiastic supporters of racial covenants, especially since realtors commonly believed property values declined as
neighborhoods lost their homogeneous (white) character. NAREB
amended its *Code of Ethics* in 1924 to include an article that declared: "A
Realtor should never be instrumental in introducing into a neighborhood a character of property or occupancy, members of any race or
nationality, or any individuals whose presence will clearly be detrimental
to property values in that neighborhood." State and local real estate
boards incorporated this caveat into their own guidelines, with strict
sanctions for anyone who disobeyed it.[4]

The federal government was another target of Abrams' diatribes.
According to him, the FHA "indulged in the most flagrantly discriminatory practices," a claim he could make without much exaggeration.
"Homogeneous development of properties in a neighborhood tends to
reduce mortgage risk," stated the FHA's 1938 *Underwriting Manual.* "If a
neighborhood is to retain stability," the *Manual* cautioned, "it is necessary that properties shall continue to be occupied by the same social and
racial class." FHA underwriters therefore decided a high valuation
should be given "only where adequate and enforced zoning regulations
exist or where effective restrictive covenants are recorded against the
entire tract, since these are the surest protection against undesirable
encroachment and inharmonious use." And, as Abrams pointed out on
more than one occasion, the FHA had even published a model covenant
to illustrate how to prevent certain races from occupying or otherwise
using a particular building or lot.[5]

Abrams eventually suggested why he believed the federal government
took these actions. "Many of the people in private enterprise" who had
been "accustomed" to discriminating, he observed, were "taken into government to administer the [housing] programs" during the 1930s and
1940s. This was related to a shift in "ethics" Abrams identified with the
emergence of a business welfare state. "As long as government and private activities functioned in separate spheres," he noted, "they also functioned under separate levels of ethics." But when the state became concerned about the success of the undertakings it insured and subsidized,
it lowered its ethical standards to those of the marketplace. Much to
Abrams' consternation, the shift from public to private ethics "hardly

[touched] the public conscience." Most people simply assumed "what was right under a private enterprise system" was "right under a public-private venture." "I talked to Federal officials at the time," Abrams recalled, "and they couldn't see anything wrong with it." For this and other reasons, Abrams advocated revision of the FHA's *Underwriting Manual* and amendments to the National Housing Act and federal civil rights laws "barring discrimination by the FHA." He also thought "a further provision forbidding insurance of mortgages on houses subject to a restrictive covenant would help reestablish an ethical responsibility for government agencies."[6]

In discussing different ethical standards, Abrams was asserting a tenuous proposition: left alone, public officials and agencies would naturally adhere to a high moral code. Such a belief might be theoretically consistent with American governance, but it often crumbled under the weight of close scrutiny. Public administrators can and sometimes do work to achieve their own ends just as private businesses pursue their own goals. In failing to acknowledge this, Abrams was not trying to dodge a potential objection to government expansion. Rather, he was expressing, as he had done on previous occasions, an almost childlike faith in the ability of public enterprises to elicit public spiritedness from those involved in them. While Abrams would have probably described this as optimistic instead of blind faith in government, the distinction was sometimes hard to see.

Another sort of optimism prompted Abrams—via speeches and articles in the mid to late 1940s—to focus unprecedented attention on the menace of segregation. Uncover the evil, he seemed to think, and people will clamor for its extinction. Rarely did heightened public awareness, however, translate into changed attitudes, at least where residential segregation was concerned. Restrictive covenants persisted as a feature of most neighborhoods even when inequality in other areas was beginning to trouble white America. Housing remained immune to broader civil rights activism partially because liberals themselves were sometimes ambivalent about or opposed to integration. As a 1953 law review article averred, "of all discrimination encountered by the Negro and other minority groups, none has proved more difficult to overcome than exclusion from housing."[7]

Recognizing the limits to moral suasion, Abrams and civil rights groups rechanneled their energies into legal action. Civil libertarians had initially contended that covenants violated the Fourteenth Amendment's due process and equal protection clauses. This argument depended on proving state action was involved, since the Fourteenth Amendment did not proscribe discriminatory conduct by private individuals. The Supreme Court eventually rebuffed this line of attack in *Corrigan v. Buckley* (1926), which upheld the constitutionality of restrictive covenants by arguing they were agreements between private parties. As a result, instead of attacking covenants per se, the NAACP had to challenge their judicial enforcement since courts were agents of the state.[8]

Civil rights organizations called upon Abrams and others to prepare arguments utilizing this strategy. In mid-July of 1947, after the Supreme Court had agreed to hear *Shelley v. Kraemer* (an important convenant case), the NAACP contacted Abrams, asking him for advice and inviting him to an important brainstorming session later that fall. Abrams himself would not argue any of the cases (two others were eventually grouped with *Shelley*), but his brief-writing skills, especially in composing *amicus curiae*, were well known. Furthermore, his work on *Dorsey v. Stuyvesant*, which had just begun, indicated he was a tenacious and uncompromising opponent of discrimination. Perhaps this was one reason the American Civil Liberties Union (ACLU) also sought Abrams' counsel and asked him to sign its brief for *Shelley*.[9]

Additional groups helping prepare *Shelley* posed legal questions to Abrams, and his responses revealed much about evolving civil rights tactics. He remarked to Norman Levy of the American Jewish Committee, "I have always viewed the function of the *amici* to take up and emphasize those points which are novel or which, if stressed in the main brief, might dilute or weaken the main forceful arguments." He was therefore unimpressed by *amici* that concentrated only on the "cumulative force" of logic. "Unlike good poetry," logic had a "tendency to bore." The primary purpose of an *amicus* brief was to create "healthy doubt" or insinuate "even a slight justification for itself on moral grounds." By doing so, it would "bend the judge toward adopting the law advocated in the main Brief." Persuasion of this sort would rely on "factual and social arguments" that might not be "legally relevant" but would nevertheless "furnish the moral background for a judicial holding." These arguments, more sociological than legal, extended the so-called Brandeis brief (summations containing nonlegal data) and anticipated the full-blown

THE QUEST FOR OPEN HOUSING   151

socio-psychological jurisprudence at the core of the plaintiffs' case in *Brown v. School Board of Topeka, Kansas* (1954).[10]

Abrams, the NAACP, and civil rights supporters were ultimately successful. On May 3, 1948, the Supreme Court, while maintaining that *private* discriminatory conduct did not violate any constitutional rights, affirmed that judicial (public) enforcement of restrictive covenants did. The decision prompted action on a number of fronts. The FHA amended its *Underwriting Manual* in 1950, adding restrictions against using race as a loan or valuation criterion. A year later, NAREB dropped the reference to "race and nationality" from Article 34 of its *Code of Ethics*, suggesting a less explicit emphasis on racial considerations in the future. These developments notwithstanding, alternative restrictive devices often replaced more formal ones. Violence, intimidation, withholding of credit, gentlemen's agreements, and tacit racism would assure the survival of segregation. As Abrams realized, the fight against discrimination in housing was far from over.[11]

"Forging a Tool" Against the "Barricade of Discrimination"

The trajectory of civil rights activism after *Shelley* was conditioned by what was possible within the context of national politics. Harry S. Truman knew his electoral coalition depended on the support of African Americans and liberal whites. He also realized the defection of southern Democrats could irrevocably damage America's oldest political party. Truman therefore avoided potentially divisive legislative battles in favor of executive branch action centering mainly on issuance of executive orders and legal briefs.[12]

Republicans also had a tricky balancing act to perform. Elements within the Grand Old Party, especially in the Northeast, remained supportive of civil rights throughout the late 1940s, 1950s, and early 1960s. Yet many of these same "liberal" Republicans opposed the interventionist federal government necessary for effective policy enforcement. Still other Republicans (and some Democrats) insisted neither legislation nor court decisions would have much effect on private conduct. They thought it better to leave race relations in the hands of local institutions, like churches and families.[13]

National political calculations had direct consequences for civil rights strategists. Spending time and effort trying to enact federal legislation seemed unwise since Democrats would oppose it on political grounds and Republicans would reject it for ideological reasons. Executive orders might be effective (as Truman's desegregation of the armed services proved), but they were often narrowly focused with understandably narrow results. Thus, many civil rights organizations decided the best strategy was litigation.

Abrams himself would adopt a variety of strategies in his antidiscrimination work, including litigation and executive/administrative regulations. Initially, however, he stressed the role housing projects could play (as he had during the Stuyvesant Town controversy). By fostering "mixed" housing, projects were *already* providing successful examples of interracial living arrangements. "In some cases," he admitted, there had been "problems and managerial headaches," while in other instances "disappointments" had occurred. Yet these cases "only pointed up the need for a proper race-relations policy and the desirability of following the mixed-race practice which has so notably succeeded in other cities."[14]

"Mixed-race practices" sometimes required race-conscious criteria. As a function of demographic and social pressures, the racial balance in a given project could tip in favor of one group. To keep projects sufficiently mixed, spaces might have to be reserved for a particular race. Abrams was never entirely comfortable with this use of "benign" quotas. He even denied they were quotas, plausibly but defensively arguing, "A quota system is a device to exclude people, not include them; to effect segregation, not to break it down." Benign quotas represented a thorny issue indeed. They would reappear in debates over the jurisprudence of "group rights," a concept condoning the use of racial categories as a temporary means to rectify past wrongs (this reasoning undergirds arguments on behalf of affirmative action). In regard to housing, controversy did not focus on quotas for African Americans but on those for *whites*. What emerged was an ironic variant of the "status" versus "welfare" debate. Were economically deserving African Americans to be denied space in public housing so a certain percentage of white residents (also economically deserving) could maintain the larger principle of integration? Abrams usually responded in the affirmative, though he also sought cover in a degree of semantic dissembling, as his definition of "quotas" illustrates.[15]

Actually, municipal officials rarely worried about keeping projects racially mixed; instead, they increasingly tried to segregate them. In the South, racial etiquette required this. But even in other cities—Chicago, Detroit, San Francisco, Sacramento, and St. Louis—decisionmakers were segregating local projects. Given his hopes for public housing, why did Abrams remain uncharacteristically silent about these developments? First, his long-held support for institutional autonomy probably militated against his taking stands against the policies of specific housing authorities. Second, at a time when integrated housing had few public supporters, Abrams likely wished to emphasize examples that broke with rather than conformed to existing racial patterns. As he had argued in one of his first speeches on interracial projects, "the long range gains made by the establishment of the fact that mixed projects can succeed" would have significant "influence in shaping local policy." Some civil rights activists, however, feared local control over tenanting policies would "accentuate" the problem of discrimination by "substituting public segregation for private segregation." These more pessimistic assessments seemed valid by the early 1960s: almost three-fourths of the housing projects under the USPHA's jurisdiction were segregated. Relying on local authorities to determine project demographics thus proved to be one of the few, but nevertheless significant, miscalculations Abrams made concerning race and housing. It prevented him from ever testing whether mixed projects could be "forged into a tool with which to drive an opening wedge into the barricade of prejudice and discrimination."[16]

The Limits to Civil Rights Legislation

The problems associated with the intersection of race, public policy, and civil rights strategies were further illustrated by the Cain-Bricker amendment. In 1949, the omnibus housing act Congress had been debating for almost three years finally appeared close to passage. One of its harshest opponents was Senator John Bricker (R-Ohio). A lifelong foe of the New Deal, Bricker wanted the federal government to eliminate all regulations of rents and building materials; only then, he believed, would the market be able to produce a sufficient supply of affordable housing. Especially hostile to subsidized housing, Bricker convinced his Senate colleague, Harry P. Cain (R-Washington), to co-sponsor an amendment forbidding racial discrimination or segregation in any public housing units constructed under the pending legislation. Bricker shrewdly realized the amendment would split proponents of the proposed bill: urban liberals, because of their commitment to civil rights, would vote for it, while southern segregationists would oppose it, given their unwavering aversion to integration. The amendment was defeated in the Banking Committee, but Cain reintroduced it on the floor of the Senate. As anticipated, it caused no little conflict among public housing supporters. The NAACP endorsed the amendment as a long overdue recognition of the government's commitment to equality. Abrams, fearing the amendment would "become the forerunner of a whole series of efforts to use the civil rights issue as an instrument for killing off civil rights," fought against it. The Cain-Bricker "maneuver," according to him, was an attempt to scuttle public housing, not advance equality. If it succeeded, it would destroy the program that had "done more to point the way to real nonsegregation than any other measure in our time." As for the civil rights struggle, it had to be waged on "many fronts," although there was "no compulsion to accept the one the enemy designated."[17]

Opposed by leading liberal Senators such as Hubert Humphrey (D-Minnesota) and Paul Douglas (D-Illinois), and moderate John Sparkman (D-Alabama), the Cain-Bricker amendment was defeated on April 21, 1949. Over the next several years, opponents of public housing introduced similar amendments, illustrating how civil rights riders could become tools of those who wished to defeat, not enact legislation. Abrams remained stung by critics who suggested he had traded principle for legislative success. Clarence Mitchell of the NAACP complained to Abrams, "We may as well face the fact that when reactionary elements try to kill legislation with civil rights measures they are stepping into a breach created because some liberals simply do not have the guts to make a good fight for this just principle." Several years after the Cain-Bricker incident, Abrams again explained his views, this time at a conference of the National Association of Intergroup Relations Officials. He stressed there was "no rule which says that the fight for equality must be fought with a flagrant disregard of consequences." The battle for equality, he added, was best fought "at a time and place at which the gains already made by minorities will not be threatened and when the factors and forces which bring us closer to equality will not be endangered."

The significance of "civil rights riders and civil rights legislation," he warned, lay not in their "indiscriminate introduction" but in their "careful use at particular times and places." Presumably, this was how Abrams distinguished his opposition to Cain-Bricker from his earlier support of nondiscrimination ordinances aimed at Stuyvesant Town. In any event, he continued to believe "the disappearance of discrimination in housing" would result from "reducing racial tensions through construction of more low-rent housing," not from "antidiscrimination laws alone or even mainly."[18]

An *Uncle Tom's Cabin* for Housing

During the early 1950s, Abrams decided to turn to writing as a way to summarize his experiences and to advance his ideas concerning civil rights. The result, *Forbidden Neighbors* (1954), made him the best-known expert on housing discrimination. Written in nontechnical language with minimal footnoting, *Forbidden Neighbors* addressed a number of related topics, most of which were absent from standard housing literature. The work's first seventy pages were devoted to a comparative history of immigration. Abrams' arguments in this section were based on his distinction between slums and ghettos. The latter were simply concentrations of particular ethnic or racial groups within a certain area, while the former were blocks or districts of dilapidated housing. Abrams' unique observation was in positing the emergence of "slum-ghettos." Possessing elements of both slums and ghettos, slum-ghettos were areas in which certain groups were *forced* to live. Even slum-ghetto residents who attained middle-class status, and therefore had the economic means to afford better housing, were prevented from relocating because of legal and social barriers. As an analytical tool, the slum-ghetto was hardly precise, yet it did identify one of America's most pressing urban problems.[19]

Forbidden Neighbors was also a catalogue of discriminatory practices. Abrams revealed the racist underpinnings behind the "patriotic glow" and "crusading fervor" of community councils, home-owner groups, and neighborhood associations. He blamed them for inflammatory propaganda and the rising frequency of interracial violence. Moreover, these systemic episodes belied America's claims to equality, democracy,

and moral superiority. They also underscored the intense emotions residential integration could generate—and the kind of opposition Abrams
and his ideas often faced. By revealing a darker side of American society, Abrams hoped to galvanize efforts against discrimination.[20]

Perhaps *Forbidden Neighbors'* most important function was disabusing
the public of various preconceptions. Certain erroneous "assumptions
. . . were being taught in many colleges as fact" and "translated into policy," Abrams noted in the preface. The most common "assumption" was
that neighborhood infiltration by minorities automatically caused a
drop in property values. Almost two decades of federal policymaking
had been predicated on this notion. The HOLC had relied on theoretical frameworks advanced by Chicago sociologist Robert Park and his colleagues, who believed property values were directly tied to the social status of a community's residents. As status declined (for example, when
African Americans moved into an all-white neighborhood), so did home
and property values. Homer Hoyt, an economist, had systematically
refined Park's model for the FHA, presenting his findings in *The
Structure and Growth of Residential Neighborhoods in American Cities* (1939).
According to Abrams, HOLC assumptions and FHA policies had
inspired a new "Gresham's Law of Neighborhoods," which posited that
"just as bad dollars drive out good ones, so do bad people of the wrong
complexion or status drive out good people and depress neighborhood
values."[21]

Abrams argued that fallacious assumptions about integrated neighborhoods reinforced three fears among white home owners: "loss of
social status," "loss of neighborhood associations," and "loss of investments." Abrams' contribution lay in identifying these concerns and presenting data to refute them. He cited studies by Luigi M. Laurenti,
Belden Morgan, and Lloyd Rodwin challenging certain connections
between property values and race. Abrams himself argued there were
"no fixed rules as to when minority neighbors raise or lower values." He
also thought "a neighborhood limited to people of single social status,
income, or color is more often socially and psychologically unsound
than a mixed neighborhood. Its depreciation is accelerated by one or all
of four factors—boredom, insecurity, fear, hate." "The emphasis on
homogeneity," Abrams concluded, "serves the misguided troublemaker
at home as it once served the master propagandist of the Third Reich."[22]

The recommendations Abrams offered for eliminating discrimination echoed many of his earlier proposals. His twelve specific "aims" included significant increases in housing construction; cessation of slum clearance until enough replacement housing had been built; prevention of discrimination in public or publicly assisted housing; and creation of racial commissions throughout the United States. None of these recommendations called for revolutionary changes, but they were still ambitious, perhaps even daring.[23]

Reviews of *Forbidden Neighbors* were generally positive, though commentators sometimes stopped short of associating themselves with Abrams' specific suggestions. Nathan Straus called it a "crusading book—quietly so, with the facts given in smooth, readable prose, presenting the case without pleading by the author." Another reviewer deemed it the "most comprehensive treatment available of housing segregation and discrimination," while Catherine Bauer called it "as timely in 1955 as *Uncle Tom's Cabin* was in 1852." Not satisfied with the publicity generated by reviews, Abrams sent copies of the book to Hubert Humphrey, Herbert Lehman (D-New York), Wayne Morse (R-Oregon), John Kennedy (D-Massachusetts), John Sparkman (D-Alabama), and former President Truman. Despite these efforts and Bauer's reference to *Uncle Tom's Cabin*, Abrams realized his book would not produce an immediate outcry against racial injustice. Other strategies would be necessary.[24]

Administrative Strategies Against Discrimination on the State Level

America confronted the ugly face of racism in the 1950s. An infuriated mob almost destroyed a Cicero, Illinois apartment building in 1951 because an African-American family was rumored to have signed a lease. In 1954, the Supreme Court ruled segregated schools were unconstitutional, but three years later federal troops were necessary to enforce that decision in Little Rock, Arkansas. In 1955, an unknown minister led a bus boycott in Montgomery, Alabama to abolish segregated public transportation, a crusade resulting in at least one threat against his life. "White Citizens Councils," often condoning violent resistance, sprang up throughout the South to combat the perceived evils of integration. In the North, equally pernicious devices for ensuring residential segregation flourished. High drama was often associated with this initial wave of activism and reaction, but not all battles were played out in front of television cameras. In New York, an extremely important revolution was taking place in the way the state investigated and prosecuted discrimination cases.

For Abrams, participating in that revolution was a logical if not entirely predictable step. Typical of the pattern his life had assumed, a period of 1940s activism had given way to an interregnum of reflection and analysis. During this latter period, he had made a number of powerful political and intellectual statements against segregation. He had also traveled throughout the United States denouncing discrimination. Back home in New York he had become better known in state political circles, largely because of his work on behalf of the Liberal Party. In 1955, just as *Forbidden Neighbors* was being released, Governor Averell Harriman selected him to become New York State Rent Administrator. The backgrounds of the two men could not have been more different. After becoming better acquainted with Abrams, Harriman invited him for a swim in his pool, and Abrams later used this scene to illustrate the social distance separating him from Harriman: " 'The Governor didn't have to impress anybody, and he never had had to,' " Abrams asserted. " 'He just lay on his back and floated while I, the ambitious underling, raced furiously up and down the pool with the windmill stroke I had learned at Bershadsky's Baths until I was absolutely exhausted.' "[25]

Harriman quickly grew to respect Abrams and his support of rent control and civil rights legislation. On the strength of this relationship, Harriman transferred Abrams from the State Rent Administration to the State Commission Against Discrimination (SCAD), appointing him Chairman on December 14, 1955. Declaring "no position in the State government" carried "greater responsibility . . . in providing inspiration in our cause to realize our conceptions of justice and to fulfill our highest aspirations as a democracy," Harriman praised Abrams as New York's most qualified person to assume SCAD's chairmanship.[26]

New York lawmakers had created SCAD in 1945 as part of the Law Against Discrimination (LAD), making it one of the first state laws to prohibit discrimination in employment because of "race, creed, color or national origin." A few other states had similar statutes, but they lacked adequate enforcement mechanisms. LAD therefore represented an escalation of civil rights rhetoric and sanctions. It viewed discrimination as a "matter of state concern" since this form of conduct not only deprived citizens of their rights and "proper privileges," it also threatened the "foundation of a free democratic state." To combat discrimination, SCAD's five members were authorized to receive and investigate complaints, conduct hearings, issue compliance orders, and adopt "rules and regulations" to effect the law's provisions.[27]

Though the legislature amended LAD in 1952 to include prohibitions against discrimination in places of "public accommodation, resort or amusement," civil rights activists such as Abrams wanted SCAD's powers to be expanded still further. In the housing provisions of Liberal Party platforms throughout the early 1950s, Abrams called on the New York legislature to permit SCAD to investigate "racial and religious discrimination in rent and occupancy of *all* housing [emphasis added]." He also demanded an end to discrimination in housing financed by the FHA or Veterans Administration (VA) and in developments receiving "public assistance in any form." Finally, Abrams urged lawmakers to give SCAD the power to *initiate* as well as respond to charges of discrimination.[28]

Complicating Abrams' calls for increases in SCAD's jurisdiction was the presence of parallel legislation also addressing the problem of discrimination. One of the salient features of the Appeals Court's decision in *Dorsey* had been the majority's contention that the civil rights clauses in the New York Constitution were not "self-executing." In other words, these clauses, as they stood in 1949, were only *implicit* constitutional protections. For plaintiffs to seek relief under these provisions, the legislature would have to enact statutes making them *explicit*. Interpreting the Appeals Court's decision as an invitation to pass such legislation, New York amended its Civil Rights Law in 1950 to make "discrimination because of race, color, religion, national origin or ancestry in publicly *assisted* housing accommodations [emphasis added]" illegal. Henceforth, alleged victims of discrimination could file suit against any housing development receiving local, state, or federal funds. The courts, not SCAD, would retain jurisdiction over enforcing these newly defined rights (in 1955, the Civil Rights Law was again amended to include publicly *insured* housing—multiple dwellings backed by FHA or VA mortgage insurance).[29]

This was the existing legislative framework when Harriman was elected as New York's first Democratic Governor in twelve years. Possessing enormous wealth, and having advised Presidents and world leaders, Harriman was fiscally cautious but socially liberal, more akin to moderate Republicans than New Deal Democrats. As the highest elected official of the nation's largest and perhaps most ethnically and racially diverse state, Harriman supported calls to increase SCAD's powers. In his first annual message to the legislature on January 5, 1955, Harriman echoed Abrams' views by recommending an extension of SCAD's jurisdiction to include any publicly assisted or insured housing. He also wanted SCAD to be able to "initiate investigations and regulatory action on its own motion." The Republican-dominated legislature only acted on Harriman's least controversial proposal. Effective July 1, 1955, SCAD's jurisdiction was amended to include publicly *assisted*, but not publicly *insured*, housing. SCAD, therefore, would not be able to receive complaints involving what was quickly becoming a significant percentage of the state's (and nation's) housing stock.[30]

Only a few weeks passed between Abrams' confirmation as SCAD Chairman and his announcement that a "drastic overhaul" of the Commission's policies was needed. This "overhaul" was necessary, according to Abrams, because a number of "social and economic changes" had occurred since passage of LAD. These changes included large migrations of African Americans and Puerto Ricans to New York City, displacement of minorities by slum clearance and urban renewal, concentration and automation of industry, and continuation of discriminatory policies by trade unions. To deal with these changes effectively, Abrams proposed four broad objectives for SCAD: the ability to file complaints on its own volition; jurisdiction over FHA and VA-insured housing; an increased budget to fund "independent studies and investigations of discrimination"; and a staff of "specialists" to carry out SCAD's functions.[31]

Abrams concentrated first on extending SCAD's jurisdiction over publicly insured dwellings. He directed SCAD's General Counsel to draft a bill accomplishing this purpose, and during the early months of 1956 SCAD's meetings were devoted to designing an effective lobbying campaign. By the middle of March, however, the proposed bill was still bottled up in committee in both the Senate and the Assembly. Harriman, fearing another year would pass without the legislature taking action, sent a last-minute appeal to lawmakers. Believing victims of discrimination might be "afraid to complain" or simply "ignorant of their rights," he implored the legislature to give SCAD the "necessary authority" to process such complaints administratively. After additional negotiations, the bill was finally reported out of committee and was passed by both houses, though not before lawmakers had restricted its coverage to "multiple dwellings," which the legislature defined as accommodations occupied by "three or more families living independently of each other" or ten or more housing accommodations located on contiguous land. Single-family homes with FHA or VA insurance that were not part of new subdivisions would remain untouched by the amended bill. Nonetheless, in signing the legislation extending SCAD's purview over certain types of publicly insured dwellings, Harriman accurately observed: "This bill, in effect, will remove the major portion of the complaints of discrimination in housing from the courts to the jurisdiction of the State Commission Against Discrimination."[32]

The change Harriman described—a change Abrams had supported for several years and was now helping to bring about as Chairman of SCAD—was part of a major transformation in civil rights legislation and in the law itself. Starting with the New Deal and continuing through the post-World War II period, administrative law had become one of the fastest growing and most influential fields of jurisprudence. The ability of both federal and state executive branch agencies to process complaints and enforce compliance through the courts, without the necessity of case-by-case litigation, significantly enhanced the ability of aggrieved individuals to seek relief and permitted a much broader attack on discriminatory practices.[33]

Property owners were quick to challenge SCAD's newly acquired powers. The first such challenge occurred less than a year after Abrams assumed the Commission's chairmanship. In December of 1956, Norris G. Shervington, an African-American advertising executive, attempted to lease an apartment in a development called Rochelle Arms. His application was held up by numerous delays and confusion arose over the precise occupancy date. According to Shervington, these actions were blatant attempts to prevent African Americans from moving into Rochelle Arms. SCAD agreed with his contentions, stating that " 'deliberate delay and a policy of calculated inaction' " fell within " 'the prohibitions of the law.' " At the public hearing stage of the investigation, the respondents admitted discriminating against Shervington, but they also argued SCAD's jurisdiction over FHA-insured dwellings was an unconstitutional abridgment of private property rights. Since the respondents did not deny they had discriminated, the Commissioners dismissed their arguments and ordered them to lease an apartment to Shervington.[34]

Rochelle Arms refused to comply with the Commission's order, which compelled SCAD to begin enforcement proceedings in the Westchester County Supreme Court in early 1958. "Four other states have followed the lead of New York in enacting legislation against discrimination in the field of housing receiving publicly insured financing," SCAD noted in a brief likely written by Abrams. Because of New York's pioneering role, the resolution of the issues raised by *New York State Commission v. Pelham Hall Apartments* (as the case became known) would "directly strengthen or weaken" the administration of similar laws throughout the country. The case would also determine "whether law and order invoked under the general welfare powers of the state . . . are available for preventing and solving problems of discrimination—or whether the answer must come through pressure and counter-pressure without governmental sanction or responsibility—and with, ultimately, passion and its concomitants."[35]

Almost a year after oral arguments, Judge Samuel W. Eager ruled that SCAD possessed the legal authority and power to exercise a cease and desist order to prevent discrimination in publicly insured housing. Concisely summarizing the relevant issues, Eager described the conflict as one between "the rights of the private property owner and the inherent power of the state to regulate . . . private property in the interest of public welfare." Assessing these two opposing interests, Eager unequivocally maintained that the "power of the state," if "reasonably exercised," was "supreme." In what must have been an ironic and satisfying twist for Abrams, Eager supported his ruling by pointing to the invitation in *Dorsey* for the legislature to pass specific civil rights statutes. The resulting legislation (in the form of amendments to the Civil Rights Law) was what protected Shervington from being discriminated by Rochelle Arms. The decision thus became an important link in the legal developments Abrams had helped to precipitate. While *Dorsey* had failed to extend the concept of state action to publicly aided redevelopment projects, subsequent legislation and activities—which Abrams supported and directed—had brought publicly assisted and insured multiple dwellings under SCAD's jurisdiction. Admittedly, segments of the private housing market remained free from certain restrictions, but Abrams' actions went a long way in eroding the legal basis for the "all-white FHA and VA-aided communities" he found so incompatible with America's democratic creed.[36]

If Abrams' campaign to increase SCAD's purview was a success, his attempt to secure the power to initiate complaints was not. Though Harriman remained a strong supporter of SCAD, Republicans in the state legislature were skeptical about expanding its powers, especially with Abrams as Chairman. On April 29, 1956, Oswald Heck, the Republican Speaker of the Assembly, was interviewed on a popular television show, the Citizens Union "Searchlight." Heck described Abrams as "too much of a zealot" and "unfit for the job." Heck's charges stemmed primarily from his dissatisfaction with Abrams' actions as State Rent Administrator; he thought Abrams had "aroused" too many people in support of continued rent controls. He also claimed it would be dangerous to allow SCAD to initiate and prosecute complaints. Instead, he believed the Republican Attorney General, Jacob Javits, should initiate complaints, then let SCAD prosecute them. At best, these concerns were misplaced. SCAD rarely exercised its power to issue cease and desist orders, and even when it did, this decision was subject to judicial review. Heck was more likely responding to Harriman's assertions that Republicans were soft on antidiscrimination measures.[37]

Abrams shrugged off Heck's accusation with a typical quip: " 'Well, now I can truly say I've been called everything from A to Z.' " Others, however, were clearly upset by Heck's comments. A. Philip Randolph, representing the New York State Committee on Discrimination in Housing, remarked: "Mr. Abrams' selection as Chairman was hailed by leaders of civic, labor, and religious organizations throughout the country as an appointment based on merit. His fitness for the position had been proved in a lifetime of service to the cause of equality and other non-partisan civic goals." Roy Wilkins, NAACP Executive Secretary, issued a separate statement. He called Heck's comments "incredible" and reiterated the NAACP's endorsement of Abrams' proposals.[38]

SCAD's inability to initiate complaints was not the only limitation that concerned Abrams. He feared the $12,000 increase in the Commission's appropriations would be insufficient to meet its additional responsibilities for the upcoming year (a $186,000 increase had been requested). Then, in June of 1956, the Attorney General's office announced its intention to begin initiating complaints. "Javits is just saying that he's going to do something that he's always had the power to do," Abrams tersely remarked. "But in the 10 years of SCAD's existence," he continued, "no Republican Attorney General has ever initiated a complaint with SCAD—and that included the time that Javits has been Attorney General." Relations between Abrams and Republicans remained problematic through the fall of 1956. In October, Abrams wrote—then released to the public—a letter to New York City Mayor Robert F. Wagner, who was running what would be a losing campaign against Javits for the U.S. Senate. Abrams accused Republicans in New York and throughout the country of attempting to " 'neglect or scuttle civil rights protection for minorities for employment, housing and public buildings.' " " 'The measure of Republican interest in discrimination in New York,' " he opined, " 'is the measure of its support of SCAD.' "[39]

The following January, Harriman joined the fray by again asking the legislature to expand SCAD's powers and increase its appropriations. Pointing out the decline in Commission personnel (it had fifteen fewer employees than it did in 1948), Harriman requested an additional $146,000 for twenty-six new positions and $45,000 for the "initiation of a research program to explore employment potentials for minority groups." In March, Republicans offered a compromise proposal. They would support an expansion of SCAD's powers to include industry-wide investigations (which, to some extent, SCAD was already conducting) if Harriman would promise not to veto authorization of $100,000 to establish a new civil rights bureau in the Attorney General's office. Claiming this "deal" was tantamount to "putting the protection of civil rights on the political bargaining table," Harriman refused to support it. Abrams also opposed the Republican proposal. A civil rights bureau, he told new Attorney General Louis J. Lefkowitz, would usurp SCAD's authority, diminish its appropriations, and confuse complainants by setting up two rival entities. He also decried Lefkowitz's well-publicized intention to make SCAD nothing more than a "judicial agency" confined to "conference, conciliation, and persuasion rather than militancy or instances of prosecution." As Abrams wryly noted, "it is a rare judicial agency . . . that can sit in judgment only with the tools of persuasion and conference while waiting upon another agency which receives and censors the charges that are to be brought before it." With Abrams, Harriman, and twenty-eight civil rights organizations opposing the bureau, Republicans had to concede defeat, though not before the legislature cut SCAD's budget request by $98,000.[40]

Over the next two years Abrams and Harriman succeeded in preventing the creation of a civil rights bureau but failed in their attempts to gain initiatory powers for SCAD. In 1958, Harriman lost his gubernatorial race with Nelson Rockefeller, which meant Abrams would have to complete his term as Chairman of SCAD without a valuable political ally. In his first message to the legislature, Rockefeller voiced support for a civil rights bureau and omitted any mention of expanding SCAD's powers. New York's new governor would have been hard-pressed to send his SCAD Chairman a clearer signal of potential conflict. Abrams, sensing the political tables had turned, resigned from the Commission on January 26, 1959, eighteen months before his term expired. In the following months, he blasted Rockefeller and the Republicans' record on civil rights. He specifically criticized the legislature's failure to increase SCAD's powers (which he claimed Heck had promised if he resigned); the appropriation of $50,000 to create a new civil rights bureau; reduction of SCAD's funding; and failure to pass the Metcalf-Baker Law, legislation designed to prohibit discrimination in certain types of private housing.[41]

These criticisms indicated some of the issues behind Abrams' unhappiness with the new administration in Albany. His concern over SCAD's limitations, however, was more than a disagreement over institutional parameters. As with his tenure and dismissal from NYCHA, it ultimately revealed the evolving contours of administrative governance. Like NYCHA, SCAD—while technically independent—was hardly isolated from the larger milieu of politics. That Abrams could have functioned as one of Harriman's top appointees and not become involved in various conflicts seems unlikely. Beyond the clash of politics and personalities, the legislative branch's ability to control appropriations and its ability to prevent SCAD from initiating complaints were powerful checks against the Commission's autonomy—and a refutation of the idea that public officials could be fully independent.

While Abrams might have failed to achieve all the objectives he had outlined for SCAD, his leadership and tireless efforts nonetheless illustrated the potential for administrative agencies to play influential roles in expanding the reach of public power. Inclusion of publicly assisted/insured housing and age-based discrimination within SCAD's jurisdiction led to a significant increase in the number of complaints filed during Abrams' Chairmanship. SCAD's educational program produced and distributed countless letters, pamphlets, newsletters, posters, and even films. In the field of employment, SCAD conducted investigations of the hotel, railroad, baking, and airline industries, which among other things, led to the hiring in 1957 of the first African-American flight attendant by a U.S. carrier (New York-based Mohawk Airlines). Finally, Abrams traveled throughout the state, inveighing against discrimination, castigating those who ignored civil rights issues, and organizing conferences to promote greater awareness about SCAD and LAD. Abrams' work at SCAD provided ample justification for the *Harvard Law Review*'s 1961 evaluation of civil rights initiatives: "Although it is difficult to measure the success of antidiscrimination commissions in influencing community attitudes, it seems clear that the effectiveness of at least those commissions not denied all power of enforcement depends less on the minute details of their statutes than on the efforts of commission members and staff to make full use of their express and implied regulatory authority."[42]

Abrams' colleagues acknowledged the dramatic changes SCAD had undergone during his tenure. Elmer Carter, the new Chairman, credited Abrams with making SCAD an "authoritative body whose opinions, concepts and philosophies" had "nationwide if not international importance." Harriman echoed Carter's sentiments, telling Abrams, "with a warm heart and great zeal, and in the face of sustained, if often secretive opposition, you have revitalized the State Commission Against Discrimination and made it a potent weapon in our struggle for equal rights for all our citizens . . . . Your understanding, combined with determination has achieved results others thought unattainable."[43]

Irrespective of what these encomia might say about Abrams personally, they suggest dynamic leadership could partially compensate for an agency's lack of autonomy and power. This kind of leadership could achieve even greater results in organizations insulated from direct political control or recrimination. The National Committee Against Discrimination in Housing (NCDH) was one such organization. At the NCDH Abrams would discover he could be an activist-intellectual without the remove of scholarship or the limitations of political accountability. In short, working for the NCDH would allow Abrams to be a hands-on, but not hands-tied policy intellectual.

Administrative Strategies Against Discrimination on the National Level

The election of John F. Kennedy in 1960 was hailed by civil rights activists as a potential turning point in America's treatment of African Americans. In marked contrast to Eisenhower's animus toward federal intervention, the youthful Kennedy's campaign rhetoric hinted at a more aggressive policy toward civil rights enforcement. While his actions would often fail to match his pronouncements—belying his posthumous image as a quintessential liberal—civil rights proponents had few reasons to doubt Kennedy's sincerity.[44]

Abrams assumed the presidency of the NCDH the same year Kennedy became President of the United States. Created in June of 1950 at a meeting of eleven civil rights groups, the NCDH's initial objective was to provide information about housing discrimination. The organization eventually focused on influencing state and federal legislation. It helped craft the Housing and Home Finance Administration's (HHFA) nondiscrimination policies and promoted creation of fair-housing committees in several cities.[45]

Unlike NYCHA or SCAD, the NCDH was not constrained by statutes or the majority dictates of politicians. But the NCDH conferred disadvantages as well as advantages. By being completely separate from government or its elected representatives, the only real power the NCDH exercised was moral authority. The range of legal weapons Abrams had come to rely upon, like cease and desist orders, were not part of the NCDH's arsenal. Instead, Abrams himself would have to persuade decisionmakers, including Kennedy, to take bold and perhaps politically risky measures in the fight against discrimination.

For open-housing advocates, one of Kennedy's most heartening campaign statements was his pledge to outlaw housing discrimination by a "stroke of the pen" (that is, by executive order). A memo circulated during Eisenhower's second term seems to have initially proposed this step, though whether Kennedy was actually aware of it remains unclear. The Eisenhower memo, unlike Kennedy's campaign comments, took a cautious political tack by outlining a limited policy banning discrimination only in a narrow range of housing. Having promised much more, Kennedy found himself in a difficult situation. On one hand, he had raised the hopes of civil rights activists by implicitly committing himself to a broad executive order. On the other hand, he had to be careful that such an order engendered as little southern Congressional opposition as possible (some opposition was unavoidable). Rather than grab the political bull by the horns, Kennedy decided to pursue a course of inaction. He omitted any mention of the order in his special message concerning housing and community development on March 9, 1961, and subsequently dodged reporters' questions about the issue, saying only that it was receiving "continuing attention."[46]

By the summer of 1961, an impatient Abrams began to orchestrate a NCDH campaign to pressure Kennedy into taking action. In July, Abrams helped write a draft order prohibiting discrimination by "agencies of the Federal government, by agencies of state and local governments operating housing assisted by the Federal government, and by private persons, corporations and other agencies in the housing industry that receive assistance from the Federal government, directly or indirectly." If enacted, this order would cover public housing, and FHA and VA-financed housing, as well as the mortgage lending practices of federal savings and loans, federally chartered commercial banks, member banks of the Federal Reserve System, and banks covered by federal deposit insurance. In a nutshell, such an order would outlaw discrimination in almost all housing. Sending this version to Kennedy might have been a tactical decision since it was bound to make a moderate option seem more acceptable. Yet, given Abrams' commitment to equality and his support of broad regulatory powers, it probably represented his true feelings.[47]

Abrams' bold policy initiative was coupled with his desire to provide the President with some flexibility. Before sending the NCDH's proposed order to Kennedy, Abrams, along with Roy Wilkins, Eleanor Roosevelt, and Algernon D. Black (the NCDH's Chairman), asked to meet with the President to give him an opportunity to digest and react to their proposal. Harris Wofford, one of Kennedy's closest advisers, thought the President should meet with the small delegation, calling Abrams and Wilkins the "top leaders" of two influential civil rights groups. The White House took more than two months to reply to Abrams' request, by which time he had already sent the draft order to Kennedy. Speaking for the President, Kenneth O'Donnell told Abrams they would keep a meeting with the NCDH "in mind" and "try to work something out."[48]

Perhaps anticipating this setback, and still concerned Kennedy might not follow through on his promise, the NCDH had launched its own "Stroke of the Pen" campaign a few weeks earlier. "Activities over the nation for the next few weeks," Abrams, Black, and the NCDH's Director Frances Levenson counseled, "will determine when and if the Order will be issued, and—most important—its scope." They advised the NCDH's member organizations to urge Kennedy to issue a "*broad* Executive Order immediately" [emphasis in original], to encourage "key political figures" to call the White House, to mobilize editorial support in newspapers, magazines, and periodicals, and to support the NCDH's efforts with financial contributions. These tactics kept pressure on the White House, which was especially important since opponents of a broad executive order, such as Atlanta Mayor William B. Hartsfield, were insisting the President had to "reckon with public sentiment" and take into account "conditions as they are instead of what they should be."[49]

Abrams was unsuccessful in arranging a personal meeting with Kennedy, but he and other representatives from the NCDH and the housing industry did meet with Attorney General Robert Kennedy on November 8, 1961. While Kennedy was "friendly, attentive, and sympathetic," he remained noncommittal. When another month passed without action, Abrams fired off a telegram to the White House. "Failure to sign the order now," he told Kennedy, "will result in resentment from minority groups, increased resistance from the South, and encumber the administration's legislative program." Abrams also wrote White House Special Assistant Arthur Schlesinger Jr., suggesting Kennedy's delay in signing the executive order on housing discrimination was beginning to resemble Eisenhower's equivocal statements regarding school desegregation.[50]

Abrams was basically correct: Kennedy was hesitating, again for political reasons. In addition to concern over Southern opposition to his legislative program, Kennedy was in the midst of trying to establish a cabinet department devoted to urban affairs, a long cherished goal of reformers and public housing advocates. He was thinking of nominating Robert Weaver to be the department's first Secretary. Both Weaver (who was an African American) and the department would be targets of rural and Southern protests, and Kennedy did not want to complicate matters further by issuing the housing order before the new cabinet position was established. The NCDH's leaders grudgingly accepted this logic, though largely because they believed Kennedy was still considering issuing a broad order. Nevertheless, until the order was actually signed, the NCDH urged its supporters to "keep the pressure up."[51]

Kennedy continued to equivocate throughout the first half of 1962. His indecisiveness was compounded by an analysis conducted by the National Association of Home Builders (NAHB). It claimed an executive order would lead to a significant drop in housing construction since whites would be unwilling to move into racially integrated subdivisions. In a letter to Kennedy, Abrams methodically highlighted several flaws in the NAHB study, calling it "propaganda, not fact." Despite this and assurances from the HHFA, the study's conclusions were sufficiently dire to make Kennedy contemplate issuing a narrower order than the one submitted to him by his staff several months earlier. Another element Kennedy and his advisers had to consider was the political orientation of various financial institutions. Commercial banks, usually considered Republican-dominated institutions, had already had their tax exemptions reduced by the Kennedy administration; another "poke" at them, Presidential assistant Lee White asserted, would not be advisable. Moreover, the legal authority for the President to regulate commercial banks, whose ties to the federal government were often limited to deposit insurance, was deemed shaky at best by the Justice Department. Savings and loans, which issued far more home mortgages than commercial banks, were traditionally Democratic allies; any attempt to cover them by an executive order could also produce undesirable political consequences.[52]

Ultimately, these considerations affected the timing and substance of Kennedy's order. Several northern Democratic Representatives, themselves hardly enthusiastic about residential integration, worried that an order promulgated before November would endanger their chances of reelection. As Martha Griffiths (D-Michigan) argued, it would be interpreted as "political and as an attempt to buy votes." Kennedy therefore decided to wait until after the midterm election to issue the long-delayed order banning discrimination in housing. Even then, Kennedy chose Thanksgiving weekend—traditionally a time when breaking news received little coverage—to sign it.[53]

The order itself was far more limited than the NCDH and other civil rights organizations had hoped. It covered only housing directly owned or financed by the government, and was not retroactive. In a joint statement, Abrams and Algernon D. Black called it an important "first step," but also noted the exemptions concerning federally supervised lending institutions and existing federally aided housing. These exceptions were troubling because FHLBS savings and loans issued approximately 60 percent of all mortgages under $20,000. Still, Abrams and Black could hail the order's "moral impact," which they believed would have "far-reaching influence on the housing market and the structure of America." Fittingly, though perhaps anti-climatically, Kennedy sent the NCDH one of the pens he had used during the signing ceremony.[54]

As discussed earlier, numerous factors besides pressure from the NCDH compelled Kennedy to issue an executive order. Nevertheless, the eighteen-month battle waged by Abrams and the NCDH was important. It focused the public spotlight on Kennedy's campaign promise, reducing his ability to renege on a professed commitment to open housing. Even if such a victory was notable more for its symbolism than its substance, Abrams recognized how this achievement could be used as a rallying point in subsequent battles. It would be misleading, however, to pigeonhole Abrams as nothing more than a half-a-loaf strategist. His real talent lay in the ability to sense when the moment was right for a particular line of attack. In this regard, his life mirrored the civil rights movement itself: activists were coming to realize that no single strategy or tactic was sufficient. A comprehensive, multi-front attack on discrimination was the only way to bring about full racial equality.[55]

Abrams' experiences also have important implications for our understanding of modern political culture. His frustrations demonstrated that whites, regardless of their political persuasion, almost never equated *equal* housing with *integrated* housing. Including racial integration within the larger push for equitable urban policies thus risked a lot, since individuals like Abrams could have been branded—purposely or not—as the tip of a dangerous liberal iceberg. If political conservatives played such a race card they might easily cleave white support from the New Deal coalition. Abrams himself was willing to take this high stakes policy gamble. By 1960, though, he realized he had lost. With a mixture of anguish and prescience, he predicted that anti-New Deal Republicans might soon join with southern Democrats to form a new political alliance based primarily on their common racial views.[56]

The extended critique Abrams mounted identifying the discrepancies between the tenets and practices of the post-New Deal state helped push the federal government away from supporting discrimination and toward a more active role in combating it. But Abrams did not stop there. He raised similar questions about American attitudes toward newly emerging countries in Asia, Africa, and Latin America. In his opinion, the same obligations, potential, and limitations characterizing U.S. domestic policies were inherent in its foreign assistance programs. Abrams would face these new challenges while working abroad as an international housing consultant.

Chapter Nine

⁂

COLD WAR, THE UNITED NATIONS, AND "TECHNICAL ASSISTANCE"

In a letter written to Ruth Abrams shortly after her husband's death in 1970, Eric Carlson, Chief of the United Nations' Housing Section, noted he had recently "paid tribute" to the "great contributions [Abrams] had made to the international cause of improving and providing better housing, especially for the poor." Carlson praised Abrams' international housing reports as "landmarks or guidebooks in much use by the government officialdom as well as being respected texts by the younger professionals whom he [Abrams] had reached." He concluded by asking Ruth to help establish a Charles Abrams chair in international housing at a prominent university.[1]

Carlson's observations hint at the impact Abrams' work had on housing policies throughout the world. Between 1953 and his death, he was an adviser to twenty-one countries, undertaking UN missions to such places as Bolivia, Ghana, Pakistan, the Philippines, and Turkey. What prompted him to pursue these endeavors? While he himself never provided a definitive answer, the growing tensions between communist and noncommunist nations certainly played a role. Abrams was not, however, a rigid ideologue or a cardboard anti-communist. The East-West conflict, in his estimation, was more than just a battle for geopolitical supremacy. It was a larger struggle to determine whether democracy or totalitarianism would triumph in developing nations.

Abrams' views on U.S. domestic policies influenced his overseas work as well. America, according to Abrams, had already experienced an "industrial" and an "urban revolution." By the late 1940s and early 1950s, other countries were beginning to undergo these transformations, which heralded increased state intervention. "There are some perversions and misuses of the new [governmental] powers," Abrams admitted, "and occasionally the interests of the many are subordinated to those of the few in the interplay of pressures." Nevertheless, he maintained there was "no longer even the pretense that the state must stand aside as people rot in their hovels or sleep on the streets." These comments implied that developing countries could avoid what American decisionmakers had endorsed: business welfare policics. Working on UN assignments would allow Abrams to make sure this was the case (at least to the extent his recommendations were implemented).[2]

Abrams' advice to various countries also illuminated his problem-solving abilities, which emphasized flexibility and pragmatism. Each country, he insisted, had its own unique predicaments and resources; only after consultants had taken these factors into account could they formulate appropriate policies. Consequently, Abrams would never draw a master blueprint for combating urban woes in developing nations. Except for a few general principles, his recommendations were tailored to fit particular countries and specific situations.

Finally, Abrams' philosophical outlook intersected with the political trajectory of other intellectuals during this period. The post-World War II era has been characterized as one in which an older generation of radical critics shifted from "revolutionary anti-Stalinism" to "liberal anti-communism." In moving ever rightward, they momentarily joined Abrams at a point left of the American political center. Some moved even farther to the right, eventually identifying themselves as neoconservatives, but Abrams' own ideological compass remained fixed. This would become clear in his criticisms of American assistance policies.[3]

The United Nations and Cold War Constraints

Impressed by *Revolution in Land,* Ernest Weissmann, director of the UN's Housing, Building, and Planning Branch, asked Abrams in 1952 to conduct an examination of international land problems. This study "sparked" Abrams' interest in the "evolving problems of the less developed nations" and, as he himself noted, "widened a focus that until then had been concentrated mainly on the American scene." The report ("Urban Land Problems and Policies") began with an analysis of land acquisition, then focused on related policies in fourteen different countries. Its significance lay not in the details but in two general propositions. First, Abrams believed shelter problems were caused by a lack of well-conceived policy initiatives, not a shortage of land. Second, he cautioned that "few urban land policies" were "applicable universally." The "differences of national patterns and [in] social, economic and political backgrounds" had to be "considered in applying the policies of another country." Both these themes would reappear throughout Abrams' international housing work.[4]

Though Abrams completed "Urban Land Problems and Policies" without complication, Cold War imperatives often impeded other UN activities. For instance, the prospect of being investigated by the FBI deterred qualified individuals from becoming technical advisers. As Abrams later observed: "The 1950s were hardly marked by calm impartiality . . . loyal Americans often shunned UN service when they learned that investigators would visit their former landladies, employers, and disgruntled employees, scour their pasts, and compile all the hearsay into a file." These investigations worked against attempts to promote America's influence since "nationals from other countries" often "preempted most of the [UN] jobs."[5]

Along with discouraging American involvement in various programs, security concerns made UN findings "restricted" information. "Some of the UN reports on specific countries," Abrams complained in 1964, "might compose an initial literature on housing and urbanization problems," but "few" had been published; most remained sealed in the UN's archives. Of the sixteen book-length reports Abrams helped write for the UN, only *Housing in Ghana* was published during his lifetime. In Abrams' opinion, desire for domestic political stability was the main reason client governments demanded secrecy. Praise for "private enterprise" might "stir up Russian citizens," while "recommendations for socialism" might "alarm the capitalist nations." This also meant reports were "too often written in guarded language" or failed "to grapple with all the realities."[6]

Abrams' own difficulties arose when he attempted to obtain security clearance to travel to India for a UN seminar in 1954. He filed his application materials in the summer of 1953, then waited for several months. "The damned trouble about the whole expedition is the abominable length of time it takes to get clearance for all the American delegation," he fumed in December. With still no response as Christmas neared, he wrote Albert Bender of the U.S. Mission to the UN, expressing his vexation. The seminar, he impatiently lectured Bender, was going to "deal with such innocuous subjects as building materials, urban land problems, and planning education." Abrams finally got his clearance, but the U.S. delegation arrived late to the seminar, reinforcing Abrams' negative opinion of the "unnecessary red-tape" generated by security precautions.[7]

Though delayed, Abrams' participation in the 1954 seminar was an important juncture in his evolving UN work. As rapporteur for the topic of "land development," Abrams wrote a summary anticipating points he would stress in future housing missions. "There generally exists within the power plants of governments," he asserted, "a proper policy for . . . governing land use, land mis-use, land abuse, land non-use, and land re-use." An "informed and properly staffed agency" would be necessary to effect this "policy." Abrams also emphasized the need for master planning and improvements in public financing, the legitimacy of zoning and public housing, and the advantages of new town developments. His recommendations concluded with a characteristic warning: "New neighborhoods" were to "avoid compulsory or induced segregation."[8]

The Use of "Experts" and Problem Solving in the Field

Developing countries opted for technical advisers instead of alternative forms of aid because they believed this was the best way to achieve self-sufficiency. The UN responded by recruiting and supplying individuals who would gather data about a particular country or region, train indigenous personnel, and offer advice to host countries. By the early

1960s, after more than a decade of providing assistance, UN advisers had adopted a fairly mechanical routine: they studied "general and specific problems," then reported "their appraisals, analyses, and recommendations" to government officials.[9]

Soon after he began accepting UN assignments, Abrams realized the role of advisers was not as straightforward as some analysts suggested; it was often ambiguous and open-ended. One investigator suggested the expert's responsibilities were frequently influenced by "his [own] personality, his awareness of his technical skill, and his professional approach to an assignment." If this were true, what specific qualities should the expert have? Contemporaries stressed two important characteristics. The first was good communication skills, including adeptness at listening and "awareness of nuances of meaning and emotion." Ability to gain the "confidence" of local officials was the second characteristic. "Confidence" in this context meant "respect for and trust in the integrity and judgment of the expert insofar as his expertise is concerned." The *United Nations Review* expressed a similar sentiment in 1958: "[The UN] must look for persons who have truly established themselves within their own fields, and who can, consequently, command the respect and the ear of very senior officials of the governments with which they work."[10]

Abrams possessed both attributes—and more. His work as a lawyer, teacher, and reformer had refined his ability to listen and articulate complex ideas clearly. Moreover, his scholarship and experiences in public service provided him with impressive credentials. Though not every country followed his recommendations, his competence was never questioned. As a UN administrator remarked, " 'Abrams is not just a consultant, he's a team all by himself.' " Abrams also had an indefatigable amount of energy. An African official had to remind him that "only mad dogs and Englishmen went out in the midday sun" and "not even *they* started their day's activities at 6 a.m. and went right through to late at night without a rest." This description might imply Abrams was a grim workaholic, but at least one colleague had a different impression:

Covered with a cloak of red dust, through which sweat trickled down his face, he sat in the back seat of the car as it jounced along the dirt road, working away furiously at a proposal. . . . Every once in a while, he would look up with a gleam in his eye and come out with some ridiculous pun on an African place name or some non-

sensical—but, I must admit, quite catchy—song he had impro-
vised. We were all close to exhaustion on that trip, but he kept us
in good spirits.[11]

To these qualifications Abrams added his own criteria. He argued that
sometimes the " 'best function' " of a UN adviser was to tell a government their " 'old ways of doing things' " were " 'actually as good as new-
fangled Western ways, if not better.' " This was crucial since underdeveloped areas had "a proneness to universalize problems" and "borrow
remedies" with little if any applicability. For Abrams, there had to be
"recognition in all policy that the ways of the West cannot be arbitrarily
and unconditionally imposed upon the underdeveloped areas." Every
culture had values that could be "built upon rather than destroyed."[12]
    Abrams also pointed out the need for more technical advisers.
Existing experts were "specialists largely trained only in a single phase of
the problem" or "civil servants trained only in routine administration."
"Too often," Abrams lamented, "they see the solution only within the
context of their own limited fields." As an alternative, he called for individuals with diverse backgrounds who (like himself) had mastered a
number of different skills and appreciated the interdependency of
social problems. "The field requires people who have a grasp not only of
economics," he noted, "but of the related disciplines . . . plus a large gift
of common sense." Such people also had to be "adroit enough to generate progress with the limited tools available in a given country." A corresponding problem Abrams identified was the lack of institutions to
train experts. Evaluating the situation in 1964, he determined that
"training was needed to develop a pool not only of visiting experts but of
'inperts,' i.e., qualified nationals within the countries themselves."
Ahead of his own suggestions as usual, Abrams had already acted on this
idea years earlier when he helped establish a Turkish university.[13]

Creating a University and Providing Roofs for the Needy

Turkey, under the leadership of Kemal Ataturk, underwent a crash program in westernization during the 1930s, adopting "modern" ideas and
practices. Later, following World War II, it became a much sought after
Cold War ally, especially in light of its control over the Straits (the water-

way that connects the Black and Aegean Seas) and its proximity to the
Middle East. By the time Abrams arrived as part of a 1954 UN mission,
the country was facing significant urban problems, including overcrowding and squatters.[14]

Abrams' initial mandate was to revise Turkey's building code, though
he soon realized that none of the country's regulations had been translated into English. So, while waiting for the translation, he embarked on
a 4,000-mile journey around Turkey to assess its housing conditions.
Sure enough, haphazard construction and obvious code violations were
everywhere. "There was no effort," Abrams later observed, "to teach or
discover indigenous Turkish architecture . . . . the tendency was . . . to
import foreign concepts and impose them on the Turkish scene." He
observed other problems as well: "Approvals of illegal plans by city officials were perfunctory, owing partly to [the] inability to read plans and
partly to a building code so general and confusing that it supplied no
clear directions." Furthermore, older guidelines had to be correlated
with more recent ones, creating "a bizarre pattern in which new buildings obscured ancient monuments."[15]

However bad conditions were, an antiquated building code was not
Turkey's biggest problem. At the heart of the country's urban woes was
a "dearth of architects and of men with technical training." "The deficiencies in personnel and training," Abrams commented, "were not only
in architecture and planning"; they also reflected a shortage of "engi-
neers, surveyors, lawyers, builders, legal draftsmen, people trained in
finance, economics and sociology, and the host of other professions and
talents a developing country needs." Abrams' frustration over the situation was obvious. "Any laws I might prepare," he concluded in a letter to
Ernest Weissmann, "would not be enforced and a detailed report with
elaborate recommendations would be relegated to the dust-bin."[16]

Abrams therefore decided to propose something else—construction
of a technical university. At the time of his mission, Turkey had fewer
than six licensed city planners and only two schools of architecture.
These schools accepted no more than 200 students each year out of
approximately 2,000 applications. The reluctance of Turkish officials to
pursue programs whose benefits were not immediately apparent was one
reason for this predicament. As Abrams noted about industrializing
countries in general: "Too often the development of education and
training facilities is viewed as too long-term and remote. The temptation

is to proceed at once without planning simultaneously for the wide variety of skills essential for the development and operation of a housing program."[17]

Abrams also thought other factors contributed to Turkey's hesitancy in accepting the prescription for a new university. He believed American experts viewed the UN as a rival organization. Consequently, they never gave its overseas missions any cooperation, either in terms of "money or in sympathetic interest." These same officials—who had "considerable influence in Turkey"—were hostile to the idea of a UN-sponsored university, even though "the proponent was American, the teaching was to be in English, and an American university was to be later involved." Abrams eventually found someone who supported his proposal, Vecdi Diker, an American-trained Turkish engineer. Diker introduced him to Fatin Zorlu, the Acting Prime Minister of Turkey. After their initial meeting, Abrams dashed off a memorandum to Zorlu outlining the need for a Middle East Technical University (METU). Zorlu, impressed with Abrams' recommendation, asked him to prepare a tentative budget. Abrams complied and also contacted the University of Pennsylvania, asking it for financial and educational assistance, which it eventually supplied. In late 1954, the UN and the government of Turkey announced plans for the new university. Sited on 12,000 acres, it became the largest university in the Middle East when it opened in 1956. By 1963, with schools in architecture and planning, engineering, public administration, and humanities, METU was serving 2,100 students (that figure would top 5,000 by 1967), qualifying it as the "fastest growing university in the world."[18]

Establishment of METU was consistent with Abrams' previous experiences and policy proposals. Its status as a publicly funded but educationally autonomous university reflected the kind of state intervention Abrams believed was necessary and appropriate. METU also demonstrated Abrams' ability to solve problems as a reflective practitioner. He arrived in Turkey with a certain set of assumptions, made firsthand observations, reformulated the problem, and ultimately suggested cogent recommendations. Summing things up a few years later, Abrams called this the " 'less scientific approach,' " which boiled down to sending "a person with trained instincts and pure motive to a country," then instructing him to "pick up the hood and take a look." On a broader level, the difficulties Abrams encountered in persuading officials to accept his recommendations illustrated the complexity of policy initiation and implementation. They also indicated American influence and monetary assistance might compete with international relief organizations in counterproductive ways. Still, METU's construction was a professional triumph for Abrams (he would later tell Catherine Bauer it was "probably the most important thing I've ever done in my life") and a victory for the UN's technical assistance program. Olle Sturen, head of the UN office in Turkey, believed it was the first time UN recommendations had been " 'so rapidly . . . discussed, considered and accepted on the absolutely highest governmental level.' "[19]

Similar themes were evident in Abrams' trip to Ghana in 1954. Granted self-government the same year Abrams traveled there, and full independence in 1957, the former British colony (the "Gold Coast") was a nation of contrasts. Cities possessed all the signs of modernity, while the hinterlands were, in comparison to the West, quite primitive. By the mid-1950s an economically besieged Ghana seemed to be leaning toward undemocratic socialism. Its leader, Kwame Nkrumah, an American- and British-educated admirer of Marxism, looked to the Soviet Union for inspiration, if not actual assistance. This was precisely the milieu in which Abrams believed Western aid could help shore up the cause of democracy.[20]

Ghana's particular circumstances, as Abrams soon discovered, could be a source of admiration and concern. He noted that the country's "ancient tribal structure" was a "proved social and political organization with its own culture, traditions, rituals, and loyalties." "In a precarious environment that few white men could endure," he remarked, "the primordial tribe has held its members together for centuries in simple dignity." On the other hand, despite the relative inexpensiveness of village land, few people could afford to purchase doors, windows, or roofs for their small houses. Construction of new dwellings was usually possible without the first two items, but absence of a roof presented a bigger problem. Government officials, after abandoning an unsuccessful experiment in prefabricated housing, provided $2.5 million for a state-run mortgage bank. This, they thought, would solve Ghana's roof problem.[21]

After reviewing the situation, Abrams decided mortgage loans for entire houses were unnecessary. Since many of Ghana's citizens possessed rudimentary carpentry skills, he determined that the government only needed to supply or finance windows, doors, and roofs. A "roof-loan scheme" was an integral part of this program. It involved the use of "local or municipal societies or councils" as administrators of loans distributed by a central agency. Each society would elect a chairman, vice-chairman, and secretary, with membership open to families who intended to build a house or have one built. Because loans would be repaid to the central agency, a constant supply of new homes could be financed.[22]

Ghana's policymakers endorsed Abrams' proposal. A revolving fund was capitalized with $2.1 million from the amount originally allocated to the government mortgage bank. Any member of a village housing society who was building a house was eligible to receive a loan. By 1960, nearly $1.85 million in loans had been approved, and village societies— their membership numbering approximately 25,000—were tackling a wide range of municipal problems outside of housing. "Members get together to discuss local problems, build better roads, improve sanitation, and even to advance their education status," Abrams commented with obvious pride.[23]

Key to the roof-loan scheme's success was the government's willingness and ability to supply the initial capital. In Bolivia, Abrams recommended a similar program, which the government also agreed to fund. Bolivian officials, however, raised only a fifth of the necessary $1 million. Complicating matters was America's refusal to loan Bolivia any money; according to Abrams, U.S. officials did not believe it would repaid. "Cities like La Paz are nerve centers," he protested, "and their slums are the festering places of revolt. . . . Even if housing is not a prime factor in promoting productivity, a million dollars lent for housing in La Paz could have prevented incalculable losses over the longer run."[24]

Despite frustrated efforts in Bolivia, Abrams' earlier activities in Ghana remained significant. Once again he had manifested a pragmatic, reflective style of problem solving. The roof loan scheme was a perfect example of how, in Abrams' words, "existing values" could be "built upon to meet a new problem in a changing societal pattern." It also illustrated how local control could balance central state involvement. " 'Only someone with a flexible and original mind would have thought of it,' " Weissmann subsequently observed. But it was Abrams himself who best summarized the importance of his Ghana mission. "The experience has demonstrated that out of the ancient cooperative aspects of the tribal and village system can be forged a new device not only for producing homes but also for making public improvements . . . advancing educa-

tion, consolidating community life, and developing social and communal responsibility." Here was the way Abrams hoped to make democratic alternatives more attractive than totalitarian ones.[25]

"Self-Help" and Core Housing

On several UN missions, Abrams noticed how client governments, disillusioned by the failure of mass-production techniques, were embracing
various "self-help" strategies. Patrick Geddes, the British planner, provided the intellectual inspiration for this approach, but much of its pop-
ularization was due to the efforts of Jacob Crane, head of the
International Office of the U.S. Housing and Home Finance Agency
from 1947 to 1954. An acquaintance of Abrams, Crane had coined the
phrase "aided self-help housing" to describe shelter policies that relied
on publicly assisted owner-builders. In brief, the state would provide economic assistance to encourage individuals and/or cooperatives to construct their own dwellings.[26]

As a *partial* solution for certain problems, Abrams believed self-help
housing could make a valuable contribution. To be sure, while he
described his roof-loan scheme as "installment construction," it possessed many self-help elements. He thought a self-help approach could
be especially useful in rural areas, since the periphery tended to foster,
somewhat paradoxically, both self-reliance and communalism. Even in
urban areas, self-help projects could teach construction skills, which in
turn might help individuals enter the building trades.[27]

Abrams also enumerated several disadvantages to self-help housing.
He claimed, perhaps too sweepingly, that public officials hoped to find
an easy and "cheap" solution to housing needs by "shifting the onus
from technology back to the individual"; this bootstraps philosophy
required the "homeless to provide for themselves," often with inadequate assistance and a "good deal of wishful thinking." When "offered as
the solution for the housing problem of cities [emphasis added]," self-
help programs took too long to build too few dwellings. Furthermore,
most urban wage-earners did not have adequate time to spend on such
projects in the first place.[28]

Alternatively, Abrams suggested the concept of "core housing," which
he termed a "major variant of the self-help technique." "Cores" referred

to mass-produced dwelling spaces of one or two rooms. Families could move into cores immediately and "thereafter expand the house as time and funds allow." Though Abrams did not rule out private construction, he thought public entities should build the initial cores. Occupants were then to be given the option of purchasing and enlarging their cores with the aid of government loans, preferably loans made to building societies like those in Ghana. If this was public housing by any other name, it was clearly designed to meet local needs and avoid the glaring defects of sub-sidized dwellings elsewhere. It also underscored Abrams' concern for social justice. "A country must choose," he insisted, "between building for the few and demonstrating little, building for the many and exhausting its resources, or providing for the many with a minimum outlay." While Abrams believed core housing met this third objective, he nonetheless struck a cautionary note: "No single type of core can be uniformly applied to all countries and all climates. Each country, and in fact each region, may call for a particular design." When this maxim was violated, the results would be "painful if not ludicrous." To prove the point, Abrams described a core housing project in the Philippines composed of "four toilets back to back"; individuals were to build their own cores around one of the toilets, a scheme prompting virtually no interest among Filipinos. It was subsequently dubbed the "Flushing Heights" project.[29]

The Problem of Squatting

The appearance of tent cities and barrios on the urban fringes was a mounting problem in the developing world. For Abrams, human history had been "an endless struggle for control of the earth's surface," with "the acquisition of property by force" one of its "more ruthless expedients." But "unlike other forms of conquest that were propelled by the pursuit of glory, trade routes, or revenues," squatting was "part of a desperate contest for shelter and land." It was therefore the "most condonable" type of "illegal seizure."[30]

Even so, the ramifications of squatting were alarming to Abrams and public officials alike. Squatters lived on land characterized by substandard sanitation, poor drinking water, crime, fires, disease, and overcrowding. Other dangers loomed as well. As Abrams warned the Fourth National Conference on Cooperative Housing in 1961, the homeless, blaming their plight on "industrialization and its by-products," were becoming angry and prone to riot. Spurred on by the "inequities and hardships" caused by metropolitan growth, the "troublemaker" would now assume a greater role in the world's "teeming cities."[31]

Postwar democracies had been unable to prevent squatting in the developing world, Abrams asserted, because "government policy (including our own) has tended to echo broad democratic generalizations without providing the essential roots out of which democratic government institutions can grow in the long run." As he had said before, the underlying cause was not a land shortage, but an absence of "ideas, policies, and the ability and will to face the problem." "With a relatively small outlay and some imagination," Abrams implored, "we can make a major contribution not only to the welfare of these people but to the identification and reinforcement of the principles which all democratic people should share." Beyond this plea for a kind of international Homestead Act, Abrams failed to specify what types of policies would produce the "small and humble" sites he felt squatters deserved. He did urge industrialized countries, especially the United States, to provide greater assistance and aid to the developing countries of Asia, Africa, and Latin America. Abrams hinted at how this might be accomplished in his fourth book.[32]

A Practical Guide to Housing Policy in Developing Countries

Man's Struggle for Shelter in the Urbanizing World, published in 1964, recapitulated more than a decade of Abrams' experiences as an international housing consultant. Like his previous books, *Man's Struggle* was intended for a general audience, and the appearance of British and Portuguese editions confirmed its appeal. Admittedly, one reviewer remarked on the book's "sloppiness and conceptual inadequacy." This criticism notwithstanding, the book's significance—as another reviewer put it—was in focusing on a "topic which has been given short shrift by most urban academic specialists and even by those concerned with urban and regional planning in general."[33]

True to Abrams' style and purpose, *Man's Struggle* contained data and anecdotes from the fourteen housing reports he had written so far. Abrams did attempt to draw together some lessons he had learned from his various missions, an ingredient the individual reports lacked. Yet those looking for the Rosetta Stone of international planning were bound to be disappointed. Abrams himself admonished readers to this effect: "The need is not only for general theories but for practical proposals. The answers, moreover, suggest themselves only after one has visited the country and talked to the people as well as the officials and experts."[34]

With no panaceas for the housing problem in sight, Abrams used *Man's Struggle* primarily as a forum to assess existing policies. In general, public housing of one sort or another was the most common shelter program in the developing world. Abrams supported this option as long as the public housing horse pulled the slum clearance cart, not the other way around (as had happened in the United States). There was, as he phrased it, a "public obligation . . . not only to evict but to rehouse." He also expressed skepticism over construction of "new towns." Building whole communities from scratch on the periphery was costly, and once constructed these towns would have to compete with central-city enticements. In the resulting tug-of-war for residents, existing urban centers would possess distinct advantages. They were usually seats of government, finance, and industry; any attempt to decentralize them (which was an objective of new towns) would likely run into strong opposition from political and business elites.[35]

After reviewing current policies, Abrams recommended a few of his own. To improve the "efficiency" of assistance programs, he advised industrialized nations to set up an "international nonprofit agency" to recruit "qualified people" for UN missions. This agency could also "offset the effects of firms operating in the field that use their initial retainers to secure lush architectural materials, or building contracts." In a different vein, he suggested affluent nations should create an international urban development bank. Such a bank would be authorized to make loans to member countries, public authorities within their jurisdictions, and even "private enterprises" interested in constructing low-income housing.[36]

Perhaps the most intriguing insights in *Man's Struggle* pertained to the larger framework in which Abrams placed assistance programs. Using the Cold War as a starting point, he argued that the Soviet Union could mount persuasive arguments against using capitalist countries as a model, even though its own performance had not provided much inspiration to developing nations. "[The USSR's] greatest attraction is not what it offers but in its assault on what non-Communist societies have not yet fulfilled," Abrams shrewdly observed. "Misery, bitterness, and resentment in the teeming slums and squatter colonies," he further explained, "all recall the scene that made the *Communist Manifesto* an alluring document in nineteenth-century Europe."[37]

Cities in the developing world were therefore among the primary battlegrounds where democratic capitalism would spar with undemocratic communism. As such, these cities took on a dual character: they were a possible "threat" and a potential "hope." They were the former because large-scale suffering could produce popular support for communism, and if communism failed (as Abrams thought it would), the "alternative" would "probably not be democracy." Cities symbolized "hope" because "widespread ownership of land and shelter"—which Abrams believed metropolitan areas could provide given the right policies—were "still the seeds from which larger freedoms have grown and can continue to grow in the world's new societies."[38]

There was also a simplistic, naive dimension to Abrams' big-picture formulation. In pitching his analyses to American and western policymakers, he tied deprivation and suffering to the threat of communist revolution. Abrams appears to have believed this linkage actually existed, but he could have also had a pragmatic purpose in mind. Cold War decisionmakers would more likely support technical assistance for housing if they were told it would help stem the spread of communism. In disseminating such a message, Abrams was coming dangerously close to accepting one of the era's prevailing assumptions: whatever undermined the appeal of communism necessarily strengthened democracy. This belief allowed American policymakers to overlook the abuses rightwing dictators doled out simply because they claimed to be fighting communists. Economic aid to these governments—whether for housing or some other social program—might actually strengthen the grip of oppression by reducing public discontent (a relatively full stomach dampens the kindling for revolution).[39]

Abrams seems to have been vulnerable on another issue, too. Could officials in developing countries simply use UN recommendations as intellectual cover for unwise policies? Abrams' mission to Singapore is instructive on this point. Situated between the Indian and Pacific oceans, Singapore, a longtime British colony, was granted internal self-rule in 1959. Dominated by one political party, which was headed by the authoritarian Lee Kuan Yew from 1959 to 1990, the island nation was theoretically a republic; in reality, the government significantly limited citizen input and criticism. Yew, once in office, embarked on a massive building and renewal campaign to combat the country's housing shortage and densely populated slums. At his request, the UN sent a team of advisers to analyze Singapore's living conditions in 1963.[40]

According to Rem Koolhaas, a controversial architect and design critic, the UN's final report (authored by its three Singapore advisers—Abrams, Susumu Kobe, and Otto Koenigsberger) ended up sanctioning the government's "dystopian program," which was based on the creed, "displace, destroy, replace." It did so by legitimizing "the ambitions that the regime [had] so far not revealed so explicitly," and by providing "easy steps toward megalomania." The ensuing renewal program, which Koolhaas claims the UN advisers supported, had predictably horrific results. The government razed thriving areas, built huge "slabs" of sterile public housing, and destroyed the native culture. Instead of achieving an optimal environment, the renewal plan turned Singapore into "authored chaos," "designed ugliness," and "willed absurdity."[41]

Koolhaas' critique has some merit. The UN mission *did* advocate urban renewal for Singapore. To achieve that end, the advisers recommended "action programmes," a novel strategy reflecting the mission's attempt to meet the government's request to design an approach "more positive" than Singapore's existing master plan. In short, "action programmes" assigned a significant role to state initiative. Abrams likely agreed with this recommendation since he usually believed private, not public, interests "perverted" social reform. For a country like Singapore, whose leaders' anti-democratic inclinations were already apparent, such an assumption was problematic. Furthermore, Abrams was overly impressed by the government's commitment and proven ability to rehouse a significant number of slum dwellers, a task he felt U.S. renewal programs should—but were not—undertaking. As with the issues of eminent domain, housing authorities, and racial segregation, Abrams too quickly presumed the intentions of public officials were benevolent.[42]

The UN report, however, was not an unqualified endorsement of renewal. The future city it described was quite different from the metropolis that actually emerged. To help solve Singapore's problems of disease and inadequate housing, the advisers admitted the renewal program would not be "an exercise in conservation or restoration." Nevertheless, they repeatedly warned against the dangers of "wholesale demolition." "We must be aware," they argued, "of the 'bulldozer addicts' who are straining to flatten out every hill . . . and cover the resulting flat desert with a dull network of roads, factory sheds and regimented blocks of houses." In section after section, the report emphasized *small-scale* public housing and urged new communities to "jealously guard their right to innovate against superimposed standardization." For Singapore's estimated 200,000–250,000 squatters, the advisers recommended aided self-help and core housing, stark contrasts to the monolithic projects favored by Yew.[43]

Without denying Singapore's shelter crisis could be solved without a substantial amount of new housing, the report, in typically Abramsesque prose, sang the praises of rehabilitation. "Too many people derive their livelihoods from such areas [Chinatowns] to be uprooted *en masse.* Many prefer to continue living in them rather than in the housing projects. . . . Every big city needs escape hatches from sameness and order, and areas like Chinatown can emerge into important examples—if they are treated with something more subtle than the steam shovel." In rejecting indiscriminate clearance, the report stressed "the value and attraction of many of the existing shop houses and of the way of living, working and trading that produced this particularly Singaporean type of architecture." It also advised government officials to provide new towns, like Jurong, with "the same richness of life and the same variety of opportunities for trade, employment and enjoyment, which exist now in the two square miles between Cantonment Road and the Kallang River [downtown Singapore]." In light of modern-day criticisms of Singapore, the report concluded with a prophetic warning: "If an urban renewal programme is to be successful, it must simultaneously embrace some comprehensive plan to up-grade these [dilapidated] dwellings and keep as many of them as possible from degenerating into rubble as the years go by. Unless this is done, urban renewal will become one unending and ever-expanding process."[44]

The problem, then, was not that the UN report paid nothing more than "lip service" to preservation, or recommended mammoth and unappealing high-rises, or disregarded traditions of vernacular architecture— but that officials ignored its advice to the contrary. This also suggests one reason why the government kept the UN report classified (recall, Abrams opposed this practice). There was no incentive to reveal its recommendations when they might call into question the regime's activities.[45]

U.S. Assistance Policies

As the Cold War reached a stalemate in the 1960s, Abrams became increasingly critical of international aid policies, especially American ones. In general, few developed countries contributed much money to UN sponsored housing or urban development programs. Abrams offered explanations for this trend, including "self-interest," "frustration," "vagueness of ideas on priorities," "unawareness," "inexperience in dealing with urbanization problems," and "international parsimony." Though he admitted some "experimental programs had been financed by institutions like the International Development Association," these "pilot schemes" would not replace the "laborious evolution of proper policy within a broad social and economic context."[46]

The thrust of Abrams' critiques skewered American policymakers for establishing a political litmus test for deciding who received assistance. It was one thing to *provide* housing aid in hopes of preventing a country from succumbing to communism (a policy Abrams had supported), but quite another to *deny* aid simply because a nation had already adopted socialism or aligned itself with the Soviet Union. To ensure greater consistency and fairness, Abrams believed a more inclusive standard was necessary. In 1961 he lauded the Papal encyclical *"Mater et Magistra,"* praising its call for "dispensation of technical and financial aid on the basis of 'sincere political disinterestedness.' " Two years later, frustrated by the Kennedy administration's apparent policy of extending aid almost solely on the basis of a country's political alignment, Abrams told the Senate Subcommittee on Housing, "We cannot discharge that responsibility [of helping the world's destitute nations] by preferring one poor people over another poor people." Later, in equally unequivocal language, he asserted that "aid should be provided without the profit of political motive when benevolence is warranted and at appropriate interest rates and terms when not so warranted."[47]

Abrams' disappointment over the inability of policymakers to understand the "important interplay of urbanism with democracy and peace" was augmented by his criticisms of specific agencies. Describing U.S. programs as "far from satisfactory," Abrams lambasted the International Cooperation Agency (ICA), the predecessor of the Agency for International Development (AID). In addition to faulting the ICA's performance in Turkey and the Philippines (the ICA was responsible for the

"Flushing Heights" fiasco), he described its personnel as "ignorant" and "hostile to housing aid." Abrams was also dissatisfied with the work of the Housing and Home Finance Agency (HHFA). In 1961 he urged HHFA's Administrator, Robert Weaver, to explore ways of providing more support for housing in developing countries. Inaction over the next few years prompted him to disparage the qualifications of the HHFA's foreign housing division: "The main justification for its existence has been the mistaken notion that those administering *American* housing know a good deal about housing in *other* countries [emphasis added]."[48]

As annoyed as Abrams was with HHFA, he was even more unhappy with AID. Established in 1961, AID's mission was to provide economic assistance to developing countries in order to bolster their social and political stability. While Abrams criticized AID as an "administrative jungle," and for its eagerness to "propose universal remedies," he nevertheless agreed in 1963 to serve on its Housing and Urban Development Advisory Committee. At the committee's initial meeting, he expressed concerns about AID's small housing staff and the absence of comprehensive studies of urban problems. In a letter to AID's Administrator a month later, he articulated his broader philosophy: "Housing aid in Latin America should be viewed not as housing alone but as an important lever that can guide the entire process of urban development. Properly tackled, it can generate public confidence and act as a force for political stability."[49]

Abrams also served on AID's Training and Personnel Subcommittee, where his influence was again apparent. A report issued by that committee in 1964 called on AID to "assist positively in the creation and strengthening of training and education programs in housing and urban development." It further advised that the "training and education of foreign housing personnel" was to be "an integral element of its technical assistance program," while "American housing specialists" were to be "encouraged to take refresher courses sponsored by AID." Grants, fellowships, and stipends were proposed as incentives to "encourage housing and urban development specialists to assist in teaching, training and research programs abroad." These suggestions were consistent with ones Abrams had been making since the early 1950s, though their exact impact on AID's policies remains uncertain.[50]

Abrams' international activities clearly manifested continuities with his concerns at home. Faithful to his commitment against discrimination, he warned developing countries to shun policies condoning or enforcing segregation. He emphasized the necessity of using public capital to finance housing programs and insisted on prohibiting business interests from exploiting public programs. Abrams' experiences also illustrated how fissures could exist between different organizations (the UN versus the ICA in Turkey) and among experts within the same organization (AID). Moreover, international consultants, like their counterparts in domestic programs, were rarely neutral observers but active participants in creating and sometimes opposing certain policies.

In America, Abrams remained busy teaching, writing, making speeches, and attending conferences. This was all the more amazing since his plate had been quite full even before his overseas commitments began. For example, Abrams wrote in a 1953 letter:

Meanwhile, many things are happening here which engage my spare time . . . . A fight to keep Washington Square from being cut up into a through road . . . political campaigning in the mayoralty fight, preparing a housing program for the next Mayor, running up to Harvard and MIT for a few occasional speeches, balling [*sic*] Judy out for staying out so late, cutting off Abby's television, and taking the parental consequences, entertaining visiting firemen, acting the part of host and husband, smoking my head off while trying to forget the writer's cramp in my right arm, keeping . . . Uncle Ralph satisfied about his various financial operations. On top of all this, I sit as referee . . . to hear an important case involving something completely alien to housing. Add to this meetings of various organizations, and you have a whole picture.[51]

Despite this whirlwind of professional, intellectual, and family involvement, Abrams was able to focus his critical energies on an additional policy development: urban renewal. Indeed, his last great battle was against the way public officials were "renewing" their cities. Like long-suffering characters in the final act of an opera, Abrams' enduring fears, hopes, and concerns would take center stage one more time.

Chapter Ten

▓

URBAN RENEWAL, THE "PERVERSION" OF SOCIAL REFORM, AND HOME OWNERSHIP FOR THE POOR

The 1950s and 1960s were an extremely productive period in Abrams' life. On top of teaching, fighting racial discrimination, and working overseas, he critiqued domestic programs implemented by the Eisenhower, Kennedy, and Johnson administrations. By doing so, he illustrated more clearly than at any other point how policy intellectuals could influence the legislative process. Both Democrats and Republicans, in their quest to capture the urban agenda, sought Abrams' advice, knowledge, and recommendations.[1]

In speeches, articles, and Congressional testimony, Abrams reiterated familiar arguments and advanced new ones concerning the relationship between urban growth and state-building. Unlike other commentators, he pressed for the modification and expansion of public programs, not their repeal. He took this position because he thought American cities lacked the ability to stem their own structural and economic decline. As he accurately noted, cities had collected 52 percent of all tax revenues in 1932 but only 7.3 percent in 1962. Falling revenues, combined with rising costs and the growing autonomy of suburbs, left many urban areas in dire straits. In Abrams' opinion, this situation required the federal government to assume "many of the obligations that the old city" could "no longer bear." Moreover, there would have to be a "re-deployment of revenues" and significant shifts in political power to meet these new national commitments and responsibilities. Though such transformations never occurred, federal urban programs did proliferate during the post-World War II period. Much to Abrams' dismay, they created additional problems, not solutions.[2]

Federal Intervention in Urban Redevelopment and Renewal, 1949–1964

A brief review of federal legislation indicates why Abrams remained dissatisfied with domestic policymaking. Between Truman's Fair Deal and Lyndon Johnson's "Great Society," lawmakers enacted numerous programs to improve the physical and economic conditions of urban America. The first such programs were created by the Housing Act of 1949. It provided funding for slum clearance ("redevelopment"), public housing, farm housing programs, and housing research. With respect to redevelopment, municipalities were authorized to use federal funds to purchase, clear, and discount the resale price of slum properties, but private developers had to plan and finance the projects that would subsequently occupy these sites. Furthermore, slum clearance had to be "predominantly residential": it would have to raze bad housing or increase the supply of good housing. At the time, policymakers did not seem to realize how this requirement could work against the inner-city poor. Developers might consistently opt to replace slum dwellings with lucrative commercial or industrial projects, instead of constructing moderate- or low-income housing in place of blighted business districts. Even reformers who, like Abrams, were troubled by this potential problem grudgingly supported the 1949 Housing Act because they believed its relatively generous public housing provisions, if met, would sufficiently accommodate residents uprooted by redevelopment projects.[3]

Initially, the new slum clearance and public housing programs fell far short of their goals. By 1953 only $105 million of the initial $500 million in redevelopment grants had been committed to specific projects. The attempt to build 810,000 new units of subsidized housing by 1955 shared a similar fate. Only 1,225 units were constructed in 1950, and while 161,000 units were completed between 1952 and 1954, they represented an atypically high number begun in early 1953, not a reversal of public housing's fortunes.[4]

Disillusioned, Abrams would have provided a systematic critique of these developments had he not been so busy working on UN and antidiscrimination projects. Another policy intellectual, Miles Colean, beat him to the punch. Colean, a well-known economist who had helped design New Deal housing programs, published his analysis in *Renewing Our Cities* (1953). Drawing his inspiration from efforts underway in Milwaukee and Baltimore, Colean argued that more attention should be given to "renewing" entire cities. His definition of "renewal" emphasized the use of rehabilitation, conservation, and stricter code enforcement (versus clearance) to upgrade urban conditions. It also encompassed adequate fire and police protection, enhanced educational and recreational facilities, improvements in social services and transportation, and additional low-income housing. "The renewal problem," Colean summarized, "is primarily one of how to construct, maintain and rebuild the various parts of the urban structure so that the city as a whole remains at all times in a sound economic condition."[5]

Abrams agreed with Colean's broader points: metropolitan regions, not just slums and blighted areas, had to be revitalized. This would necessitate expanded municipal services and greater federal involvement. Abrams, however, was less comfortable with Colean's concern with the "sound economic condition" of cities, an emphasis some decision-makers could interpret as a call to improve the financial rather than the social condition of American metropolises. Indeed, Colean intended renewal to address both issues, but the programs his ideas inspired—and the ones Abrams subsequently criticized—generally ignored this twofold approach.[6]

Abrams' invectives would eventually target the Housing Act of 1954, legislation directly influenced by Colean's thinking. Enacted on August 2, 1954, the new housing act liberalized requirements for FHA mortgage insurance, authorized 140,000 units of public housing over a four year period—a scant amount compared to earlier goals—and introduced the concept of renewal. The 1954 legislation also modified the 1949 Housing Act's "predominantly residential" requirement by exempting up to 10 percent of a renewal project's funding from this criterion. Developers, in collaboration with city officials, could now focus some of their efforts solely on restoring once-prosperous business districts. (Subsequent exemptions would move renewal even further from the holistic strategy Colean and others had advocated.) The 1954 Housing Act's most innovative element required municipalities to establish "workable programs" before they could qualify for federal funds. A locality was deemed to have a workable program if it practiced comprehensive code enforcement, followed a master plan, stimulated citizen participation in its renewal efforts, and provided relocation options for displaced families. These requirements were supposed to prevent renewal projects from becoming giveaways to private developers. As state and local officials soon realized, though, the cost of implementing all the criteria for workable programs was beyond the financial means of many cities. Receiving federal funds would thus hinge on finding ways to meet—or circumvent—such expenses.[7]

Reformers, including Abrams, were quick to identify flaws in the 1954 legislation. They specifically criticized it for ignoring the housing needs of the country's poorest citizens. No program would be successful, they warned, if it relied primarily on rehabilitation and code enforcement, rather than significant increases in new housing. "The rehabilitation program, which offers handsome Federal insurance to mortgage lenders and builders for rehabilitating existing slums, may help some minority families but may dispossess many more than it aids," Abrams remarked. Also troubling to reformers was the absence of community service provisions Colean had deemed imperative for renewal. These omissions notwithstanding, or perhaps because of them, the Housing Act of 1954 received widespread support from the business community, which especially liked the way it linked private and public interests.[8]

In 1961 (just as Abrams was initiating NCDH's "stroke of the pen" campaign), Congress passed another piece of significant urban legislation. The Housing Act of 1961 authorized 100,000 additional units of low-income public housing, doubled the budget for renewal programs, and raised from 20 to 30 percent the amount of land within rehabilitation areas exempt from the "predominantly residential" requirement (that figure had already been increased from 10 to 20 percent, and would be extended again to 35 percent in 1965). This last provision further shifted the emphasis of renewal projects from depressed residential areas to blighted commercial districts, precisely the trend Abrams feared contemporary policies would foster. Even when cities did concentrate on shelter needs, substandard dwellings continued to disappear far faster than newly authorized public housing units were constructed.[9]

Responses to Urban Renewal

The Ford Foundation asked Abrams to undertake an evaluation of urban renewal in 1960. Parts of Abrams' resulting analysis were designed as a response to Martin Anderson's examination of the same issues. Anderson's *The Federal Bulldozer* (1964) was both a dispassionate dissection of renewal and a passionate defense of private enterprise. His main purpose was to question certain "beliefs" concerning renewal: that it had made a "significant contribution" toward solving the housing problems of low-income groups; that it "did not really affect many people"; and that "the typical urban renewal project" could be completed relatively quickly. Anderson refuted these contentions without much difficulty since they were essentially straw men (few policymakers held such views). Another point Anderson hammered home was the necessity of employing a narrow interpretation of "public use." In fact, he implied there was seldom if ever a "public use" justifying the exercise of eminent domain. Throughout the remainder of the book, he linked his criticisms of government initiatives with praise for the housing industry: "The record of what has been achieved outside of the federal urban renewal program by private forces," he concluded, "is an eloquent testimony to what can be done by a basically free-enterprise system." What Anderson failed to acknowledge was the role federal initiatives—tax exemptions for homeowners and FHA/VA insurance for mortgage lenders—had played in the post-World War II housing boom. Without them, the private sector's accomplishments would have been far less impressive.[10]

The City Is the Frontier (1965), Abrams' study of renewal, provided a different perspective on the (re)development of American cities. Though the Marxist scholar Manuel Castells labeled the work too " 'balanced,' " a review in *The New Republic* provided a more insightful description: "This is the distillation of a man who has lived most of the roles, knows all the angles, suffered all the frustrations, enjoyed the satisfactions of creativity and genius—and perhaps the regrets of human error." Elsewhere, Chester Hartman, an influential sociologist and urbanist, paired *The City Is the Frontier* with the *Federal Bulldozer*, adjudging them the definitive assessments of urban renewal.[11]

Abrams' argument was fairly straightforward: urban renewal merited continuation, with certain modifications. He contrasted this view to Anderson's study, which, as he wryly noted, "makes some good criticism of the program, makes no mention of its virtues, and then bluntly asks for its repeal." Abrams, taking a different approach, spent an entire chapter discussing some of urban renewal's "blessings." They included encouragement of "civic interest"; "rationalization of disparate plots and traffic problems"; "civic and cultural improvements"; "institutional expansion"; construction of some additional low-income housing; and "increased tax revenues." Abrams even thought the renewal of downtown business districts might have a few benefits: "However imperfect the effort, the move by cities to revitalize their main streets is at least an acknowledgment that something more than new housing and slum clearance is needed to restore the city's health."[12]

By reviewing renewal's accomplishments, Abrams was not exonerating it from wrongdoing. The program, as he had remarked in 1959, "has developed into a device for displacing the poor from their footholds to make way for higher rental dwellings which those displaced cannot afford." By 1963, Abrams was voicing another dissent: "If I were to propose the single greatest single contribution to the renewal of neighborhoods, physical improvement, as important at that is, would take a secondary place to the provision of social facilities." "Slum elimination," he continued, "can be accomplished as often by the lifting of the human spirit as the razing of buildings." Abrams used *The City Is the Frontier*, which would be his last comprehensive evaluation of urban life, to condense these warnings into a single admonition: slum clearance was to be avoided unless there was a "substantial surplus of cheap housing."[13]

Despite Abrams' concerns, policymakers and urban officials consistently disregarded renewal's negative consequences. Admittedly, clearance projects, in order to receive federal funds, were supposed to make provisions to rehouse displaced families in the renewal district itself. But as Abrams pointed out, such a mandate was illogical: "If there are ample and well-located 'decent, safe, and sanitary dwellings' in the urban renewal area which slum dwellers can afford, presumably there is no housing problem." In other words, if an area did not have a housing problem, why would it be slated for renewal to begin with? Municipal officials rarely answered this question since they preferred to avoid discussing the plight of uprooted residents altogether. The results of a 1968 analysis of urban renewal indicate the reason for their reluctance. "Relocation," the author of the study concluded, "often became an administrative obstacle to be hurdled or circumvented, or at best, an opportunity to accomplish a minimum amount of good for the people involved within the restraints imposed by the political, social, and economic facts operative in each local instance."[14]

Connected to his criticisms of renewal was Abrams' increasing disillusionment with public housing, which was where a significant percentage of displacees were supposed to be relocated. As one of its earliest proponents, Abrams did not oppose the *concept* of public housing, just the structures themselves. The ideal project, in his estimation, was limited in both area and height, preferably three to four stories tall and integrated into its surrounding neighborhood. He often cited First Houses and Harlem River Houses, both in New York City, as actual analogs to these ideal types. His views, however, did not prevail. Instead, the most influential design ideas came from the modernist French architect and city planner Le Corbusier, who thought skyscrapers were the optimum building type for urban areas; housing advocate James Ford, who believed large projects were less likely to regress into slums; and Elizabeth Wood, who, as head of the Chicago Housing Authority during the 1940s and early 1950s, favored massive "super-blocks" of subsidized housing. The mammoth housing projects inspired by these individuals did indeed dominate their environments, but this seemed only to alienate their occupants and frighten those who had to work or live near them.[15]

By the late 1950s, the image—and sometimes reality—of decaying, "sterile" high rises dominated official and popular perceptions of public housing. Catherine Bauer, lamenting the dehumanizing size and architecture of the country's largest projects, invited several "experts," including Abrams, to suggest how the "dreary deadlock of public housing" could be broken. In his response, Abrams insisted that projects should be built on vacant sites, not in the middle of congested downtown districts. He also espoused the formation of "state-wide authorities" to supervise suburban construction of single family homes for the "less privileged." In making such a proposal, Abrams was not embracing the sentimental, often deceptive post-World War I portrayals of home ownership. Rather, he was urging policymakers to provide low-income residents with alternative places to live. Public housing, he stressed elsewhere, would continue "to have a place as one of the choices available, but a limited place, in what should be a total effort to rehouse the low-income family." If tenants wished to remain in projects, Abrams emphasized the importance of giving them the opportunity to buy their own units. This would require the construction of "more and more public housing" under "similar arrangements," which, Abrams noted, would expand the housing supply while "simultaneously desocializing the ownership." Although his support of ownership options might have inclined him toward advocating stricter admission standards (owning took more responsibility than renting), Abrams was actually growing increasingly angry over the exclusion of unwed mothers, alcoholics, "skidrowers," the mentally ill, and "chronic lawbreakers" from housing projects. In contrast to his views in the 1930s, he was now reluctant to limit public housing to "respectable" individuals, or to agree with contemporaries who associated the deterioration of projects with "problem families."[16]

The "Perversion" of Social Reform

Abrams ascribed the problems of urban renewal and public housing to the "perversion" of their initial objectives. This critique bridged his earlier concerns over business welfare policies with a more general examination of the interplay between reform and policy implementation. Abrams rooted his assertions in what he called the "Newtonian and Darwinian Laws of Social Reform," which postulated, "A law in motion tends to continue in motion." One reason for this legislative inertia was the inability of decisionmakers and administrators to acknowledge policy failures. "The local public officials are managing programs that have taken years to put through," Abrams commented; it was therefore difficult for them "to confess that the whole approach was wrong from the beginning, or that supervening circumstances have made it senseless to continue digging into the same hole." He believed reformers faced similar difficulties. They had "committed" themselves to certain positions and were "not prone to concede that all had not worked out for the best." Even when reformers did decide to question their own assumptions, their colleagues were anything but encouraging. "The protagonist of change," Abrams pessimistically ruminated, "is viewed as a turncoat or a Pharisee."[17]

Had Abrams' theory about the perversion of social reforms been limited to these observations, his insights would not have been unique. To assert people are reluctant to admit past mistakes is a truism. Abrams, though, went further. Urban policies, he argued, were distorted because they had utilized private interests to serve public ends. Reaching back to the 1949 Housing Act, he opined: "When the entrepreneurial and the general welfare are bracketed in the same legislation, it should not be surprising that the social purpose [of housing lower-income families] will be subordinated." "In the long run," he declared, "the profit motive somehow operates as the undesignated but effective legislator while the public obligation is pushed under the rug." His assessment of urban renewal followed similar lines. It was essentially a Progressive critique of how private interests had been left unsupervised in the public's candy store.[18]

These considerations caused a reluctant Abrams to conclude that renewal, despite its achievements, had undermined the democratic character of cities. Yet he did not think state involvement was, in and of itself, the problem. "The vast expansion of government interest in city and regional planning and housing," he remarked in 1962, "has not been paralleled by a federal policy sufficiently strong to effect compliance with the requirements of the national welfare which spawned the expansion." His prescription was not abandonment, but enlargement of public sector mechanisms: "In all programs that evict families there should be a requirement that the families be subsidized to the extent of the difference between what they can afford and what they are compelled to pay for decent housing in decent neighborhoods."[19]

As opposed to the 1930s and 1940s, when Abrams was a voice crying in the urban wilderness, a wide variety of sources now confirmed the business-welfare drift of federal policies. Contemporaries, however, characterized this development as essentially positive. One major periodical announced: "Housing Developers Vie for Jobs of Clearing Urban Slums," "Good Business in Urban Renewal," and "Money to be Made in Real Estate." Other mass circulation journals published similarly upbeat articles. "Slums," *U.S. News and World Report* gushed, were "coming down" and "gleaming skyscrapers, apartments, theaters, [and] shops" were "going up." Even the more reserved *Architectural Forum* joined the celebratory bandwagon in 1962: "While it was once felt that renewal's toughest problem would be attracting the private market to develop slum land . . . the situation is reversed in many cities today, where would-be redevelopers have to be turned away because cleared land cannot be made available to them."[20]

Academics and urban experts evaluated renewal in a more detached manner but failed to place it in the larger framework of twentieth-century state-building, as Abrams had. One planner, for instance, thought housing and slum clearance had been "elusive" objectives mainly because their goals were not "uniformly held" or interpreted. Pursuing different concerns, political scientists believed the "dilution of responsibility" on the national and local level had impeded renewal. According to another scholar, urban renewal's troubles had resulted from the failure to understand the "nature of urban areas"; the creation of policies by individuals with no responsibility for their "broader consequences"; and the inability to "coordinate" various federal programs. This analysis and others, by focusing almost entirely on flaws within the policymaking process itself, sometimes led investigators to pose unintentionally counterfactual questions: "Why did the private interests . . . who designed these programs fail to anticipate [their] consequences?" An examination of Abrams' experiences and scholarship suggests why such a query was misplaced. Private interests not merely anticipated, but actually applauded the outcomes of federal and state renewal programs.[21]

Even the era's two best-known urbanists, Jane Jacobs and Lewis Mumford, rarely addressed the larger state-society implications of urban policies. For Jacobs, the chief cause of metropolitan woes was the lack of diversity; by increasing the diversity (and intensity) of land use, planners and public officials could reverse the slow death of cities. Mumford, concentrating on an entirely different set of issues, blamed urban problems on the "astounding mechanical success" of "high-powered technologies," which he mystically referred to as the "Megamachine." The polemics of Jacobs and Mumford thus concentrated either on single city blocks or on the whole cosmos.[22]

Abrams' own business-welfare perspective, while generally valid, was not above criticism. By stressing the private sector's endorsement of urban renewal, he understated the role of central-city decisionmakers, the United States Conference of Mayors, and the American Municipal

Association. They, too, approved of renewal, primarily because it was the only dependable urban assistance from the federal government. Moreover, Abrams' mounting dissatisfactions with inner-city projects should have made him more sensitive to the diminishing popular and political support for public housing—the antidote he relied on to blunt the damage caused by indiscriminate slum clearance. Finally and uncharacteristically, Abrams missed a larger point he himself had made on many occasions. As long as the victims of urban policies were predominantly poor and African American, mainstream society appeared unwilling to commit the additional resources necessary to ameliorate their hardships.[23]

Providing Homes for Low-Income Groups: The Philadelphia Study

Starting in the late 1950s, Abrams began to look more positively toward home ownership as a policy goal. Frustration with public housing and mixed feelings about renewal partially explain why his views changed. Other factors, though, were also involved. One of them was Abrams' desire to counteract the long-standing bias that housing programs exhibited toward middle- and upper-income groups. As he told Representative Charles C. Diggs Jr. (D-Michigan) in the fall of 1963, "The practice of the last twenty-five years has been to extend housing aid to middle income groups, college housing and a host of other beneficiaries, but to ignore the home ownership requirements of those who need it most." To reverse this trend, he advised Diggs to enact legislation making home ownership available to the "lowest income group." A related consideration also affected Abrams' outlook. He had opposed ownership when public programs seemed to urge everyone (including families with modest means) to encumber their savings in home mortgages. Over time, the national policy pendulum had swung in the opposite direction. On the eve of the Great Society, virtually no federal program provided the poor with direct assistance to purchase homes. Contemporary rhetoric even claimed they were incapable of meeting the responsibilities of property ownership. This was exactly the kind of shibboleth Abrams enjoyed attacking.[24]

The housing study Abrams made for the city of Philadelphia was the best illustration of his shifting attitudes toward home ownership. In May of 1966, the Philadelphia Community Renewal Project (CRP) asked Abrams to conduct an investigation of the city's minority housing needs. His analysis was to be the last of eighteen technical reports the city would use in creating its urban renewal plan. Aided by a young research assistant, Robert Kolodny, Abrams reviewed data on nonwhite residence patterns, assessed the region's housing supply, and formulated an "affirmative program to expand the housing opportunities available to minority groups in the community."[25]

In most respects, Abrams' report was unexceptional. It provided a socioeconomic profile of the city's African-American residents, described their difficulties finding adequate housing and employment (the two were connected), and compared the quality of housing in white versus African-American neighborhoods. If the study had been confined to these areas, it might have been what Kolodny believed the CRP had intended: a "fair-housing and uplift-through-integration" report.[26]

Abrams' analysis, however, generated controversy by making additional observations and recommendations. He advised Philadelphia to rehabilitate its existing housing rather than tap into federal funds earmarked for building new housing. Such an approach was feasible for Philadelphia because it had a large supply of relatively cheap row houses. "Whether new or old," Abrams accurately noted, "the row house is still the most common habitation, and its proportion has actually grown since 1950." City officials, aware of this fact, had initiated a program to rehabilitate approximately 14,000 structures, including row houses. Under the appropriately named "Used House Program," private builders purchased old houses on the open market, renovated them to meet specifications mandated by the Philadelphia Housing Authority (PHA), then sold them to the PHA. In turn, the PHA used federal rent subsidies to make the rehabilitated housing affordable for low-income tenants. As of September 1966, the program was an apparent success: the PHA had acquired 229 properties, with another 336 under contract.[27]

Despite his support for rehabilitation, Abrams felt the Used House Program was a poorly designed policy. His reasoning was based on one primary consideration: cost. Early in their investigation, he and Kolodny had ascertained that row houses, many in "move-in" condition, could be bought for as little as $2,000–$4,000. Even those in the best shape sold for no more than $6,000–$8,000. Yet the PHA, by purchasing these same houses through private developers, was paying up to $12,300 per dwelling. The difference between the two prices, as entrepreneurs and speculators quickly pointed out, resulted from the renovations they were forced to make before selling their houses to the PHA. Here, Abrams concluded, was the problem. "A quick glance at these [rehabilitation] specifications discloses some twenty-six pages of requirements . . . . They apply to every house, regardless of its present condition." These mandatory and sometimes unnecessary renovations also resulted in prohibitive rents. "Standardization of specifications," Abrams remarked, "is good if its purpose is to cut costs, but it makes no sense when it raises them."[28]

Abrams believed Philadelphia could solve its housing problems by having the PHA or some other nonprofit organization (like the Philadelphia Housing Development Corporation) purchase homes directly from the private market, then sell them to low-income residents. This would eliminate middlemen from the acquisition process, provide greater public supervision of real estate interests and contractors (whatever role they might play), and give low-income families the opportunity to own rather than rent. Abrams also urged the PHA to liberalize its Procrustean renovation requirements. He admitted some homes might require structural repairs; owners living in renewal areas, though, could always apply for $1,500 federal rehabilitation grants and 3 percent loans. These loans would translate into additional expenses, but according to Abrams' calculations, they would be significantly lower than the amount private builders would charge for the same renovations.[29]

The recommendations Abrams offered to Philadelphia did not require an oversimplification of urban issues. There were, he confessed, "no universal solvents for the varying problems of all cities . . . no easy problems for which there are easy answers." Home ownership was therefore not for everyone. "There are a number of families with incomes so low," he observed, "that they can hardly sustain life, to say nothing of buying a home." Finally, he noted something national policymakers were only just acknowledging: "These [impoverished individuals] pose not simply a housing problem but call for a program meeting their basic wants. A housing program alone cannot ease their predicament."[30]

Nor did Abrams' concern over the supply of affordable housing mean he had relinquished the ideal of integration. He continued to exhort the government to make all neighborhoods open to African Americans. But as long as minority groups chose to remain in segregated areas, public agencies were obligated to "improve their lot; give them better schools, facilities, and services where they live; and simultaneously, provide them with the option to own their homes at a cost within their means." Far from advocating segregation, Abrams was just demanding equality for minorities if and when they lived apart from whites.[31]

The Philadelphia report also gave Abrams the opportunity to articulate and apply one of the lessons he had learned from his UN missions: "Only when each city is profiled in the context of its own environment and requirements will its objectives become clearer and programs be formulated to suit its particular conditions." Without this knowledge, federal housing programs might be inappropriate or "inadequate." Indeed, Abrams argued that the mismatch between local needs and federal programs was already a serious problem in American state-building. As he told the Senate Subcommittee on Executive Reorganization in 1967, there was "a predisposition to look to *existing* federal programs and to the maximum available federal subsidies rather than to the *indigenous* needs and conditions of each city [emphasis added]." "The result," he claimed, "is that every city frames its programs upon what is available under the federal hierarchal [sic] formulae, whether or not these formulae are the most suitable to its needs."[32]

Abrams' views on this point provide a flip side to subsequent examinations of urban policymaking. According to these analyses, a "progrowth coalition" operating on both the local and national level sustained particular programs. Abrams asserted that the reverse was also possible: programs themselves could generate specific constituencies (just as his earlier arguments had stressed the ability of various policies to create a certain type of state). Moreover, Abrams saw this as problematic. While some cities might benefit from federally funded programs, their haphazard implementation elsewhere might prevent municipal officials from adopting better-suited alternatives. Phrased more simply, federal money did not always translate into local solutions.[33]

Creating a National Low-Income Home Ownership Program

While he had confined his immediate investigations of low-income home ownership to Philadelphia, Abrams' writings and lobbying during the 1960s attracted the attention of various elected officials. Representatives Warren G. Magnuson (D-Washington), William F. Ryan (D-New York) and James H. Scheuer (D-New York); Senators Robert Kennedy (D-New York), Jacob J. Javits (R-New York), and Abraham Ribicoff (D-Connecticut); Republican Presidential nominee Richard Nixon; and future Senator Paul Simon (D-Illinois) all sought Abrams' counsel. No one, however, was more impressed with Abrams' ideas than the junior Senator from Illinois, Charles Percy.

Other than having the same first name, Percy, a Chicago Republican and Christian Scientist, seemingly had little in common with Abrams, a New York City Democrat and immigrant Jew. Percy's father lost his job and life's savings during the Depression, forcing the family to rely on relief for a brief period. Percy subsequently worked his way through the University of Chicago, then served in the United States Navy, eventually attaining the rank of lieutenant. His career at Bell and Howell (he was its chief executive for fourteen years) was enormously lucrative, placing him in an economic stratum far above the admittedly well-off Abrams. In 1966 Percy estimated his net worth at $6 million. That same year, he was elected to the United States Senate, an office he would hold for almost twenty years.[34]

What brought these two personal and political opposites together was their commitment to affordable housing. Despairing over the near absence of any mention of urban problems in President Johnson's 1967 State of the Union message, Percy and twenty-eight other Republican Senators issued a challenge to their colleagues. "Nineteen sixty-seven," they announced, "must be a year for the beginning of a national effort to win the war against slums, and to bring a new dawn of opportunity to those now living in these desperate circumstances." Specifically, they endorsed programs to advance home ownership for the " 'economically underprivileged,' with its associated value of pride, dignity, and independence." Prior to this Republican manifesto, Percy had asked Abrams for his help in preparing new housing legislation. "I expect to work closely with others," he wrote Abrams on December 31, 1966, "without regard to ideology or party lines to bring a sound, workable program into being."[35]

By early spring of 1967, Percy had finished drafting a bill containing many of the ideas Abrams had championed during the previous decade. As he candidly told his new colleague, "I will be the first to acknowledge

. . . that a tremendous amount of the thinking underlying this program to help low income families become home owners can be traced to your own seminal works dating back at least to *The Future of Housing* in 1946." Rather than his books, Abrams' statement to the Senate's Committee on Banking and Currency in 1959 provided policymakers with a legislative blueprint. On that occasion, Abrams had lamented the skewed nature of assistance policies: "The extensive federal home credits and guarantees . . . seem to be allotted largely to those who neither need nor deserve government subvention . . . . It smacks of the philosophy of socialism for the rich and private enterprise for the poor." As a solution, he outlined a program targeted at the working poor—families not indigent enough to qualify for public housing, but not affluent enough to afford housing in the private market. This program would help low-income families purchase their own homes by creating a quasi-public corporation to extend low-interest loans. The use of a separate corporation reflected Abrams' long standing commitment to public authorities and nonprofit organizations as the institutional mechanisms to provide better housing, though it probably also indicated his continuing disillusionment with existing federal agencies, especially the FHA.[36]

The similarities between Abrams' policy recommendations and the bill Percy introduced on April 20, 1967, were evident. The National Home Ownership Act (NHOA), as the bill was titled, would establish a public/private corporation, the National Home Ownership Foundation (NHOF), whose services would duplicate some of those already offered by the Department of Housing and Urban Development (HUD) and the FHA. The NHOF, through the sale of federal bonds, would create a Home Ownership Loan Fund (capitalized at $2 billion). This fund would issue loans to local nonprofit housing associations, cooperatives, limited dividend and neighborhood corporations, labor and church groups, and the newly created community action agencies. These local organizations would supervise the construction and/or rehabilitation of private housing for sale to low-income buyers; they could also issue mortgages directly if private-market funds were unavailable. To reduce monthly payments, the NHOA authorized the U.S. Treasury to pay part of the interest on mortgage premiums. Its "sweat equity" provision permitted a potential home buyer to contribute his own labor to defray construction or rehabilitation costs. Furthermore, a "home owner's insurance program" protected residents from losing their homes in case of temporary illness, disability, or unemployment (Percy conceded this benefit was "identical" to the one Abrams had been advocating for almost twenty-one years). the NHOA also proposed a "Technical Assistance Service" to help "eligible borrowers" obtain "access to supporting programs in the fields of training, employment and counseling, and other related programs necessary to the success of a home ownership program." The need for such assistance underscored the insufficiency of housing as the sole remedy for inner-city poverty, an argument Abrams had been making throughout the 1960s.[37]

In Congress, the NHOA received an enthusiastic, almost giddy reception, especially among Republicans. Several of the NHOA's co-sponsors in the Senate rose to give homilies on the virtues of home ownership and self-help. Senator Edward W. Brooke (R-Massachusetts) was the only one whose remarks were guarded. Home ownership, he stressed, would have to be "linked to programs of education and job retraining." In the House, where a companion bill had been introduced by Representative William B. Widnall (R-New Jersey), platitudes were equally plentiful. The young Republican Representative from Texas, George Bush, described Percy's plan as "dynamic in that it unleashes the creativeness of the private sector of our economy on a national problem which the public sector has not been able to solve alone." Representative Donald E. Lukens (R-Ohio) also added his views: "In contrast to the model cities program, which will reach a very limited number of our urban areas, the home ownership plan would be available and practical for every city in the country."[38]

Praise for the NHOA was not just a product of its emphasis on property ownership. For Republicans still reeling from the barrage of Great Society legislation passed since 1964, the NHOA not only permitted them to recapture part of the legislative momentum, it also gave them moral capital as advocates of home ownership for low-income groups. Their efforts were amplified by the Democrats' apparent apathy regarding this issue, as well as the Johnson administration's quick and vocal opposition to Percy's recommendations. A day after NHOA was introduced, Robert Weaver, Secretary of HUD, released a statement claiming the legislation failed to provide for municipal involvement, intergovernmental coordination, relocation programs, or "the means for families of low incomes to own their own home." Though largely partisan blustering, Weaver's response put Abrams in an awkward position. As a defender of home ownership for low-income groups, he found himself on the wrong side of a Democratic administration and at odds with a long-time friend. Fortunately, this tension quickly evaporated: sensing home ownership was an issue Republicans could exploit, Johnson himself took the lead in urging Democrats to introduce similar legislation. Within a few months there were no fewer than thirty-five bills (many authored by Democrats) to be reviewed by the Senate Subcommittee on Housing and Urban Affairs.[39]

Percy continued to solicit Abrams' advice throughout the spring and summer of 1967, meeting with him in New York City on at least one occasion. He eventually asked Abrams to provide Congressional testimony, which he did in late July. His statement not only lauded the NHOA, but also outlined some of its limitations. The NHOA, Abrams counseled, would not solve every housing problem, nor would it fulfill the need for "social services, recreation, school aid and other neighborhood improvements" in America's central cities. Abrams also took the opportunity to lobby for the creation of "local information services." These programs, modeled along the lines of the NHOA's Technical Assistance Services, would teach residents "some of the skills and simple crafts required for maintaining and improving their homes."[40]

The outcome of Percy's legislation, embodying Abrams' hopes to make home ownership a reality for low-income groups, was ultimately influenced by national politics and contested policy visions. On November 28, 1967, the Senate Banking and Currency Committee reported out a Housing and Urban Redevelopment Bill containing elements of the various proposals introduced in the Senate during the past several months. Its main feature, dubbed "Section 235," was a new home owner assistance program authorizing HUD to subsidize mortgages for moderate- and low-income housing. Lawmakers believed the increased availability of cheap mortgage money would stimulate home sales, which in turn would encourage developers to build or renovate more houses. Funding for 235, though, was limited so the additional demand it generated would result in no more than 200,000 units of new or renovated housing over a three-year period (the same amount the NHOA had contemplated via the Home Ownership Loan Fund). The bill's authors hoped that keeping this number relatively modest would maintain the program's focus on the quality, not quantity of Section 235 housing. Another provision, Section 236, extended similar assistance for rental housing. Finally, the bill authorized a weakened NHOF, but omitted an insurance program for home owners. Democratic Senators, perhaps realizing Johnson's views might differ from theirs, decided to postpone consideration of the bill until after the president's special message on cities.[41]

On February 22, 1968, Johnson outlined his vision for urban America in a speech apocryphally entitled "The Crisis of the Cities." He called for construction of twenty-six million new homes and apartments over the next ten years. Six million of these units were to receive federal subsidies. The Senate Banking and Currency Committee, retreating from its earlier recommendations, quickly revised the 1967 bill to reflect Johnson's emphasis on housing production. In doing so, the Committee opened up the new ownership and rental programs to a larger, poorer clientele (mortgage interest rates could be set as low as 1 percent versus 3 percent under the original bill). These provisions were incorporated into the 1968 Housing Act, which Congress passed on August 1, 1968.[42]

On one level, these events might fit into a facile interpretation of Republican stringency overridden by Democratic largesse. Yet the 1968 Housing Act's production goals actually indicated a more problematic shift in policy objectives. "If," one of Percy's legislative aids later wrote, "the . . . programs [supported by Percy and Abrams] were to be available only in neighborhoods that had formed a [nonprofit] housing corporation . . . then it was clearly impossible to attain anything like the national housing goals proposed by the Johnson Administration." By calling for significantly more housing than the NHOF had countenanced, and by ruling out a prominent role for local, nonprofit housing organizations, it was the Democratically influenced Housing Act of 1968—not the Republican-initiated and Abrams-inspired NHOA—that was predicated on virtually unrestricted private sector participation.[43]

The results substantiated Percy and Abrams' worries about any approach that inordinately stressed ownership and Abrams' more specific fear concerning the potential abuse of public programs by private interests. "Merely installing lower income families in a decent structure that they own," Percy accurately predicted, "may well not, absent other considerations, result in the achievement of the goals of this program." Moreover, whatever technical and financial supervision the NHOF could have provided fell victim to Nixon's anger over Percy's opposition to the Safeguard antiballistic missile system during the summer of 1969.

Having counted on Percy's vote, Nixon retaliated by preventing the NHOF from being funded. No appropriations were ever made, nor was anyone ever appointed to its eighteen-member Board, which would likely have included both Percy and Abrams.[44]

If the NHOF was stillborn, the performance of Section 235 was more ambiguous. As of 1974, 453,791 families had become home owners under the 235 program, a significant achievement given the financial barriers historically impeding home ownership for low-income groups. Section 235 mortgages also allowed some whites and African Americans to move from central cities to better (albeit segregated) suburban neighborhoods. And, perhaps equally important, Section 235 housing developments helped reduce public antipathy toward subsidized dwellings by eschewing the size and design of inner-city projects.[45]

The accomplishments of Section 235, however, were overshadowed by its failures. Without the social services Abrams and Percy had advocated, some individuals were clearly unprepared to meet monthly mortgage payments. Worse still, Section 235 transactions, lacking strict public oversight and management, were characterized by fraud and deceit. As subsequent investigations would show, speculators had bought dilapidated housing, made superficial repairs, received FHA inspections, then sold the dwellings at inflated prices to unsuspecting buyers. A random audit by HUD in 1971 revealed the magnitude of the problem. HUD discovered that FHA appraisers had certified a large number of Section 235 properties for sale (43 percent of existing homes and 26 percent of new ones) even though they did not meet minimum building standards. Unable to afford repairs that were soon necessary, the new owners simply abandoned their homes, leaving the government to repay holders of Section 235 mortgages. Foreclosure rates for Section 235 units thus averaged 10.05 percent, more than five times the default rate for basic FHA mortgages. These factors—plus negative publicity—led to a series of Congressional investigations that prompted President Nixon to suspend the Section 235 and 236 programs on January 5, 1973. They were never reactivated, but were subsumed in different forms under the Housing and Community Development Act of 1974.[46]

Whether the fate of low-income home ownership would have been different if Congress had enacted the unrevised NHOA is difficult to determine. Sponsors of the original bill certainly thought the NHOF's limited clientele would stem private-sector abuses. Furthermore, the

NHOF's bypassing of the FHA might have eliminated other problems as well (for example, certification of substandard dwellings). Even when the 1968 Housing Act confirmed Section 235 as the primary mechanism to expand home ownership, NHOF funding and reduced production goals might have minimized mismanagement and malfeasance. At the very least, the Technical Assistance Service could have informed home buyers about various educational and vocational programs.

Why had Abrams' ideas resulted in an array of unintended consequences? First and foremost, Democrats—responding to the gauntlet thrown down by Republicans and anxious to appear in tune with the *zeitgeist*—eagerly affirmed Johnson's hyperbolic policy goals. In this case, though, more was not necessarily better. The sheer number of housing units called for in the Housing Act of 1968 required the services of large-scale developers, individuals far less willing to adhere to local code requirements than smaller, community-based contractors.[47]

The deceptive simplicity of home ownership also influenced policy-making in unanticipated ways. The majority of lawmakers had purchased their own homes; for them, this had been a straightforward proposition resulting in enhanced financial security. Home ownership did not necessarily have the same effect on those who had lived in poverty for most if not all of their lives. Percy and Abrams understood this. Their sentiments would be echoed in a statement made in 1968 by the President's Committee on Urban Housing: "Better housing alone will not uplift the poor. The Committee emphasizes that stepped up efforts in urban housing must be supported by concentrated and accelerated public and private actions for equipping and enabling the poor to help themselves enter the mainstream of American life." Without acknowledging the complexity of the problem (poverty), lawmakers unwisely assumed that home ownership per se was the solution.[48]

Insufficient regulation of private sector involvement probably contributed most to the distortion of Abrams' proposals. To be sure, the results of the 235 program confirmed the potential dangers that inhered in the government's persistent reliance on a generally unregulated market economy as the medium to convey benefits to the American public. Abrams had been a long-time critic of this approach, believing profit-driven enterprises possessed a kind of moral calcium deficiency. That was why he advocated strict regulation of business interests when they participated in public initiatives. The original NHOA legislation introduced in 1967 illustrated Percy's agreement with him on this point: absent restrictions or safeguards, entrepreneurs would be tempted to use public programs to maximize private profits.

Like his work in other areas, Abrams' criticisms of urban renewal and his push for low-income home ownership were characterized by originality, creativity, and the willingness to challenge firmly held opinions. On the broadest analytical level, he remained troubled by the contradictions and limitations of liberal politics. As he faced his final years, he would continue to use his writing and speaking skills to highlight the necessity of keeping public, not private, interests dominant.

Chapter Eleven

"WHEN THE GREY MIST SUBSIDES"

The late 1960s were just as frenetic for Abrams as the previous four decades. In 1965 he was appointed chairman of Columbia University's Division of Urban Planning; he became head of the New York City Housing Task Force in 1966; between 1966 and 1967 he was a housing consultant on Ford Foundation missions to Chile and India; in 1968 he was a visiting lecturer at University College in London, while the following year he was Williams Visiting Professor at Harvard's School of Design.

Activities and commitments were numerous during this period because Abrams was enjoying public recognition for his accomplishments, especially after the appearance of a two part "Profile" on him in *The New Yorker* magazine in February of 1967. The article generated dozens of letters from people Abrams had never met. His good-natured reply to Edwin P. Uhl of Grand Rapids, Michigan was typical: "I have received several requests to take people around New York since *The New Yorker* profile. . . . The trouble with these trips is that they cannot be done like a tour. They are interesting only if you are accompanied by a few people." His increased visibility caught the attention of his publisher,

Harper & Row, who indicated a desire to reprint *The Future of Housing* and *Forbidden Neighbors*, as well as publish a new book on squatters, a long awaited urban "dictionary," and an "anthology" of his other works. Amid this welter, several of Abrams' projects—participation in the Lawndale Community Conference, work at Columbia University, and the drafting of his final book—illustrated his continuing ability to move from one arena to another, to link the worlds of academia, politics, and everyday life.[1]

Lawndale and the Changing Role of Policy Intellectuals

In the summer of 1967, Abrams was invited to attend the Lawndale Community Conference. Lawndale, an impoverished neighborhood on Chicago's West Side, exemplified many of America's inner-city problems. In an attempt to generate public outrage over its plight, Martin Luther King and his wife had rented a four-room apartment there in early 1966. The following year, local residents learned of an upper-middle-income housing development slated for the area. Fearing its construction would push them into adjacent slums, residents planned and hosted a two-day conference to discuss how to combat the proposed project.[2]

Two of the best-known participants in the conference were Abrams and Jane Jacobs. Though they were invited as "planning experts," neither could claim that distinction. Moreover, despite Abrams' past accomplishments, he had never actually planned a city or even a neighborhood. The selection of Abrams and Jacobs was likely based on their well-publicized sympathy for slum residents, especially those who had become the victims rather than the beneficiaries of state and federal policies. Inviting Abrams and Jacobs might have also symbolized the growing distrust inner-city residents had for professional planners, the putative driving force behind urban renewal.[3]

During the conference, Abrams sat down with residents, listened to their problems, asked them questions, translated their proposals into policy recommendations, and served as a source of information. Ultimately, the conference did not identify anything novel about Lawndale's problems. Attendees complained about the lack of mortgage money and the negative consequences of inconsistent code enforcement. They stressed the need for tenant education and the pernicious effects racial discrimination had on their lives (many Lawndale residents were African American). Beyond these specifics, the conference revealed the important role citizen empowerment was assuming in the late 1960s and early 1970s. This was illustrated by the discussion Abrams led over the proposed charter for the West Side Federation, the entity designated to present Lawndale's grievances and recommendations. "Residents," the charter asserted, could "best plan the kind of redevelopment" for their community; "poor people" should not be asked to bear the "major social and economic costs of urban renewal"; the "official planning process" should include "people based community organizations"; and "ultimate ownership and responsibilities of new or rehabilitated housing" should "rest mainly with the people who live in them, and/or community based non-profit housing corporations."[4]

In supporting the goals of the conference and the West Side Federation, Abrams acknowledged that experts like himself could no longer operate in a top-down fashion. By the 1960s, activists of every stripe were demanding a greater say in the decisions affecting their lives. If this "participatory democracy" fell short of pure democracy, it was nonetheless a grass-roots form of policymaking, one in which ordinary citizens would help create and run various programs. Abrams seemed to have been moving in this direction ever since the 1950s; by 1967 he clearly supported involvement of inner-city residents in policy initiatives. As he told them at the beginning of the Lawndale conference: "I can't talk as an expert by visiting the community for a few hours and then trying to talk to the people on what I think. I think that you're the experts; you live here." Once residents had identified the actual "housing problem," they and Abrams could collectively "structure the program" to solve it. This interactive, bottom-up approach certainly differed from the 1930s, when Abrams and others formulated various policies, campaigned for their enactment, then assisted in their implementation.[5]

Protests at Columbia University

Successful as both a teacher and administrator at Columbia University, Abrams was also involved in one of that institution's most traumatic incidents, a milestone in the increasing militancy of student protest. His reaction to this episode revealed his legal and political skills, his concern for justice, and his own conception of participatory democracy. Like many urban universities, Columbia often found itself at odds with the surrounding community. As the school expanded, it acquired—sometimes in an arrogant and heavy-handed manner—many nearby properties (more than 100 in the 1950s and 1960s alone). The *New York Times* subsequently observed that this process often entailed the "eviction of many long-time residents of low-cost rent-controlled housing." Columbia's plan for a new gym in the 1960s was a catalyst for another round of university-community conflict. The school hoped to build the gym on a site in Morningside Park, which was virtually the only public land left between campus and West Harlem. As part of the project, Columbia agreed to provide local residents with a few facilities, though it would spend far less on them than on its gym. The building's proposed architecture was also galling to some African Americans: the entrance for Columbia's students would be at the top of the sloping site, while the entrance for Harlemites would be at the bottom. When the foundations were laid in February of 1968, neighborhood leaders immediately referred to it as "Gym Crow." Halting construction soon became a rallying cry for members of Columbia's chapter of Students for a Democratic Society (SDS), one of the country's most influential youth protest organizations.[6]

On April 23, several hundred Columbia students gathered to hear SDS members address a number of issues, including the Vietnam War, university discipline policies, and the new gym. After a few speeches, the crowd marched to the building site, where several fights broke out between students and the police. Regrouping, a smaller band marched back to campus and occupied Hamilton Hall. Shortly thereafter, they issued a set of demands: demonstrators were to be granted amnesty; the university was to disassociate itself from the Institute for Defense Analysis (an organization conducting weapons research); and construction of the gym was to be halted. Over the next few days, both sides became more recalcitrant, with compromise apparently impossible. Students seized five more buildings, and President Grayson Kirk, in no mood to negotiate, flatly refused to provide amnesty to anyone.[7]

As tensions escalated, the administration scheduled an emergency meeting of all Columbia's faculty on April 28. With more than 500 people in attendance, the faculty voted overwhelmingly to condemn the students' actions and to support the administration's position on amnesty. Later that day, Abrams expressed his views in a letter to David Truman, Columbia's Provost: "It involves what I consider to be a misunderstanding by both sides of the meaning of the term 'amnesty.' " In an enclosed, hastily drawn memo, Abrams claimed students themselves, by raising the issue of amnesty, admitted to the illegality of their actions and were "simply requesting that a concept of public law be invoked conceding a voluntary extinction from memory of a crime they have committed." In short, students wanted to be absolved from the criminal consequences of their actions. This demand, Abrams pointed out, "should not be viewed as freedom from guilt or as a pardon." The university had recently granted amnesty to "all book borrowers and book stealers alike," and "they were not required to identify themselves as they did so." Admitting the two issues were not identical, Abrams nevertheless thought the university had set a useful precedent.[8]

Abrams also outlined a peace settlement of sorts. He thought it was important at the outset "to learn why the students [had] acted illegally and wantonly." The findings of a "responsible committee," he added, would have "a more salutary, more wholesome and more lasting effect than a disciplinary warning or any punishment meted out to any individuals." Abrams then offered a six-point proposal: A "fact-finding" committee composed of faculty and students was to be created; students in the occupied buildings were to present their views through their own committee; work on the gym was to be suspended until a modified plan won community approval; students were to leave the buildings if these terms were acceptable (no criminal charges would be brought against them); the fact-finding committee was to report its recommendations within thirty days; and finally, establishment of such a committee was "in no way to be considered a sanction of violence or of the seizure of property."[9]

The administration resolved Columbia's sit-in far differently than Abrams had suggested. During the early hours of April 30, after a final warning, more than 1,000 New York City policemen cleared the occupied buildings. Forty-eight people were injured and 722 were arrested. At a faculty meeting later that day, Abrams attempted to make a motion to drop the charges against all demonstrators, but it was blocked. The following day, in a letter to Daniel Bell of Columbia's Executive Committee, he again urged leniency toward the students. He went on to discuss the issues raised by the administration's handling of the situation: "A criminal charge that is based on spontaneous decisions made under the stress of emotion at 3 a.m. and which releases others with the presence of mind to walk out is neither fair nor equitable." He also questioned whether using the police had been an "intelligent" or "humane" way of "dealing with student misfeasances." It would have been much better, he believed, if school officials had provided students with an "act of grace" rather than punitive consequences. Turning to the students' substantive grievances, Abrams stated they had highlighted "important failings in the administration by whom they are being charged." The students had also "insinuated a morality into the issue of the gymnasium," a "morality" the administration now "belatedly conceded."[10]

Abrams' analysis and reaction to the sit-in were consistent with positions he had taken throughout his professional life. For him, the gym symbolized any and all such projects that ignored the needs, wishes, and desires of urban residents. As for the ensuing confrontation, it was not unlike other social problems. It had several sides, and until a careful search for the facts had been conducted, the university would have to withhold judgment. This relatively dispassionate approach did not immunize the protesters' tactics from criticism; Abrams felt they were ethically dubious (the right of all students to attend class had been denied) and politically naive (Columbia's old-guard administration would never retreat beyond a certain point). Characteristically, Abrams had offered a legal compromise. But even if it had received serious consideration, partial victories—which is what Abrams' technical definition of "amnesty" would have effected—were no longer acceptable to either the student left or its opponents.[11]

The Columbia crisis affected other New York intellectuals, many of whom possessed liberal credentials going back to the 1920s and 1930s. For some, like Dwight Macdonald, the students were an inspirational example of invigorated radical protest. The majority of progressive thinkers, though, did not take their cue from Macdonald, but from the more conservative Diana Trilling, wife of the noted literary critic, Lionel Trilling. In an article published in *Commentary* a few months after the sit-in, she expressed a growing sense of frustration, anger, and fear over the direction organized protest had taken. Specifically and almost obsessively, she focused on the means students had employed, as well as their apparent intention to effect "large social destructiveness." Trilling implied that this signaled the bankruptcy of liberalism, writ large. The responses of Trilling and Abrams were thus in sharp contrast. Like so many other times, Abrams had pointed to a pragmatic middle ground. He could not, like Macdonald, speak glowingly of the students as modern-day "communards" (which suggested approval of their tactics). But, since he condoned some of their objectives, he refrained from the shrillness of Trilling-esque diatribes. In this instance, Abrams viewed means and ends as discrete and separable.[12]

Even after the sit-in, Abrams attempted to play the role of peacemaker between the administration and community leaders. On May 8, 1968, he offered Bayard Rustin, a prominent civil rights activist, several proposals, including a "modification of the gymnasium plans to eliminate the present segregated pattern." "It is a strategic time," Abrams wrote David Truman the next day, "to identify the possible areas of cooperation between the community and the University so that the long-standing underlying misunderstandings can be settled." Over the summer, university officials met with both Rustin and A. Philip Randolph, a veteran civil rights leader. Consequently, Columbia decided to cease construction of the gym. Instead, the school built a different facility inside its main campus several years later.[13]

Black Power

Abrams clearly expressed his feelings toward white student protest but said tantalizingly little about the increasingly strident rhetoric of some African Americans. In word and deed, he had been a supporter of civil rights in the 1940s, 1950s, and early 1960s, fighting important battles himself and condemning those who stood in the way of social justice. In 1959 he told a professor at Louisiana State University: "Trained in the law, I am also trained to respect it and to frown on those who nullify or violate it instead of proceeding through the available processes for changing it." While this comment foreshadowed Abrams' equally critical assessments of younger African-American activists, his reactions to the doctrine of "Black Power" varied. He hoped the philosophy was "more likely to imply 'black pride' rather than 'black coercion,' " but he was also concerned that black power's emphasis on racial separatism might undo the decades-long struggle for an integrated society. Furthermore, he worried the movement's broader goals were fueling a "white backlash" that had already produced support for anti-civil-rights legislation and George Wallace's 1968 presidential bid. He reserved his harshest criticism for African-American protesters who supported violence, individuals whom he vaguely referred to as "militants." According to Abrams, before the "rise of black militancy" there had been "real signs of progress in Negro-white relations." Now, however, fear was "gnawing at the white city dweller," which was forcing him to flee the city. If fear continued to plague urban areas, Abrams speculated, "the city and the Negro problems will become synonymous and both will suffer irretrievably." These remarks, coming only a couple of years before his death, suggest a degree of pessimism had crept into Abrams' normally hopeful outlook. They also accurately gauged how whites would react when they believed (rightly or wrongly) violence was being enlisted in the struggle for racial equality.[14]

Learning the Language of Cities

Published after his death, *The Language of Cities: A Glossary of Terms* (1971) was the most creative book Abrams wrote. Almost twenty years earlier, he had compiled a far smaller urban glossary to be appended to his 1953 study on land problems, but as Abrams later remarked, "the U.N.'s budget people excluded it in the interests of economy." Over the intervening years, he made it available to his students at MIT, the University of Pennsylvania, Columbia, and elsewhere. The dictionary grew by accretion, and by the mid-1960s contained several hundred definitions. Hoping to publish it, Abrams approached his friend Louis Winnick of the Ford Foundation for a small grant to defray costs. Winnick rejected his proposal, but countered with an offer of a $400,000 grant. Abrams subsequently explained why he declined Winnick's generosity: "What he [Winnick] evidently wanted was a 'project' entailing the hiring of a team of scholars for the production of a definitive urban dictionary—authentic, scholarly, impersonal, and precisely the opposite of what I was then prepared to do."[15]

In preparing *The Language of Cities*, Abrams again called upon the help of Robert Kolodny. Together, they pored over hundreds of potential entries, adding, eliminating, revising, and checking various definitions. They eventually created an enormous urban dictionary with three objectives: identification of the most salient terms; defining those terms "simply and accurately"; and providing "personal opinions or biases" where they were "useful and relevant." In reviewing the finished product, political scientist Clement E. Vose concisely described this admixture of objective and subjective analysis: "The resulting art form is really different from a dictionary, and as such it seems to me to succeed when it is handled both with imagination and competence."[16]

The impressive range of terms (979 items) was a testament to Abrams' experience and knowledge. As promised, he articulated his opinions. Defining "school busing," he noted that even were busing a "politically acceptable policy," it probably would not achieve desegregation because of white flight and the availability of private schools. In discussing "capitalism," he suggested "government [had] substantially supplanted the individual as the exclusive activator of enterprises." Under "socialism," he called attention to the blurring of private and public interests. "The issue that may well have to be resolved," he concluded, "is not whether there shall be socialism or capitalism, but socialism for whom."[17]

Reflective of Abrams' own personality, *The Language of Cities* was also full of sly humor. In explaining the evolution of the word "entrepreneur," he commented: "The term was originally used as an alternative name for 'employer.' Adam Smith used the word 'undertaker' (now a live entrepreneur engaged in burying dead ones)." For "desocialization," he playfully observed: "The old Marxian concept was that with the socialization of all enterprises, the state would 'wither away,' but with complete socialization it might not have a place whither to wither to."[18]

If the glossary was purposely an informal, nonacademic work, it was also a summation of Abrams' life as an urbanist. "As the gusto in all this suggests," Vose noted, "Abrams has prepared a highly personal tour of the urban world from the experience of a man who was at once a lawyer, a political figure, and a careful reader in the literature of city planning, law, history and the social sciences." Perhaps even more than a "personal tour," it was a powerful, even profound humanist manifesto ringing with hope, tolerance, and exuberance for mankind's struggle to create a more livable world. When Abrams defined the "ideal city," he wrote:

The search for the ideal city will nevertheless go on—as it should. It will be sought in new towns, in cities of 30,000 people and of 500,000, in the new suburbs of the great metropolises. . . . But it is in the vast miscellany rather than in the prototype that the ideal will be found. For what is ideal can neither be one man's concept nor remain a constant. Life can be ideal in a garret for some, or at Walden Pond for others, and as it goes on both the garret and the pond may ultimately prove restrictive. The existence of many forms makes choice possible, and the existence of choice makes the search for the ideal and the ideal city hopeful. Choice, however, implies not only a choice of physical forms and a variety in the types of houses, streets, sites, neighbors, and facilities, but also the existence of institutions and devices that allow men to move about and develop their potential free of unreasonable restraints—free to reject the creations of what some planners see as the ideal.[19]

On another topic, "hippies," Abrams revealed far more understanding and charity than did most Americans nearing seventy:

Though much has been written on the hippie phenomenon, one of the missing commentaries is on the activities of meeting and mating in these youth movements, whether hippies or yippies, civil rights, draft resistance, or the anti-war campaign. It should be said that the hippie movement, like the others, supplied a purpose, cause, or pretext that gave the youth the right, the opportunity, and the freedom to meet and mate. The city was failing as a context for bringing people together, and just as young communism and [the] Spanish Loyalist movement of the 1930s supplied an "honorable cause" for coming together, so did the hippie movement—adding its element of universal love, flowers, and the "trip." Perhaps someday urban renewal will be more broadly defined; not simply as the demolition of buildings, but the renewal of the human spirit, the provision of space for social assemblage, and creation of better devices for the young to meet in an expanding arena of wholesome opportunities.[20]

And, in what could have been a fitting conclusion, Abrams eloquently mused on the ultimate meaning of "community":

Community, finally, is that mythical state of social wholeness in which each member has his place and in which life is regulated by cooperation rather than by competition and conflict. It has had brief and intermittent flowerings through history but always seems to be in decline at any given historical present. Thus community is that which each generation feels it must rediscover and recreate.[21]

The "Grey Mist" of Time

Abrams maintained his hectic pace despite declining health. In October of 1967 he had a malignant tumor removed from his bladder, which was followed by radiation therapy. Six weeks later he was back in the hospital to have another tumor removed, a lymph node dissection, and an appendectomy. He was also diagnosed with high blood pressure and mild diabetes. In late 1968 he had yet another tumor removed, and in May of 1969, a metastatic lesion was discovered on his hip. With the cancer spreading, Abrams underwent several weeks of radiation treatment in the fall of 1969. It was unsuccessful.[22]

The "lover of cities" confronted mortality in the same spirit he had embraced life. As early as the 1950s, he had expressed his desire to be cremated. Years later, in May of 1969, he explained to his friend Henry Goldschmidt:

> I prefer to be cremated. My reason is not because of a deviation from the Jewish tradition, which I have always respected in principle and heritage, though not always in ritual, but because as one who has written on the urban land problem, I have found cemeteries to be one of the most competitive bidders for valuable urban land. Traditional or untraditional, I do not believe in the tyranny of the dead over the living. I hope my family will understand.[23]

This mixture of principle and subtle humor was an appropriate epitaph for Abrams. Just a few months earlier, he had written an equally apt description of where he wanted to spend his last days:

> I am and always have been a New Yorker and Cambridge with all its attractions cannot hold me. I enjoyed Harvard this year . . . and enjoyed seeing the squirrels instead of rats, breathing clean air and the scent of flowers at Grey gardens. But I felt I had either to go

back to New York or give up my subscription to the *New York Times*. New York is where the action and the trouble are, and I've been either a trouble-shooter or a trouble-maker. It's in my tiring bones and when at last they fail, they will rest on the Lower East Side streets on a final walk with a few students.[24]

Faced with these challenges, Abrams kept pushing on. In March 1969 he agreed to participate in the Blazer Lectures at the University of Kentucky, where other speakers would include Richard Wade, an influential urban historian, and Carl Stokes, the first African-American mayor of a large U.S. city (Cleveland). Abrams also hoped to teach a full load of classes when he returned to Columbia in the fall. He was unable, however, to follow through on these commitments. In late December 1969, after extensive radiation therapy, he remained confined to bed and limited to two short daily walks. Word came on February 12, 1970 that Abrams had been named as the recipient of the American Society of Planning Officials' Medal for "leadership and contributions to the advancement of planning." Past recipients had included Catherine Bauer, Lewis Mumford, and Rexford Tugwell. It was a fitting, though perhaps belated recognition of his accomplishments. Always the punster, Abrams kept his sense of humor to the very end. When a colleague visited him in the hospital and asked how he was doing, Abrams answered, "The doctor says I nined." Receiving a puzzled look, he explained: "I over-eight." Approximately two weeks later, on February 22, the pen, the voice, and the life of Charles Abrams ended.[25]

Following his death, tributes poured in from friends, colleagues, and organizations alike. The National Committee Against Discrimination in Housing called him the "beloved Renaissance Man of the vital metropolis," while Dorothy Gazzolo wrote in the *Journal of Housing*: "There are hundreds of thousands of people—not only in the U.S.A., but around the world—who did not have the fun of knowing Charlie Abrams but who have benefited by the combination of talents, training, and experience that made him who he was." Judge Bernard Botein, who had known Abrams since their days at Brooklyn Law School, remarked that he was "the most unstuffy and the most amiably disciplined person I have ever known, he would fight grimly and tenaciously for what Abrams, the planner and crusader held dear; but he was never grim about himself as a person." Perhaps the most eloquent praise for Abrams came from the

American Society of Planning Officials (ASPO), which conferred its Medal Award to him posthumously on April 7, 1970. In a citation presented to Ruth, ASPO declared:

Rarely is preeminence achieved with enduring influence in so many fields as it was by Charles Abrams. Charles Abrams was unique as a planner, houser, author, lawyer and public servant. Among the few in the planning profession whose ideas have significantly changed the art and science of planning, he ranks with the foremost. Among the pioneers in housing whose humanity gave planning many of its insights into the plight of racial and economic minorities, none excels him. Among those whose authoritative studies have paved the way for others, he is renowned. Among lawyers whose creativity has aided and affected the practice of planning, his impact is one of the greatest. Among public servants—city, state, national and international—his voice was one of the influential.[26]

On a rare occasion when Abrams had revealed his own thoughts about death, he noted: "But death strikes with an inevitability which leaves us little choice. Only the inspiration one leaves behind, the influence, thought, wisdom and humor are the lasting monuments. They become more manifest when the grey mist subsides." Abrams did indeed bequeath a legacy of inspiration, influence, wisdom, and humor. His work helped to bring about public housing, the elimination of certain forms of discrimination, the improvement of living conditions in the developing world, and a greater understanding of the increasingly complex urban environment.[27]

By the early 1990s, all of Abrams' books were out of print. Abrams himself might not have been too distressed by this fact; he believed each generation must define its own problems, propose its own solutions, follow its own collective *tachlis*. Yet, were he still alive, Abrams would likely be disturbed by much of what he would see. Already in severe trouble by the 1960s, high-rise public housing projects in America's largest cities have become palpable symbols of America's continuing urban crisis. Other types of public housing, including low-rises, retirement complexes, and even Abrams' own First Houses in New York City are mostly successful. What would be unsettling to Abrams is the bipartisan branding of *all* public housing with the image and reality of a few notorious projects.

He would also be disarmed by the political revolution that began in 1980. He did not think government programs were always the solution to society's problems, or that unsuccessful policies should be retained. To this extent, Abrams would be comfortable with some aspects of contemporary political discourse. It is unlikely, however, that he would agree with the notion that government itself is society's overriding problem. He had witnessed and substantiated too many instances where the private sector was either unwilling or unable to address certain issues. This lifetime of documentation would have prevented him from supporting those who thought a return to laissez-faire governance was either possible or desirable.

Above all else, Abrams would be alarmed at the precariousness of American race relations. He never believed establishment and enforcement of civil rights would, by themselves, bring about racial equality. Rights had to be coupled with social and economic opportunities in order for minorities, especially African Americans, to achieve upward social mobility. Nonetheless, he would be disturbed that legal equality has seemingly done little to reduce the divide separating most whites from most African Americans. He would be discouraged by continuing resistance to African-American entry into predominantly white neighborhoods. He would also be upset that African Americans are disproportionately denied mortgage loans and often find themselves trapped in the grim battlefields of inner-city ghettos.[28]

Studying Abrams' ideas and actions reveals the distance separating contemporary society from the ideal community he wanted to help create. Like most visionaries, his expectations were sometimes unrealistic. His support of massive, direct federal aid and his critique of business welfare policies were part of a larger struggle to force mainstream American politics out of long-standing and deeply dug channels. Maybe it was he, not his adversaries, who tried to "pervert" certain traditions and assumptions.

Irony lurks in another aspect of Abrams' career. Given his opinions on urban development and civil rights, we might see him as an *ubermensch* conjured up by the forces of twentieth-century liberalism to battle inequality and discrimination. That, however, would be too simplistic an interpretation. Abrams consistently favored public agencies free from politicians and partisanship. His belief in government removed from politics—and thus to a degree removed from the people—unconsciously insinuated an undemocratic *potential* into social reform. With respect to public authorities, Abrams never appears to have realized how others, like Moses, might exploit that potential. Admittedly, Abrams' scorn for Moses was undiluted. Describing him in 1954, he wrote: "He is as unscrupulous in the public interest as in his own; as skillful with an epithet as he is mischievous with a monkey wrench." Though this attack might have been an accurate personality assessment, it failed to acknowledge the factors and forces that had enabled Moses to wield his "monkey wrench" in the first place.[29]

Concerning the more narrow issue of eminent domain, Abrams belatedly recognized the negative uses to which that mechanism might be put; he would spend the rest of his life trying to prevent its abuse. Whether the latter fully compensated for the former is a difficult question. At the very least it indicated Abrams was far from perfect, a statement with which he would likely agree. He would have disagreed, though, with the assertion that his policy miscalculations underscored a fundamental flaw in liberal state-building, as political conservatives then and now might argue in their support of a minimal federal government. The contingent nature and unexpected outcomes of policymaking, he would have insisted, did not suggest government expansion was, by definition, wrong—just more complicated than he and others had realized.

Whatever shortcomings Abrams possessed, his conception of life-affirming cities and his courageously democratic stances against prejudice aimed at racial minorities and the polychromatic poor remain worthy of emulation. In trying to achieve his goals, Abrams never looked down on people but instead reached out to them. Nor did he allow his copious scholarship to suffocate his abundant humanity. It is only fitting to allow Abrams, the public/policy intellectual, to have the last word. In 1965 he issued this challenge to policymakers and reformers:

Put simply . . . there is no single simple answer to the complex needs and demands of human beings with their eccentricities and the diverse requirements called forth by the alternations in human yearnings and in life's cycles. The big city is one answer but only one; the new town is another, but only another. The real answer lies in expanding the options available to the individual with his mysterious urges and his unswerving search for something new, different, better—or worse but cheaper. Variety of cities and sections, new towns, existence of movement and movability from one scene to another are among the essential ingredients for the transient, unpredictable, and dissimilar Americans.[30]

Notes

❖

Introduction

1. Robert Reich, *The Power of Public Ideas* (Cambridge, Massachusetts: Ballinger, 1988), 75; Russell Jacoby, *The Last Intellectuals: American Culture in the Age of Academe* (New York: Basic Books, 1987), 5.

2. Abrams, "Vital Plans," photocopy of review of Lewis Mumford, *City Development* (New York: Harcourt, Brace, 1945), reel 26, Charles Abrams Papers, Cornell University Archives (hereafter AP).

3. Michael Berube, "Public Perceptions of Universities and Faculty," *Academe: Bulletin of the American Association of University Professors* 82, no. 4 (July–August 1996), 10–17; Loic J. D. Wacquant, "The Self-Inflicted Irrelevance of American Academics," ibid., 18–23; Stephen T. Leonard, "Introduction: A Genealogy of the Politicized Intellectual," in *Intellectuals and Public Life: Between Radicalism and Reform*, eds. Leon Fink, Stephen T. Leonard, and Donald M. Reid (Ithaca: Cornell University Press, 1996), 19.

4. Alexander Bloom, *Prodigal Sons: The New York Intellectuals and Their World* (New York: Oxford University Press, 1986), 6. Additional studies of the "New York intellectuals" include Terry A. Cooney, *The Rise of the New York Intellectuals: Partisan Review and Its Circle* (Madison: University of

Wisconsin Press, 1986); Alan M. Wald, *The New York Intellectuals: The Rise and Decline of the Anti-Stalinist Left from the 1930s to the 1980s* (Chapel Hill: University of North Carolina Press, 1987); Neil Jumonville, *Critical Crossings: The New York Intellectuals in Postwar America* (Berkeley and Los Angeles: University of California Press, 1991); Hugh Wilford, *The New York Intellectuals: From Vanguard to Institution* (New York: Manchester University Press, 1995); Harvey M. Teres, *Renewing the Left: Politics, Imagination, and the New York Intellectuals* (New York: Oxford University Press, 1996). For biographies that portray their subjects as symbols of twentieth-century liberalism, see Jordan A. Schwarz, *Liberal: Adolph A. Berle and the Vision of an American Era* (New York: Free Press, 1987); Laura Kalman, *Abe Fortas: A Biography* (New Haven: Yale University Press, 1990); Steven M. Neuse, *David E. Lilienthal: The Journey of an American Liberal* (Knoxville: University of Tennessee Press, 1996).

5. For investigations of business sector influence on policymaking, see David Vogel, *Fluctuating Fortunes: The Political Power of Business in America* (New York: Basic Books, 1989); Scott R. Bowman, *The Modern Corporation and American Political Thought: Law, Power, and Ideology* (University Park: Pennsylvania State University Press, 1996).

6. Hugh Davis Graham, "The Stunted Career of Policy History: A Critique and an Agenda," *Journal of Policy History* 15, no. 2 (Spring 1993), 26, 29. See also Richard L. McCormick, "The Party Period and Public Policy: An Exploratory Hypothesis," *Journal of American History* 66, no. 2 (September 1979), 279–298; J. Morgan Kousser, "Restoring Politics to Political History," *Journal of Interdisciplinary History* 12, no. 4 (Spring 1982), 569. A recent analysis of the subfield of political history is Steven M. Gillon, "The Future of Political History," *Journal of Policy History* 9, no. 2 (1997), 240–255.

7. The most important work of Skocpol and her colleagues includes, Theda Skocpol and Kenneth Finegold, "State Capacity and Economic Intervention in the Early New Deal," *Political Science Quarterly* 97, no. 2 (Summer 1982), 255–278; Peter B. Evans, Dietrich Rueschemeyer, and Theda Skocpol, eds., *Bringing the State Back In* (New York: Cambridge University Press, 1985); Margaret Weir, Ann Shola Orloff, and Theda Skocpol, eds., *The Politics of Social Policy in the United States* (Princeton: Princeton University Press, 1988); Kenneth Finegold and Theda Skocpol, *State and Party in America's New Deal* (Madison: University of Wisconsin Press, 1995). In addition, see Stephen Skowronek, *Building a New American State: The Expansion of National Administrative Capacities, 1877–1922* (New York: Cambridge University Press, 1982). For scholarship concerning the rise of institutions and corporations (the "organizational synthesis"), see Samuel P. Hays, *The Response to Industrialism, 1885–1914* (Chicago:

University of Chicago Press, 1957); Robert H. Wiebe, *The Search for Order, 1877–1920* (New York: Hill and Wang, 1967); Louis Galambos, "The Emerging Organizational Synthesis in Modern American History," *Business History Review* 44, no. 3 (Autumn 1970), 279–290; Louis Galambos, "Technology, Political Economy, and Professionalization: Central Themes of the Organizational Synthesis," ibid. 57, no. 4 (Winter 1983), 471–493; Brian Balogh, "Reorganizing the Organizational Synthesis: Federal-Professional Relations in Modern America," *Studies in American Political Development* 5, no. 1 (Spring 1991), 119–172. Developments in political science are outlined in Paul J. DiMaggio and Walter W. Powell, *The New Institutionalism in Organizational Analysis* (Chicago: University of Chicago Press, 1991).

8. Brian Balogh, *Chain Reaction: Expert Debate and Public Participation in American Commercial Nuclear Power, 1945–1975* (New York: Cambridge University Press, 1991); Linda Gordon, *Pitied But Not Entitled: Single Mothers and the History of Welfare, 1890–1935* (New York: Free Press, 1994); Blanche D. Coll, *Safety Net: Welfare and Social Security, 1929–1979* (New Brunswick: Rutgers University Press, 1995); Judith Sealander, *Private Wealth and Public Life: Foundation Philanthropy and the Reshaping of American Social Policy from the Progressive Era to the New Deal* (Baltimore: Johns Hopkins University Press, 1997); Donald L. Critchlow, *Intended Consequences: Birth Control, Abortion, and the Federal Government in Modern America* (New York: Oxford University Press, 1999). Investigations that use housing or housing policies as foci are Timothy L. McDonnell, *The Wagner Housing Act: A Case Study of the Legislative Process* (Chicago: Loyola University Press, 1957); Richard O. Davies, *Housing Reform During the Truman Administration* (Columbia: University of Missouri Press, 1966); John F. Bauman, *Public Housing, Race, and Renewal: Urban Planning in Philadelphia, 1920–1974* (Philadelphia: Temple University Press, 1987); Robert B. Fairbanks, *Making Better Citizens: Housing Reform and the Community Development Strategy in Cincinnati, 1890–1960* (Urbana: University of Illinois Press, 1988); Thomas J. Sugrue, *The Origins of the Urban Crisis: Race and Inequality in Postwar Detroit* (Princeton: Princeton University Press, 1996); Peter H. Henderson, "Local Deals and the New Deal State: Implementing Federal Public Housing in Baltimore, 1933–1968" (Ph.D. diss., Johns Hopkins University, 1993). One of the first national studies of housing and policy development is Gail Radford, *Modern Housing for America: Policy Struggles in the New Deal Era* (Chicago: University of Chicago Press, 1996). See also Daniel T. Rodgers, *Atlantic Crossings: Social Politics in a Progressive Age* (Cambridge: Harvard University Press, 1998), especially chaps. 9 and 10.

9. Nathaniel S. Keith, *Politics and the Housing Crisis Since 1930* (New York:

Universe Books, 1973), 24; Stephen Labaton, "Power of the Mortgage Twins: Fannie and Freddie Guard Autonomy," *New York Times* (hereafter *NYT*), November 12, 1991, C1, C7; Alvin Rabushka, "Flat Tax Lite," ibid., January 23, 1996, A11. In 1995, the mortgage interest deduction cost the federal government $58.3 billion. Peter Dreier, "Billions for the Rich, Pennies for the Poor," *Shelterforce* 18, no. 1 (January–February 1996), 6, 21. For a discussion of related points, see Christopher Howard, "The Hidden Side of the American Welfare State," *Political Science Quarterly* 108, no. 3 (1993), 403–436.

10. Even Skocpol has begun to argue that extra-state variables are important considerations in understanding policy development. Theda Skocpol, *Protecting Soldiers and Mothers: The Political Origins of Social Policy in the United States* (Cambridge: Harvard University Press, 1992). Alan Brinkley has called the distinction between state-centered and society-centered analyses "deep but ultimately artificial." Alan Brinkley, "For Their Own Good," review of *Protecting Soldiers and Mothers*, by Theda Skocpol, *New York Review of Books*, May 26, 1994, 40–43, quote at 43. See also Ira Katznelson and Bruce Pietrykowski, "Rebuilding the American State: Evidence from the 1940s," *Studies in American Political Development* 5, no. 2 (Fall 1991), 301–339. For another indication that debates over state-building are moving toward a middle-ground, see Meg Jacobs, " 'How About Some Meat?': The Office of Price Administration, Consumption Politics, and State Building from the Bottom Up," *Journal of American History* 84, no. 3 (December 1997), 910–941.

1. Immigration and Community

1. Bernard Taper, "A Lover of Cities," I, *The New Yorker*, February 4, 1967, 39–42, 44, 47–48, 50, 55–56, 58, 61–62, 64, 69–70, 72, 75–76, 78, 83–84, 86, 89–91; Taper, "A Lover of Cities," II, ibid., February 11, 1967, 45–50, 53–54, 56, 59–60, 62, 67–68, 70, 73, 76, 78, 80, 85–86, 88, 90, 92, 95, 97–98, 103–104, 106, 109–110, 112, 115. For an example of a biographical entry on Abrams, see "Charles Abrams," in *Current Biography Yearbook: 1969*, ed. Charles Moritz (New York: H. W. Wilson, 1970), 1.

2. Taper, "A Lover of Cities," II, 47; Samuel Joseph, *Jewish Immigration to the United States* (New York: Columbia University Press, 1914), 158; U.S. Industrial Commission, *Reports* (Washington, D.C., 1901–1902), 15:254; Israel Cohen, *Vilna* (Philadelphia: Jewish Publication Society of America, 1943), 337; Martin Gilbert, *Atlas of Russian History*, 2d ed. (New York: Oxford University Press, 1993), 70; Leo Errera, *The Russian Jews: Extermination or Emancipation?*, trans. Bella Lowy (New York: Macmillan,

1894), 29, 114; Simon M. Dubnow, *History of the Jews in Russia and Poland,* trans. I. Friedlaender (Philadelphia: Jewish Publication Society of America, 1920), 3:23–24; Chimen Abramsky, Maciej Jachimczyk, and Antony Polonsky, eds., *The Jews in Poland* (London: Basil Blackwell, 1986), 79; Thomas Kessner, *The Golden Door: Italian and Jewish Immigrant Mobility in New York City, 1880–1915* (New York: Oxford University Press, 1977), 18.

3. Cohen, *Vilna,* 341–342; Dubnow, *History of the Jews in Russia and Poland,* 3:56; Salo W. Baron, *The Russian Jew Under Tsars and Soviets* (New York: Macmillan, 1964), 169–170; Irving Howe, *World of Our Fathers: The Journey of the East European Jews to America and the Life They Found and Made* (New York: Simon & Schuster, 1976), 21. On Hillman's early activities in the Bund, see Steven Fraser, *Labor Will Rule: Sidney Hillman and the Rise of American Labor* (New York: Free Press, 1991), chap. 1.

4. Abraham Cahan, *The Education of Abraham Cahan,* trans. Leon Stein, Abraham P. Conan, and Lynn Davison (Philadelphia: Jewish Publication Society of America, 1969), 18; Howe, *World of Our Fathers,* 7–15.

5. Vilna quote from Joseph Buloff, *From the Old Marketplace,* trans. Joseph Buloff (Cambridge: Harvard University Press, 1991), 3; Abrams, *The Language of Cities: A Glossary of Terms* (New York: Viking, 1971), quote at 277; Hugh Seton Watson, *The Russian Empire, 1801–1917* (New York: Oxford University Press, 1967), 50–51, 494; Gerard Israil, *The Jews in Russia,* trans. Sanford L. Chernoff (New York: St. Martin's, 1975), 55; Hans Rogger, *Russia in the Age of Modernization and Revolution, 1881–1917* (New York: Longman, 1983), 200; Gilbert, *Atlas of Russian History,* 51, 69; Errera, *The Russian Jews,* 42; Abramsky, Jachimczyk, and Polonsky, *The Jews in Poland,* 79; Howe, *World of Our Fathers,* 21; Cohen, *Vilna,* 295; Joseph, *Jewish Immigration to the United States,* 57, 62, 63, 64; Kessner, *The Golden Door,* 37; Cahan, *The Education of Abraham Cahan,* 195–196; U.S. Immigration Commission, *Reports* (Washington, D.C., 1911), 1:246; Simon M. Dubnow, *History of the Jews: From the Congress of Vienna to the Emergence of Hitler,* trans. Moshe Spiegel (Cranbury, New Jersey: Thomas Yoseloff, 1973), 5:717.

6. Dubnow, *History of the Jews in Russia and Poland,* 3:717–719; Howe, *World of Our Fathers,* 29; Marcus E. Ravage, *An American in the Making: The Life Story of an Immigrant* (1917; reprint, New York: Dover, 1971), 27.

7. Gilbert, *Atlas of Russian History,* 70; Howe, *World of Our Fathers,* 28, 41; Philip Taylor, *The Distant Magnet: European Emigration to the U.S.A.* (London: Eyre & Spottiswoode, 1971), 147–148, 150–151, 156–157; Cahan, *The Education of Abraham Cahan,* 187; Isaac Metzker, ed., *A Bintel Brief: Sixty Years of Letters from the Lower East Side to the Jewish Daily Forward* (New York: Ballantine Books, 1971), 95; Immigration Commission, *Reports,* 1:185, 187,

190; Ida M. Van Etten, "Russian Jews as Desirable Immigrants," *Forum*, April 1893, 180; Industrial Commission, *Reports*, 15:xv, 245–246.

8. Francis A. Walker, "Restriction of Immigration," *Atlantic Monthly*, June 1896, 822, quote at 823. Immigration Commission, *Reports*, 1:56, 60, 168–169; Joseph, *Jewish Immigration*, 173.

9. "Map of the City of New York City, New York, Showing the Density of the Population by Wards in 1890," in New York Tenement House Committee of 1894, *Report of the Tenement House Committee of 1894* (Albany, New York: James B. Lyon, 1895), no page number given; Industrial Commission, *Reports*, 15:465, 471, 476–477; Immigration Commission, *Reports*, 1:247.

10. "Exodus from East Side to New 'Promised Land,' " *Brooklyn Daily Eagle* (hereafter *BDE*), April 10, 1904, quote at 5; "Brownsville Development Remarkable in a Few Years," ibid., May 1, 1904, quote at 1; Industrial Commission, *Reports*, 15:477; Burton J. Hendrick, "The Great Jewish Invasion," *McClure's*, January 1907, 309, 320.

11. Henry R. Stiles, *History of the City of Brooklyn*, (Brooklyn: Munsell, 1884), 1:403; Samuel P. Abelow, *History of Brooklyn Jewry* (Brooklyn: Scheba Publishing Company, 1937), 9; Harold Coffin Syrett, *The City of Brooklyn, 1865–1898: A Political History* (New York: Columbia University Press, 1944), 239.

12. New York Tenement House Committee of 1894, *Report*, 49; Taper, "A Lover of Cities," II, 47.

13. J. T. Bailey, *Historical Sketch of the City of Brooklyn* (Brooklyn: n.p., 1840), 7; Stephen M. Ostrander, *A History of the City of Brooklyn and Kings County* (Brooklyn: n.p., 1894), 26; Stiles, *History of the City of Brooklyn*, 1:23; Kenneth T. Jackson, *Crabgrass Frontier: The Suburbanization of the United States* (New York: Oxford University Press, 1985), 25–30; Syrett, *The City of Brooklyn*, 235, 237–238. Brooklyn became one of New York City's five boroughs in 1898.

14. "Early Spring Will See Big Boom in Building Line," *BDE*, January 30, 1904, quote at 3; "High Rents on East Side Send Jews to Brooklyn," ibid., April 6, 1904, 2; "Local Building Boom Has Reached Top Notch," December 27, 1904, ibid., quote at 1; David W. McCullough, *Brooklyn . . . and How It Got That Way* (New York: Dial Press, 1983), 198.

15. "Activity in the Suburbs," *BDE*, February 17, 1904, quote at 4; Abrams, *Language of Cities*, quotes at 44 and 118; Ebenezer Howard, *Garden Cities of To-Morrow*, ed. F. J. Osborn (Cambridge: MIT Press, 1965), 48. See also William H. Wilson, *The City Beautiful Movement* (Baltimore: Johns Hopkins University Press, 1989); Stanley Buder, *Visionaries and Planners: The Garden City Movement and the Modern Community* (New York: Oxford University Press, 1990).

16. "In the Real Estate Field: Avenues of Travel to be Created by Williamsburg Bridge," *NYT*, February 8, 1903, 20; "Want Big Eviction Put Off: East Siders Say Bridge Terminal Notice Will Make Thousands Idle," ibid., November 2, 1907, 4; "Tenants Won't Move," ibid., November 25, 1907, 16; Joel Schwartz, *The New York Approach: Robert Moses, Urban Liberals, and Redevelopment of the Inner City* (Columbus: Ohio State University Press, 1993), 14; Moses Rischin, *The Promised City: New York's Jews, 1870–1914* (Cambridge: Harvard University Press, 1962), 93.

17. "They Want No Colored Neighbor," *NYT*, October 1, 1894, quotes at 2; "Caste in Brooklyn," ibid., October 2, 1894, 4; "Race Riot in East New York," *BDE*, July 12, 1904, quote at 20; Abrams, *Language of Cities*, quote at 244; U.S. Census Bureau, *Negro Population in the United States, 1790–1915* (Washington, D.C., 1918), 101; U.S. Census Bureau, *Negroes in the United States, 1920–1932* (Washington, D.C., 1935), 62; U.S. Census Bureau, *Fourteenth Census of the United States* (Washington, D.C., 1922), 2:47. See also Harold X. Connolly, *A Ghetto Grows in Brooklyn* (New York: New York University Press, 1977), 54–55.

18. Frederic C. Howe, *The City: The Hope of Democracy* (New York: Charles Scribners' Sons, 1906), 21; Fred H. Matthews, *Quest for an American Sociology: Robert E. Park and the Chicago School* (Montreal: McGill-Queen's University Press, 1977), 121–156; John Fairfield, *The Mysteries of the Great City: The Politics of Urban Design, 1877–1937* (Columbus: Ohio State University Press, 1993), 8–10. For an introduction to Park's views, see Robert Park, Ernest W. Burgess, and Roderick D. McKenzie, *The City* (Chicago: University of Chicago Press, 1925).

19. *Report of the Mayor's Push-Cart Commission* (New York: n.p., 1906), 11, 12, 54; Ravage, *An American in the Making*, 91–102; Taper, "A Lover of Cites," II, 47; Charles S. Bernheimer, ed., *The Russian Jew in the United States* (Philadelphia: John C. Winston, 1905), 108–109; Kessner, *The Golden Door*, 19, 55; Hendrick, "The Great Jewish Invasion," 314; Edward A. Steiner, "The Russian and Polish Jew in New York," *Outlook*, November 1902, 530; "Peddlers Rush for Stands," *NYT*, July 22, 1904, 3. See also Daniel M. Bluestone, " 'The Pushcart Evil': Peddlers, Merchants, and New York City's Streets, 1890–1940," *Journal of Urban History* 18, no. 1 (November 1991), 68–92.

20. Taper, "A Lover of Cites," II, 47; Howe, *World of Our Fathers*, 125.

21. Taper, "A Lover of Cites," II, 47; Ravage, *An American in the Making*, 83; Jewish Publication Society of America, *American Jewish Yearbook, 1908–1909* (Philadelphia: Jewish Publication Society of America, 1909), 191–192, 194; Daniel Burnstein, "The Vegetable Man Cometh: Political and Moral Choices in Pushcart Policy in Progressive Era New York City," *New York History* 77, no. 1 (January 1996), 54.

22. "City Relief for the Poor," *BDE*, December 14, 1904, quote at 4; Abelow, *History of Brooklyn Jewry*, 200, 289; Steiner, "The Russian and Polish Jew in New York," 534; Jacob Rader Marcus, *United States Jewry, 1776–1985* (Detroit: Wayne State University Press, 1993), 4:181, 189; Daniel Soyer, *Jewish Immigrant Associations and American Identity in New York, 1880–1939* (Cambridge: Harvard University Press, 1997), 1–9; Beth S. Wenger, *New York Jews and the Great Depression: Uncertain Promise* (New Haven: Yale University Press, 1996), 136–165.

23. Abelow, *History of Brooklyn Jewry*, 335; Ezra S. Brudno, "The Russian Jew Americanized," *World's Work*, 7, no. 5 (March 1904), 4557; Marcus, *United States Jewry, 1776–1985*, 4:185.

24. "Rowdies Attack Jews," *NYT*, June 6, 1904, quote at 14. See also Metzker, *A Bintel Brief*, 58; Abelow, *History of Brooklyn Jewry*, 12–13.

25. Taper, "A Lover of Cities," II, 48, Abrams quoted at 47.

26. Taper, "A Lover of Cities," II, 47, 50, Abrams quoted at 48.

27. Lloyd Rodwin, interview by author, Cambridge, Massachusetts, October 12, 1994, 11 (transcript in possession of author); Taper, "A Lover of Cities," I, 40. The quote from Socrates can be found in Edith Hamilton and Huntington Cairns, eds., *The Collected Dialogues of Plato* (New York: Pantheon, 1961), 479.

28. Lewis Mumford, *Sketches from Life: The Autobiography of Lewis Mumford* (New York: Dial Press, 1982), 13, 16, 20, quote at 18; Donald L. Miller, *Lewis Mumford: A Life* (New York: Weidenfeld & Nicolson, 1989), 378; Robert A. Caro, *The Power Broker: Robert Moses and the Fall of New York* (New York: Random House, 1974), 12.

29. Robert Moses, *Public Works: A Dangerous Trade* (New York: McGraw-Hill, 1970), 161; Caro, *The Power Broker*, 65–66.

30. Mumford and Abrams quoted in Caro, *The Power Broker*, 12, 777.

31. Lewis Mumford, *Technics and Civilization* (New York: Harcourt, Brace and Company, 1934), 109; Miller, *Lewis Mumford*, 375.

32. Caro, *The Power Broker*, 484.

33. Abrams, "Robert Moses vs. 'Robert Moses,' " quote at 5, reel 29, AP; Miller, *Lewis Mumford*, 361.

34. *New York Post*, February 23, 1970, no page number given, reprinted in *Congressional Record—House*, 91st Cong., 2d sess., February 25, 1970, 4741–4742. See also Alexander Crosby to Bernard Taper, September 4, 1956, reel 1, AP.

35. Taper, "A Lover of Cities," II, quotes at 48.

36. Taper, "A Lover of Cities," I, quote at 84.

37. Abrams to Esther Abrams Tarshis, August 7, 1936, reel 54, AP.

2. Law, Real Estate, and Praxis

1. Joseph Freeman, *An American Testament* (New York: Farrar & Rinehart, 1936), 29; Bloom, *Prodigal Sons*, 29; Fraser, *Labor Will Rule*, 23; Brudno, "The Russian Jew Americanized," 4562.

2. Abrams to Shirley Adelson Siegel, November 22, 1949, reel 8, AP; Harry Tugend to Bernard Taper, October 4, 1956, reel 1, ibid.; Bernard Botein, "Charles Abrams," reprinted from The Association of the Bar of the City of New York, *Memorial Book*, 1970, reel 1, ibid.; Alexander M. Dushkin, *Jewish Education in New York City* (New York: Bureau of Jewish Education, 1918), 156, 413; Oscar I. Janowsky, ed., *The American Jew: A Reappraisal* (Philadelphia: Jewish Publication Society of America, 1964), 128–132; Taper, "A Lover of Cities," II, 50; Rodwin, interview, 7.

3. "Identification and Personnel Data for Employment of United States Citizen," 1952, reel 1, AP; "Data Form" for Abrams' entry in *Current Biography*, not dated (probably 1968), reel 1, ibid.; "Polytechnic," advertisement in "Education Supplement," *BDE*, September 8, 1904, 10. Abrams told Brooklyn Law School he was born on September 20, 1901. Abby Abrams, telephone interview by author, May 13, 1998.

4. Edward T. Lee, "The Evening Law School," *The American Law School Review* 1, no. 9 (Spring 1905), 290–291; Robert Stevens, *Law School Legal Education in America from the 1850s to the 1880s* (Chapel Hill: University of North Carolina Press, 1983), 74, 391, 397, 401–402; Louis H. Pink and Rutherford E. Delmage, *Candle in the Wilderness: A Centennial History of the St. Lawrence University, 1856–1956* (New York: Appleton-Century-Crofts, 1957), 240; David G. Trager, "Back to the Future: A History of Brooklyn Law School," *Brooklyn Law School News* (Winter, 1993), 3; "Education Supplement," 10.

5. Alfred Zantzinger Reed, *Training for the Public Profession of the Law* (New York: Carnegie Foundation for the Advancement of Teaching, 1921), 448–449; Lee, "The Evening Law School," 292–293; Stevens, *Law School Education*, 102, 131; Jerold S. Auerbach, *Unequal Justice: Lawyers and Social Change in Modern America* (New York: Oxford University Press, 1976), 80, 96–101.

6. Reed, *Training for the Public Profession of the Law*, quote at 400; Jerome Frank, "What Constitutes a Good Legal Education?," *American Bar Association Journal* 19, no. 12 (December 1933), quote at 726; Jerome Frank, "Why Not a Clinical Lawyer-School?," *University of Pennsylvania Law Review* 81, no. 8 (June 1933), 923; Stevens, *Law School Education*, 156; N.E.H. Hull, *Roscoe Pound & Karl Llewellyn: Searching for an American Jurisprudence*

(Chicago: University of Chicago Press, 1997), 34–36; Edward A. Purcell, Jr., "American Jurisprudence Between the Wars: Legal Realism and the Crisis of Democratic Theory," *American Historical Review* 75, no. 2 (December 1969), 429–430; Laura Kalman, *Legal Realism at Yale, 1927–1960* (Chapel Hill: University of North Carolina Press, 1986), 3–44.

7. Arthur Garfield Hays, *City Lawyer: The Autobiography of a Law Practice* (New York: Simon and Schuster, 1942), 17, 22, 24, 213–215, 219, quotes at x and xi; Samuel Walker, *In Defense of American Liberties: A History of the ACLU* (New York: Oxford University Press, 1990), 53; Edward J. Larson, *Summer for the Gods: The Scopes Trial and America's Continuing Debate Over Science and Religion* (New York: Basic Books, 1997), 89.

8. Taper, "A Lover of Cities," II, 53, 54; untitled and undated memo (probably 1950), reel 4, AP; Abrams, "Cigar Agreement," July 31, 1956, reel 1, ibid.

9. Taper, "A Lover of Cities," II, 53, 54; Hays, *City Lawyer*, quotes at 222 and 224; American Civil Liberties Union, *Annual Report* 1, no. 2 (1923; reprint, New York: Arno Press, 1970), 27; Larson, *Summer for the Gods*, 68–69.

10. Hays, *City Lawyer*, quote at 246; Rodwin, interview, 31.

11. Taper, "A Lover of Cities," II, 53.

12. Undated biographical data for Bernard Botein, box 17, Bernard Botein Papers, New York Historical Society; *The Reminiscences of Charles Abrams* (1963), 35, in the Oral History Collection of Columbia University (hereafter Abrams, COHC); "Memorandum Re Charles Abrams," February 14, 1933, reel 1, AP; "Identification and Personnel Data," reel 1, ibid.; Taper, "A Lover of Cities," II, 54. Data concerning salaries for Harvard Law School graduates come from Schwarz, *Liberal*, 45.

13. "Botein and Abrams Schedule of Fees, January 1, 1937 to December 31, 1937," reel 54, AP; Gershon & Streel, CPA, to Abrams, February 26, 1955, reel 54, ibid.; Abrams to Daniel Gutman, April 26, 1955, reel 17, ibid.; Abrams to Benjamin Rabin, September 12, 1936, reel 7, ibid.; Benjamin Rabin to Abrams, July 12, 1937, reel 7, ibid.; Nathan Klein to Morton J. Schussheim, February 28, 1967, reel 5, ibid.

14. Taper, "A Lover of Cities," II, 54, 56; Abrams to Morris Strunsky, September 12, 1933, reel 8, AP. There is some confusion over marriage and birth dates. Ruth, never one who wanted her real age known (especially later in life), gave 1912 as her birthday and 1930 as her marriage date. The former conflicts with the one given by Abrams and his daughters (1907), while the latter is at odds with what Abrams indicated on official forms, what appeared in biographical dictionaries, and what *The New Yorker* asserted (1928). For these reasons, the present study uses 1907 as Ruth's birthday and adheres to December 22, 1928 as her marriage date. Abby Abrams, telephone interview by author, July 10, 1998.

15. Quote from Ruth Abrams to Carnegie Institute, November 19, 1957, in folder marked, "Ruth Abrams: Philosophy of Painting," in Ruth Abrams Papers, The Archives of American Art, Washington, D.C. (hereafter RAP); "First Exhibition, Paintings and Sculpture, Ruth Abrams," loose item, ibid.; Rodwin, interview, 10; Judy Abrams, letter to author, August 2, 1996; Thomas A. Livesay, *Ruth Abrams: Paintings, 1940–1985* (New York: Grey Art Gallery, 1986), 9.

16. Livesay, *Ruth Abrams*, 10.

17. Ruth's quote from "Kids Tugging at the Easel? Go Get a Room of One's Own," *Village Voice*, March 21, 1956, no page number given, loose item, RAP; Ruth Abrams to Wallace Harrison, not dated, ibid.; "A First Showing," *NYT*, December 2, 1934, sec. 10, 8; Livesay, *Ruth Abrams*, 10–11.

18. Ruth Abrams to Marc Moldawer, not dated, in folder marked, "Ca. 1956," RAP; Livesay, *Ruth Abrams*, 11–16; "Ruth Abrams," *NYT*, July 25, 1986, C26; "Ruth Abrams," *Arts Magazine* 51, no. 7 (March 1977), 46. Quotes from Lewis Mumford to Ruth Abrams, March 2, 1956, loose item, RAP and Ruth Abrams to Wallace Harrison, not dated, ibid.

19. Ruth quoted in Livesay, *Ruth Abrams*, 12; Abrams to Ruth Abrams, July 30 (no year given, but probably 1963), loose item, RAP; Ann Eden Gibson, *Abstract Expressionism: Other Politics* (New Haven: Yale University Press, 1997), 152–153.

20. Rick Beard and Leslie Cohen Berlowitz, eds., *Greenwich Village: Culture and Counterculture* (New Brunswick: Rutgers University Press, 1993), 38, 43, 44, 47, 53; "New Homes in Old Greenwich Village," *NYT*, May 23, 1915, sec. 8, 1; "Housing Plan for Greenwich Village," ibid., March 28, 1920, sec. 8, 1; "Many Lower Greenwich Village Landmarks Doomed by Jersey Vehicular Tunnel," ibid., October 31, 1920, sec. 8, quotes at 6.

21. Caroline Ware, *Greenwich Village, 1920–1930* (1935; reprint, New York: Harper, 1965), 5, 82, 93, 142, quotes at 89 and 422.

22. Abrams, *Language of Cities*, quote at 46; Abrams, *The City is the Frontier* (New York: Harper, 1965), quotes at 201; Jane Jacobs, *The Death and Life of Great American Cities* (New York: Random House, 1961), 14, 145, 150–151, 244–245, quote at 241.

23. Abrams, untitled acceptance speech, Greenwich Village Community Brotherhood Award, February 11, 1958, quotes at 1 and 2, reel 31, AP; Alfred Kazin, *A Walker in the City* (New York: Harcourt, Brace, & World, 1951), quote at 12. The "cosmopolitan ideal" is discussed in David Hollinger, *In The American Province: Studies in the History and Historiography of Ideas* (Bloomington: Indiana University Press, 1985), 72.

24. Louis Adamic, *My America, 1928–1938* (New York: Harper, 1938), 87–93, quote at 91; Judy Abrams, letter, August 2, 1996; Abby Abrams, inter-

view, July 10, 1998; Taper, "A Lover of Cities," II, 56; Frances Spencer to
Abrams, July 29, 1938, reel 2, AP; Abrams to Calverton, July 26, 1936, reel
2, ibid.; Calverton to Abrams, July 18, July 23, and October 16, 1936, all in
box 1, V. F. Calverton Papers, New York Public Library; Leonard Wilcox, *V.
F. Calverton: Radical in the American Grain* (Philadelphia: Temple University
Press, 1992), 244.

25. Quote from Harry Tugend to Bernard Taper, October 4, 1956, reel
1, AP; Abrams to Morris Strunsky, April 1, 1933, reel 8, ibid.; Abrams to
Morris Strunsky, November 15, 1944, reel 8, ibid.; Taper, "A Lover of Cities,"
II, 56, 59. According to Taper, Ira Gershwin ended up using only a few of
Abrams' suggestions—the words "whereas" and "hereby." For the actual
lyrics of "Impeachment Proceeding," as well as background information on
Of Thee I Sing, see Robert Kimball, ed., *The Complete Lyrics of Ira Gershwin*
(New York: Knopf, 1994), xiii, 185, 186.

26. All the examples come from the collection of undated puns and
jokes, reel 53, AP. The only exception is the one about Ghana, which is cited
in Taper, "A Lover of Cities," I, 47. The definition of "city planning" is in
Abrams, *Language of Cities*, 228. See also Taper, "A Lover of Cities," II, 92, 95.

27. Dwight Macdonald, "Commentary on a Glommentary," review of *The
Language of Cities*, by Charles Abrams, *The New Yorker*, May 6, 1972, quote at
130; Judy Abrams, letter, August 2, 1996. For an example of Abrams' "nose"
signature, see his letter to Ruth, dated "Friday, 1960," loose item, RAP.

28. Livesay, *Ruth Abrams*, 10; Taper, "A Lover of Cities," I, quote at 76.

29. Ware, *Greenwich Village, 1920–1930*, quote at 86; Abrams, untitled
acceptance speech, quote at 4, reel 31, AP.

30. Abrams, COHC, 36, quotes at 37; "Housing Plan for Greenwich
Village," 1; Beard and Berlowitz, *Greenwich Village*, 19, 97; Taper, "A Lover of
Cities," II, 57, 92, salesman quoted at 59; Judy Abrams, letter, August 2,
1996; James Boylan, *Revolutionary Lives: Anna Strunsky and William English
Walling* (Amherst: University of Massachusetts Press, 1998), 132; James
Boylan, letter to author, November 29, 1998; Abrams, "Rider" to 1941
resume, 1942, reel 1, AP; Abrams to Morris Strunsky, June 2 and September
12, 1933, reel 8, ibid.; Harry Tugend to Bernard Taper, October 4, 1956,
reel 1, ibid.; Abrams, application, *Who's Who in New York*, September 9, 1937,
reel 1, ibid.; Abrams, "Personal Report Form," *Martindale Hubbell Law
Directory*, August 2, 1951, reel 1, ibid.; Gershon & Streel, CPA, to Abrams,
February 22, 1955, reel 54, ibid.; Abrams to Daniel Gutman, April 26, 1955,
reel 17, ibid.; Abrams to Averell Harriman, January 5, 1955, reel 4, ibid.;
"Qualifications of Abrams: Activities Since 1927," not dated, reel 10, ibid.

31. Abrams quoted in Taper, "A Lover of Cities," I, 84; Abrams to Averell
Harriman, May 27, 1960, reel 4, AP.

32. "Charles Abrams," in *National Cyclopedia of American Biography* (Clifton, New Jersey: James T. White, 1975), 56:109; Taper, "A Lover of Cities," II, 59; "Charles Abrams," *NYT*, February 23, 1970, 27; Abrams, *City Is the Frontier*, 200–201.

33. Beard and Berlowitz, *Greenwich Village*, 114–115, 120, 126–127; Abrams, *Forbidden Neighbors: A Study of Prejudice in Housing* (1955; reprint, Port Washington, New York: Kennikat Press, 1971), 23; "Charles Abrams," *National Cyclopedia*, 109; Abrams, COHC, 37–38; Taper, "A Lover of Cities," II, 60; Abrams, *City Is the Frontier*, quote at 323.

34. Louise Cooper Campbell, "Charles Abrams: 1901–1970," *Architectural Forum* 132, no. 3 (April 1970), 63; "Charles Abrams," *National Cyclopedia*, 109; Taper, "A Lover of Cities," II, quote at 60.

35. For general works on Mumford and Moses, see Miller, *Lewis Mumford*; Caro, *The Power Broker*.

36. Frank, "What Constitutes a Good Legal Education?," 726; Donald A. Schon, *The Reflective Practitioner: How Professionals Think in Action* (New York: Basic Books, 1983), viii-ix, 14–15, 40–41, quotes at 61 and 68. I am indebted to Lloyd Rodwin for first suggesting that Abrams was a reflective practitioner. For Abrams' background in "practical affairs," see Taper, "A Lover of Cities," II, 60; Dorothy Gazzolo, "Charles Abrams," *The Journal of Housing* 27, no. 4 (April 1970), 178.

37. Taper, "A Lover of Cities," I, 50, 58, 75; Abrams to Ernest Weissman, February 15, 1960, reel 9, AP. Reflective practice also resembles what Charles E. Lindblom has described as the "science of muddling through," a model of policymaking that emphasizes "past experience with small policy steps" instead of theoretical frameworks. See Charles E. Lindblom, "The Science of 'Muddling Through,' " *Public Administration Review* 19, no. 2 (Spring 1959), 79. See also David Braybrooke and Charles E. Lindblom, *A Strategy of Decision: Policy Evaluation as a Social Process* (New York: Free Press, 1963).

38. Taper, "A Lover of Cities," I, 61; Abrams, "How Increased Cooperation Might Change Our Cities," untitled speech, Princeton Conference, April 19, 1968, 4, reel 34, AP; Abrams, preface to *Downtown U.S.A.*, by Oscar H. Steiner (Dobbs Ferry, New York: Oceana Publications, 1964), quote at xii; Abrams' dialogue with Bauer quoted in Abrams to William Wurster, March 27, 1969, reel 10, AP; *House and Home* quote in Abrams to Averell Harriman, June 9, 1958, reel 4, ibid.

39. Taper, "A Lover of Cities," I, 42; Abrams, *Language of Cities*, 148–149, 325, quote at 206; Abrams, *City is the Frontier*, 337–344; "Cities and the Single Girl," *Newsweek*, November 15, 1965, 120.

40. Rodwin, interview, 9, 18–19; Morris R. Cohen, "The Conception of

Philosophy in Recent Discussion," *Journal of Philosophy* 7, no. 14 (July 1910), 402–403, 405, 408–409; David Hollinger, *Morris R. Cohen and the Scientific Ideal* (Cambridge: MIT Press, 1975), chap. 3; Martin Bulmer, *The Chicago School of Sociology: Institutionalization, Diversity, and the Rise of Sociological Research* (Chicago: University of Chicago Press, 1984), 5–6; Abrams, *Man's Struggle for Shelter in an Urbanizing World* (Cambridge: MIT Press, 1964), quote at 211.

41. Rodwin, interview, 31; Harriman's quote from Taper, "A Lover of Cities," I, 42; Thomas Haskell, *The Emergence of Professional Social Science: The American Social Science Association and the Nineteenth-Century Crisis of Authority* (Chicago: University of Illinois Press, 1977), 14; Sealander, *Private Wealth and Public Life*, 244; Charles Merriam, "The Present State of the Study of Politics," *American Political Science Review* 15, no. 2 (May 1921), 181, 184, 185; Barry D. Karl, *Charles E. Merriam and the Study of Politics* (Chicago: University of Chicago Press, 1974), 106; Barry D. Karl, *Executive Reorganization and Reform in the New Deal: The Genesis of Administrative Management, 1900–1939* (Cambridge: Harvard University Press, 1963), 50, 74; Raymond Seidelman, *Disenchanted Realists: Political Science and the American Crisis, 1884–1984* (Albany: SUNY Press, 1985), 109, 115.

42. Taper, "A Lover of Cities," I, quotes at 42, 44. My notion of a "public intellectual" is informed primarily by Jacoby, *The Last Intellectuals*.

43. Abrams, untitled and undated pun, reel 53, AP.

3. From Tenement Laws to Housing Authorities

1. "Mayor Names Five to Housing Board," *NYT*, February 14, 1934, 21. Unless otherwise noted, all statutes cited in this book refer to the state of New York.

2. General treatments of housing reform, especially in New York, are Dorothy Schaffter, *State Housing Agencies* (New York: Columbia University Press, 1942); Roy Lubove, *The Progressives and the Slums: Tenement House Reform in New York City, 1890–1917* (Pittsburgh: University of Pittsburgh Press, 1962); Robert Ingalls, *Herbert H. Lehman and New York's Little New Deal* (New York: New York University Press, 1975); Anthony Jackson, *A Place Called Home: A History of Low-Cost Housing in Manhattan* (Cambridge: MIT Press, 1976); Richard Plunz, *A History of Housing in New York City: Dwelling Type and Social Change in the American Metropolis* (New York: Columbia University Press, 1990); Schwartz, *The New York Approach*.

3. Abrams' quote from *Laws of 1934*, chap. 4, sec. 61. For national trends in institutional and administrative growth during this period, see Alan Dawley, *Struggles for Justice: Social Responsibility and the Liberal State*

(Cambridge: Harvard University Press, 1991), 362–363; Morton Keller, *Regulating a New Society: Public Policy and Social Change in America, 1900–1933* (Cambridge: Harvard University Press, 1994).

4. Anwar Syed, *The Political Theory of American Local Government* (New York: Random House, 1966), 155.

5. For the legislative history of housing reform in New York, see New York Assembly, *Report of the Select Committee Appointed to Examine Into the Condition of Tenant Houses in New York and Brooklyn,* March 9, 1857, A. Doc. 205; New York Assembly, *Report of the Committee on Public Health, Medical Colleges and Societies, Relative to the Condition of Tenement Houses in the Cities of New York and Brooklyn,* March 8, 1867, A. Doc. 156; *Laws of 1867,* chap. 908; New York Senate, *Report of the Tenement House Commission,* February 17, 1885, S. Doc. 36; New York Senate, *Report on the Tenement-House Problem,* January 13, 1888, S. Doc. 16; *Laws of 1887,* chap. 84; New York Assembly, *Report of the Tenement House Commission,* January 17, 1895, A. Doc. 37; *Laws of 1895,* chap. 567; *Laws of 1901,* chap. 334; New York City Tenement House Department, *First Report, January 1, 1902–July 1, 1903,* (New York, 1903); Lawrence Veiller, "The Proposed Code of Tenement House Laws," in *The Tenement House Problem,* eds. Robert W. DeForest and Lawrence Veiller (1903; reprint, New York: Arno Press, 1970), 2:101–146; Lawrence Veiller, "The Act for the Creation of a Separate Tenement House Department," ibid., 2:147–160.

6. Jacob A. Riis, *How the Other Half Lives* (1890; reprint, New York: Sagamore Press, 1957), 220, 224, quote at 205. Model tenements are discussed in Alfred T. White, *Improved Dwellings for the Laboring Classes* (New York: n.p., 1877); Lawrence Veiller, "Tenement House Reform in New York City, 1834–1900," in *The Tenement House Problem,* 1:85–86, 97–98, 107–109; "New York's Great Movement for Housing Reform," *Review of Reviews,* December 1896, 693, 699; Eugenie Ladner Birch and Deborah S. Gardner, "The Seven-Percent Solution: A Review of Philanthropic Housing, 1870–1910," *Journal of Urban History* 7, no. 4 (August 1981), 403–438.

7. Abrams, *The Future of Housing* (New York: Harper, 1946), 197, quotes at 178 and 190.

8. For use of the terms "autonomy" and "capacity," see Skocpol and Finegold, "State Capacity and Economic Intervention in the Early New Deal," 255–275.

9. Lawrence Veiller, "The Non-Enforcement of the Tenement House Laws in New Buildings," in *The Tenement House Problem,* 2:257; New York Assembly, *Report of the Tenement House Commission of 1900,* February 25, 1901, A. Doc. 76, 42–59. See also Charles A. Beard, *American City Government* (New York: Century, Co., 1912), 302. The specific duties and functions of the

Tenement House Department are enumerated in the revised New York City Charter (1901), chap. 19a, sec. 1326; chap. 4, sec. 110.

10. Abrams, *Future of Housing*, quotes at 206; Charity Organization Society Committee on Housing, *Housing Administration in New York City* (New York: Charity Organization Society, 1938), 4–5; "Success of the Tenement Law," *The Nation*, January 15, 1903, 46–47; Robert W. DeForest, "Recent Progress in Tenement-House Reform," *Annals of the American Academy of Political and Social Sciences* 23 (1904), 104; "The Appointment of Tenement-House Commissioner," *Charities* 7, no. 24 (December 14, 1901), 532–534; Bureau of Municipal Research, *Tenement House Administration: Steps Taken to Locate and to Solve Problems of Enforcing the Tenement House Law* (New York: Bureau of Municipal Research, 1909), 39, 43, 77–78, 87; Lubove, *Progressives and the Slums*, 156–157.

11. New York State Board of Housing, *Report*, February 28, 1930, Leg. Doc. 84, 71; New York City Tenement House Department, *Third Report, 1906* (New York, 1906), 33–34; New York City Tenement House Department, *Fourth Report, 1907–1908* (New York, 1908), 19–20, 23, 25, 37–38; James Ford, "The Enforcement of Housing Legislation," *Political Science Quarterly* 42, no. 4 (December 1927), 551, 553–554; Langdon W. Post, *The Challenge of Housing* (New York: Farrar & Rinehart, 1938), 115–116, 118–119; Lubove, *Progressives and the Slums*, 160, 165.

12. Abrams, *Future of Housing*, quote at 206.

13. Lawrence Veiller, "The Tenement House Problem," in *The Tenement House Problem*, quote at 1:44; Roger Biles, "Lawrence Turnure Veiller," in *The Biographical Dictionary of Social Welfare in America*, ed. Walter Trattner (New York: Greenwood Press, 1986), 731–733; John F. Sutherland, "Lawrence Turnure Veiller," in *Encyclopedia of Urban America: The Cities and Suburbs*, ed. Neil Larry Shumsky (Santa Barbara: Abc-Clio, 1998), 2:856–857; Assembly, *Report*, February 25, 1901, 70; Lawrence Veiller, "The National Housing Association," *Survey* 23 (March 5, 1910), 841; Lawrence Veiller, *A Model Housing Law*, 2d ed. (New York: Russell Sage Foundation, 1920), 5. See also Lawrence Veiller, *Housing Reform: A Hand-Book for Practical Use in American Cities* (New York: Charities Publication Committee, 1910), 71–72, 81–82, 85; Lawrence Veiller, "The Effect of the New Tenement House Law," *Real Estate Record and Builders' Guide*, January 18, 1902, 105–109.

14. Edith Elmer Wood, *Recent Trends in American Housing* (New York: Macmillan, 1931), quote at 11; Edith Elmer Wood, *The Housing of the Unskilled Wage Earner: America's Next Problem* (New York: Macmillan, 1919), 276; Peter Kivisto, "Edith Elmer Wood," in *Biographical Dictionary of Social Welfare in America*, 789–792; Radford, *Modern Housing for America*, 36.

15. Ray Lyman Wilbur, foreword to *Slums, Large-Scale Housing, and*

Decentralization, vol. 3 of *The President's Conference on Home Building and Home Ownership,* eds. John M. Gries and James Ford (Washington, D.C., 1932), quotes at xi; Editors of Fortune, *Housing America* (New York: Harcourt, 1932), quote at 131.

16. Mary Kingsbury Simkhovitch, *Here Is God's Plenty: Reflections on American Social Advance* (New York: Harper, 1949), quote at 39; *The Reminiscences of Louis H. Pink* (1949), 40–42, in the Oral History Collection of Columbia University (hereafter Pink, COHC); Bauman, *Public Housing, Race, and Renewal,* chap. 1; Fairbanks, *Making Better Citizens,* 79; Elizabeth Hughes, "Chicago Takes Another Step," article reprinted from *Welfare Magazine,* March 1927, 6, in Chicago Municipal Research Library; Joel Schwartz, "Mary Melinda Kingsbury Simkhovitch" and "Louis Heaton Pink," in *Biographical Dictionary of Social Welfare in America,* 673–676, 594–597; Helen L. Alfred, *Municipal Housing* (New York: League for Industrial Democracy, 1932), 25–26; "Seek Laws to Let City Build Homes," *NYT,* February 12, 1932, 21; "Open Drive to Build Low-Cost Homes," ibid., March 23, 1932, 15; "Asks City to Provide $25,000,000 Housing," ibid., July 7, 1932, 19; "City is Urged to Build Low-Rent Homes at Once with Federal Loan to Aid Jobless, End Slums," ibid., October 3, 1932, 19; "Municipal Board for Housing Urged," ibid., October 31, 1932, 17; "Asks City to Form Own Housing Board," ibid., November 6, 1932, sec. 10–11, 2; "New Housing Plan Offered for City," ibid., February 16, 1933, 21; "Suggest Reviving War Housing Body," ibid., March 30, 1933, 4; "Federal Aid Plans Urged by Straus," ibid., November 6, 1933, 3; "Slum Clearance by City Authority," ibid., November 12, 1933, sec. 10–11, 1, 2.

17. Simkhovitch, *Here is God's Plenty,* 43; Gilbert A. Cam, "United States Government Activity in Low-Cost Housing, 1932–1938," *Journal of Political Economy* 47, no. 3 (June 1939), 358; "Housing Session Urged," *NYT,* July 13, 1933, 21; "Backs City Housing Plan," ibid., August 6, 1933, sec. 2, 9; Herbert H. Lehman, "Radio Address," January 2, 1934, in *Public Papers of Herbert H. Lehman, 1934* (Albany: J. B. Lyon Company, 1936), 691–692; Lehman, "Annual Message," January 3, 1934, ibid., 47; Ernest M. Fisher, "Housing Legislation and Housing Policy in the United States," *Michigan Law Review* 31, no. 3 (January 1933), 344; Ingalls, *Herbert H. Lehman,* 189. PWA's enabling legislation is located at 48 Stat. 195.

18. "Jimmy Walker Beats the Boot," *The New Republic,* September 14, 1932, 112–113; Abrams, COHC, 38; James E. Finegan, *Tammany At Bay* (New York: Dodd, Mead, 1933), 213–214; Herbert Mitgang, *The Man Who Rode the Tiger: The Life and Times of Judge Samuel Seabury* (Philadelphia: Lippincott, 1963), 297, 299; Edward J. Flynn, *You're the Boss: The Practice of American Politics* (New York: Collier, 1962), 72–73; Thomas Kessner, *Fiorello*

H. LaGuardia and the Making of Modern New York (New York: Penguin, 1989), 236; Charles Garrett, *The LaGuardia Years: Machine and Reform Politics in New York City* (New Brunswick: Rutgers University Press, 1961), 103, 107, 109; Arthur Garfield Hays, "LaGuardia for Mayor of New York," *The Nation,* July 19, 1933, 71–72.

19. Abrams, COHC, quotes at 38, 40, and 41.

20. For discussions of federalism and intergovernmental relations, see Daniel J. Elazar, "The Shaping of Intergovernmental Relations in the Twentieth Century," *Annals of the American Academy of Political and Social Science"* 359 (May 1965), 10–22; Morton Grodzins, *The American System,* ed. Daniel J. Elazar (Chicago: Rand McNally, 1966), v-vi; Paul E. Peterson, *City Limits* (Chicago: University of Chicago Press, 1981), 13–15.

21. Hays, "LaGuardia for Mayor of New York," quote at 711; Post's quote from "LaGuardia Speeds Action on Housing," *NYT,* December 30, 1933, 15. See also "Post Pledges Aid on Public Works," ibid., October 17, 1933, 4; "Post Urges Reform in Housing Control," ibid., October 19, 1933, 3; Karl, *Executive Reorganization,* 24, 184; Martin J. Schiesl, *The Politics of Efficiency: Municipal Administration and Reform in America, 1800–1920* (Berkeley and Los Angeles: University of California Press, 1977), 3, 5.

22. Flynn, *You're the Boss,* 155; Garrett, *LaGuardia Years,* 108; Paul Blanshard, "LaGuardia Versus McKee," *The Nation,* October 25, 1933, 477.

23. Arthur Mann, *LaGuardia Comes to Power, 1933* (Chicago: University of Chicago Press, 1965), 123, 154–155, 159; Kessner, *Fiorello LaGuardia,* 431; Charles Willis Thompson, "Meaning of the Elections," *Commonweal,* December 1, 1933, 124–126. A Fusionist mayoral victory resulted in part from the fact that the Democrats ran both an incumbent (John P. O'Brien) and an "independent" (Joseph V. McKee).

24. LaGuardia quoted in "LaGuardia Scores M'Kee in Wall Street," *NYT,* November 3, 1933, 3. See also "Group to End Slums is Organized Here," ibid., October 17, 1933, 5; Abrams, COHC, 44.

25. Arthur C. Holden, "Facing Realities in Slum Clearance," *Architectural Record* 71, no. 2 (February 1932), 75–82, quotes at 77, 78, 79, and 82. For an explanation of the "redevelopment districts" advocated by real estate interests, see "NAREB Suggests Plan for Reclaiming Blighted Areas," *National Real Estate Journal* 36, no. 10 (October 1935), 33–34.

26. Fisher, "Housing Legislation," 321, 344–345; E. H. Foley, Jr., "Some Recent Developments in the Law Relating to Municipal Financing of Public Works," *Fordham Law Review* 4, no. 1 (January 1935), 14–15; Peter R. Nehemkis, Jr., "The Public Authority: Some Legal and Practical Aspects," *Yale Law Journal* 47, no. 1 (November 1937), 14, 21; Robert G. Smith, *Public Authorities, Special Districts, and Local Government* (Washington, D.C.:

National Association of Counties Research Foundation, 1964), 13, 27, 31; Annette Baker Fox, "The Local Housing Authority and the Municipal Government," *Journal of Land and Public Utility Economics* 7, no. 3 (August 1941), 289.

27. Abrams, COHC, quote at 42; Charles Kettleborough, "Special Municipal Corporations," *American Political Science Review* 8, no. 4 (November 1914), 614; Smith, *Public Authorities*, 9–10; Leonard D. White, *Trends in Public Administration* (New York: McGraw-Hill, 1933), 171–175; E. H. Foley Jr., "Revenue Financing of Public Enterprises," *Michigan Law Review* 35, no. 1 (November 1936), 2–3; "Table 2: Laws Governing Establishment of Housing Authorities," in *Housing Officials' Yearbook, 1936*, ed. Coleman Woodbury (Chicago: National Association of Housing Officials, 1936), 222–225. For a sense of how uncertain the process of policymaking was on the national level, see Thomas H. Eliot, *Recollections of the New Deal: When the People Mattered* (Boston: Northeastern University Press, 1992).

28. Taper, "A Lover of Cities," II, 48; *Laws of 1934*, chap. 4, sec. 1.

29. Abrams, COHC, quotes at 33, 43; *Laws of 1934*, chap. 4, secs. 63, 64, 76. For subsequent changes made to the public authorities law, see *Laws of 1939*, chap. 808.

30. *Laws of 1934*, chap. 4, secs. 66, 72–74; E. H. Foley, Jr., "Legal Aspects of Low-Rent Housing in New York," *Fordham Law Review* 6, no. 1 (January 1937), 14–16. See also B. J. Hovde, "The Local Housing Authority," *Public Administration Review* 1, no. 2 (Winter 1941), 168.

31. *Laws of 1934*, chap. 4, sec. 70; Philip Nichols, Jr., "The Meaning of Public Use in the Law of Eminent Domain," *Boston University Law Review* 20, no. 4 (November 1940), 617.

32. Table 2, *Housing Officials Yearbook, 1936*, 222–225.

33. "Slum Clearance," *NYT*, December 19, 1933, quotes at 20; Lehman's quote from "Memorandum Filed with Senate Bill, Int. No. 249, Pr. No. 412," in *Laws of 1934*, chap. 4, Governor's Bill Jacket, January 31, 1934, not paginated; NYCHA, *Toward the End To Be Achieved: The New York City Housing Authority—Its History in Outline* (New York: NYCHA, 1937), 5–6.

4. Vision and Reality

1. John W. Kingdon, *Agendas, Alternatives, and Public Policies* (Boston: Little, Brown, 1984), 204.

2. For a general overview of Abrams' work at NYCHA, see Abrams to Robert L. Crawford, April 15, 1943, reel 1, AP.

3. "Mayor Names Five to Housing Board," 21; NYCHA, *Toward the End to be Achieved*, 6. See also NYCHA, *First Houses* (New York: NYCHA, 1935), 14;

Rebecca B. Rankin, ed., *New York Advancing: A Scientific Approach to Municipal Government* (New York: Municipal Reference Library, 1936), 195; NYCHA, *Twenty-Five Years of Public Housing, 1935–1960* (New York: NYCHA, 1960). For legal reasons, Abrams had to drop the title "counsel" and use "consultant" instead.

4. *Laws of 1934*, chap. 4, secs. 1, 61, 70.

5. Emphasis on slum clearance can be found in "Housing Leaders Defend City Plan," *NYT*, February 15, 1934, 21; Joseph Platzker, "Replanning Old Areas for New Housing," *Architectural Record* 75, no. 2 (February 1934), 103, 132; Harold L. Ickes, "The Place of Housing in National Rehabilitation," *Journal of Land and Public Utility Economics* 11, no. 2 (May 1935), 113; Harold L. Ickes, "The Federal Housing Program," *The New Republic*, December 19, 1934, 155. Vacant land advocates expressed their views in Catherine Bauer, "Slum Clearance or Housing," *The Nation*, December 27, 1933, 730–731; Henry Wright, *Rehousing Urban America* (New York: Columbia University Press, 1935), 6; Albert Mayer, "New Homes for a New Deal, I: Slum Clearance—But How?," *The New Republic*, February 14, 1934, 7–9; Henry Wright, "New Homes for a New Deal, II: Abolishing Slums Forever," ibid., February 21, 1934, 41–43; Lewis Mumford, "New Homes for a New Deal, III: The Shortage of Dwellings and Direction," ibid., February 28, 1934, 69–72; Albert Mayer, Henry Wright, and Lewis Mumford, "New Homes for a New Deal, IV: A Concrete Program," ibid., March 7, 1934, 91–94.

6. Abrams quoted in "Opposes Changes in Housing Rules," *NYT*, March 4, 1934, sec. 10–11, 1, 2.

7. Abrams, *Future of Housing*, quotes at 269, 314; "Opposes Changes in Housing Rules," 1. Peter Marcuse has argued that public housing in New York City was important because of its relative, not its absolute numbers (it accounted for 23 percent of all new units built between 1934–1941). Though this contention might be valid, public housing nonetheless remained limited in its ability to rehouse those living in slums or displaced by slum clearance. This situation was actually exacerbated by the Housing Act of 1937, which mandated the "elimination" of "unsafe or unsanitary dwellings . . . substantially equal in number" to the amount of new dwellings provided by a housing project (50 Stat. 888, quote at 892). In 1938, for example, 6,670 units were slated for construction in New York City, while 6,744 were targeted for demolition. See Peter Marcuse, "The Beginnings of Public Housing in New York," *Journal of Urban History* 12, no. 4 (August 1986), 354; United States Housing Authority, *Annual Report, 1938*, (Washington, D.C., 1938), 23, 25. For the legal aspects of "equivalent elimination," see John I. Robinson and Sophie Robinson, "Equivalent

Elimination Agreements in Public Housing Projects," *Boston University Law Review* 22, no. 3 (June 1942), 375–389.

8. Theda Skocpol, "Bringing the State Back In: Strategies of Analysis in Current Research," in *Bringing the State Back In*, 4, 7, 9; Edward D. Berkowitz, *America's Welfare State: From Roosevelt to Reagan* (Baltimore: Johns Hopkins University Press, 1991), xvii. Additional state-centered analyses include Hugh Heclo, *Modern Social Politics in Britain and Sweden: From Relief to Income Maintenance* (New Haven: Yale University Press, 1974); Stephen D. Krasner, *Defending the National Interest: Raw Materials Investments and U.S. Foreign Policy* (Princeton: Princeton University Press, 1978); Susan S. and Norman I. Fainstein, "National Policy and Urban Development," *Social Problems* 26, no. 2 (December 1978), 125–146; Martha Derthick, *Policymaking for Social Security* (Washington, D.C.: Brookings Institution, 1979); Katznelson and Pietrykowski, "Rebuilding the American State," 301–339. For articulations of the "classical model" of policy implementation, see Woodrow Wilson, "The Study of Administration," *Political Science Quarterly* 2, no. 2 (June 1887), 197–222; Luther Gulick and Lyndall Urwick, eds., *Papers on the Science of Administration* (New York: Institute of Public Administration, 1937). More recent theorizing on policy implementation can be found in Michael M. Lipsky, "Implementation on Its Head," in *American Politics and Public Policy*, eds. Walter D. Burnham and Martha W. Weinberg (Cambridge: MIT Press, 1978), 390–402; Robert T. Nakamura and Frank Smallwood, *The Politics of Policy Implementation* (New York: St. Martin's Press, 1980), 12–19.

9. Harold L. Ickes, *The Autobiography of a Curmudgeon* (1943; reprint, Chicago: Quadrangle Books, 1969), 283; T. H. Watkins, *Righteous Pilgrim: The Life and Times of Harold L. Ickes, 1874–1952* (New York: Henry Holt, 1990), 55–109.

10. "$25,000,000 Put Up for Housing Here," *NYT*, January 5, 1934, 3. NIRA's enabling legislation is located at 48 Stat. 195.

11. Harold L. Ickes, "Housing Corporation to Hasten Slum Clearance," *Architectural Record* 74, no. 6 (December 1933), 1; Harold L. Ickes, *Back to Work: The Story of PWA* (New York: Macmillan, 1935), 183; Cam, "United States Government Activity in Low-Cost Housing," 362; Eugene H. Klaber, "Limited Dividend Corporations Under the National Housing Act," *Architectural Record* 77, no. 2 (February 1935), 78; Radford, *Modern Housing for America*, 94; Robert Moore Fisher, *Twenty Years of Public Housing* (New York: Harper, 1959), 81–82.

12. 48 Stat. 195; Michael W. Straus and Talbot Wegg, *Housing Comes of Age* (New York: Oxford University Press, 1938), 124–125; "State Housing: American Style," *Fortune*, February 1934, 33; Ickes, "Housing Corporation to Hasten Slum Clearance," 1; Cam, "Government Activity in Low-Cost

Housing," 360. The PWA's early views are cited in *PWA Bulletin 5343*, as quoted in Abrams, *Future of Housing*, 252.

13. Ickes, "Housing Corporation to Hasten Slum Clearance," 1; Cam, "Government Activity in Low-Cost Housing," 360; Radford, *Modern Housing for America*, 99.

14. Abrams, *Future of Housing*, quote at 257; "The New Housing Board," *NYT*, February 15, 1934, quote at 18; "Opposes Changes in Housing Rules," Abrams quoted at 2. See also "Post Seeks Funds for Slum Removal," *NYT*, December 22, 1933, 39; "Post Visits Roosevelt," ibid., January 19, 1934, 22; "Housing Plan Ready Soon," ibid., March 9, 1934, 15; U.S. Senate, *Hearings Before the Committee on Education and Labor on S. 1685 (To Create a United States Housing Authority)*, 75th Cong., 1st sess., April 14, 1937, 21; "City Planning Merges Into National Planning," *American City* 48, no. 11 (November 1933), 65; Howard A. Gray, "The Housing Division's Third Year," in *Housing Officials' Yearbook, 1937*, ed. Coleman Woodbury (Chicago: National Association of Housing Officials, 1938), 3.

15. "Confidential Report of Washington Trip, March 7, 1934," quote at 1, box 0055D2, folder 4, New York City Housing Authority Records, LaGuardia and Wagner Archives, LaGuardia Community College (hereafter NYCHAR); Abrams, *Future of Housing*, quote at 252; "Wider Housing Aim Outlined by Post," *NYT*, March 20, 1934, quote at 25.

16. Straus and Wegg, *Housing Comes of Age*, 96; Post, *Challenge of Housing*, 235; "Brooklyn Picked for Model Housing," *NYT*, May 16, 1934, 21; Abrams, "The Significance and Importance of the Plan Proposed by the NYCHA for the Development and Construction of the Low Cost Housing Projects in NYC," July 19, 1934, 1, box 0053A2, folder 4, NYCHAR.

17. "PWA to Allot $25,000,000 on Slum Clearance Here," *NYT*, June 23, 1934, 1; "$25,000,000 for City Held Up by PWA," ibid., September 3, 1934, Ickes quoted at 1; Post, *Challenge of Housing*, quote at 177; Norbert Brown, "Confusion Attends the New York Housing Program," *Real Estate Record and Builder's Guide*, July 14, 1934, 4; Kessner, *Fiorello H. LaGuardia*, 325–326.

18. "$25,000,000 for City Held Up by PWA," 1; "Housing to Go Forward," *NYT*, September 4, 1934, 18; "Temporary Board on Housing Urged," ibid., September 7, 1934, 24; "Ickes and Mayor Agree on Housing," ibid., September 11, 1934, quote at 1; "Ickes Awaits Sites for Housing Here," ibid., September 21, 1934, 41; "Federal Housing Aid Is Held Temporarily," ibid., September 23, 1934, 38; "Agreement Hinted on Slum Work Here," ibid., October 12, 1934, 32; "PWA Takes Sites to End Slums Here," ibid., October 13, 1934, 6; Post, *Challenge of Housing*, 234; Harold Ickes to LaGuardia, September 7, 1934, reel 51, AP; LaGuardia to Ickes, September 18, 1934, reel 51, ibid.; Ickes to Post, October 1, 1934, reel 51, ibid.; "Washington

Conference of September 25 and 26, 1934," box 0053A4, folder 1, NYCHAR.

19. Post, *Challenge of Housing*, quote at 177; Abrams to Hamilton Rogers, April 30, 1935, reel 16, AP; Ickes to LaGuardia, May 14, 1935, reel 51, ibid.; "General Information on Proposed Assemblage in the Williamsburg Area of Brooklyn," not dated, reel 51, ibid.; NYCHA, *Toward the End to be Achieved*, 10–11; "City to Get $13,000,000 More," *NYT*, January 1, 1935, 4; "Government Sues for Housing Land," ibid., April 18, 1935, 11; "City Plan to Speed Slum Site Buying Accepted by Ickes," ibid., May 15, 1935, 1, 6; "New Housing Here Near Action Stage," ibid., May 31, 1935, 27; "Push Slum Projects Despite Court Ruling," ibid., July 17, 1935, 38; "$12,500,000 Housing Begun in Brooklyn by Ickes and Mayor," ibid., January 4, 1936, 1, 17; "Low Rents Sought on Projects Here," ibid., November 19, 1936, 18; New York State Board of Housing, *Report*, January 12, 1934, Leg. Doc. 41, 28; Arnold H. Diamond, "The New York City Housing Authority: A Study in Public Corporations" (Ph.D. diss., Columbia University, 1954), 8.

20. PWA, *Williamsburg Houses: A Case History of Housing* (Washington, D.C., 1937), 15, quote at 5; Post, *Challenge of Housing*, 177–178, 191–192; NYCHA, *Third Annual Report, December 1, 1935-November 30, 1936* (New York: NYCHA, 1936), 281, in unnumbered box labeled "Annual Reports," NYCHAR; NYCHA, *Fifth Annual Report, 1938* (New York: NYCHA, 1938), 11. See also Rosalie Genevro, "Site Selection and the New York City Housing Authority, 1934–1939," *Journal of Urban History* 12, no. 4 (August 1986), 344.

21. Post, *Challenge of Housing*, 235; NYCHA, *Fifth Annual Report, 1938*, quote at 24; Genevro, "Site Selection," 344.

22. *Laws of 1934*, chap. 4; Abrams, COHC, quote at 45; "Mayor is Stirred by Job Prospects," *NYT*, April 14, 1934, 5.

23. Abrams, COHC, quotes at 46, 47, and 48; NYCHA, *First Houses* (New York: NYCHA, 1935), quote at 19; NYCHA, *Report of the Secretary for the Period December 1-November 30, 1935*, unnumbered box labeled "Annual Reports," NYCHAR. See also, Taper, "A Lover of Cities," II, 76.

24. "Astor Would Sell Tenements to City," *NYT*, March 15, 1934, quotes at 3; "Tenement Owners Spur Slum Drive," ibid., March 16, 1934, 23; Abrams, COHC, 51–52.

25. Abrams, COHC, quote at 49; Post, *Challenge of Housing*, 181–182; "City Will Revamp Section of Slums," *NYT*, December 8, 1934, 17; NYCHA, *Toward the End to be Achieved*, 9; NYCHA, *First Houses*, 20–21.

26. NYCHA, *First Houses*, 20, 24–25; "City Will Revamp Section of Slums," 17; Marcuse, "Beginnings of Public Housing," 363; Abrams, COHC, 61. Ultimately, First Houses was composed of three renovated and five new

buildings. For a critical assessment of the project, see John F. St. George, "An Analysis of the City's 'Astor' Housing Project," *Real Estate Record and Builders' Guide*, May 4, 1935, 4–5.

27. Abrams, COHC, 62, 63; "Families Chosen for City Housing," *NYT*, October 28, 1935; NYCHA, *First Houses*, 29–31; Rankin, *New York Advancing*, 196; May Lumsden, "First Families," *Survey Graphic* 25, no. 2 (February 1936), 103–105; NYCHA, *Fifth Annual Report, 1938*, 24–25; U.S. Census Bureau, *Historical Statistics of the United States, Colonial Times to 1970* (Washington, D.C., 1975), 166, 167, 169. See also Maxwell H. Tretter, "Public Housing Finance," *Harvard Law Review* 54, no. 8 (June 1941), 1325–1355.

28. Straus and Wegg, *Housing Comes of Age*, 82–83; Mayer, "New Homes for a New Deal," 9; "PWA Pledges Action on Low-Cost Housing and Slum Clearance," *American City* 49, no. 9 (September 1934), 99; Ickes, *Back to Work*, 185. The *Louisville* decision is located at 9 F. Supp. 137. For discussions of the case and the issues it involved, see William Ebenstein, *The Law of Public Housing* (Madison: University of Wisconsin Press, 1940), 34, 36; Edward S. Corwin, "Constitutional Aspects of Federal Housing," *University of Pennsylvania Law Review* 84, no. 2 (December 1935), 131–156; Ira S. Robbins, "The Use of Eminent Domain for Housing Purposes," in *Housing Officials' Yearbook, 1936*, 116–127.

29. Post, *Challenge of Housing*, 183–184; Abrams, COHC, 52–56; New York State Board of Housing, *Report*, March 18, 1936, Leg. Doc. 41, 27–28.

30. Abrams, COHC, 52–56; "Post Hits Snag in Slum Project," *NYT*, February 22, 1935, 19; NYCHA, *Minutes*, February 27 and March 5, 1935, box 0078A7, folder 8, NYCHAR; NYCHA, *Minutes*, May 28, 1935, box 0078A2, folder 9, ibid. Abrams wrote briefs for the *Louisville* case when it was argued in the District and Federal Appeals Courts. The government lost both times, and had arranged to argue its appeal before the United States Supreme Court, but withdrew the case at the last moment. The Roosevelt administration apparently feared that a loss before the nation's highest tribunal might endanger other New Deal programs. See 78 F.(2d) 684; 294 U.S. 735; Alfred Bettman to Abrams and Ira S. Robbins, February 21, 1935, reel 16, AP; Abrams, COHC, 56–57; Harold L. Ickes, *The Secret Diary of Harold Ickes* (New York: Simon and Schuster, 1953), 1:530–531; New York State Board of Housing, *Report*, March 12, 1937, Leg. Doc. 41, 13.

31. Abrams' briefs for the lower and Appeals Court were virtually identical, and unless otherwise noted, quotes are from the latter. A copy of the lower court brief can be found in box 0055D2, folder 4, NYCHAR. For the Appeals court brief, see note 32 below. Muller's arguments can be found in "Appellants' Brief" for *New York City Housing Authority v. Muller* in *Cases and*

Points: New York Court of Appeals, 4636:14, 27, 29, 30, 39, 40, quote at 16, located in the New York State Supreme Court library in Buffalo, New York.

32. Abrams, "Amicus Curiae Brief," *New York City Housing Authority v. Muller* in *Cases and Points*, 4636:6–7, 51, quotes at 36–37 and 40. Even though the right of housing authorities to condemn land was the issue in question, New York City had been granted the power of "excess condemnation" prior to World War I; this allowed the city to condemn excess land around improvements for later sale or development. See Herbert Croly, "Civic Improvements: The Case of New York," *Architectural Record* 21, no. 5 (May 1907), 350–351; Lawson Purdy, "Subsidized Housing in New York," *National Municipal Review* 16, no. 11 (November 1927), 702.

33. Abrams, "Amicus Brief," 74–75. Abrams' quote comes from the Federal Appeals, not the District Court, decision in the *Louisville* case.

34. Abrams, "Amicus Brief," 60, quotes at 57, 58, 61, 63, and 66. See also Philip Nichols, *The Power of Eminent Domain*, 2d ed. (Boston: Boston Book Company, 1917); J. A. C. Grant, "The Higher Law Background of the Law of Eminent Domain," *Wisconsin Law Review* 6, no. 2 (February 1931), 67–85; Philip Nichols, Jr., "The Meaning of Public Use in the Law of Eminent Domain," *Boston University Law Review* 20, no. 4 (November 1940), 615–641; Myres S. McDougal and Addison A. Mueller, "Public Purpose in Public Housing: An Anachronism Reburied," *Yale Law Journal* 52, no. 1 (December 1942), 42–73.

35. Abrams, "Amicus Brief," 80.

36. "City Condemnation for Housing Upheld," *NYT*, April 13, 1935, 17; *New York City Housing Authority v. Muller* (1935), 155 Misc. 681, quote at 683; *New York City Housing Authority v. Muller* (1936), 270 N.Y. 333, quote at 342; Post, *Challenge of Housing*, 184; Edith Elmer Wood to Ira S. Robbins, April 19, 1935, box 91, folder 23, Edith Elmer Wood Papers, Avery Architectural and Fine Arts Archives, Columbia University.

37. NYCHA, *Toward the End to be Achieved*, 6–7. See also NYCHA, *Real Property Inventory: City of New York*, 5 vols. (New York: NYCHA, 1934).

38. "The High Cost of Slums," *Review of Reviews*, June 1934, 47; Post, *Challenge of Housing*, 31–32; "Blue Sky for All Is Slum Clearance Goal," *Literary Digest*, April 28, 1934, 19; "New York's War on Fire-Trap Tenements," ibid., March 24, 1934, 21; Abrams, COHC, 67; New York State Board of Housing, *Report*, April 5, 1933, Leg. Doc. 112, 29; "City Housing Law Arouses Protests," *NYT*, February 18, 1934, sec. 10–11, 22; "Post Will Order Firetraps Closed," ibid., February 24, 1934, 14; "Tenement Owners Defy Firetrap Law," ibid., March 5, 1934, 1, 5; "Drive on Firetraps Will Begin Today," ibid., March 20, 1934, 25; "10,000 Hear Mayor Say Unsafe Slums Will Be Wiped Out," ibid., April 9, 1934, 1, 12.

39. "Post Says Slum Plan Is To Break Values," *NYT*, January 24, 1935, quote at 20; "Safeguards Asked in Tenement Law," ibid., January 24, 1935, 38; "Hears Property Owners," ibid., January 25, 1935, 4; "Fight Moratorium on Tenement Laws," ibid., March 4, 1936, 6; "Slum Tenements by Hundreds Shut," ibid., July 22, 1936, 21; "Tenement Repairs Up Sharply in Year," ibid., September 8, 1936, 29; Abrams, COHC, 66–67; Post, *Challenge of Housing*, 150–151; *Laws of 1935*, chap. 866; *Laws of 1935*, chap. 904; *Laws of 1936*, chap. 271; Rankin, *New York Advancing*, 192.

40. Rankin, *New York Advancing*, 190–191; "Cheaper Tenements Being Boarded Up," *NYT*, December 9, 1936, 29; "LaGuardia Urges Action to Prevent Housing Shortage," ibid., December 16, 1936, 1, 2; Post, *Challenge of Housing*, 150–151; NYCHA, *Must We Have Slums?* (New York: NYCHA, 1937), 13–16; Joseph A. Spencer, "Tenant Organization and Housing Reform in New York City: The Citywide Tenants' Council, 1936–1943," in *Community Organization for Urban Social Change*, eds. Robert Fisher and Peter Romanofsky (Westport, Connecticut: Greenwood Press, 1981), 142–143. See also Catherine Bauer, "We Face a Housing Shortage," in *Housing Officials' Yearbook, 1937*, 62.

41. NYCHA, *Report to His Honor Fiorello H. LaGuardia, Mayor of the City of New York, by the New York City Housing Authority, Pursuant to Article Five of the State Housing Law, on Its Investigation and Public Hearings on Living and Housing Conditions in the City of New York*, January 25, 1937, Leg. Doc. 85, 44–58, quote at 53; Post to LaGuardia, December 31, 1935, box 0055D3, folder 20, NYCHAR; Abrams, "Memorandum of Law on Proposed Emergency Rent Laws," March 25, 1937, quote at 15, box 0058C8, folder 2, ibid.; "LaGuardia Urges Action to Prevent Housing Shortage," 2; Mrs. Samuel I. Rosenman to Abrams, March 19, 1937, folder 119, United Neighborhood Houses Papers, Social Welfare History Archives, University of Minnesota; Stanley Isaacs to Abrams, March 19, 1937, folder 119, ibid.; "Housing Meeting Today," *NYT*, December 17, 1936, 25; "2,000,000 in Slums Face Housing Crisis," ibid., December 18, 1936, 21; "Remodeling Urged as Best Slum Plan," ibid., December 22, 1936, 5; "Court Stay of Evictions Possible as Housing Board Drafts Actions for Today," ibid., December 31, 1936, 1; "City Seeking To Avert Shortage of Housing," ibid., January 3, 1937, sec. 4, 10; "Emergency Steps on Housing Asked," ibid., February 17, 1937, 23; "Citizens Organize To Aid Slum Fight," ibid., February 27, 1937, 23.

42. Post, *Challenge of Housing*, 152; Spencer, "Tenant Organization," 138; "LaGuardia Urges Action to Prevent Housing Shortage," 1. The legislature eventually passed a six-month exemption from criminal liability and penalties for tenement owners who agreed to comply with code requirements or

vacate their buildings. The legislature also passed a bill declaring the condition of old law tenements an "emergency," which permitted appropriate municipal departments to make repairs/renovations if tenement owners did not comply within twenty-one days. After that point, municipalities could place liens on noncomplying properties to pay for renovations. "Mayor's Slum Bill is Sent to Albany," *NYT*, February 23, 1937, 2; *Laws of 1937*, chaps. 1 and 353.

43. Kessner, *Fiorello H. LaGuardia*, 430; Abrams, COHC, 74; "10-Year Program of Housing Urged," *NYT*, October 21, 1937, 19; Ickes' quotes from Harold L. Ickes, *The Secret Diary of Harold L. Ickes* (New York: Simon and Schuster, 1954), 2:218; Rodwin, interview, 13; Roger Biles, "Nathan Straus and the Failure of U.S. Public Housing, 1937–1942," *The Historian* 53, no. 1 (Autumn 1990), 37–44.

The Housing Act of 1937 established the Federal Housing Authority, which replaced Ickes' Housing Division. Abrams was among a small group of advisers who met with Senator Robert F. Wagner (D-NY) to help craft the bill. After its passage, Abrams wrote a pamphlet entitled *Housing and the Law*, which explained the law's major provisions. The act is located at 50 Stat. 888. See William V. Reed and Elizabeth Ogg, *New Homes for Old: Public Housing in Europe and America* (New York: Foreign Policy Association, 1940), 105; "Mss. minutes of meeting, March 25, 1936," box 6, Warren J. Vinton Papers, Cornell University Archives; "Mss. account of Wagner Bill meeting, February 18, 1937," "Notes on Treasury negotiations," "Notes by Charles Abrams, May 21, 1937," and "Memorandum by American Federation of Housing Authorities," all in box 5, ibid.; McDonnell, *Wagner Housing Act*, 158, 267, 284; NYCHA to Abrams, November 23, 1937, reel 16, AP. See also Abrams to Herbert H. Lehman, October 18, 1938, reel 6, ibid.

44. Kessner, *Fiorello H. LaGuardia*, 411–414, 419; Rodwin, interview, 12–13; LaGuardia quoted in "City Housing Body and Mayor Clash," *NYT*, November 24, 1937, 5.

45. "Mayor's Statement," November 23, 1937, reel 513, Fiorello H. LaGuardia Papers, LaGuardia and Wagner Archives, LaGuardia Community College; LaGuardia to Helen Alfred, November 22, 1937, reel 141, ibid.; Abrams, Letter of Resignation, November 22, 1937, box 0058L8, folder 2, NYCHAR (also printed in "Housing Counsel Quits in Protest," *NYT*, November 23, 1937, 7). The American Federation of Housing Authorities was set up by Post, with Abrams as general counsel, to push for legislation to decentralize public housing and to augment the role of housing authorities. Its single most important activity was helping pass the Housing Act of 1937. See Abrams, COHC, 76; Abrams, *Future of Housing*, 257.

46. LaGuardia quote from "City Housing Body and Mayor Clash," 5;

"House Counsel Quits in Protest," 7; NYCHA to Abrams, November 23, 1937, reel 16, AP; "Concerning Housing," *NYT*, November 24, 1937, 22.

47. Post's quotes from Post, *Challenge of Housing*, 261 and Post, "My Clash with LaGuardia," *The Nation*, January 29, 1938, 126; Hays' quote from Arthur Garfield Hays to Herbert Lehman, December 5, 1937, reel 16, AP; Abrams, COHC, 77; "Post Defies Mayor; Quits Housing Body," *NYT*, December 2, 1937, 1, 10; "Mayor Forces Post Off Housing Board," ibid., December 3, 1937, 1, 8; "The Housing Squabble," ibid., December 4, 1937, 16; "Delay on Housing Charged to Mayor," ibid., December 20, 1937, 1, 2; "Evans Clark Quits Housing Body," ibid., December 21, 1937, 8; "Mayor Supported by Housing Group," ibid., December 23, 1937, 2; LaGuardia to Post, December 1, 1937, reel 163, LaGuardia Papers; Evans Clark to LaGuardia, December 1, 1937, reel 513, ibid.; Post to LaGuardia, December 1, 1937, reel 513, ibid.; Post to LaGuardia, December 2, 1937, reel 163, ibid.; Abrams to Alfred Rheinstein, January 10, 1938, reel 16, AP; Abrams to LaGuardia, January 13, 1938, reel 16, ibid.; Abrams to Post, January 18, 1938, reel 7, ibid. Abrams sent two additional letters criticizing LaGuardia's actions to the *New York Times* that were never published. See "Letter to the Editor," December 17, 1937, reel 26, AP and "Municipal Housing Authorities: The Latest Phase," January 1, 1938, reel 26, ibid. LaGuardia attempted to run New York City's Planning Commission in a fashion similar to the way he handled NYCHA. See Mark I. Gelfand, "Rexford G. Tugwell and the Frustration of Planning in New York City," *American Planning Association Journal* 51, no. 2 (Spring 1985), 151–160.

48. Fairbanks, *Making Better Citizens*, 88–90; Bauman, *Public Housing, Race, and Renewal*, 27, 29, 37, 39, 44; Henderson, "Local Deals," chap. 3; John H. Mollenkopf, *The Contested City* (Princeton: Princeton University Press, 1983), chap. 1.

49. Post, *Challenge of Housing*, 202; Abrams, *Future of Housing*, 251–252, 255, 256–258.

50. Maxwell H. Tretter, "Legal Foundations of Housing in New York: The Constitution and the Occupancy Tax Plan," *New York University Law Quarterly Review* 16, no. 1 (November 1938), 90; Annette Baker Fox, "The Local Housing Authority and the Municipal Government," *Journal of Land and Public Utility Economics* 7, no. 3 (August 1941), 281; Abrams' quote is from Abrams to Herbert H. Lehman, May 15, 1939, reel 11, AP. See also Abrams, untitled speech, Conference of Local Housing Authorities of Pennsylvania, June 17, 1938, reel 26, AP; Abrams, "Looking Ahead in Housing," *Shelter* 3, no. 3 (October 1938), 23–24. For a discussion of how state agencies and policymakers can be "insulated" from societal pressures, see Krasner, *Defending the National Interest*, 11. Conversely, Brian Balogh's work on nuclear power

regulation has concluded that policymakers are often less insulated than some state-centered analyses have suggested. See Balogh, *Chain Reaction*, 312.

51. Abrams lamented in early 1938 that "housing had not been developed into a movement," though he felt that increasing the number of housing courses taught at universities might help. Abrams to Josephine Gomon, January 12, 1938, reel 3, AP.

5. The Practitioner as Scholar

1. "Society League Starts a Revolt," *NYT*, February 17, 1919, 1, 3; "History Professor Quits Columbia," ibid., May 6, 1919, 10; "Research School to Open," ibid., September 30, 1919, 20; Richard Hofstadter, *The Progressive Historians: Turner, Beard, Parrington* (New York: Random House, 1968), 72, 174–178, 285–288; Charles Beard, "A Statement," *New Republic*, December 29, 1917, 249–251; James Harvey Robinson, *The New History: Essays Illustrating the Modern Historical Outlook* (New York: Macmillan, 1912), 24; Peter M. Rutkoff and William B. Scott, *New School: A History of the New School for Social Research* (New York: Free Press, 1986), xii, 8, 9, 26, 36, 37, 47, 66, 78–79; Miller, *Lewis Mumford*, 171–172; Frank G. Novak, Jr., ed., *Lewis Mumford and Patrick Geddes: The Correspondence* (New York: Routledge, 1995), 12, 49, 53, 93, 96, 98, 149, 158, 183; Bloom, *Prodigal Sons*, 34.

2. Rutkoff and Scott, *New School*, quote at 38; Claus-Dieter Krohn, *Intellectuals in Exile: Refugee Scholars and the New School for Social Research*, trans. Rita and Robert Kimber (Amherst: University of Massachusetts Press, 1993), 39, 52, 54, 111.

3. Abrams to Josephine Gomon, April 1, 1939, reel 3, AP; Abrams, "Lecture Notes, Fall 1939," New School for Social Research, reel 16, ibid.

4. Benjamin G. Rader, *The Academic Mind and Reform: The Influence of Richard T. Ely in American Life* (Lexington, Kentucky: University of Kentucky Press, 1966), 28–38; Richard T. Ely, *Ground Under Our Feet* (New York: Macmillan, 1938), 179, 192; Richard T. Ely and George S. Wehrwein, *Land Economics* (1940; reprint, Madison: University of Wisconsin Press, 1964), vii; Leonard A. Salter, Jr., *A Critical Review of Research in Land Economics*, rev. ed. (Madison: University of Wisconsin Press, 1967), 22, 23; Barton J. Bledstein, *The Culture of Professionalism: The Middle Class and the Development of Higher Education in America* (New York: Norton, 1978), 328–329; Richard T. Ely, "Research in Land and Public Utility Economics," *Journal of Land and Public Utility Economics* 1, no. 1 (January 1925), 6; Marc A. Weiss, "Richard T. Ely and the Contribution of Economic Research to National Housing Policy, 1920–1940," *Urban Studies* 26, no. 1 (February 1989), 116, 117.

5. Frederick J. Adams and Gerald Hodge, "City Planning Instruction in the United States: The Pioneering Days, 1900–1930," *Journal of the American Institute of Planners* 31, no. 1 (February 1965), 43–51; M. Christine Boyer, *Dreaming the Rational City: The Myth of American City Planning* (Cambridge: MIT Press, 1983), 229; Mel Scott, *American City Planning Since 1890* (Berkeley and Los Angeles: University of California Press, 1969), 163; Arnold Whittick, ed., *Encyclopedia of Urban Planning* (New York: McGraw-Hill, 1974), 1108.

6. New School for Social Research, *Course Catalogue*, Spring 1939, no page numbers given, reel 52, AP; Abrams, "Lecture Notes"; Abrams to Edith Elmer Wood, September 21, 1936, Wood to Abrams, September 24, 1936, and Abrams to Wood, September 25, 1936, all in box 58, folder A, Edith Elmer Wood Papers; "Lists Five Courses on Housing Topics," *NYT*, August 27, 1939, sec. 11, 1.

7. Hans B. C. Spiegel, letter to author, April 21, 1998; Lois Dean, letter to author, April 15, 1998; Walter Thabit, letter to author, May 19, 1998; unsigned letter (probably from Abrams' secretary) to Abrams, February 5, 1954, reel 30, AP.

8. Quote from Abrams to Robert L. Crawford, April 15, 1943, reel 1, AP; Abrams to Josephine Gomon, January 12, 1938, reel 3, ibid.; "Course Announcement," 1951, New School for Social Research, reel 15, ibid.

9. O. H. Koenigsberger, S. Groak, and B. Bernstein, eds., *The Work of Charles Abrams: Housing and Urban Renewal in the USA and the Third World* (New York: Pergamon Press, 1980), 21, 22, 29, 41, quote at 36; Abrams to Social Science Research Council, not dated, reel 8, ibid.; Abrams, "Lecture Notes"; Taper, "A Lover of Cities," I, 76; Rutkoff and Scott, *New School*, 81–82.

10. Koenigsberger, Groak, and Bernstein, *The Work of Charles Abrams*, 22.

11. Abrams to Mrs. Albert A. List, March 8, 1963, reel 15, AP; Alvin Johnson to Abrams, April 19, 1963, box 1, folder 3, Alvin Saunders Johnson Papers, Manuscripts and Archives, Yale University Library.

12. Abrams quoted in Taper, "A Lover of Cities," II, 41; "Charles Abrams," *National Cyclopedia of American Biography*, 56:109; Abrams' comment about MIT from Abrams to Lloyd Rodwin, March 23, 1945, reel 7, AP.

13. Abrams to Lloyd Rodwin, March 23, 1945, reel 7, AP; Rodwin to Abrams, November 15, 1965, reel 7, ibid.; Louis Sert to Abrams, May 28, 1968, reel 12, ibid.; Abrams to Louis Sert, June 26, 1968, reel 12, ibid.; Louis Sert to Abrams, June 28, 1968, reel 12, ibid.; Abrams, "City College Final Exam," May 23, 1949, reel 11, ibid.; Abrams to Blanche Ittleson, December 22, 1965, reel 11, ibid.; Taper, "A Lover of Cities," II, 112, 115.

14. Abrams, *Revolution in Land* (New York: Harper, 1939), xiii; Abrams to

Robert L. Crawford, April 15, 1943, reel 1, AP. See also Taper, "A Lover of Cities," II, 90.

15. C. E. Lively, untitled review of *Revolution in Land*, by Charles Abrams, *Rural Sociology* 6, no. 1 (March 1941), quote at 76; Abrams, *Revolution in Land*, 3, 5, 19, 20, quotes at 13.

16. Abrams, *Revolution in Land*, quotes at 6, 21, and 27. For a discussion of Depression-era debates over monopolies, see Ellis W. Hawley, *The New Deal and the Problem of Monopoly* (Princeton: Princeton University Press, 1966).

17. Abrams, *Revolution in Land*, 78, quotes at 6, 25, and 80.

18. Ibid., 87–90, quote at 87.

19. Maurice Stein, *The Eclipse of Community: An Interpretation of American Studies*, 2d ed. (Princeton: Princeton University Press, 1972), 45, 46.

20. Abrams, *Revolution in Land*, quote at 7–8; Adolf A. Berle, Jr. and Gardiner C. Means, *The Modern Corporation and Private Property* (New York: Macmillan, 1932), 1, quotes at 349 and 357.

21. Abrams, *Revolution in Land*, 38, 47, 51–53, quotes at 73.

22. Ibid., 73, 76, quotes at 77.

23. Henry George, *Progress and Poverty* (New York: D. Appleton & Company, 1882), 3, 11, 148–149, 295–304, 362–366, 490, 495–496.

24. Abrams, *Revolution in Land*, 118–119, quotes at 197.

25. Ibid., 118, 121, quotes at 119 and 125.

26. Ibid., quotes at 119, 120, 127, and 128.

27. Carol Aronovici, *Housing the Masses* (New York: Wiley, 1939), quote at xii; Catherine Bauer, *Modern Housing* (Boston: Houghton Mifflin, 1934), quote at 122.

28. Abrams, *Revolution in Land*, 233, quotes at 28, 246, and 263.

29. Ibid., 93, 294–295, 298, quotes at 287 and 289. For Lewis Mumford's views on regionalism, see his articles, "Regionalism and Irregionalism," *Sociological Review* 19, no. 4 (October 1927), 277–288, "The Theory and Practice of Regionalism (I)," ibid. 20, no. 1 (January 1928), 18–33, and "The Theory and Practice of Regionalism (II)," ibid. 20, no. 2 (April 1928), 131–141. The evolution of Abrams' approach to regional planning can be found in the following items written by him: "Regional Planning in Under-Developed Areas," UN Housing Seminar, Tokyo, Japan, July 1958, reel 31, AP, "City Planning, Master Planning, and Regional Planning," March 25, 1963, reel 32, ibid., "Regional Planning Legislation in Underdeveloped Areas," *Land Economics* 35, no. 2 (May 1959), 85–103, and "Regional Planning in an Urbanizing World," *Ekistics* 18, no. 107 (October 1964), 243–248.

30. Abrams, *Revolution in Land*, 282, 284, 285, 295, quotes at 228.

31. Ibid., quotes at 303 and 307. For organized labor's positions during the New Deal, see Steve Fraser, "The 'Labor Question,' " in *The Rise and Fall of the New Deal Order, 1930–1980*, eds. Steve Fraser and Gary Gerstle (Princeton: Princeton University Press, 1989), 55–84.

32. For the views of Leon Henderson and Thurmond Arnold, see Hawley, *New Deal*, 421–424.

33. Abrams, *Revolution in Land*, xiii; Lewis Mumford, *The Culture of Cities* (New York: Harcourt, Brace, 1938), quote at 9.

34. Abrams to Perry Prentice, October 20, 1960, reel 7, AP.

35. See the following reviews of *Revolution*: Bertram M. Cross, "Without Architect or Plan," *The Nation*, January 27, 1940, quote at 103; Karl Brandt (untitled), *Annals of the American Academy of Political and Social Science* 208 (March 1940), quote at 236; B. H. Hibbard (untitled), *Journal of Political Economy* 49, no. 6 (December 1941), 909–912; Joseph Milner, "Which Way Land Planning," *Survey Graphic* 28, no. 12 (December 1939), quote at 760; Leo Grebler (untitled), *Social Research* 7, no. 5 (September 1940), quote at 380. For Abrams' reaction to these reviews, see Bernard Taper, "A Lover of Cities," II, 90; Koenigsberger, Groak, and Bernstein, *The Work of Charles Abrams*, 36.

6. Federal Housing Policies

1. Abrams to Lloyd Rodwin, May 27, 1943, reel 7, AP; John B. Marsh to Abrams, June 22, 1943, reel 1, ibid.; Abrams to Josephine Gomon, July 23, 1942, reel 4, ibid. See also Abrams to Mary H. Fairbanks, January 15, 1942, reel 1, AP; Mary H. Fairbanks to Abrams, September 5, 1942, reel 1, ibid.; Mary H. Fairbanks to Abrams, September 24, 1942, reel 1, ibid.; Francis L. Blewer to Abrams, April 3, 1943, reel 1, ibid.; Abrams to Robert Wagner, April 14, 1943, reel 1, ibid.; Warren J. Vinton to Abrams, April 14, 1943, reel 1, ibid.; Abrams to Bernard Botein, April 15, 1943, reel 1, ibid.; Abrams to Lee Johnson, April 22, 1943, reel 1, ibid.; Warren J. Vinton to Abrams, April 23, 1943, reel 1, ibid.; Abrams to Lee Johnson, April 24, 1943, reel 1, ibid.; Abrams to Lewis Lorwin, April 28, 1943, reel 1, ibid.

Parts of this chapter originally appeared in "Charles Abrams and the Problem of a Business Welfare State," *Journal of Policy History* 9, no. 2 (Summer 1997), 211–239. Copyright 1997 by The Pennsylvania State University. Reproduced by permission of The Pennsylvania State University Press.

2. Abrams, untitled radio address, WEVD, New York, May 13, 1937, 5, reel 26, AP.

3. Abrams, *Future of Housing*, 16. Other housing studies that appeared

during this period were Clarence Arthur Perry, *Housing for the Machine Age* (New York: Russell Sage Foundation, 1939); Miles Colean, *American Housing: Problems and Prospects* (New York: Twentieth Century Fund, 1944); Nathan Straus, *The Seven Myths of Housing* (New York: Knopf, 1944); Henry Churchill, *The City is the People* (New York: Reynal & Hitchcock, 1945); Dorothy Rosenman, *A Million Homes a Year* (New York: Harcourt, 1945).

4. Hoover, "Press Statement," July 22, 1932, in *The State Papers and Other Public Writings of Herbert Hoover*, ed. William Starr Myers (Garden City, New York: Doubleday, 1934), 2:238–240; U.S. Congress, *Hearings Before the Temporary National Economic Committee*, 76th Cong., 1st sess., pt. 11, July 14, 1939, 5380 (hereafter *TNEC Hearings*). The Federal Home Loan Bank Act is located at 47 Stat. 725. Additional information on the FHLBS can be found in U.S. House, *Creation of Not Less Than 8 and Not More Than 12 Federal Home Loan Banks*, 72d Cong., 1st sess., May 25, 1932, H. Rept. 1418, 3–18. See also E. S. Wallace, "Survey of Federal Legislation Affecting Private Home Financing Since 1932," *Law and Contemporary Problems* 5, no. 4 (Autumn 1938), 483–489; Miles Colean, *The Impact of Government on Real Estate Finance in the United States* (New York: National Bureau of Economic Research, 1950), 91–93; R. J. Saulnier, Harold G. Halcrow, and Neil H. Jacoby, *Federal Lending and Loan Insurance* (Princeton: Princeton University Press, 1958), 293–297; Albert U. Romasco, *The Poverty of Abundance: Hoover, the Nation, the Depression* (New York: Oxford University Press, 1965), 191; William J. Barber, *From New Era to New Deal: Herbert Hoover, the Economists, and American Economic Policy, 1921–1933* (New York: Cambridge University Press, 1985), 179. For a discussion of the general principles of the Federal Reserve System, see Robert Craig West, *Banking Reform and the Federal Reserve, 1863–1923* (Ithaca: Cornell University Press, 1977), chap. 9.

5. Abrams, *Future of Housing*, quote at 240; FHLBB, *Second Annual Report, from creation to December 31, 1934* (Washington, D.C., 1935), 115; TNEC, *Monograph No. 8: Toward More Housing* (Washington, D.C., 1940), 82; *TNEC Hearings*, pt. 11, July 6, 1939, 5085 and July 14, 1939, Fahey's quote at 5383. See also Thomas B. Marvell, *The Federal Home Loan Bank Board* (New York: Praeger, 1969), 27, 29. Chartering of federal savings and loans was authorized by the Home Owners Loan Act in 1933. The funds appropriated to "incite" communities to organize saving and loans ($150,000) had been a point of Congressional debate, with some Representatives fearful they would be used to disseminate misleading government "propaganda." See *Congressional Record—House*, 73d Cong., 1st sess., April 28, 1933, 2579–2581.

6. Abrams, *Future of Housing*, 241–242, quote at 243; TNEC, *Monograph No. 8*, 82. Interest rate calculations are given in Rosenman, *A Million Homes a Year*, 11.

7. Abrams, *Future of Housing*, quote at 242; *Congressional Record—Senate*, 72d Cong., 1st sess., July 6, 1932, Couzens' quote at 14664; *TNEC Hearings*, pt. 11, July 14, 1939, 5397, Fahey's quote at 5398. By 1936, the twelve Home Loan Banks were "operating at a substantial profit." See John H. Fahey, "The Federal Home Loan Bank Board," in *Housing Officials' Yearbook, 1937*, 14. To become a member of the FHLBS, a thrift initially had to purchase only $1,500 of the capital stock of the Home Loan Bank in its region. This was eventually lowered to $500. See FHLBB, *Second Annual Report*, 1.

8. Abrams, *Future of Housing*, 242; *TNEC Hearings*, pt. 11, July 14, 1939, Fahey's quote at 5395; John H. Fahey, "Competition and Mortgage Rates," *Journal of Land & Public Utility Economics* 15, no. 2 (May 1939), quote at 152; Morton Bodfish, "Toward an Understanding of the Federal Home Loan Bank System," ibid. 15, no. 4 (November 1939), quote at 424; FHLBB, *Tenth Annual Report, 1942* (Washington, D.C., 1943), 16; Ray B. Westerfield, "An Analysis of F.H.L.B. Lending Policies," *Bankers Monthly* 56, no. 7 (July 1939), 387; Marvel, *Federal Home Loan Bank Board*, 23. Building and loans had long argued that they needed to charge from 3 to 4.5 percent on mortgage loans, yet in 1931 actual interest rates were 8 percent. By 1936, federal savings and loans had lowered their rate to 6.3 percent, but much of the mortgage risk (calculated at .5 to 1 percent) had been absorbed by the federal government through FHA insurance. See TNEC, *Monograph No. 8*, 82–83. The public character of the FHLBS was clear by 1936, when over $124 million (82 percent) of its capitalization came from the U.S. Treasury. In 1946 the federal government still held more than half of the FHLBS's assets. See FHLBB, *Fourth Annual Report, 1936* (Washington, D.C., 1937), 15; Ray B. Westerfield, *Money, Credit, and Banking* (New York: Ronald Press, 1947), 1059–1060.

9. Abrams, *Future of Housing*, 242–244.

10. For another instance where Abrams felt that relatively large firms/corporations were not necessarily a liability, see Abrams, "Homeless America: Illusions About Housing," *The Nation*, December 21, 1946, 725.

11. Abrams, *Future of Housing*, 248, quote at 247; U.S. Senate, *Hearings Before the Subcommittee on Housing and Urban Redevelopment of the Special Committee on Post-War Economic Policy and Planning*, 79th Cong., 1st sess., January 10, 1945, 1413; *TNEC Hearings*, pt. 11, July 14, 1939, 5382; "Commissioner Fahey on Inflationary Lending," *Federal Home Loan Bank Review* 9, no. 3 (December 1943), 61; Fahey, "The Federal Home Loan Bank Board," 13; FHLBB, *Ninth Annual Report, 1941* (Washington, D.C., 1941), 24; FHLBB, *Tenth Annual Report*, 2; Marvell, *Federal Home Loan Bank Board*, 23; John H. Fahey, "The Federal Home Loan Bank Administration, 1942," in *Housing Yearbook, 1943*, ed. Coleman Woodbury (Chicago: National

Association of Housing Officials, 1943), 64. The inability of federal housing policies to insure economic stability is discussed in Leo Grebler, "Stabilizing Residential Construction—A Review of the Post-War Test," *American Economic Review* 39, no. 5 (September 1949), 898–910; U.S. Congress, *Hearings Before the Joint Committee on the Economic Report (Anti-Inflation Program as Recommended in the President's Message of November 17, 1947)*, 80th Cong., 1st sess., November 25, 1947, 166–168.

12. *TNEC Hearings*, pt. 11, July 14, 1939, 5386, Fahey's quote at 5382; *Congressional Record—House*, 73d Cong., 1st sess., April 27, 1933, 2506; Roosevelt, "A Message Asking for Legislation to Save Small Home Mortgages from Foreclosure," April 13, 1933 and "The Home Owners Loan Act is Signed," June 13, 1933, in *The Public Papers and Addresses of Franklin D. Roosevelt*, ed. Samuel I. Rosenman (New York: Random House, 1938), 2:233–237, quote at 135; Miles L. Colean, *A Backward Glance: An Oral History* (Washington, D.C.: Mortgage Bankers Association of America, 1975), 22.

13. U.S. Senate, *The Home Owners' Loan Corporation*, 73d Cong., 1st sess., June 6, 1933, S. Doc. 74, 1–3; U.S. House, *Loans to Home Owners*, 73d Cong., 1st sess., April 25, 1933, H. Rept. 55, 1–2; TNEC, *Monograph No. 8*, 84–85; Marvel, *Home Loan Bank Board*, 24. The Home Owners' Loan Act of 1933 is located at 48 Stat. 128. See also C. Lowell Harriss, *History and Policies of the Home Owners' Loan Corporation* (New York: National Bureau of Economic Research, 1951), 1; Paul F. Wendt, *Housing Policy: The Search for Solutions* (Berkeley and Los Angeles: University of California Press, 1962), 149–150; Nathaniel S. Keith, *Politics and the Housing Crisis Since 1930s* (New York: Universe Books, 1973), 24–25; James S. Olson, *Saving Capitalism: The Reconstruction Finance Corporation and the New Deal, 1933–1940* (Princeton: Princeton University Press, 1988), 45, 95.

14. "Note" appended to Roosevelt, "The Home Owners Loan Act is Signed," 234–235, quote at 236; Jackson, *Crabgrass Frontier*, quote at 196; Marc A. Weiss, "Marketing and Financing Home Ownership: Mortgage Lending and Public Policy in the United States, 1918–1989," *Business and Economic History*, 2d ser., 18 (1989), 115. See also Kenneth Jackson, "Race, Ethnicity, and Real Estate Appraisal: The Home Owners Loan Corporation and the Federal Housing Administration," *Journal of Urban History* 6, no. 4 (August 1980), 419–452.

15. 48 Stat. 128, quote at 131; FHLBB, *Sixth Annual Report, 1938* (Washington, D.C., 1938), 70; Abrams, unpublished article for *Life* magazine, July 16, 1958, reel 31, AP; Abrams, *Future of Housing*, 245; Harriss, *History and Policies of the Home Owners' Loan Corporation*, 50. Congress did grant a three-year moratorium on payments of mortgage principal, but dropped this option less than a year after the HOLC was established. A

review of state mortgage moratoria can be found in J. Douglass Poteat, "State Legislative Relief for the Mortgage Debtor During the Depression," *Law and Contemporary Problems* 5, no. 4 (Autumn 1938), 517–544.

16. *Congressional Record—House*, 73d Cong., 1st sess., April 27, 1933, Cochran's quote at 2483; *Congressional Record—Senate*, 73d Cong., 1st sess., June 5, 1933, Trammel's quote at 4984; Abrams, *Future of Housing*, 246; Westerfield, *Money, Credit, and Banking*, 1068. Others who publicly supported direct loan provisions included Representatives Ralph Lozier (D-MO), John MacCormack (D-MA), Andrew May (D-KY), Marion Zioncheck (D-WA), and Senators Sam Bratton (D-NM) and Lynn Frazier (R-ND). See *Congressional Record—House*, 73d Cong., 1st sess., April 27, 1933, 2504–2505 and April 26, 1933, 2570; *Congressional Record—Senate*, 73d Cong., 1st sess., June 5, 1933, 4975, 4981.

17. Abrams, *Future of Housing*, 246. To combat the frequent fluctuations in mortgage markets, efforts were underway in the 1930s to improve appraisal methods. These reforms emphasized risk potential and a borrower's income, rather than temporary economic conditions (like real estate booms) as determining factors in the long-range value of housing and mortgages. The growing sophistication of appraisal practices can be traced by comparing pages 114–132 in Ernest Fisher, *Principles of Real Estate Practice* (New York: Macmillan, 1923) to pages 129–156 in Frederick M. Babcock, *The Valuation of Real Estate* (New York: McGraw-Hill, 1932). The influence of the HOLC's appraisal policies on the FHA can be seen in FHA, *Underwriting Manual* (Washington, D.C., 1938), secs. 6, 8, 9. See also Frederick M. Babcock, "Influence of the Federal Housing Administration on Mortgage Lending Policy," *Journal of Land & Public Utility Economics* 15, no. 1 (February 1939), 1–5; Marc Weiss, "Richard T. Ely and the Contribution of Economic Research to National Housing Policy, 1920–1940," *Urban Studies* 26, no. 1 (February 1989), 122–123. Abrams remained skeptical that real estate appraisal could ever become an exact science. The term " 'value,' " he argued, had become "a concept increasingly divorced from reality." See Abrams, *Future of Housing*, 394–395.

18. Roosevelt, "The Home Owners Loan Act is Signed," quote at 233; Abrams, *Future of Housing*, 246. *TNEC Hearings*, pt. 11, June 29, 1939, 5044 and July 14, 1939, 5404; FHLBB, *Sixth Annual Report*, 70. Initial data on HOLC operations confirm that adjustments represented mortgage debt relief of only 6.4 percent. The average purchase price of HOLC mortgages was $3,027, while average indebtedness before refinancing was $3,233. See Fahey, "The Federal Home Loan Bank Board," 11.

19. M. Ada Beney, *Wages, Hours, and Employment in the United States, 1914–1936* (New York: National Industrial Conference Board, 1936),

28–33; Weiss, "Marketing and Financing Home Ownership," 115; Abrams, *Future of Housing*, 246.

20. Abrams, *Future of Housing*, 246–247, quote at 248; Colean, *A Backward Glance*, 23; Ernest M. Fisher, "Speculation in Suburban Lands," *American Economic Review* 23, no. 1 (March 1933), 161; Herbert D. Simpson, "Real Estate Speculation and the Depression," ibid., 163–167. For an early discussion of periodicity in real estate fluctuations, see Lewis A. Maverick, "Cycles in Real Estate Activity," *Journal of Land & Public Utility Economics* 8, no. 2 (May 1932), 191–199.

21. Abrams to Dorothy Rosenman, October 18, 1944, reel 14, AP.

22. Abrams, *Future of Housing*, chap. 17; Roosevelt, "Recommendation for Legislation to Provide Assistance for Repairing and Construction of Homes," May 14, 1934, in *Public Papers*, 3:232; Mariner Eccles, *Beckoning Frontiers: Public and Personal Recollections* (New York: Knopf, 1951), 148; Colean, *A Backward Glance*, 37. The National Housing Act of 1934 is located at 48 Stat. 1246. For Congressional acknowledgment that the bill was essentially an attempt to revive the building trades, see U.S. House, *Hearings Before the Committee on Banking and Currency on H.R. 9620 (National Housing Act)*, 73d Cong., 2d sess., May 18, 1934, 11 and May 28, 1934, 137 (hereafter *Hearings on National Housing Act*); *Congressional Record—House*, 73d Cong., 2d sess., June 12, 1934, 11191, 11194, 11198, 11205, 11210, 11222 and June 13, 1934, 11383; *Congressional Record—Senate*, 73d Cong., 2d sess., June 16, 1934, 11973, 11981.

23. *Hearings on National Housing Act*, May 28, 1934, 122 and May 31, 1934, 225, 249; U.S. Senate, *Hearings Before the Committee on Banking and Currency on S. 3603 (National Housing Act)*, 73d Cong., 2d sess., May 18, 1934, 109, May 19, 1934, 152, May 22, 1934, 254, 258, 276–278, Bodfish's quote at 271, May 23, 1934, 294, and May 24, 1934, 421–422, 424; *Congressional Record—Senate*, 73d Cong., 2d sess., June 16, 1934, 11975; Eccles, *Beckoning Frontiers*, 148, 153, 155; Colean, *A Backward Glance*, 30, 50; Josephine Hedges Ewalt, *A Business Reborn: The Savings and Loan Story, 1930–1960* (Chicago: American Savings and Loan Institute Press, 1962), 144. In addition to interest, borrowers also had to pay a 1 percent (later reduced to between one-quarter and one-half percent) insurance premium that covered the operating costs and reserve requirements of the FHA.

24. Abrams, *Future of Housing*, 227, quotes at 224, 226, 228, and 229; FHA, *Second Annual Report, 1935* (Washington, D.C., 1936), 4; Fahey, "The Federal Home Loan Bank Board," 6; Rosenman, *A Million Homes a Year*, 29, 264–265. For subsequent analyses that supported Abrams' concerns over the FHA's loan policies, see Charles Haar, *Federal Credit and Private Housing*, 65; Paul F. Wendt, *The Role of the Federal Government in Housing* (Washington,

D.C.: American Enterprise Association, 1956), 15; Saulnier, Halcrow, and Jacoby, *Federal Lending and Loan Insurance*, 361; Henry J. Aaron, *Shelter and Subsidies: Who Benefits from Federal Housing Policies?* (Washington, D.C.: Brookings Institution, 1972), 84. For general discussions of the FHA's effects on mortgage financing, see Frederick M. Babcock, "FHA Mortgage Risk Rating System," in *Housing Officials' Yearbook, 1937*, 90–96; Babcock, "Influence of the Federal Housing Administration on Mortgage Lending Policy," 1–5.

25. Abrams, *Future of Housing*, quote at 224; John M. Gries and James S. Taylor, *How To Own Your Home* (Washington, D.C., 1923), Hoover's quote at v; James S. Taylor, "The Division of Building and Housing," in *The Better Homes Manual*, ed. Blanche Halbert (Chicago: University of Chicago Press, 1931), 760, 765; Ellis W. Hawley, "Herbert Hoover, the Commerce Secretariat, and the Vision of an 'Associative State,' 1921–1928," *Journal of American History* 61, no. 1 (June 1974), 125; Janet Huchison, "Building for Babbitt: The State and Suburban Home Ideal," *Journal of Policy History* 9, no. 2 (1997), 194.

26. Rose M. Stein, "More Home or More Mortgages?," *The New Republic*, September 7, 1932, 90; Stuart Chase, "The Case Against Home Ownership," *Survey Graphic* 27, no. 5 (May 1938), 267; Post, *Challenge of Housing*, 246. See also "The Second New York Own-Your-Home Exposition," *Building Age* 42, no. 6 (June 1920), 50–52; Arthur C. Holden, "The Home Sales Racket," *Survey* 68, no. 17 (December 1, 1932), 651–653; Charles F. Lewis, "Large-Scale Rental Developments as an Alternative to Home Ownership," *Law and Contemporary Problems* 5, no. 4 (Autumn 1938), 602–607; Weiss, "Marketing and Financing Home Ownership," 109.

27. Roosevelt, "A Letter on the Progress Made Under the National Housing Act," March 6, 1935, in *Public Papers*, quote at 4:94–95; FHA, *Better Selling of Better Housing* (Washington, D.C., 1935), quotes at 1; C. C. McGehee, "Significance of New Title I Provisions and Regulations to Realtors," in *Proceedings of the Realtors' Housing Conference Discussing the National Housing Act* (Washington, D.C., 1938), quote at 5; "Nation-Wide Home Building Drive Planned to Aid Private Business," *American Builder* 59, no. 12 (December 1937), quote at 32; F. L. Newton, "Using Movies in Selling Homes," *Freehold* 8, no. 9 (September 1, 1941), quote at 21; "Realtor Builders on the Newsfront," ibid. 5, no. 5 (September 1, 1939), 152; FHA, *Selling Better Housing* (Washington, D.C., 1935), 8; FHA, *How to Have the Home You Want* (Washington, D.C., 1936), 3; FHA, *First Annual Report, 1934* (Washington, D.C., 1935), 10–11; "Models Build a Subdivision," *Architectural Forum* 69, no. 4 (October 1938), 304–305; John Dean, *Home Ownership: Is It Sound?* (New York: Harper, 1945), 51.

28. Abrams, *Future of Housing*, 229–230, 237; FHA, "How to Have the Home You Want," 9; Dean, *Home Ownership*, 55; Abrams, "Your Dream Home Foreclosed," *McCall's Magazine*, May 1945, 76–79; Taper, "A Lover of Cities," I, 64. For a discussion of shifting attitudes towards consumer spending, including the emergence of "modern moralism," see Daniel Horowitz, *Attitudes Toward the Consumer Society in America, 1875–1940* (Baltimore: Johns Hopkins University Press, 1985), 162–169.

29. Abrams, *Future of Housing*, 240, 400, quotes at xviii and 322; Abrams, "How Sound Are Our Institutions?," speech, League for Mutual Aide, March 6, 1954, 9, reel 30, AP; Abrams, untitled speech, Conference on Urban Design, Harvard University, April 10, 1956, 2, reel 31, ibid.

30. Abrams to Catherine Bauer, October 2, 1940, reel 10, AP; Abrams, untitled speech, Convention of the National Public Housing Conference, March 24, 1944, 2–3, quote at 1, reel 26, ibid.; Abrams, "The Future of America and the Role of Cooperatives," Group Housing Cooperative, speech, Washington D.C., March 28, 1947, no page numbers given, reel 26, ibid.; Abrams, *Future of Housing*, quotes at 16 and 317; Abrams, "Real Estate Radicals," *Public Housing* 10, no. 4 (April 1944), 6–7; Abrams, "Housing Is News Again," *The New Republic*, March 19, 1945, 380–381; Rodwin, interview, 15–16; Ralph H. Cake, "The Future of Real Estate," *Savings and Loans* 18, no. 3 (March 1943), 17–19.

31. Abrams to Herbert U. Nelson, March 3, 1947, 1, reel 14, AP.

32. Abrams, untitled speech, Convention of the National Public Housing Conference, quote at 4; U.S. House, *Hearings Before the Select Committee on Lobbying Activities (Housing Lobby)*, 81st Cong., 2d sess., pt. 2, April 19, 1950, Nelson's quotes at 20 and 21 (hereafter *Housing Lobby*). In addition, see Abrams, "The Threat to Public Housing," in *Postwar Planning for Peace and Full Employment*, ed. Harry W. Laidler (New York: League for Industrial Democracy, 1944), 54.

33. Abrams, *Democracy in Crisis*, unpublished manuscript, 1950, 21, 38, quotes at 39 (chap. 7), reel 36, AP.

34. James Burnham, *The Managerial Revolution* (New York: John Day, 1941); James Burnham, "Is Democracy Possible?," in *Whose Revolution?*, ed. Irving DeWitt Talmadge (New York: Howell, Soskin, 1941), 193–194; Friedrich Hayek, *The Road to Serfdom* (Chicago: University of Chicago Press, 1944); Ludwig von Mises, *Omnipotent Government* (New Haven: Yale University Press, 1944); John T. Flynn, *The Road Ahead* (New York: Devin-Adair, 1949), 132.

35. Abrams, "Homeless America: Bailing Out the Builders," *The Nation*, December 28, 1946, 755; Abrams, "Homeless America: Illusions About Housing," 723. For opposition to the FHLBS by mortgage bankers, see U.S.

House, *Hearings Before a Subcommittee of the Committee on Banking and Currency on H.R. 7620 (Creation of a System of Federal Home Loan Banks)*, 72d Cong., 1st sess., March 16, 1932, 36 and March 25, 1932, 360.

36. Albert U. Romasco, *The Politics of Recovery: Roosevelt's New Deal* (New York: Oxford University Press, 1983), 246; Thomas McGraw, "The New Deal and the Mixed Economy," in *Fifty Years Later: The New Deal Evaluated*, ed. Harvard Sitkoff (New York: McGraw-Hill, 1985), 37–67, 58.

37. Abrams, *Future of Housing*, quote at 243; Abrams, "How Sound Are Our Institutions?," quote at 11; Morton Bodfish, *History of Building of Loan in the United States* (Chicago: U.S. Building and Loan League, 1931), quote at 143; "Between the Housers and the Planners: The Recollections of Coleman Woodbury," in *The American Planner: Biographies and Recollections*, ed. Donald A. Krueckeberg (New York: Methuen, 1983), quote at 327; *TNEC Hearings*, pt. 11, July 6, 1939, 5084–5085; U.S. Department of Commerce, *National Associations of the United States* (Washington, D.C., 1949), 353; Eccles, *Beckoning Frontiers*, 153–154. For discussions of the dynamics among interest groups, federal agencies, and Congressional committees, see Theodore J. Lowi, *The End of Liberalism: Ideology, Policy, and the Crisis of Public Authority* (New York: Norton, 1969), chap. 4; John E. Chubb, *Interest Groups and the Bureaucracy: The Politics of Energy* (Stanford: Stanford University Press, 1983), chap. 2.

38. Abrams, *Future of Housing*, quote at 243; Ewalt, *A Business Reborn*, 141; Marc A. Weiss, *The Rise of the Community Builders: The American Real Estate Industry and Urban Land Planning* (New York: Columbia University Press, 1987), 146.

39. Abrams, "The FHA System Enriches the Speculators," *The New Leader*, June 2, 1952, 8, quote at 9; Department of Commerce, *National Associations*, 353; U.S. Department of Commerce, *Trade Association Activities* (Washington, D.C., 1927), 150–151.

40. Abrams, untitled speech, The League for Industrial Democracy, April 15, 1950, quote at 3, reel 27, AP; Abrams, "The FHA System," 8–9; Abrams, untitled speech, Convention of the National Public Housing Conference, 1–4. Nelson's remarks about Abrams can be found in U.S. Senate, *Hearings Before the Committee on Banking and Currency, on S. 287, S. 866, S. 701, S. 801, S. 802, S. 803, and S. 804 (Bills Pertaining to National Housing)*, 80th Cong., 1st sess., March 26, 1947, 344 (hereafter *Bills Pertaining to National Housing*). The positions taken on housing policies in the 1930s and 1940s by various banking, building, and real estate lobbies can be found in several sources, including the Chicago-based publication of the U.S. Savings and Loan League, *Savings and Loan Annals* (known as the *Building and Loan Annals* from 1930–1939). See, for example: *Annals, 1934*, 486; *Annals, 1935*,

20–27, 78–90, 501–505; *Annals, 1936,* 510, 513–515; *Annals, 1937,* 415–417, 422–423; *Annals, 1939,* 470–471; *Annals, 1940,* 520–521; *Annals, 1941,* 208–213; *Annals, 1942,* 46–68, 277–280; *Annals, 1943,* 252–259; *Annals, 1944,* 290–291; *Annals, 1945,* 229–233; *Annals, 1946,* 254–255; NAREB, press releases, November 7, 1946 and March 11, 1947, reel 14, AP; "Memorandum on the Program Committee on Housing and Blighted Areas," *Freehold* 8, no. 8 (August 1941), 16; *Housing Lobby,* April 19, 1950, 10–13, 21, 22 and April 20, 1950, 53, 66; U.S. House, *U.S. Savings and Loan League,* 81st Cong., 2d sess., October 31, 1950, H. Rept. 3139, 1, 605, 616–617, 626, 636; *Bills Pertaining to National Housing,* March 26, 1947, 342, 344, 347, 363–364; Karl Schriftgiesser, *The Lobbyists* (Boston: Little, Brown, 1951), 98; Pearl Janet Davies, *Real Estate in American History* (Washington, D.C.: Public Affairs Press, 1958), 176–182; McDonnell, *Wagner Housing Act,* 315–316; Davies, *Housing Reform During the Truman Administration,* 21–22, 66, 118–119, 126. The National Association of Home Builders remained opposed to public housing in the 1940s and 1950s, though it reversed that position in the 1960s. See *Bills Pertaining to National Housing,* March 28, 1947, 389, 393–395; William Lilley III, "The Homebuilders' Lobby," in *Housing Urban America,* eds. Jon Pynoos, Robert Schafter, and Chester W. Hartman (Chicago: Aldine, 1973), 30–31. More ideologically consistent than other lobbies, the National Association of Manufacturers opposed all subsidies to housing. See Morris Sayre, "The Stake of Industry," *Annals of the American Academy of Political and Social Science* 259 (September 1948), 113–121.

41. Quotes from Adam Smith, *The Wealth of Nations* (Chicago: University of Chicago Press, 1976), 244, Abrams to Robert Taft, February 11, 1943, reel 8, AP, and Abrams, "The Subsidy and Housing," *Journal of Land & Public Utility Economics* 22, no. 2 (May 1946), 134; Abrams, "A Plank in a Platform," *The Nation,* May 15, 1948, 549; Abrams to Dorothy Rosenman, October 18, 1944, reel 14, AP; Abrams, "New Roles of Private Enterprise in Housing," in *Cooperation of the Public and Private Sectors in Housing,* Princeton University Conference #88 (Princeton: Princeton University Press, 1968), 66.

42. Discussions of mixed economies can be found in Stuart Chase, "Freedom from Want," *Harpers,* October 1942, 469; Lillian Symes, "Define 'Mixed Economy,' " *The Call,* July 9, 1943, 2; Lewis Corey, "Mixture for a Mixed Economy," *Common Sense,* February 1944, 67–68; Charles E. Lindblom, "Empirical Problems and Particular Goals," *The American Scholar* 19, no. 4 (Autumn 1950), 488; Theodore Rosenof, *Patterns of Political Economy in America: The Failure to Develop a Democratic Left Synthesis, 1933–1950* (New York: Garland, 1983), 212–214.

43. Quotes from Abrams, "Housing—The Ever-Recurring Crisis," in

Saving American Capitalism, ed. Scymour E. Harris (New York: Knopf, 1948), 190 and Abrams, "Homeless America: Illusions About Housing," 725; Abrams, *Future of Housing*, 365–368; Abrams, "One World—One Housing Problem," *Citizens Housing Council News* 5, no. 3 (November–December 1946), 3; Abrams, *A Housing Program for America* (New York: League for Industrial Democracy, 1946).

44. Abrams, *Future of Housing*, 391, 399, quotes at 360–361, 389; Abrams, "Housing—The Ever-Recurring Crisis," in *Saving American Capitalism*, ed. Seymour E. Harris (New York: Knopf, 1948), 186, quote at 190; Abrams, "A Plank in a Platform," 550; Abrams, "Government and Housing," *The Nation*, October 21, 1944, 498; Abrams, "What's Wrong With G. I. Bill?," *Public Housing* 11, no. 1 (January 1945), 3; Abrams to Herbert Nelson, September 29, 1948, reel 14, AP.

45. Mary Earhart Dillon, "Pressure Groups," *American Political Science Review* 36, no. 3 (June 1942), quote at 481; Pendelton Herring, *Group Representation Before Congress* (New York: Russell and Russell, 1929), quote at 268; Abrams, "Homeless America: Bailing Out Builders," 755. See also U.S. House, *Report and Recommendations on Federal Lobbying Act*, 81st Cong., 2d sess., January 1, 1951, H. Rept. 3239, 4 (hereafter *Rept. 3239*); Truman, "Special Message to the Congress Upon Signing the Housing and Rent Act," June 30, 1947, in *Public Papers of the Presidents of the United States: Harry S. Truman, 1945–1953*, vol. 3 (Washington, 1963), 317; Schriftgiesser, *The Lobbyists*, 96, 225. The Federal Lobbying Act, which was part of the Legislative Reorganization Act of 1946, is printed in *Rept. 3239*, 39–41.

46. John Kenneth Galbraith, *American Capitalism: The Concept of Countervailing Power* (Boston: Houghton Mifflin, 1952), 113, 151, quote at 111. Galbraith's views are in marked contrast to the conclusions that the TNEC had reached a little over a decade before. In examining a wide range of interest groups, the TNEC noted: "In essence, the New Deal has tried to equalize the bargaining power of business, farmers, and labor vis-a-vis government. Even after 8 years, an adequate method for doing so has not been worked out, although some progress has perhaps been made." The strongest pressures, the TNEC asserted, came from business groups. TNEC, *Monograph No. 26: Economic Power and Political Pressure* (Washington, D.C., 1941), 10, 187.

47. Daniel T. Rodgers, *Contested Truths: Keywords in American Politics Since Independence* (New York: Basic Books, 1987), 207–211; David B. Truman, *The Governmental Process* (New York: Knopf, 1951), 50, 51, and chap. 16; Arthur F. Bentley, *The Process of Government* (Cambridge: Harvard University Press, 1908); Robert A. Dahl, *A Preface to Democratic Theory* (Chicago: University of Chicago Press, 1956), chap. 3.

48. Alan Brinkley, "The New Deal and the Idea of the State," in *Rise and Fall of the New Deal Order*, 87, 100 ["regulatory" versus "compensatory"]; Margaret Weir and Theda Skocpol, "State Structures and the Possibilities for 'Keynesian' Responses to the Great Depression in Sweden, Britain, and the United States," in *Bringing the State Back In*, 108 ["social" Keynesianism]; Robert Lekachman, *The Age of Keynes* (New York: Random House, 1966), 287 ["commercial" Keynesianism]; Katznelson and Pietrykowski, "Rebuilding the American State," 306 ["developmental" versus "fiscalist"]. For slightly different views of state-building during this period, see Michael K. Brown, "State Capacity and Political Choice: Interpreting the Failure of the Third New Deal," *Studies in American Political Development* 9, no. 1 (Spring 1995), 187–212; Brian Waddell, "Economic Mobilization for World War II and the Transformation of the U.S. State," *Politics & Society* 22, no. 2 (June 1994), 165–194. Keynes' theories and influence are discussed in John Maynard Keynes, *General Theory of Employment, Interest and Money* (New York: Harcourt, 1936), 113–131, 245–254, 372–384; Lauchlin Currie, "Comments on Pump Priming, [ca. 1935]," printed in *History of Political Economy* 10, no. 4 (Winter 1978), 527; Leon H. Keyserling, "The Middle Way for America," *The Progressive*, May 1949, 5–9; Alan Brinkley, *The End of Reform: New Deal Liberalism in Recession and War* (New York: Knopf, 1995), 232. One prominent Keynesian, Marriner Eccles, helped craft the FHA's initial policies. For his influence and the attempts of others to use the FHA for macroeconomic purposes, see Eccles, *Beckoning Frontiers*, chap. 6; Colean, *A Backward Glance*, 37, 39, 41, 46–47; Robert F. Wagner, untitled radio address, December 27, 1937, box 121, book 2, sec. 3, Robert F. Wagner Papers, Georgetown University Archives. Analyses of the influence of Keynesian economics on American policymaking are provided in Alan Sweezy, "The Keynesians and Government Policy, 1933–1939," *American Economic Review* 62, no. 2 (May 1972), 116–124; Alfred H. Bornemann, "The Keynesian Paradigm and Economic Policy," *American Journal of Economics and Sociology* 35, no. 2 (April 1976), 125–136; Donald T. Critchlow, "The Political Control of the Economy: Deficit Spending as a Political Belief, 1932–1952," *The Public Historian* 3, no. 2 (Spring 1981), 22; John W. Jeffries, "The 'New' New Deal: FDR and American Liberalism, 1937–1945," *Political Science Quarterly* 105, no. 3 (Fall 1990), 397–418; Richard P. Adelstein, " 'The Nation as an Economic Unit': Keynes, Roosevelt, and the Managerial Ideal," *Journal of American History* 78, no. 1 (June 1991), 160–187.

49. Leon Keyserling to Abrams, March 24, 1945, reel 26, AP.

50. Abrams, "The Threat to Public Housing," 50. The phrase "fiscal revolution" comes from Herbert Stein, *The Fiscal Revolution in America* (Washington, D.C.: American Enterprise Institute Press, 1968). The impor-

tance of consumption in the early post-World War II period is discussed in Conference on Economic Progress, *Consumption: Key to Full Prosperity* (Washington, D.C.: Conference on Economic Progress, 1957). As early as 1935, Walter Lippmann predicted that the "management of money and the use of the national credit to expand and to contract government expenditures" were likely to become "permanently new functions of the American government." Walter Lippmann, "The Permanent New Deal," *Yale Review* 24, no. 4 (June 1935), 666.

51. Abrams, *Future of Housing*, 216; Lewis H. Brown, "Using Private Business Agencies to Achieve Public Goals in the Postwar World," *American Economic Review* 33, supplement, pt. 2 (March 1943), 74; Lawrence N. Bloomberg, "The Role of the Federal Government in Urban Housing," *American Economic Review* 41, no. 2 (May 1951), 592; Barry Checkoway, "Large Builders, Federal Housing Programmes, and Postwar Suburbanization," *International Journal of Urban and Regional Research* 4, no. 1 (March 1980), 29. The policy analyst Charles Haar suggested why business interests found "insurance and guarantee devices" so appealing: they provided the least amount of disruption to the private market. Haar, *Federal Credit and Private Housing*, 70. Business support of government housing policies can also be found in William L. C. Wheaton, "The Evolution of Federal Housing Programs" (Ph.D. diss., University of Chicago, 1953), 68, 436–438, 469. Elsewhere, Charles Linblom has argued that government subsidies are necessary compensations for the limitations of exchange relations in market-driven economies. See Charles Linblom, *Politics and Markets: The World's Political-Economic Systems* (New York: Basic Books, 1977), 173.

52. Jordan A. Schwarz, *The New Dealers: Power Politics in the Age of Roosevelt* (New York: Knopf, 1993), 86, quote at xi. See also William E. Leuchtenburg, *Franklin Roosevelt and the New Deal, 1932–1940* (New York: Harper, 1963), 193; Arthur M. Schlesinger, Jr., *The Coming of the New Deal* (Boston: Houghton Mifflin, 1958), 298. For views closer to Abrams, though without specific discussions of housing policies, see Barton J. Bernstein, "The New Deal: The Conservative Achievements of Liberal Reform," in *Towards a New Past: Dissenting Essays in American History*, ed. Barton J. Bernstein (New York: Vintage, 1969), 263–288.

53. Richard Polenberg, *One Nation Divisible: Class, Race, and Ethnicity in the United States Since 1938* (New York: Penguin, 1980), 54–55, 72–74, 78; Nicholas Lemann, *The Promised Land: The Great Migration and How It Changed America* (New York: Knopf, 1991), 6–7; Joe William Trotter, Jr., *Black Milwaukee: The Making of an Industrial Proletariat, 1915–1945* (Urbana: University of Illinois Press, 1985), 179–188; Arnold Hirsch, *Making of the*

Second Ghetto: Race and Housing in the Second Ghetto, 1940–1960 (New York: Cambridge University Press, 1983), 4–9.

7. "The Walls of Stuyvesant Town"

1. Ecker quoted in Abrams, "The Walls of Stuyvesant Town," *The Nation*, March 24, 1945, 328.

2. *Laws of 1892*, chap. 35, sec. 13; *Laws of 1906*, chap. 228; New York Legislature, *Joint Committee of the Senate and Assembly Appointed to Investigate the Affairs of Life Insurance Companies*, 1906, A. Doc. 41, 379–380; Superintendent of Insurance of the State of New York, *Annual Report, part 1, 1908* (Albany, 1908) 17; *Laws of 1909*, chap. 33; *Laws of 1922*, chap. 658; New York Legislature, *Intermediate Report of the Joint Legislative Committee on Housing*, 1922, Leg. Doc. 60, 250; "Legislature Kills 2 Lockwood Bills," *NYT*, March 15, 1922, 1; "9 Lockwood Bills Pass Legislature," ibid., March 18, 1922, 1; "Untermyer Asks Special Session," ibid., March 20, 1922, 1; "Governor Refuses an Extra Session on Housing Bills," ibid., March 21, 1922, 1; "The Defeated Bills," ibid., March 22, 1922, 12; Marquis James, *Metropolitan Life: A Study in Business Growth* (New York: Viking, 1947), 252–253; Louis I. Dublin, *A Family of Thirty Million: The Story of the Metropolitan Life Insurance Company* (New York: Metropolitan Life Insurance Company, 1943), 348.

3. *Laws of 1926*, chap. 12, secs. 14, 16, 20, 30, 39; Alfred E. Smith, *Up to Now: An Autobiography* (New York: Viking, 1929), 272–275; Alfred E. Smith, "A Housing Policy for New York," *Survey* 45, no. 1 (October 2, 1920), 3–4; Edith Elmer Wood, *Slums and Blighted Areas in the United States* (1934; reprint, College Park, Maryland: McGrath Publishing, 1969), 105; Schaffter, *State Housing Agencies*, 254–255; Foley, "Legal Aspects of Low-Rent Housing in New York," 7–8. The first and one of the largest housing developments built under the State Housing Law was the Amalgamated Housing Project in the Bronx, which was constructed for members of the Amalgamated Clothing Workers of America. See New York State Board of Housing, *Report*, February 29, 1928, Leg. Doc. 76, 16–17. For a contemporary assessment of the State Housing Law, see Louis H. Pink, *The New Day in Housing* (New York: John Day, 1928), chap. 12.

4. "Louis Heaton Pink," in *Biographical Dictionary of Social Welfare in America*, 594–597; Pink, *New Day in Housing*, quotes at 143; *Laws of 1938*, chap. 25; James, *Metropolitan Life*, 306–307; John Stanton, "Town Within a City," *New York Times Magazine*, May 11, 1941, 27. See also Pink, COHC, 52–56. Data on life insurance investments in housing during the 1930s can be found in *TNEC Hearings*, pt. 10-A, 258. The general role of insurance

companies in real estate investment is discussed in R. J. Saulnier, *Urban Mortgage Lending by Life Insurance Companies* (New York: National Bureau of Economic Research, 1950); Leo Grebler, David M. Blank, and Louis Winnick, *Capital Formation in Residential Real Estate: Trends and Prospects* (Princeton: Princeton University Press, 1956); J. E. Morton, *Urban Mortgage Lending: Comparative Markets & Experience* (Princeton: Princeton University Press, 1956); Robert E. Schultz, *Life Insurance Housing Projects* (Homewood, Illinois: Richard D. Irwin, 1956); Wayne Snider, *Life Insurance Investment in Commercial Real Estate* (Homewood, Illinois: Richard D. Irwin, 1956); Saul B. Klaman, *The Postwar Residential Mortgage Market* (Princeton: Princeton University Press, 1961); Herman E. Kroos and Martin R. Blyn, *A History of Financial Intermediaries* (New York: Random House, 1971); Karen Orren, *Corporate Power and Social Change: The Politics of the Life Insurance Industry* (Baltimore: Johns Hopkins University Press, 1974); George A. Bishop, *Capital Formation Through Life Insurance* (Homewood, Illinois: Richard E. Irwin, 1976).

5. The Housing Article is Article 18 of the New York Constitution. General suggestions for redevelopment during the 1940s can be found in Frederic A. Delano, "Must Urban Redevelopment Wait on Bombing?," *American City* 56, no. 5 (May 1941), 35; Charles S. Asher, "Better Cities After the War," ibid. 57, no. 6 (June 1942), 55–57; Ira S. Robbins, "Subsidy and Taxation for Urban Redevelopment," ibid., 59, no. 6 (June 1944), 76–78; Philip V. I. Darling, "Some Notes on Blighted Areas," *The Planners' Journal* 9, no. 1 (January–March 1943), 9–18; Walter H. Blucher, "Urban Redevelopment," in *American Planning and Civic Annual, 1943*, ed. Harlean James (Washington, D.C.: American Planning and Civic Association, 1943), 157–166; Hugh Potter, "The Need for Federal Action in Rebuilding Cities," ibid., 175–179; Thomas S. Holden, "Postwar Urban Redevelopment," ibid., 180–190; Ira S. Robbins, "The Role of the State," in *Proceedings of the National Conference on Postwar Housing* (New York: National Committee on Housing, 1944), 20–25; Roger S. Nelson, "Federal Aid for Urban Land Acquisition," *Journal of Land & Public Utility Economics* 21, no. 2 (May 1945), 125–135. The "model" redevelopment statute crafted by the American Society of Planning Officials (ASPO) in 1943 represented an attempt to reconcile conflicting viewpoints over how to ensure private sector participation in urban reconstruction. See "Report of the Committee on Urban Redevelopment," in ASPO, *Proceedings of the National Conference on Planning, 1943* (Chicago: ASPO, 1943), 98–100.

6. Abrams to Lee Johnson, February 19, 1945, box 9, folder 3, Catherine Krouse Bauer Wurster Papers, Manuscript Division, Bancroft Library, University of California, Berkeley; Abrams to Robert Taft, February 11, 1943, reel 6, AP. In addition to the works cited throughout this chapter,

Abrams' evolving ideas concerning housing and redevelopment can be found in Abrams, "Housing in the Post-War World," *Bulletin of Economics* (May 1943), 2–5; Abrams to Senator Robert F. Wagner, September 1, 1944, reel 9, AP; Abrams, *Future of Housing,* chaps. 24, 25, 27; Abrams, "The Segregation Threat in Housing," in *Two-Thirds of a Nation: A Housing Program,* ed. Nathan Straus (New York: Knopf, 1952), 210–235.

7. Robert Moses, "Slums and City Planning," *Atlantic Monthly,* January 1945, quotes at 66; Herbert H. Lehman, "Memorandum filed with Assembly Bill, Int. No. 1678, Pr. No. 2757," April 27, 1940, in *Public Papers of Herbert H. Lehman, 1940* (New York: Publishers Printing Company, 1940), 291–292; *New York Legislative Record and Index* (1940), Assembly Int. No. 1678, Senate Int. No. 1333; "Albany Bill Bares Housing Authority," *NYT,* March 11, 1943, 34; Schwartz, *The New York Approach,* 80–81. Also see Thomas S. Holden, "New York Suggests a Plan for Urban Rehabilitation by Private Initiative," *Architectural Record* 87, no. 5 (May 1940), 86–87.

8. New York Life quoted in Moses, "Slums and City Planning," 66; *Laws of 1941,* chap. 892; *Laws of 1942,* chap. 845; Thomas C. Desmond, "Blighted Areas Get a New Chance," *National Municipal Review* 30, no. 11 (November 1941), 629; Moses, *Public Works,* 430. See also "New York Legislature Passes Rebuilding Bill," *Freehold* 8, no. 6 (June 1941), 53–54; H. M. Olmstead, "Private Rehabilitation of Blighted Areas Encouraged," *National Municipal Review* 30, no. 7 (July 1941), 435; Thomas Holden, "Urban Redevelopment Corporations: A Legislative Victory in New York," in ASPO, *Proceedings of the National Conference on Planning, 1941* (Chicago: ASPO, 1941), 222–234; Holden, "Postwar Urban Redevelopment," 187. The urban redevelopment corporations sanctioned by the 1941 legislation were similar to the "neighborhood protective and improvement districts" that NAREB had advocated as early as 1933. Both were to be composed of local property owners who would be able to exercise limited powers of taxation and eminent domain. For the NAREB proposal, see "NAREB Suggests Plan for Reclaiming Blighted Areas," 33.

9. Moses, *Public Works,* 431; *Laws of 1943,* chap. 234. For an additional explanation of "superior public use," see FHA, *Handbook on Urban Redevelopment for Cities in the United States* (Washington, D.C., 1941), 17.

10. Abrams to Dewey, April 3, 1943, reel 11, AP; "Is Metropolitan Life Project the Answer?," *Public Housing* 9, no. 4 (April 1943), 2; Thomas E. Dewey, "Memorandum filed with Senate Bill, Int. No. 812, Pr. No. 1874," March 30, 1943, in *Public Papers of Thomas E. Dewey, 1943* (Albany: Williams Press, 1944), 218. See also Abrams, "Urban Redevelopment Laws Leave Slum Problem Unsolved," *Citizens' Housing Council of New York Housing News,* March 1943, 2.

11. James, *Metropolitan Life*, quote at 385; "East Side 'Suburb in City' to House 30,000 After War," *NYT*, April 19, 1943, 1; "Hearing Advances Big Housing Plan," ibid., May 6, 1943, 36. See also "Proposed Postwar Housing Project," *Architectural Record* 93, no. 6 (June 1943), 16; Boyden Sparkes, "Can the Cities Come Back?," *Saturday Evening Post*, November 4, 1944, 29; "Metropolitan Life Makes Housing Pay," *Fortune*, April 1946, 216; "One Way to Invest," *Business Week*, May 8, 1943, 103, 105; Henry Reed, "The Investment Policy of the Metropolitan Life," *Task* 4 (1945), 38–39. Contemporary distinctions between slums and blighted areas are discussed in Bauer, *Modern Housing*, 244–245; James Ford, *Slums and Housing*, vol. 1 (Cambridge: Harvard University Press, 1936); National Resources Committee, *Our Cities: Their Role in the National Economy* (Washington, D.C., 1937), 60; Mabel Walker, *Urban Blight and Slums* (Cambridge: Harvard University Press, 1938), 3–7; Wright, *Rehousing Urban America*, 3–6. A brief summary of Metropolitan's housing activities through 1947 can be found in *Bills Pertaining to National Housing*, March 26, 1947, 340–342.

12. "Proposed Postwar Housing Project," 16; Isaacs quoted in "Housing Plan Seen as a 'Walled City,' " *NYT*, May 20, 1943, 23. Also see Harold S. Buttenheim, "A Few Warnings on Private Enterprise Housing Plan," *National Municipal Review* 32, no. 7 (July 1943), 384–385; Alfred Bettman, "Problems of Planning and Democracy in Urban Redevelopment Legislation," *Journal of the American Institute of Planners* 10, no. 1 (Autumn 1944), 3–8; Tracy B. Augur, "An Analysis of the Plan of Stuyvesant Town," ibid., 8–13.

13. Arthur Simon, *Stuyvesant Town, U.S.A.: Pattern for Two Americas* (New York: New York University Press, 1970), 32; "Housing Plans Disapproved," *NYT*, June 1, 1943, 22; "We Mean Some White Folks," *New York Age* (hereafter *NYA*), May 29, 1943, 6. See also "New Housing Unit is Approved," *NYT*, May 21, 1943, 8; Abrams and Algernon D. Black to "Friends" of the City-Wide Citizens Committee on Harlem, May 27, 1943, reel 50, AP; Charles V. Hamilton, *Adam Clayton Powell, Jr.: The Political Biography of an American Dilemma* (New York: Atheneum, 1991), 127. Additional evidence of Metropolitan's intention to bar African Americans from Stuyvesant Town can be found in George Gove to William T. Andrews, April 22, 1943, reel 50, AP. For the reaction of the African-American press to Stuyvesant Town, see "Metropolitan Life Again," *NYA*, June 5, 1943, 6; "Our Estimate Was Wrong," ibid., June 12, 1943, 1, 6, 7; "The Board of Estimate Vote," ibid., June 19, 1943, 6; "Another Foe—Metropolitan Life," *Amsterdam News*, May 29, 1943, 10; "Citizens Make Protest Against Metropolitan 'Walled City,' " ibid., June 5, 1943, 1, 2. Contemporaries believed that Metropolitan's actions were one reason for the Harlem riot of 1943. See Dominic J. Capeci,

Jr., *The Harlem Riot of 1943* (Philadelphia: Temple University Press, 1977), 140–141.

14. "Stuyvesant Town," *NYT*, June 2, 1943, 24; Moses quoted in "Stuyvesant Town Approved by Board," ibid., June 4, 1943, 23; Moses' letter printed as "Stuyvesant Town Defended," ibid., June 3, 1943, 20.

15. *NYT*, June 5, 1943, 14; "Metropolitan Life Again," 6.

16. Lewis Mumford, "Prefabricated Blight," *The New Yorker*, October 30, 1948, quotes at 70 and 72; "New Nightmares for Old?," *Time*, December 13, 1948, 27; Catherine Bauer, "Cities in Flux: A Challenge to Postwar Planners," *The American Scholar* 13, no. 1 (Winter 1943), 80; Mumford to Abrams, July 28, 1948, reel 6, AP.

17. Moses' remarks are from his letter to the editors of *The New Yorker*, which was reprinted in Mumford, "Stuyvesant Town Revisited," *The New Yorker*, November 27, 1948, quotes at 61 and 63; Moses, "Mr. Moses Dissects the 'Long-Haired Planners,' " *New York Times Magazine*, June 23, 1944, quote at 16; "City Planning: Battle of the Approach," *Fortune*, November 1943, 165. Even Mumford admitted that Moses was popular because he "concentrates his resources on a particular job, and carries it through till the improvement is finished." See Lewis Mumford, *City Development* (New York: Harcourt: 1945), 115.

18. Abrams to Bauer, December 28, 1948, reel 10, AP.

19. Taper, "A Lover of Cities," II, 95, 97; quotes from Abrams, "Robert Moses, the City's No. 1 Housing Bottleneck," *New York Post*, July 16, 1947, 4 and Abrams, "Stuyvesant Town Race Ban Ruling Dangerous," ibid., July 30, 1947, 18, both on reel 35, AP. See also Raymond M. Hilliard to Abrams, May 27, 1948, reel 1, ibid.

20. Abrams, "The Walls of Stuyvesant Town," 328. For a general discussion of tax subsidies, as well as a specific discussion of Abrams' calculations, see Walter J. Blum and Norman Bursler, "Tax Subsidies For Rental Housing," *University of Chicago Law Review* 15, no. 2 (Winter 1948), 269.

21. "East Side 'Suburb in City' to House 30,000 After War," 1; "Rent and Readers," *NYT*, April 20, 1943, 22; "Moves to Enlarge Slum Clearance Area," ibid., April 22, 1943, 24. Stuyvesant Town's rents would be high enough to exclude more than one-half of New York City's families of two or more persons. See Blum and Bursler, "Tax Subsidies for Rental Housing," 270–72. Robert Caro contends that in subsequent redevelopment projects, Moses consistently misrepresented the number of spaces available in New York City's public housing for dislocated tenants. See Caro, *The Power Broker*, 962–965.

22. Abrams, "The Walls of Stuyvesant Town," 329; "Uprooted Thousands Starting Trek From Site of Stuyvesant Town," *NYT*, March 3, 1945, 15;

"Metropolitan Life Makes Housing Pay," 209; Edwin S. Burdell, "Rehousing Needs of the Families on the Stuyvesant Town Site," *Journal of the American Institute of Planners* 11, no. 4 (October–December 1945), 16–17. See also Abrams, *Future of Housing*, 321–322. A legislative subcommittee investigating Stuyvesant Town did not seem concerned about this aspect of tenant relocation, noting only that housing for "300 to 400 families" had not yet been found. See New York Legislature, *Report of the Sub-Committee of the Joint Legislative Committee to Recodify the Multiple Dwelling Law*, 1947, Leg. Doc. 47, 9. For suggestions on how to handle similar problems that were a byproduct of the Housing Act of 1949, see George B. Nesbitt, "Relocating Negroes From Urban Slum Clearance Sites," *Land Economics* 25, no. 3 (August 1949), 275–288.

23. Abrams, "Race Bias in Housing: The Great Hypocrisy," *The Nation*, July 19, 1947, quotes at 67 and 68; Abrams, "Our Chance for Democratic Housing," *The Nation*, August 16, 1947, quote at 162; Abrams, "The Segregation Threat in Housing," *Commentary*, February 1949, quote at 131.

24. Abrams, "Our Chance for Democratic Housing," quote at 161; Abrams, "The Segregation Threat," quote at 130. See also Abrams to Julian D. Steele, June 9, 1943, reel 11, AP; Abrams, "Mixed Projects in New York City," speech, New York State Conference on Social Work, November 18, 1943, reel 26, ibid.; Abrams, "Discrimination in Housing," speech, Civic Unity Committee, November 9, 1950, reel 27, ibid.; Abrams, "Living in Harmony," *Opportunity: Journal of Negro Life* 24, no. 3 (Summer 1946), 116, 166–167; Abrams, "Will Interracial Housing Work?," *The Nation*, August 2, 1947, 123; Abrams, "Human Rights in Slum Clearance," *Survey* 86, no. 1 (January 1950), 27–28; Thomas F. Farrel, "Object Lesson in Race Relations," *New York Times Magazine*, February 12, 1950, 16, 36–37.

25. Abrams, "The Walls of Stuyvesant Town," 328.

26. James, *Metropolitan Life*, 386–387; Moses, *Public Works*, 431; "Insurance Housing," 64; Metropolitan's remarks are quoted in Simon, *Stuyvesant Town*, 38, 39.

27. Quotes from Abrams, "Memorandum Re: Riverton Project," October 4, 1944, reel 11, AP; Abrams, "The Walls of Stuyvesant Town," 328; James Q. Wilson, *Negro Politics: The Search for Leadership* (New York: Free Press, 1960), 185. For a discussion of this conflict in Chicago, see Hirsch, *Making the Second Ghetto*, 250–251.

28. Abrams, "Race Bias in Housing," quote at 68; Abrams, "The Segregation Threat," quote at 131; Abrams to Louis S. Weiss, November 9, 1944, reel 9, AP; Louis S. Weiss to Abrams, December 21, 1944, reel 9, ibid.

29. Quotes from Abrams, "The Segregation Threat," 125, 127; Abrams, "Stuyvesant Town's Threat to Our Liberties," *Commentary*, November 1949, 427. See also Abrams, untitled speech, American Jewish Congress, November 6, 1950, reel 27, AP; Abrams, "Freedom to Dwell Together," *Congress Weekly*, November 27, 1950, 17, reel 27, ibid.

30. Abrams, "The Segregation Threat," 131.

31. Abrams, "Stuyvesant Town's Threat to Our Liberties," quotes at 429, 430, and 432; Abrams to Elizabeth Wood, May 7, 1947, reel 50, AP; Abrams, "Freedom to Dwell Together," 17; Abrams, *Forbidden Neighbors*, 256.

32. Abrams, "Stuyvesant Town's Threat to Our Liberties," 429; Abrams, *Future of Housing*, 400; Abrams, *Forbidden Neighbors*, 256; Abrams, "Notes for Finance Committee Meeting at City Hall on February 4, 1944 on Race Discrimination Bill," 8, Reel 11, AP. See also Abrams, *Democracy in Crisis*, chap. 7.

33. Citizen's Housing Council of New York, *Minutes*, January 25, 1944, reel 11, AP; Abrams, *Future of Housing*, 322; *Laws of 1939*, chap. 808, sec. 223; *Revised Record of the Constitutional Convention of the State of New York, 1938* (Albany: J. B. Lyon, 1938), 4:2626–2627; *Proposed Amendments of the Constitutional Convention of the State of New York, 1938* (Albany: J. B. Lyon, 1938), Pr. Nos. 10, 18, 49, 203, 380, 625, 691, 750, 809; Carl Eric Carlson, "Urban Redevelopment Legislation Needs Critical Study," *American City* 61, no. 11 (November 1946), 94. Henry Epstein, another lawyer on CHC's Board, might have assisted Abrams in drafting an antidiscrimination ordinance. See Charles A. Collier Jr. to Abrams, January 25, 1944, reel 11, AP. By 1950, with redevelopment laws on the books of twenty-seven states and the District of Columbia, only Pennsylvania's would contain an unequivocal antidiscrimination clause. See "Recent Cases," *Minnesota Law Review* 34, no. 4 (March 1950), 338.

34. Citizen's Housing Council of New York, *Minutes*.

35. Abrams, "Notes for Finance Committee Meeting," 8, 10. For Myrdal's explanation of the "American Dilemma," see Gunnar Myrdal, *An American Dilemma* (New York: Harper, 1944), xliii. The gap between America's beliefs and actions is also emphasized in President's Committee on Civil Rights, *To Secure These Rights: The Report of the President's Committee on Civil Rights* (Washington, D.C., 1947), 9–10, 13.

36. "New Era Held Near for City Housing," *NYT*, February 5, 1944, Moses quoted at 6; "City Bill Bars Bias Toward Tenants," ibid., May 16, 1944, 23; "Race Bias Measure Approved by Board," ibid., June 9, 1944, 17; "Anti-Bias Law Signed," ibid., July 6, 1944, 13; Isaacs to Abrams, April 24, 1944, reel 11, AP; Abrams to Richard Clark, February 13, 1951, reel 50, ibid.

37. Hugh Davis Graham, *The Civil Rights Era: Origins and Development of National Policy* (New York: Oxford University Press, 1990), 82. For a comprehensive history of Title VI, see Stephen Halpern, *On the Limits of the Law: The Ironic Legacy of Title VI of the 1964 Civil Rights Act* (Baltimore: Johns Hopkins University Press, 1995).

38. See the *New York Legislative Record and Index* (1944–1948) for descriptions of the following antidiscrimination bills: 1944, Assembly Int. Nos. 29, 1216, 1333; 1945, Int. Nos. 176, 340, 1716; 1947, Int. Nos. 34, 35, 72; 1948, Int. Nos. 127, 128, 217, 715, 1177, 1270.

39. The *Civil Rights Cases* is located at 109 U.S. 3; James D. Barnett, "Public Agencies and Private Agencies," *American Political Science Review* 18, no. 1 (February 1924), quote at 48; Charles E. Merriam, *Public and Private Government* (New Haven: Yale University Press, 1944), 11–19. For contemporary discussions of legal issues surrounding "state action" and urban redevelopment, see Philip Nichols, Jr., "The Meaning of Public Use in the Law of Eminent Domain," 615–641; "Urban Redevelopment," *Yale Law Journal* 54, no. 1 (December 1944), 116–140; Isaac N. Groner and David M. Helfeld, "Race Discrimination in Housing," ibid. 57, no. 3 (January 1948), 426–458; James D. Barnett, "What Is 'State' Action Under the Fourteenth, Fifteenth, and Nineteenth Amendments of the Constitution?," *Oregon Law Review* 24, no. 4 (June 1945), 227–243; Shirley Adelson Siegel, "Real Property Law and Mass Housing Needs," *Law and Contemporary Problems* 12, no. 1 (Winter 1947), 30–46.

40. *Murray v. LaGuardia* (1943), N.Y. 180 Misc 760; *Murray v. LaGuardia* (1943), 266 App. Div. 912; *Murray v. LaGuardia* (1943), 291 N.Y. 320; "Stuyvesant Town Wins," *NYT*, June 3, 1943, 23; "Stuyvesant Town Stayed by Court," ibid., June 6, 1943, 27; "Housing Case Hearing Set," ibid., June 12, 1943, 14; "Court Asks Reason for Housing Haste," ibid., June 16, 1943, 23; "Stuyvesant Plan Upheld by Court," ibid., July 3, 1943, 15; "To Hear Housing Suit," ibid., August 19, 1943, 33; "Stuyvesant Town Strikes New Snag," ibid., August 28, 1943, 13; " 'Walled City' in High State Court," ibid., September 10, 1943, 26; "Court Sanctions Stuyvesant Town," ibid., December 3, 1943, 8; "Housing," *Survey Midmonthly* 80, no. 1 (January 1944), 25–26.

41. *Pratt v. LaGuardia* (1944), N.Y. 182 Misc. 462; *Pratt v. LaGuardia* (1944), 268 App. Div. 972; *Pratt v. LaGuardia* (1945), 294 N.Y. Rep. 842. See also, "Plaintiff-Appellant's Brief in Support of Motion for Leave to Appeal," in the Appeals Court records for *Pratt v. LaGuardia*; "Sue to Enjoin City on Housing Project," *NYT*, August 16, 1943, 27; "Stuyvesant Town Wins in Court," ibid., December 16, 1944, 30.

42. William J. Butler to Charles Collier, December 6, 1946, reel 50, AP;

Abrams to Richard Clarke, February 8, 1951, reel 50, ibid.; Mitgang, *The Man Who Rode the Tiger*, 352–353.

43. *Dorsey v. Stuyvesant Town* (1947), N.Y. 190 Misc. 187, with defendants' arguments summarized at 191–192. See also "Race Housing Plea Quashed by Court," *NYT*, July 29, 1947, 23.

44. Ibid., plaintiffs' brief quoted by Judge Benvenga at 191. Other quotes from Abrams, "Stuyvesant Town's Threat to Our Liberties," 429 and Abrams, "The Threat to Public Housing," 55.

45. Ibid., Benvenga's quotes at 192 and 193. For Gove's testimony, see *Bills Pertaining to National Housing*, March 26, 1947, quote at 338.

46. *Dorsey v. Stuyvesant Town* (1948), 274 App. Div. 992; *Dorsey v. Stuyvesant Town* (1949), 299 N.Y. 512, with briefs listed at 512–520.

47. *Dorsey v. Stuyvesant Town*, 299 N.Y. 512, quotes at 519 and 520.

48. Ibid., quotes at 519 and 520.

49. Ibid., quotes at 515 and 516; *Smith v. Allwright*, 321 U.S. 663; *Marsh v. Alabama*, 326 U.S. 501. For a more detailed discussion of these two cases, see Robert L. Hale, "Rights Under the Fourteenth and Fifteenth Amendments Against Injuries Inflicted by Private Individuals," *Lawyers Guild Review* 6, no. 5 (November–December 1946), 627–639.

50. *Dorsey v. Stuyvesant Town*, 299 N.Y. 512, quotes at 535 and 536.

51. Ibid., quotes at 535. See also "Ask Mayor to Quit Case," *NYT*, April 11, 1949, 27; "State Held Aiding Negro Tenant Ban," ibid., April 12, 1949, 4; "Stuyvesant Town Negro Ban Upheld by Court of Appeals," ibid., July 20, 1949, 1, 19.

52. Abrams, "Stuyvesant Town's Threat to Our Liberties," quotes at 426, 427, and 428; *Dorsey v. Stuyvesant Town*, 339 U.S. 981; Memo on *Dorsey v. Stuyvesant Town*, signed "WMC," November 24, 1949, container 191, William O. Douglas Papers, Library of Congress. As in *Murray*, where Fourteenth Amendment issues were involved, the plaintiffs had the right to ask the Supreme Court to hear their case.

53. *Notre Dame Lawyer* 25, no. 1 (Fall 1949), 149; *Nebraska Law Review* 29, no. 3 (March 1950), 473; *University of Pennsylvania Law Review* 98, no. 2 (December 1949), 249.

54. Morroe Berger, *Equality by Statute* (New York: Columbia University Press, 1952), 192; Abrams, "The Limits of Law," review of *Equality by Statute*, by Morroe Berger, *Commentary*, October 1952, 402; Lynn W. Ely and Thomas W. Casstevens, eds., *The Politics of Fair Housing Legislation* (San Francisco: Chandler Publishing Company, 1968), 38–40.

55. Abrams, "The Subsidy and Housing," 131. Abrams defined "subsidy" as "any kind of grant or aid extended to an undertaking in which the public interest is imputed."

8. The Quest for Open Housing

1. Abrams, "Will Interracial Housing Work?," 122. Parts of this chapter originally appeared in "The New York State Commission Against Discrimination and the Quest for Equality in Housing," in *Proceedings of the Sixth National Conference on American Planning History* (Richmond: Society for American City and Regional Planning History, 1996), 243–255.

2. Teres, *Renewing the Left*, quote at 223.

3. Helen C. Monchow, *The Use of Deed Restrictions in Subdivision Development* (Chicago: Institute for Research in Land Economics and Public Utilities, 1928), 50; M. T. Van Hecke, "Zoning Ordinances and Restrictions in Deeds," *Yale Law Journal* 37, no. 4 (February 1928), 413. By 1940, the NAACP estimated that 80 percent of Chicago's dwellings were covered by restrictive covenants. See "Iron Ring in Housing," *The Crisis* 47, no. 7 (July 1940), 205. The poor condition of African-American housing is outlined by data quoted from FHA, *Real Property Inventories*, as cited in Richard Sterner, *The Negro's Share: A Study of Income, Consumption, Housing, and Public Assistance* (New York: Harper, 1943), 190. The case that struck down racially restrictive ordinances was *Buchanan v. Warley* (1917), 245 U.S. 60.

4. Abrams, "Home for Aryans Only," *Commentary*, May 1947, quotes at 421 and 422; NAREB, *Code of Ethics* (Washington, D.C.: NAREB, 1924), pt. 3, quote at article 34; Abrams, "Living in Harmony," 118; Abrams, "Our Chance for Democratic Housing," 160–162; Davis McEntire, *Residence and Race* (Berkeley and Los Angeles: University of California Press, 1960), 244–245; William H. Brown, Jr., "Access to Housing: The Role of Real Estate Industry," *Economic Geography* 48, no. 1 (January 1972), 68.

5. Abrams, "Homes for Aryans Only," 422; FHA, *Underwriting Manual* (Washington, D.C., 1938), secs. 933, 934, quotes at 909, 937, and 980(1); FHA, *Planning Profitable Neighborhoods*, Technical Bulletin No. 7 (Washington, D.C., n.d.), 6; FHA, *Successful Subdivisions*, Land Planning Bulletin No. 1 (Washington, D.C., n.d.), 9.

6. Abrams, COHC, 15, quotes at 13, 14, and 16; Abrams, untitled speech, NAACP meeting, Atlanta, Georgia, July 6, 1962, quote at 5, reel 32, AP; Abrams, "Race Bias in Housing," quote at 69. See also Abrams, untitled speech, Conference of the Councils of the New York State Commission Against Discrimination, May 5, 1956, 5, reel 31, AP; Robert C. Weaver, *The Negro Ghetto* (New York: Harcourt, 1948), 70.

7. Will Maslow and Joseph B. Robison, "Civil Rights Legislation and the Fight for Equality, 1862–1952," *University of Chicago Law Review* 20, no. 3 (Spring 1953), quote at 407; John P. Dean, "Only Caucasian: A Study of Race Covenants," *Journal of Land & Public Utility Economics* 23, no. 4

(November 1947), 429. For opposition to restrictive covenants, see Robert C. Weaver, "Race Restrictive Housing Covenants," *Journal of Land & Public Utility Economics* 20, no. 3 (August 1944), 183–193; Robert C. Weaver, "Housing in a Democracy," *Annals of the American Academy of Political and Social Science* 244 (March 1946), 95; D. O. McGovney, "Racial Residential Segregation by State Court Enforcement of Restrictive Agreements, Covenants or Conditions in Deeds is Unconstitutional," *California Law Review* 33, no. 1 (March 1945), 5–39; Loren Miller, "Race Restrictions on Ownership or Occupancy of Land," *Lawyers Guild Review* 7, no. 3 (May-June 1947), 99–111; Loren Miller, "The Power of Restrictive Covenants," *Survey Graphic* 36, no. 10 (October 1947), 541–543, 558–559; "Restrictive Covenants Directed Against Purchase or Occupancy of Land by Negroes," *American City* 62, no. 5 (May 1947), 103–104; "Supreme Court Test," *Architectural Forum* 87, no. 4 (October 1947), 16; Irwin M. Taylor, "The Racial Restrictive Covenants in the Light of the Equal Protection Clause," *Brooklyn Law Review* 14, no. 1 (December 1947), 80–101; I. N. Groner and D. M. Helfeld, "Race Discrimination in Housing," *Yale Law Journal* 57, no. 3 (January 1948), 426.

8. *Corrigan v. Buckley* is located at 271 U.S. 323; Jack Greenberg, *Crusaders in the Courts: How a Dedicated Band of Lawyers Fought for the Civil Rights Revolution* (New York: Basic Books, 1994), 111.

9. Thurgood Marshall to "Friend," July 11 and July 17, 1947, reel 50, AP; Phineas Indritz to Abrams, July 23, August 14 and August 22, 1947, reel 50, ibid.

10. Abrams to Newman Levy, November 13, 1947, reel 50, AP; Clement Vose, *Caucasians Only: The Supreme Court, the NAACP, and the Restrictive Covenant Cases* (Berkeley and Los Angeles: University of California Press, 1959), 165–167. For a comprehensive treatment of Jewish involvement in civil rights campaigns, see Stuart Svonkin, *Jews Against Prejudice: American Jews and the Fight for Civil Liberties* (New York: Columbia University Press, 1997).

11. "Constitutional Aspects of Legislation Prohibiting Discrimination in Housing," *Fordham Law Review* 26 (1957–1958), 677. *Shelley v. Kraemer* is located at 334 U.S. 1. See also B. T. McGraw and George B. Nesbitt, "Aftermath of Shelley Versus Kraemer on Residential Restriction by Race," *Land Economics* 29, no. 3 (August 1953), 283, 285, 287.

12. William C. Berman, *The Politics of Civil Rights in the Truman Administration* (Columbus: Ohio State University Press, 1970), 238–240; Robert A. Garson, *The Democratic Party and the Politics of Sectionalism, 1941–1948* (Baton Rouge: Louisiana State University Press, 1974), 316. See also Donald R. McCoy and Richard T. Ruetten, *Quest and Response: Minority*

Rights and the Truman Administration (Lawrence: University Press of Kansas, 1973); Abrams to Walter Lippmann, August 17, 1956, reel 6, AP.

13. Nicol C. Rae, *The Decline and Fall of the Liberal Republicans from 1952 to the Present* (New York: Oxford University Press, 1989), 163.

14. Abrams, "The Time Bomb That Exploded in Cicero," *Commentary*, November 1951, 412, quotes at 414; Abrams, "Will Interracial Housing Work?," quote at 123; Abrams, "Living in Harmony," 116; Abrams, untitled speech, Open Forum on Civil Rights, New York Chapter, Americans for Democratic Action, May 23, 1957, 3, reel 31, AP.

15. Abrams, *Forbidden Neighbors*, quote at 312; Oscar Cohen, "The Case for Benign Quotas in Housing," *Phylon* 21 (1960), 20–29; Paul Moreno, *From Direct Action to Affirmative Action: Fair Employment Law and Policy in America, 1933–1972* (Baton Rouge: Louisiana State University Press, 1997), 141.

16. Abrams, "Living in Harmony," quote at 116; Abrams, "Mixed Projects in New York City," speech, New York Conference on Social Work, November 18, 1943, quote at 6, reel 26, AP; Milton R. Konvitz to Abrams, January 24, 1944, reel 26, ibid. See also Jack Greenberg, *Race Relations and American Law* (New York: Columbia University Press, 1959), 287–291; Milton L. McGhee and Ann Fagan Ginger, "The House I Live In: A Study of Housing for Minorities," *Cornell Law Quarterly* 46, no. 2 (Winter 1961), 199; Jordan D. Luttrell, "The Public Housing Administration and Discrimination in Federally Assisted Low-Rent Housing," *Michigan Law Review* 64 (March 1966), 871; McGraw and Nesbitt, "Aftermath of Shelley Versus Kraemer," 284. Chicago's policy of systematic segregation is detailed in Martin Meyerson and Edward C. Banfield, *Politics, Planning, and the Public Interest: The Case of Public Housing in Chicago* (New York: Free Press, 1955).

17. Abrams' quotes from *Congressional Record—Senate*, 81st Cong., 1st sess., April 21, 1949, 4853. See also Abrams to *New York Herald Tribune*, October 29, 1952, reel 29, AP; Richard O. Davies, *Defender of the Old Guard: John Bricker and American Politics* (Columbus: Ohio State University Press, 1993), 110, 111, 120, 137; Paul H. Douglas, *In the Fullness of Time: The Memoirs of Paul H. Douglas* (New York: Harcourt, 1971), 272. The evolution of Abrams' views can be seen by contrasting his remarks in 1955 to those he made in 1944: "I am prepared to see housing lost if a larger issue, such as race equality, can be won." See Abrams to Milton Konvitz, February 1, 1944, reel 26, AP.

18. Abrams, "Should Federal Laws Contain Prohibitions of Racial Discrimination and Segregation?," speech, Ninth Annual Conference of the National Association of Intergroup Relations Officials, Milwaukee, Wisconsin, December 1, 1955, quotes at 4 and 8, reel 30, AP; Mitchell to

Abrams, July 29, 1955, NAACP Washington Bureau Papers, box 91, Library of Congress; *Congressional Record—Senate*, 81st Cong., 1st sess., April 21, 1949, 4860; Davies, *Defender of the Old Guard*, 137. See also Abrams, "The Choice is Nixon or Sparkman," *The New Leader*, September 22, 1952, 14–15.

19. Abrams, *Forbidden Neighbors*, 10–81. For a contemporary discussion of slums versus ghettos, see Thomas Lee Philpott, *The Slum and the Ghetto: Neighborhood Deterioration and Middle-Class Reform, Chicago, 1880–1930* (New York: Oxford University Press, 1978).

20. Abrams, *Forbidden Neighbors*, chaps. 8–12, 15, quote at 182.

21. Ibid., 150–168, quotes at ix and 158. See also Homer Hoyt, *One Hundred Years of Land Values in Chicago* (Chicago: University of Chicago Press, 1933); Homer Hoyt, *The Structure and Growth of Residential Neighborhoods in American Cities* (Washington, D.C.: FHA, 1939). Among the other "fallacies" that Abrams attempted to refute were: 1) "Negroes and Whites Do Not Mix"; 2) "Negroes (or Other Nonwhites) Are Dirty and Spoil the Neighborhood"; 3) "Entry of Minority Families into a Neighborhood Hurts Social Status"; 4) "The Minority Always Goes Where It Is Not Wanted"; and 5) "Once the Minority Establishes a Beachhead, Many More Will Soon Follow and Displace the Once Dominant Majority." See Abrams, *Forbidden Neighbors*, 265–277.

22. Abrams, *Forbidden Neighbors*, 157, 158, 161, 261, 278, quotes at 262, 263, 279 and 292; Belden Morgan, "Values in Transition Areas: Some New Concepts," *The Review of the Society of Residential Appraisers* 18, no. 3 (March 1952), 5–10; Luigi M. Laurenti, "Effects of Nonwhite Purchases on Market Prices of Residences," *The Appraisal Journal* 20, no. 3 (July 1952), 314–329; Lloyd Rodwin, "The Theory of Residential Growth and Structure," ibid. 18, no. 3 (July 1950), 295–317. See also Abrams, "The New 'Gresham's Law of Neighborhoods'—Fact or Fiction," *The Appraisal Journal* 10, no. 8 (July 1951), 324–328. For additional studies that refute a direct relationship between minority occupancy and a decline in property values, see Luigi M. Laurenti, *Property Values and Race: Studies in Seven Cities* (Berkeley and Los Angeles: University of California Press, 1960), 47; Ernest A. T. Barth and L. K. Northwood, *Urban Desegregation: Negro Pioneers and Their White Neighbors* (Seattle: University of Washington Press, 1965), 64–65. Older studies that posited such a link include Stanley L. McMichael and R. F. Bingham, *City Growth and Values* (Cleveland: Stanley McMichael, 1923), 181, 182; John Spiler, *Real Estate Business as a Profession* (Cincinnati: Stewart Kidd, 1923), 123, 128; Babcock, *The Valuation of Real Estate*, 89, 91; Henry E. Hoagland, *Real Estate Principles* (New York: McGraw-Hill, 1940), 148; Arthur A. May, *The Valuation of Residential Real Estate* (New York: Prentice-Hall, 1942), 99. The most comprehensive study of the real estate industry's racial attitudes dur-

ing this period remains Rose Helper, *Racial Policies and Practices of Real Estate Brokers* (Minneapolis: University of Minnesota Press, 1969).

23. Abrams' twelve specific "aims" included: 1) "A Comprehensive Long-Range Housing Program for All Groups"; 2) "Adequate Protection by Law of the Opportunity to Secure Shelter"; 3) "An Executive Policy Prohibiting Discrimination by Those Dispensing Federal Funds or Benefits Funds or Benefiting from Public Power"; 4) "Curtailment of Slum-Clearance Operations for the Duration of the Housing Emergency"; 5) "Adequate Land for Housing Open to Minorities"; 6) "Adequate Financing"; 7) "An Effective Program for the Repair and Improvement of Existing Housing and Maintenance of Adequate Occupancy Standards"; 8) "Housing for Migratory Labor"; 9) "Local, State, and Federal Racial Commissions"; 10) "A More Effective Federal Civil Rights Section"; 11) "Expansion of Racial Relations Services in Housing and Other Related Departments"; 12) "Planned Integration of Minorities into Neighborhoods." See Abrams, *Forbidden Neighbors*, 346–381.

24. See the following reviews of *Forbidden Neighbors*: Nathan Straus, "The Man Next Door," *Saturday Review of Literature*, April 2, 1956, 29; Frank S. Loescher (untitled), *Annals of the American Academy of Political and Social Science*, 300 (July 1955), 154; Catherine Bauer, "The Issue that Cannot Wait," *The Nation*, September 3, 1955, 207. For a list of the individuals to whom Abrams sent copies of *Forbidden Neighbors*, see Abrams, untitled memo, 1955 (no date given), reel 37, AP.

25. The swimming-pool anecdote is recounted in Taper, "A Lover of Cities," II, 110.

26. Harriman, "Appointments" and "Statement Accompanying Appointments of Charles Abrams to Discrimination Commission and Robert C. Weaver as Rent Administrator," December 14, 1955, both in *Public Papers of Averell Harriman, 1955* (Albany: n.p., 1958–1961), 397, 541, quote at 755 (hereafter *Harriman Papers*).

27. *Laws of 1945*, chap. 118 (LAD was also known as the Ives-Quinn Bill). For additional background on antidiscrimination efforts, see Ruth G. Weintraub, *How Secure These Rights?* (Garden City, New York: Doubleday & Company, 1949), 33; Greenberg, *Race Relations and American Law*, 192; Andrew Edmund Kersten, "Fighting for Fair Employment: The FEPC in the Midwest, 1941–1946," (Ph.D. diss., University of Cincinnati, 1997). By 1957, SCAD's Chairman received a salary of $16,000, while the remaining four members received $15,200. See *New York State Redbook, 1957–1958* (Albany: Williams Press, 1958), 368. Only two other state commissions had paid commissioners. See Michael A. Bamberger and Nathan A. Lewin, "The Right to Equal Treatment: Administrative Enforcement of Antidiscrimi-

nation," *Harvard Law Review* 74, no. 3 (January 1961), 568. SCAD was also assisted by a Labor Advisory Committee, a Commerce and Industry Advisory Committee, and a Housing Advisory Council. Moreover, twelve community councils (representing Albany County, Bronx County, Broome County, Buffalo, Kings County, Manhattan County, Queens County, Richmond County, Rochester, Syracuse and Onondaga County, Troy, and Westchester County) helped implement SCAD's policies on the local level. See SCAD, *Report of Progress, 1958* (Albany: SCAD, n.d.), 120–127; Jay Anders Higbee, *Development and Administration of the New York State Law Against Discrimination* (University, Alabama: University of Alabama Press, 1966), chap. 5. Other states quickly followed New York's lead, and by 1960 seventeen similar antidiscrimination laws existed throughout the country. See Hanes Walton, Jr., *When the Marching Stopped: The Politics of Civil Rights Regulatory Agencies* (Albany, New York: SUNY Press, 1988), 11. A review of fair housing laws in operation though 1961 can be found in Joseph B. Robison, "Housing—The Northern Civil Rights Frontier," *Western Reserve Law Review* 13, no. 1 (December 1961), 101–127.

28. Abrams, "Liberal Party State Legislative Program, 1951," quote at 2, reel 12, AP; Abrams, "Liberal Party State Legislative Program, 1955," 8, reel 13, ibid. See also Abrams, "Liberal Party Municipal Program, 1953," 3, reel 13, ibid.; Abrams, "Liberal Party State Legislative Program, 1954," 8, reel 13, ibid.

29. *Dorsey v. Stuyvesant* (1949), 299 N.Y. 512, quote at 531; *Laws of 1950*, chap. 287; Robert C. Weaver, "The Effect of Anti-Discrimination Legislation Upon the FHA- and VA-Insured Housing Market in New York State," *Land Economics* 31, no. 4 (November 1955), 303–313. The New York Civil Rights Law was initially passed in 1909, and its provisions covering "publicly aided" housing are located in Article 2a. See *Laws of 1909*, chap. 14; Book Eight ("Civil Rights Law") of *McKinney's Consolidated Laws of New York* (St. Paul, Minnesota: West Publishing, 1992), 30–40.

30. Harriman, "Annual Message," January 5, 1955, *Harriman Papers, 1955*, quote at 34; Abrams to Harriman, January 4, 1956, reel 16, AP; Harriman to Abrams, December 14, 1955, reel 16, ibid.; Abrams, untitled speech on civil rights for Harriman, May 21, 1956, reel 16, ibid.; Rudy Abramson, *Spanning the Century: The Life of W. Averell Harriman, 1891–1986* (New York: William Morrow, 1992), 516–520; *Laws of 1955*, chap. 340; Harriman, "Annual Message," January 4, 1956, *Harriman Papers, 1956*, 23; SCAD, *Report of Progress, 1956* (Albany: SCAD, n.d.), 84; J. Harold Saks and Sol Rabkin, "Racial and Religious Discrimination in Housing: A Report of Legal Progress," *Iowa Law Review* 45, no. 3 (Spring 1960), 515; Arnold Forster and Sol Rabkin, "The Constitutionality of Laws Against

Discrimination in Publicly Assisted Housing," *New York Law Forum* 6, no. 1 (January 1960), 43.

31. SCAD, "Press Release," February 27, 1956, Abrams' quotes at 1 and 2, reel 30, AP; Abrams, untitled speech, Workmen's Circle Division, Jewish Labor Committee, January 8, 1956, 1, reel 30, ibid.; Abrams, untitled speech, Governor Harriman's Conference on Discrimination and Low Incomes, March 12, 1958, 2, reel 31, ibid.; Abrams, interview on the WCBS program, "Let's Find Out," December (no date given), 1958, 2, reel 31, ibid. Demographic shifts in the 1950s were indeed profound. Between 1950 and 1960, the population of "nonwhites" in central cities (the ten largest urban areas in the United States) increased by 56 percent. At the same time, affluent whites were moving to the suburbs in record numbers. See U.S. Housing and Home Finance Agency, *Our Nonwhite Population and Its Housing: The Changes Between 1950 and 1960* (Washington, D.C., 1963), 5; Morton Grodzins, "Metropolitan Segregation," *Scientific American*, October 1957, 33. A detailed analysis of how this process worked in Baltimore can be found in W. Edward Orser, *Blockbusting in Baltimore: The Edmondson Village Story* (Lexington: University Press of Kentucky, 1994).

32. Harriman's quotes from Harriman, *Message of the Governor in Relation to Extending Authority of State Commission Against Discrimination*, March 16, 1956, Leg. Doc. 15L, 1 and SCAD, *Report of Progress, 1956*, 85. See also SCAD, *Minutes*, January 5, 12, and 26, 1956 (all minutes located in the New York State Division of Human Rights, New York City); Harriman, "Annual Message," January 9, 1957, *Harriman Papers, 1957*, 28; *Laws of 1956*, chap. 563; *New York State Legislative Annual, 1956* (New York: New York Legislative Service, 1956), 464–465; Bamberger and Lewin, "The Right to Equal Treatment," 526.

33. SCAD, *Report of Progress, 1956*, 86. For the growth of administrative law see Alexander H. Pekelis, "Administrative Discretion and the Rule of Law," *Social Research* 10, no. 1 (February 1943), 36–37; Joseph Vining, *Legal Identity: The Coming of Age of Public Law* (New Haven: Yale University Press, 1978). For a critical account, see Jeremy Rabkin, *Judicial Compulsions: How Public Law Distorts Public Policy* (New York: Basic Books, 1987), 3–35. In New York, aggrieved parties retained the option of filing suit in court to recover damages, but they could not seek monetary relief in that forum *and* administrative relief through SCAD. See Higbee, *Development and Administration*, 31.

34. SCAD, *Report of Progress, 1957* (Albany: SCAD, n.d.), 90, 92–93, unidentified SCAD Commissioner quoted at 91; Abrams, testimony, President's Commission on Civil Rights, December 1959 (no date given, but delivered on February 2), 8, reel 17, AP.

35. SCAD, *Report of Progress, 1957,* 93, quotes at 94. Pelham Hall Apartments managed Rochelle Arms.

36. *New York State Commission v. Pelham Hall Apartments* is located at 170 N.Y. S.2d 750, quotes at 757; SCAD, "Press Release," March 21 (no year given, but probably 1956), Abrams' quote at 1, reel 35, AP; "2 Appeals Dropped on S.C.A.D. Order," *NYT,* October 1, 1958, 28. In 1959, Abrams estimated that despite recent legislation, only 250,000 out of 5,000,000 dwellings in New York were covered by antidiscrimination provisions. In 1961, after several failed attempts, the New York Legislature finally passed the so-called Metcalf-Baker bill outlawing discrimination in all private housing accommodations (irrespective of federal mortgage insurance), with the exception of one- and two-family homes, and three-family homes in which the owner was an occupant. This brought an additional 520,000 units outside New York City under antidiscrimination laws. See *Laws of 1961,* chap. 414; Abrams, testimony, President's Commission on Civil Rights, 7; Higbee, *Development and Administration,* 54.

37. Citizens Union "Searchlight" transcript, April 29, 1952, 1, quotes at 2, reel 11, AP; "Heck-Abrams Re-union," March 14, 1957, 1–3, reel 10, ibid. A 1961 analysis of state commissions against discrimination concluded that none abused its abilities to investigate and prosecute cases. See Bamberger and Lewis, "The Right to Equal Treatment," 569–570.

38. Abrams quoted in Taper, "A Lover of Cities," II, 106; SCAD Board to Oswald D. Heck, May 1, 1956, reel 16, AP; NAACP, "Press Release," May 3, 1956, reel 14, ibid.; Abrams, Harriman speech draft, December 6, 1956, 7, reel 16, ibid.

39. *New York Post,* June 5, 1956, Abrams' quote at 14; Abrams quoted in "Abrams-Wagner Press Release," October (no date given), 1956, 1, reel 12, AP. See also "28 Cents for Democracy," *NYT,* March 5, 1956, 22; Abrams, Harriman speech draft, 5; Abrams, untitled speech, 25th Semi-Annual Conference of the New York State Council of Machinists, Buffalo, New York, February 23, 1957, 10, reel 31, AP; Abrams, untitled speech, Annual Conference of the National Committee Against Discrimination in Housing, Philadelphia, Pennsylvania, December 11, 1958, 5, reel 31, ibid.

40. Harriman, "Transmitting the Executive Budget and Recommended Appropriations for 1957–1958," February 1, 1957, *Harriman Papers, 1957,* quote at 127; "Statement Concerning Rejection by the Governor and the Democratic Legislative Leaders of a Republican 'Deal' To Broaden the Powers of the State Commission Against Discrimination To Conduct Industry-Wide Investigations," March 29, 1957, ibid., Harriman quoted at 909, 910; Abrams' quotes from Abrams to Louis J. Lefkowitz, March 28, 1957, reel 16, AP. See also Harriman, "Annual Message," January 9, 1957;

Harriman to the New York Legislature, March 28, 1957 and March 30, 1957, *Harriman Papers, 1957,* 544, 549; Harriman, "Statement by the Governor Relative to the Legislative Session Just Concluded," March 31, 1957, ibid., 913; Abrams to the *New York Times,* March 13, 1957, reel 17, AP; Abrams to Herbert Hill, March 18, 1958, reel 14, ibid.; Abrams to Marvin H. Riseman, February 28, 1958, reel 11, ibid.; SCAD, *Minutes,* March 2, 1956.

41. Harriman, "Annual Message," January 8, 1958, *Harriman Papers, 1958,* 51; SCAD, *Report of Progress, 1958* (Albany: SCAD, n.d.), 23; Rockefeller, "Annual Message," January 7, 1959, *Public Papers of Nelson A. Rockefeller, 1959* (New York: n.p., 1959–1973), 26; Abrams to Nelson A. Rockefeller, January 26, 1959, reel 17, AP; Rockefeller to Abrams, January 30, 1959, reel 17, ibid.; SCAD, "Press Release," March 31, 1959, reel 31, ibid.; "Pro and Con" transcript, June 18, 1959, 1–6, reel 31, ibid.; "Rockefeller Lags, Abrams Asserts," *NYT,* January 29, 1959, 56. For a detailed account of Rockefeller's campaign, see Cary Reich, *The Life of Nelson Rockefeller: World to Conquer, 1908–1958* (New York: Doubleday, 1996), 727–769. Elmer Carter's views on SCAD can be found in his article, "Practical Considerations of Anti-Discrimination Legislation—Experience Under the New York Law Against Discrimination," *Cornell Law Quarterly* 40, no. 1 (Fall 1954), 40–59.

42. Bamberger and Lewin, "The Right to Equal Treatment," 588. Precise data on complaints are located in SCAD, *Report of Progress, 1958,* 103. For New York's law against age discrimination, see *Laws of 1958,* chap. 738. SCAD's activities during Abrams' chairmanship are described in SCAD, *Minutes,* February 2, April 24, May 4, June 20, June 26, November 8, 11, and December 13, 1956; January 16, April 11, June 7, and November 12, 1957; April 15, June 10, September 25, and October 12, 1958; SCAD, *Report of Progress, 1956,* 67–82; SCAD, *Report of Progress, 1957,* 26–34, 98–104; SCAD, *Report of Progress, 1958,* 18–22, 62–67, 77–87, 98–99; SCAD, *Report of Progress, 1959* (Albany: SCAD, n.d.), 60–68; Harriman, "Annual Message," January 9, 1957, *Harriman Papers, 1957,* 27–28; Harriman, "Annual Message," January 1958, *Harriman Papers, 1958,* 48–50; SCAD, "Press Release," December 3, 1956, 1–14, reel 31, AP; SCAD, "Press Release," November 20, 1957, 1, reel 17, ibid.; Abrams, testimony, President's Commission on Civil Rights, 10–11. By the end of Abrams' tenure, SCAD's personnel included a Director of Housing, Director of Education, Director of Employment Discrimination, Director of Investigations, and Director of Research.

43. Carter's quotes from SCAD, *Minutes,* February 5, 1959; Harriman's quote from Harriman to Abrams, December 28, 1950, reel 4, AP.

44. Kennedy's views on civil rights are discussed in Carl M. Brauer, *John F. Kennedy and the Second Reconstruction* (New York: Columbia University Press, 1977); Irving Bernstein, *Promises Kept: John F. Kennedy's New Frontier* (New York: Oxford University Press, 1991), chap. 2; Richard Reeves, *President Kennedy: Profile of Power* (New York: Simon & Schuster, 1993), 59–63.

45. Abrams to David Dubinsky, March 17, 1952, reel 14, AP; "Ghettos: The Last Barrier to Civil Rights," NCDH brochure, not dated, reel 14, ibid. See also Juliet Saltman, *Open Housing as a Social Movement* (Lexington, Massachusetts: D.C. Heath, 1971), 33–39; Juliet Saltman, *Open Housing: Dynamics of a Social Movement* (New York: Praeger, 1978), 44–47, 50–59.

46. Kennedy, "The President's News Conference of March 1, 1961," in *Public Papers of the Presidents of the United States: John F. Kennedy, 1961–1963*, vol. 1 (Washington, D.C., 1962), 137; Kennedy, "Special Message to the Congress on Housing and Community Development," March 9, 1961, ibid., 162–170; Kennedy, "The President's News Conference of March 23, 1961," ibid., quote at 218; Norbert A. Schlei, recorded interview by John Stewart, February 20–21, 1968, 34–35, John F. Kennedy Library Oral History Program (hereafter JFKOHP); "Ban on Color Line in Housing Due," *NYT*, September 28, 1961, 1, 33; "Stroke of the Pen: Dimensions of a Presidential Decision," a film for the John F. Kennedy Library produced by Envision Corporation (shown at the Kennedy Library).

47. "Proposed Executive Order to Bar Discrimination in Housing Receiving Federal Assistance," July 27, 1961, quotes at 1 and 2, reel 14, AP. Abrams estimated that 90 percent of all home mortgages were "affected by some government activity." See Abrams to Kennedy, November 1, 1961, box 21, Lee White Files, John F. Kennedy Presidential Library (hereafter WF). Still more pressure was brought to bear on Kennedy when the 1961 Report of the U.S. Commission on Civil Rights echoed NCDH's recommendations. In 1959 the Commission conducted hearings in New York City, Atlanta, and Chicago. At the New York hearings, Abrams forcefully outlined his position: "I believe there should be an executive policy prohibiting discrimination in housing receiving Federal subsidies or mortgage guarantees or benefiting from the exercise of Federal power." See U.S. Commission on Civil Rights, *Hearings Before the United States Commission on Civil Rights on Housing*, February 2, 1959, 158; U.S. Commission on Civil Rights, *Report of the United States Commission on Civil Rights—1959* (Washington, D.C., 1959), 536–540.

48. Quotes from Harris Wofford to Kenneth O'Donnell, September 6, 1961, box 71, White House Subject Files, John F. Kennedy Presidential Library (hereafter WHSF) and Kenneth O'Donnell to Abrams, October 30, 1961, box 71, ibid.; Abrams, Black, Roosevelt, and Wilkins to Kennedy, August 22, 1961, box 71, ibid.

49. Quotes from Abrams, Black, and Frances Levenson to NCDH Board of Directors, October 4, 1961, 1, reel 14, AP and William B. Hartsfield to Kennedy, October 19, 1961, box 21, WF; Burke Marshall, recorded interview by Louis Oberdorfer, May 29, 1964, 54, JFKOHP; Abrams to Kennedy, September 22, 1961, box 21, WF; NCDH, "A Call on the President of the United States for the Issuance of an Executive Order Ending Discrimination in All Federal Housing Programs," box 21, ibid.; Abrams to Kennedy, November 1, 1961, box 21, ibid. Among NCDH's member organizations were the Amalgamated Clothing Workers of America, the American Civil Liberties Union, the American Friends Service Committee, the American Jewish Congress, Americans for Democratic Action, the Congress for Racial Equality, the League for Industrial Democracy, the National Association for the Advancement of Colored People, the National Council of Churches, the National Urban League, the United Auto Workers of America, and the United Steelworkers of America. Members of its advisory council included Ralph Bunche, Ralph Ellison, Harry Emerson Fosdick, Senator Philip Hart (D-MI), Senator Hubert Humphrey (D-MN), Senator Jacob Javits (R-NY), Senator Henry Jackson (D-WA), Martin Luther King, Jr., Herbert Lehman, George Meany, Walter Reuther, and Eleanor Roosevelt.

50. For the description of Robert Kennedy, see Frances Levenson to NCDH Board of Directors, November 30, 1961, quote at 2, reel 14, AP; Abrams' quote from "Confirmation of Telegram Sent December 14, 1961," box 371, WHSF. See also Abrams to O'Donnell, November 1, 1961, box 371, WHSF; Kenneth O'Donnell to Abrams, November 21, 1961, box 371, ibid.; Lee White to Abrams, December 16, 1961, box 371, ibid.; Schlesinger to Wofford, December 16, 1961, box 371, ibid.; Abrams to Kennedy, March 26, 1962, box 371, ibid.; O'Donnell to Abrams, April 4, 1962, box 371, ibid.; Abrams to Schlesinger December 13, 1961, reel 8, AP; Schlesinger to Abrams, December 15, 1961, reel 8, ibid.; Marshall, interview, 55–56; "Order to Ban Bias in Housing Ready," *NYT*, November 27, 1961, 1, 22; "Mr. Kennedy Should Sign," ibid., December 25, 1961, 22. Abrams' increasing visibility in the campaign for a housing order sometimes generated hostility toward him personally. At least one letter writer, asserting that New York City was "fast becoming a dump thanks to Puerto Ricans and Negroes," mocked Abrams' efforts and called him a "Jew Bastard." See "Disgusted Citizen" to Abrams, April 11, 1962, reel 10, AP.

51. Quote from Frances Levenson to Board of Directors and Friends, December 29, 1961, reel 14, AP. See also Theodore Sorensen, *Kennedy* (New York: Harper, 1965), 480. Kennedy's plans for a Department of Urban Affairs were defeated; the Department of Housing and Urban Development was established under his successor, Lyndon B. Johnson.

52. Abrams to Kennedy, July 16, 1962, box 21, WF; Lee White, recorded interview by Milton Guirtzman, May 25, 1964, 85–86, quote at 87, JFKOHP; Kennedy, "The President's News Conference of January 15, 1962," in *Public Papers of the Presidents of the United States: John F. Kennedy, 1961–1963*, vol. 2 (Washington, D.C., 1963), 21; Kennedy, "The President's News Conference of July 5, 1962," ibid., 544; "Home Builders Report to Kennedy Called Biased," *Trends in Housing* 6, no. 3 (May–June, 1962), 1–3; White to Kennedy, July 17, 1962, box 371, WHSF; NCDH, "Press Release," July 18, 1962, 1–2, box 21, WF; Milton P. Semer to Lee White, August 17, 1962, box 21, ibid.; Lee White to Kennedy, August 28, 1962, box 21, ibid.; "Proposed Executive Order Entitled 'Equal Opportunity in Housing,' " unsigned memorandum, September 19, 1962, ibid.; Marshall, interview, 56–58; Schlei, interview, 28, 31–32. Among other critics of the NAHB report was *Architectural Forum*, which asserted that there was "little reason . . . to take this survey too seriously." See "Kennedy Again Ponders Antibias Edict," *Architectural Forum* 117, no. 2 (August 1962), 5. Four years earlier, the California Commission on Race and Housing reached a similar conclusion, arguing that the "fear" over the effects of banning discrimination "had not been confirmed by the experience of those who have built for an unrestricted market." See California Commission on Race and Housing, *Where Shall We Live? Report of the Commission on Race and Housing* (Berkeley and Los Angeles: University of California Press, 1958), 52. For comments by the building industry, see "Too Many 'Ifs' in 1963," *Business Week*, November 17, 1962, 33–34.

53. Martha Griffiths to Larry O'Brien, September 18, 1962, box 21, WF; Larry O'Brien to Lee White, September 11 and 15, 1962, box 21, ibid.; Kennedy, "The President's News Conference of November 20, 1962," in *Public Papers of the Presidents of the United States: John F. Kennedy, 1961–1963*, vol. 2, 831–832, 835; "President Bars Bias in Housing," *NYT*, November 21, 1962, 1, 19. Senator Philip Hart's office was alone among communicants to the White House in asserting that a pre-election executive order would have positive political consequences. See Bill Walsh to Lee White, October 4, 1962, box 21, WF.

54. "Victory! President Signs Housing Order," *Trends in Housing* 6, no. 5 (September-October, 1962), 1, 4, Abrams and Black's quotes at 3. For the complete text of the order, see *Federal Register* 27 (November 24, 1962), 11527–11530. The U.S. Civil Rights Commission was also critical of Kennedy's order and his reluctance to enforce it. See U.S. Commission on Civil Rights, *Civil Rights—Report of the United States Commission on Civil Rights, 1963* (Washington, D.C., 1963), 95–103.

55. For an analysis that stresses the symbolic nature of Kennedy's execu-

tive order, see Brauer, *John F. Kennedy*, 210–211. If the positive aspects of the order were limited, so were its negative consequences. See "The Shoe Drops for Builders," *Business Week*, December 1, 1962, 30; Robert C. Weaver to Timothy Reardon, December 4, 1962, reel 6, Housing and Home Finance Agency microfilms, John F. Kennedy Library; Sorensen, *Kennedy*, 481; NCDH, "Press Release," November 19, 1964, reel 14, AP; NCDH, "Press Release," May 7, 1965, reel 14, ibid.

56. For the rise of the Republican Party in the South, see Kevin P. Phillips, *Post-Conservative America: People, Politics, & Ideology in a Time of Crisis* (New York: Random House, 1982), chap. 4. Abrams' views on political coalitions can be found in Abrams, untitled speech written for Robert Wagner, March 10, 1955, 9, reel 10, AP; Abrams, untitled speech, National Catholic Charities, September 20, 1957, 4, reel 10, ibid.; SCAD, "Press Release," March 21 (no year given, but probably 1956), 1, reel 35, ibid.; Abrams, untitled speech, Conference of the Councils of the New York State Commission Against Discrimination, 3–4; Abrams, untitled speech, Open Forum on Civil Rights, 6–7.

9. Cold War

1. Eric Carlson to Ruth Abrams, May 6, 1970, reel 54, AP. Abrams summarized most of his housing reports in his book, *Man's Struggle*. Generally, this chapter will discuss and cite that work, rather than individual reports. Copies of the reports themselves can be found on the following AP microfilm rolls: "Report to the Barbados Government and the Barbados Housing Authority on Land Tenure, Housing Policy, and Home Finance," reel 19; Report on Housing Financing in Bolivia, reel 19; "Housing in Ghana," reel 21; "Urban Renewal Project in Ireland," reel 22; "Report of Housing Mission of International Cooperation Administration to the United States Operations Mission," reel 22; "Planning and Action Program for the Development of the Hanshin Metropolitan Region of Japan," reel 22; "United Nations Mission to Kenya on Housing," reel 22; "Metropolitan Lagos," reel 23; "Report on Housing in Pakistan," reel 23; "Report on the Housing Program of the Commonwealth of Puerto Rico," reel 24; "Growth and Urban Renewal in Singapore," reel 24; "The Need for Training and Education for Housing and Planning [in Turkey]," reel 25; "Report on the Development of Ciudad Guayana in Venezuela," reel 25.

2. Abrams, *Man's Struggle*, 270, 275, quotes at 276.

3. Wald, *New York Intellectuals*, quote at 268; Jumonville, *Critical Crossings*, xi.

4. Abrams, *Man's Struggle*, quote at v; Abrams, "Urban Land Problems and Policies," *Bulletin on Housing and Town and Country Planning*, no. 7 (New

York: United Nations, 1953), quotes at 55 and 58. Additional information concerning the UN's technical assistance work can be found in Francis O. Wilcox, "The United Nations Program for Technical Assistance," *Annals of the American Academy of Political and Social Science* 268 (March 1950), 48; Clyde Eagleton and Richard N. Swift, eds., *Annual Review of United Nations Affairs, 1951* (New York: New York University Press, 1952), 222; "Technical Assistance Under the Regular Programmes of the United Nations," *Yearbook of the United Nations, 1951* (New York: Columbia University Press, 1952), 393; Clyde Eagleton and Richard N. Swift, eds., *Annual Review of United Nations Affairs, 1953* (New York: New York University Press, 1954), 157–158; David Mitrany, "The International Technical Assistance Program," *Proceedings of the Academy of Political Science* 25, no. 2 (January 1953), 145–155; "Trading in 'Know-How,' " *The Economist*, July 18, 1953, 185; "A Review of the New Projects Approved for Special Fund Assistance," *United Nations Review* 6, no. 8 (February 1960), 13–17; Clark M. Eichelberger, *UN: The First Twenty Years* (New York: Harper, 1965), 108; UN Technical Assistance Board, *15 Years and 150,000 Skills: An Anniversary Review of the United Nations Expanded Programme of Technical Assistance* (New York: United Nations, 1965), 1.

5. Abrams, *Man's Struggle*, quotes at 93.

6. Ibid., quotes at 93 and 94; Koenigsberger, Groak, and Bernstein, *The Work of Charles Abrams*, 45.

7. Quotes from Abrams to Jacqueline Tyrwhitt, December 10, 1953, reel 30, AP and Abrams to Albert Bender, December 22, 1953, reel 30, ibid.; Albert Bender to Abrams, January 21, 1954, reel 30, ibid.; "U.N. Special Service Agreement," January 21, 1954, reel 30, ibid.; "Housing and Town and Country Planning," *Yearbook of the United Nations, 1954*, 261; Abrams, *Man's Struggle*, 93. In addition to Abrams, Jacob Crane, a prominent American housing official, also had difficulty obtaining a visa to the UN conference. See Richard Harris, " 'A Burp in Church': Jacob L. Crane's Vision of Aided Self-Help Housing," *Planning History Studies* 11, no. 1 (1997), 12.

8. "Report on Section III: Physical Planning: Urban Land Policies," not dated, 3, 4, 5, 6, quotes at 1, reel 30, AP; "Description of the Seminar: January 8, 1964," 2, reel 30, ibid.; "Delhi Seminar on Housing and Planning," *Ekistics* 1, no. 6 (March 1955), 19–36.

9. Yonah Alexander, *International Technical Assistance Experts: A Case Study of the U.N. Experience* (New York: Praeger, 1966), 63, 69, quote at 67; Philip Glick, "The Choice of Instruments for Technical Cooperation," *The Annals of the American Academy of Political and Social Science* 323 (May 1959), 59–67.

10. Alexander, *International Technical Assistance Experts*, quote at 65; Lyton K. Caldwell, "The Role of the Technical Expert," *Annals of the American Academy of Political and Social Science* 323 (May 1959), quotes at 96; "Finding the Expert," *United Nations Review* 5, no. 1 (July 1958), quote at 34.

11. Taper, "A Lover of Cities," I, administrator quoted at 41, official paraphrased at 44, colleague quoted at 46.

12. Abrams to Ernest Weissmann, February 15, 1960, reel 9, AP; Abrams, "From Cooperation to Disorganization in a Changing World," speech, Fourth National Conference on Cooperative Housing, Washington, D.C., February 13–14, 1961, quotes at 20 and 21, reel 32, ibid.; Taper, "A Lover of Cities," I, 75, Abrams quoted at 50.

13. Abrams, *Man's Struggle*, quotes at 103 and 104; H. Peter Oberlander, "Planning Education for Newly Independent Countries," *Journal of the American Institute of Planners* 28, no. 2 (May 1962), 116. See also Abrams, "The World Housing Crisis," not dated, 1, reel 34, AP.

14. Sydney Nettleton Fisher, *The Middle East: A History*, 3d ed. (New York: Knopf, 1979), 516–518; Abrams, *Man's Struggle*, 196.

15. Abrams, *Man's Struggle*, quotes at 197 and 198.

16. Ibid., 197–198, quote at 201–202; Abrams' letter to Weissmann reprinted in ibid. at 202. See also Taper, "A Lover of Cities," I, 89–91.

17. Abrams, "Emerging Social Problems in an Urbanizing World," *Ekistics* 24, no. 145 (December 1967), quote at 460; Abrams, *Man's Struggle*, 197; Abrams, "Memorandum on the Establishment of a School of Architecture and Community Planning in Ankara, Turkey," October 1, 1954, reel 51, AP; Abrams, "The Middle East University in Ankara," *Ekistics* 24, no. 143 (October 1967), 346.

18. Abrams, *Man's Struggle*, 202, 205, 207, quotes at 203; "Technical University at Ankara Begins 6th Year with Big Plans," *NYT*, October 21, 1963, quote at 2; Abrams to Catherine Bauer, July 15, 1959, reel 10, AP.

19. Abrams, untitled speech, Organization for American States Advisory Committee on Housing in Latin America, Bogota, Columbia, September 4–9, 1961, quote at 1, reel 32, AP; Abrams to Catherine Bauer, July 15, 1959, reel 10, ibid.; Sturen quoted in Abrams, *Man's Struggle*, 205.

20. Felix Gilbert, *The End of the European Era, 1890 to the Present*, 3d ed. (New York: Norton, 1984), 444; John D. Hargreaves, *Decolonization in Africa* (London: Longman, 1988), 113–121.

21. Abrams, *Man's Struggle*, 184, 186, quotes at 183; Taper, "A Lover of Cities," I, 55–56.

22. Abrams, *Man's Struggle*, 185–186, 188, quote at 187.

23. Ibid., 187–188, quote at 189.

24. Ibid., quote at 193.

25. Ibid., quotes at 191 and 194; Weissmann quoted in Taper, "A Lover of Cities," I, 56.

26. Harris, " 'A Burp in Church,' " 3–10; Richard Harris, "The Silence of the Experts: 'Aided Self-Help Housing,' 1939–1954," *Habitat International* 22, no. 22 (1998), 165–167. A seminal article by Crane on aided self-help housing is "Huts and Houses in the Tropics," *Unasylva* 3, no. 3 (May–June 1949), 99–105.

27. Abrams, *Man's Struggle*, 173–174. Abrams never really acknowledged Jacob Crane's influence on aided self-help housing policies. This is partly explained by Abrams' pragmatic approach to problem solving, which eschewed copious or systematic research. That Abrams' own recommendations advanced a different version of self-help housing might be another reason.

28. Ibid., 171, 172, quotes at 168 and 174.

29. Ibid., 175, 176, quotes at 176, 177, 179, 180; Taper, "A Lover of Cities," I, 63.

30. Abrams, *Man's Struggle*, 21–23, quotes at 12.

31. Abrams, "From Cooperation to Disorganization in a Changing World," quotes at 19.

32. Abrams, "From Cooperation to Disorganization in a Changing World," quotes at 18 and 19; Abrams, "Emerging Social Problems in an Urbanizing World," quote at 458; Abrams, *Man's Struggle*, 17, 23, quote at 24; Abrams, "Freedom and the City," not dated (probably 1960), 17–19, reel 32, AP.

33. See the following reviews of *Man's Struggle*: William Petersen (untitled), *American Sociological Review* 30, no. 6 (December 1965), 957; Norton Ginsburg (untitled), *Economic Geography* 41, no. 3 (July 1965), 275.

34. Abrams, *Man's Struggle*, quote at vi–vii.

35. Ibid., 127–128, 133, 136–137, 139–140, quote at 130.

36. Ibid., 261, quotes at 253.

37. Ibid., 268–269, quotes at 287 and 291. Housing and land policies in the Soviet Union are examined in S. Strumilin, "Family and Community in the Society of the Future," *Soviet Review* 2, no. 2 (February 1961), 3–29; A. Zhuravlev and M. Fyodorov, "The Microdistrict and New Living Conditions," ibid. 2, no. 4 (April 1961), 37–40; Robert J. Osborn and Thomas A. Reiner, "Soviet City Planning: Current Issues and Future Perspectives," *Journal of the American Institute of Planners* 28, no. 4 (November 1962), 239–250.

38. Abrams, *Man's Struggle*, quotes at 288, 295–296. Despite Abrams' emphasis on housing as an important part of a developing country's economy, he did not subscribe to economic determinism (the belief that certain "stages" of economic growth generate certain kinds of political regimes).

For the now classic example of this approach, see W. W. Rostow, *The Stages of Economic Growth: A Non-Communist Manifesto* (New York: Cambridge University Press, 1960). Another contemporary, Adolph Berle, similarly suggested that exporting America's form of state capitalism could help make developing countries U.S. allies. See Schwarz, *Liberal*, 260.

39. Harris, " 'A Burp in Church,' " 10.

40. Koenigsberger, Groak, and Bernstein, *The Work of Charles Abrams*, 85–86.

41. Rem Koolhaas, "Singapore Songlines," in Rem Koolhaas and Bruce Mau, *Small, Medium, Large, Extra-Large: Office for Metropolitan Architecture, Rem Koolhaas and Bruce Mau*, ed. Jennifer Sigler (New York: Monacelli Press, 1995), 1013, 1033, 1037, 1044, 1077, quotes at 1011, 1021, 1029, 1035, 1083.

42. Charles Abrams, Susumu Kobe, and Otto Koenigsberger, *Growth and Urban Renewal in Singapore* (New York: United Nations, 1963), 12–13, 20, 48, 127, quotes at 11 and 45. An accessible, though edited, version of the report can be found in Koenigsberger, Groak, and Bernstein, *The Work of Charles Abrams*, 85–127. A copy of the report exists in AP, but it does not contain chap. 1. Unless otherwise noted, the page numbers in these notes refer to the copy of the report in the law library of the State University of New York at Buffalo. For a detailed discussion of "action programmes," see "action planning" in F. Stuart Chapin, Jr. and Edward J. Kaiser, *Urban Land Use Planning* (Urbana: University of Illinois Press, 1979), 70–72.

43. Abrams, Kobe, and Koenigsberger, *Growth and Urban Renewal in Singapore*, 51, 68, 73, 115–117, 123, 140, quotes at 9, 18, 62, and 67.

44. Ibid., 20, 118, 149, quotes at 18, 55, 122, and 148. Koolhaas believes that urban renewal in Singapore has become a perpetual process. See Koolhaas, "Singapore Songlines," 1035, 1037, 1075.

45. Koolhaas, "Singapore Songlines," quote at 1025. Though Koolhaas's prose is sometimes difficult to parse, he seems to argue that the UN report was kept secret because it would have revealed the regime's master strategy, which was bound to have generated public opposition. Koolhaas, ibid., 1025, 1053

46. Abrams, *Man's Struggle*, quotes at 244 and 245; Eric Carlson to Ruth Abrams, May 6, 1970, reel 54, AP.

47. Quotes from Abrams, *Man's Struggle*, 248, Abrams to George Hunton, July 24, 1961, reel 11, AP, and Abrams to U.S. Senate Subcommittee on Housing, January 14, 1963, 26, reel 32, ibid.

48. Quotes from Abrams to Bernard Taper, April 26, 1960, reel 1, AP, Abrams, "From Cooperation to Disorganization in a Changing World," 19, and Abrams, *Man's Struggle*, 249.

49. AID Housing and Urban Development Committee, *Minutes*, September 25, 1963, reel 11, AP. Quotes from Abrams, *Man's Struggle*, 100 and 251 and Abrams to David Bell, October 28, 1963, reel 11, AP. See also Osborne T. Boyd to Abrams, February 4, 1964, reel 11, ibid.; AID Housing and Urban Development Committee, *Minutes*, December 18, May 27, and September 17, 1963, December 16, 1964, and March 3, 1966, reel 11, ibid.

50. "Recommendations on AID Policy for the Training of Housing and Urban Development Personnel," May 11, 1964, quotes at 1 and 2, reel 11, AP.

51. Abrams to Jacqueline Tyrwhitt, December 10, 1953, reel 30, AP.

10. Urban Renewal

1. For renewed political interest in urban problems during the 1960s, see Francis E. Rourke, "Urbanism and the National Party Organizations," *Western Political Quarterly* 18, no. 1 (March 1965), 149–163.

2. Abrams, *City Is the Frontier*, 12, 211–212, quotes at 364; Abrams, "Freedom and the City," 22. For discussions of urban agendas and the limits to accomplishing them during this period, see Jon C. Teaford, *Rough Road to Renaissance: Urban Revitalization in America, 1940–1984* (Baltimore: Johns Hopkins University Press, 1990), 11, 26, 42, 83, 106; Peterson, *City Limits*, 4, 29.

3. The Housing Act of 1949 is located at 63 Stat. 413. The most complete treatment of the 1949 Housing Act is Davies, *Housing Reform During the Truman Administration*. See also "The Housing Act of 1949: A Federal Program for Public Housing and Slum Clearance," *Illinois Law Review* 44, no. 5 (November–December, 1949), 685–708; Lee Johnson, "The Housing Act of 1949 and Your Community," in *Two-Thirds of a Nation*, 194–209; Jewel Bellush and Murray Hausknecht, "Urban Renewal: An Historical Overview," in *Urban Renewal: People, Politics, and Planning*, eds. Jewel Bellush and Murray Hausknecht (Garden City, New York: Doubleday, 1967), 3–16; Lawrence M. Friedman, *Government and Slum Housing* (1968; reprint, New York: Arno Press, 1978), 148–151; Leonard Freedman, *Public Housing: The Politics of Poverty* (New York: Holt, Rinehart and Winston, 1969), 19–23; R. Allen Hays, *The Federal Government and Urban Housing: Ideology and Change in Public Policy* (Albany: SUNY Press, 1985), 89. Contemporary data on the supply of and demand for housing can be found in Robert Lasch, *Breaking the Building Blockade* (Chicago: University of Chicago Press, 1946), chap. 2. For an account of one of the first cities to utilize the provisions of the 1949 Housing Act, see Harold Kaplan, *Urban Renewal Politics: Slum Clearance in Newark* (New York: Columbia University Press, 1963). New York City's efforts are detailed in Schwartz, *The New York Approach*.

4. Housing and Home Finance Agency, *Fourteenth Annual Report, 1960* (Washington, D.C., 1961), 287; U.S. Senate, *Hearing Before the Committee on Banking and Currency on S. 2889, S. 2938, and S. 2949 (Bills to Expand and Extend Title III, Servicemen's Readjustment Act of 1944, National Housing Act, and Housing Act of 1949)*, 83d Cong., 2d sess., March 12, 1954, 233 (hereafter *1954 Housing Act Hearings*); National Commission on Urban Problems, *Building the American City* (New York: Praeger, 1969), 111; Catherine Bauer, "Redevelopment: A Misfit in the Fifties," in *The Future of Cities and Urban Redevelopment,* ed. Coleman Woodbury (Chicago: University of Chicago Press, 1953), 1:9; Keith, *Politics and the Housing Crisis,* 102; Mark I. Gelfand, *A Nation of Cities: The Federal Government and Urban America, 1933–1965* (New York: Oxford University Press, 1975), 170.

5. Miles L. Colean, *Renewing Our Cities* (New York: Twentieth Century Fund, 1953), 7–11, 37–58, 142–168, quote at 40. Baltimore took the lead in urban rehabilitation, and thus early descriptions of renewal were often said to be following the "Baltimore Plan." See Edgar L. Jones and Burke David, "Slum Clearance at a Profit," *Atlantic Monthly,* May 1949, 35–38; Martin Millspaugh, "Rehabilitation—The Human Problems," in *The Human Side of Urban Renewal,* eds. Martin Millspaugh and Gurney Breckenfeld (Baltimore: Fight-Blight, 1958), 2–64.

6. One reason that Colean's call for comprehensive renewal was ignored was the costs involved. City planners estimated that to renew all American cities with 2,500 or more inhabitants would cost $1.3 trillion over a twelve-year period. See John W. Dyckman and Reginald R. Isaacs, *Capital Requirements for Urban Development and Renewal* (New York: McGraw-Hill, 1961), 17; William L. C. Wheaton, "The Cost of Comprehensive Renewal," in *Ends and Means of Urban Renewal: Papers from the Philadelphia Housing Association's Fiftieth Anniversary Forum* (Philadelphia: Philadelphia Housing Association, 1961), 59–75. A more general analysis of cost estimates can be found in William Nash, *Residential Rehabilitation: Private Profits and Public Purpose* (New York: McGraw-Hill, 1959).

7. House Committee on Banking, Currency and Housing, Subcommittee on Housing and Community Development, *Evolution of Role of the Federal Government in Housing and Community Development: A Chronology of Legislative and Selected Executive Actions, 1892–1974,* 94th Cong., 1st sess., 1975, Committee Print, 41; J. Paul Mitchell, "The Housing Act of 1954: Impacts on Housing," *Planning History Present* 8, no. 1 (1994), 3. The Housing Act of 1954 is located at 68 Stat 590. Even though Eisenhower had recommended 140,000 new units of public housing, the Housing Act of 1954 authorized 35,000 for the following fiscal year, but none for the ensuing three years. See Keith, *Politics and the Housing Crisis,* 115.

8. U.S. Senate, *1954 Housing Act Hearings*, March 15, 1954, 249, March 19, 1954, 620–625, March 24, 1954, 829, 832, 836, 838–846; Abrams, "Slums, Ghettos, and the G.O.P.'s 'Remedy,' " *The Reporter*, May 11, 1954, quote at 29–30. For business support of the 1954 Housing Act, see U.S. Senate, *1954 Housing Act Hearings*, March 15, 1954, 243, 245, March 18, 1954, 412, 416, and March 22, 1954, 651, 680, 690, 692, 708; "Growing Problem of Federal Housing Aid," *Congressional Digest* 38, no. 3 (March 1959), 67; Michael Harrington, "The Housing Scandal," *Commonweal*, July 2, 1954, 311–313. See also Michael Harrington, "Slums, Old and New," *Commentary*, August 1960, 118. Another reason pubic housing supporters might have been skeptical of the bill's effectiveness was because of its implicit reliance on "filtering down." "Filtering" is the general process by which housing stock is passed down to lower socioeconomic groups; this process provides the newest housing to upper-income groups, while giving the oldest, least desirable housing to lower-income groups. In the 1954 Housing Act, rehabilitation was seen as one mechanism to initiate filtering. See U.S. Senate, *1954 Housing Act Hearings*, 15 March 1954, 250. For additional information on the various meanings of "filtering," see William G. Grigsby, *Housing Markets and Public Policy* (Philadelphia: University of Pennsylvania Press, 1963), 84–130.

9. Keith, *Politics and the Housing Crisis*, 145; National Commission on Urban Problems, *Building the American City*, 157. The Housing Act of 1961 is located at 75 Stat 149. The 1961 Housing Act also included two additional provisions, 221(d)(3) and 221(d)(4), aimed at stimulating construction of more housing for displacees, but neither resulted in a substantial increase in dwellings. See Paul L. Niebanck, *Relocation in Urban Planning: From Obstacle to Opportunity* (Philadelphia: University of Pennsylvania Press, 1968), 22–23.

10. Abrams, *City is the Frontier*, ix; Martin Anderson, *The Federal Bulldozer: A Critical Analysis of Urban Renewal, 1949–1962* (Cambridge: MIT Press, 1964), 13, 18, 183, 230, quotes at 1, 220, 221, 222, and 228. Anderson's arguments are also presented in his article, "Fiasco of Urban Renewal," *Harvard Business Review* 43, no. 1 (January–February 1965), 6–21. Even James Q. Wilson, Director of the MIT-Harvard Joint Center for Urban Studies—which published *The Federal Bulldozer*—cast doubt on some of Anderson's arguments, stating that " 'the Anderson book meets only the minimum standards of scholarship that the center applies to its studies.' " Wilson quoted in Warren Lehman, "Thinking Small About Urban Renewal," *Washington University Law Quarterly*, no. 4 (December 1965), 397.

11. Manuel Castells, *The Urban Question: A Marxist Approach*, trans. Alan Sheridan (Cambridge: MIT Press, 1977), quote at 286; Walter Thabit, "The

Cities of Charles Abrams," review of *The City is the Frontier*, by Charles Abrams, *The New Republic*, May 14, 1966, quote at 44; Chester W. Hartman, "A Critique and a Blueprint," review of *The City is the Frontier*, by Charles Abrams, *Progressive Architecture* 47, no. 1 (January 1966), 198, 200, 206, 214, 222. Several other reviewers believed that *The City Is the Frontier* was the single best analysis of urban renewal to date. See the following reviews: James King, "Prime and Pertinent," *Journal of Housing* 22, no. 10 (November 1965), 556; unsigned review (untitled), *Atlantic Monthly*, December 1965, 151; C. W. Griffin, Jr., "The State of the Cities," *The Reporter*, December 16, 1965, 52–54. In 1960, the Ford Foundation extended grants to nine other individuals to provide analyses of urban renewal. As of the spring of 1966, Abrams was the only one who had published his findings. See Edward C. Banfield, review of *The City Is the Frontier*, by Charles Abrams, *Commentary*, March 1966, 93.

12. Abrams, *City Is the Frontier*, ix, 155–181, quotes at 155 and 169. For a recent study that discusses the contributions of urban renewal, see Thomas H. O'Connor, *Building a New Boston: Politics and Urban Renewal, 1950–1970* (Boston: Northeastern University Press, 1993), 285–286.

13. Abrams, "Statement . . . Before the United States Senate, Committee on Banking and Currency, Subcommittee on Housing," Thursday, May 14th, 1959, quote at 1, reel 31, AP; Abrams, untitled speech, Harvard Divinity School, January 31, 1963, quotes at 10 and 11, reel 32, ibid.; Abrams, *City Is the Frontier*, quote at 28; Abrams, "U.S. Housing: A New Program," Special Supplement, *The New Leader*, January 13, 1958, 6, reel 31, ibid.; Abrams, "Housing Policy—1937 to 1967," in *Shaping an Urban Future: Essays in Memory of Catherine Bauer Wurster*, eds. Bernard J. Frieden and William W. Nash, Jr. (Cambridge: MIT Press, 1969), 35–45. Abrams first noted the problems of clearing slums without supplying new housing in his article "Slum Clearance or Vacant Land Development," *Shelter* 3, no. 7 (February 1939), 23–24. A number of scholars subsequently echoed Abrams' concerns. See Grigsby, *Housing Markets and Public Policy*, 286; Bernard Frieden, *The Future of Old Neighborhoods* (Cambridge: MIT Press, 1964), 619.

14. Abrams, *City Is the Frontier*, quote at 135; Niebanck, *Relocation in Urban Planning*, quote at 14; National Commission on Urban Problems, *Building the American City*, 125; Peter Marris, "A Report on Urban Renewal in the United States," in *The Urban Condition: People and Policy in the Metropolis*, ed. Leonard J. Duhl (New York: Basic Books, 1963), 123. The sociologist Chester Hartman reached a conclusion similar to the one articulated by Abrams. See Chester Hartman, "The Housing of Relocated Families," *Journal of the American Institute of Planners* 30, no. 4 (November 1964), 266. See also

Herbert Gans, "The Human Implications of Current Redevelopment and Relocation Planning," *Journal of the American Institute of Planners* 25, no. 1 (February 1959), 15; Martin Millspaugh, "Problems and Opportunities of Relocation," *Law and Contemporary Problems* 26, no. 1 (Winter 1961), 6–8. Robert Weaver suggested in 1963 that the trend toward displacing minority residents had been reversed, though the data were still discouraging for African Americans; in 1957, 53 percent of displacees were nonwhite, a figure that dropped to 51.5 percent in 1961, and to 46.1 percent in March of 1963. See Robert Weaver, "Current Trends in Urban Renewal," *Land Economics* 39, no. 4 (November 1963), 341. Another scholar has concluded that renewal was not the primary cause of urban segregation in Atlanta, but simply conformed to existing patterns established by municipal officials. See Ronald H. Baylor, "Urban Renewal, Public Housing and the Racial Shaping of America," *Journal of Policy History* 1, no. 4 (1989), 419–439.

15. Abrams, *City Is the Frontier*, 32–33; Gwendolyn Wright, *Building the American Dream: A Social History of Housing in America* (Cambridge: MIT Press, 1981), 234–237; "Low-Income Housing," *America*, January 7, 1956, 391. A good discussion of Le Corbusier can be found in Robert Fishman, *Urban Utopias in the Twentieth Century: Ebenezer Howard, Frank Lloyd Wright, and Le Corbusier* (New York: Basic Books, 1977). See also Abrams, "Criteria for Urban Renewal," *Architectural Record* 131, no. 5 (May 1962), 156–157; Abrams, "City Planning and Housing Policy in Relation to Crime and Juvenile Delinquency," *International Review of Criminal Policy*, no. 16 (October 1960), 25; Abrams, "Land, Homes, and People: Policies for Growth and Renewal," speech, Philadelphia Housing Association, May 23, 1963, reel 32, AP; Abrams, "Determining the Priorities for New York City," recommendations for the City Planning Commission, October 16, 1964, reel 33, ibid. The city that gained the most notoriety for its high-rise projects was Chicago. For a review of projects built by the Chicago Housing Authority between the 1930s and 1970s, see Meyerson and Banfield, *Politics, Planning, and the Public Interest*, especially chap. 6; Devereux Bowly, Jr., *The Poorhouse: Subsidized Housing in Chicago, 1895–1978* (Carbondale, Illinois: Southern Illinois University Press, 1978); Raymond J. Struyk, *A New System for Public Housing: Salvaging a National Resource* (Washington, D.C.: Urban Institute, 1980), 24–29. Contemporary evaluations of public housing, mostly negative, are Oscar Newman, *Defensible Space: Crime Prevention Through Urban Design* (New York: Macmillan, 1972); William Moore Jr., *The Vertical Ghetto: Everyday Life in an Urban Project* (New York: Random House, 1969); Lee Rainwater, *Behind Ghetto Walls: Black Families in a Federal Slum* (New York: Penguin, 1973).

16. Catherine Bauer, "The Dreary Deadlock of Public Housing," *Architectural Forum* 106, no. 5 (May 1957), 140–142, 219, 221; "The Dreary Deadlock of Public Housing—How to Break It," ibid., 106, no. 6 (June 1957), Abrams' quote at 218; Abrams, *City Is the Frontier*, 30, quotes at 34 and 36; Abrams, "Public Housing: A New Look," *Real Estate News* (August 1957), quote at 276. See also Abrams, "Report of the Housing and Urban Renewal Task Force to Mayor John V. Lindsay," reprinted in *Taming Megalopolis*, ed. H. Wentworth Eldredge (New York: Praeger, 1967), 1:498; Abrams, "U.S. Housing: A New Program," 11–12; Abrams, untitled speech, Lexington Democratic Club, March 4, 1961, reel 32, AP; Abrams, untitled speech, Cooper Square Association, October 24, 1961, reel 32, ibid.; Abrams, "The Sociological Needs of Low Income Families in Public Housing Design," Princeton Design Seminar, March 8, 1965, reel 33, ibid.; Abrams, untitled speech, Boston College, April 22, 1969, reel 34, ibid. Robert Weaver held views similar to Abrams, asserting the need to "develop more tolerance to variations from established middle-class values and behavior." See Robert Weaver, "Class, Race and Urban Renewal," *Land Economics* 36, no. 3 (August 1960), 251. For discussions of "problem tenants," see "Unwed Mothers: Even Experts Are Stumped About How to Treat Them," *Journal of Housing* 16, no. 8 (September 1959), 289–290; Richard S. Scobie, *Problem Tenants in Public Housing: Who, Where, and Why Are They?* (New York: Praeger, 1975); Alvin Rabuska and William G. Weissert, *Caseworkers or Police? How Tenants See Public Housing* (Stanford: Hoover Institution Press, 1977), 83. For a survey of the treatment of public housing in the popular press, see A. Scott Henderson, "Tarred with the Exceptional Image": Public Housing and Popular Discourse, 1950–1990," *American Studies* 36, no. 1 (Spring 1995), 31–52.

17. Abrams, *City Is the Frontier*, quotes at 22 and 23.

18. Abrams, *City Is the Frontier*, quotes at 84 and 85. Perhaps the most egregious example of private-public fraud (the type of corruption Abrams criticized) had occurred during the so-called 608 scandals. The 608 program, a provision of the 1942 Housing Act, was originally designed to stimulate war housing, but was modified in 1946 to provide incentives for construction of rental housing. With little administrative oversight, builders inflated their cost estimates, received mortgage funds for these amounts (with FHA approval), and pocketed enormous profits that accrued from the difference between projected and actual costs. Abrams called attention to these practices at the time, blaming government officials as well as private entrepreneurs. See Abrams, "The FHA System," 8–9; Abrams, *City Is the Frontier*, 87–89.

19. Abrams, "The Legal Basis for Reorganizing Metropolitan Areas in a

Free Society," *Proceedings of the American Philosophical Society* 106, no. 3 (June 1962), quote at 188; Abrams, *City Is the Frontier,* 147, quote at 153. In addition to remaining an advocate of federal and state programs, Abrams continued to be a strong supporter of urban planning, refusing to identify himself with those who, in the wake of urban renewal's failures, expressed "anti-planning" views. See Robert Fishman, "The Anti-Planners: The Contemporary Revolt Against Planning and Its Significance for Planning History," in *Shaping an Urban World,* ed. Gordon E. Cherry (New York: St. Martin's, 1980), 243–252.

20. "Housing Developers Vie for Jobs of Clearing Slums," *Business Week,* February 22, 1958, 80–82, 84, 87; "Good Business in Urban Renewal," ibid., April 15, 1961, 153–154, 156; "Money to be Made in Real Estate," ibid., June 24, 1961, 121–122; "Big Cities Try for a Comeback," *U.S. News and World Report,* December 28, 1964, 34–38, quote at 34; David B. Carlson, "Urban Renewal: Running Hard, Sitting Still," *Architectural Forum* 116, no. 4 (April 1962), quote at 99. Similar discussions of urban renewal can be found in "Urban Renewal Reviving Centers of Nation's Cities," *NYT,* April 6, 1964, 1, 22; "The City: Under the Knife, or All for Their Own Good," *Time,* November 6, 1964, 60–72. For the popular press's tendency to ignore the problematic aspects of urban renewal, see Herbert J. Gans, "The Failure of Urban Renewal: A Critique and Some Proposals," *Commentary,* April 1965, 29.

21. William G. Grigsby, "Housing and Slum Clearance: Elusive Goals," *Annals of the American Academy of Political and Social Science* 352 (March 1964), quote at 107; Scott Greer and David W. Minar, "The Political Side of Urban Development and Redevelopment," *Annals of the American Academy of Political and Social Science* 352 (March 1964), quote at 62; Anthony Downs, "The Successes and Failures of Federal Housing Policy," *The Public Interest,* no. 34 (Winter 1974), quotes at 131.

22. Jane Jacobs' views on urban problems can be found in her major work, *The Death and Life of Great American Cities.* Mumford's quotes are from "Statement of Mr. Lewis Mumford Before the Senate Subcommittee on Executive Reorganization," April 21, 1967, 11, unmicrofilmed portion, AP. Abrams was impressed with *The Death and Life of Great American Cities* largely because of Jacobs' iconoclastic views, which he collectively called an "abattoir for sacred cows." To be sure, Jacobs excoriated the views of Catherine Bauer, Henry Wright, Clarence Stein, and above all, Lewis Mumford, whose *Culture of Cities* she called a "morbid and biased catalogue of ills." Mumford returned the favor by describing Jacobs as a "dreary fanatic," and accusing Abrams of being part of her "uncritical following." See Jacobs, *The Death and Life of Great American Cities,* quote at 20; Lewis Mumford, *The Urban Prospect*

(New York: Harcourt, 1968), 182–207; Abrams, "Abattoir for Sacred Cows," *Progressive Architecture* 43, no. 4 (April 1962), 196; Abrams to Mumford, March 30 and April 1, 1968, with Mumford's description of Jacobs from Mumford to Abrams, April 3, 1967, all in the Lewis Mumford Papers, folders 14 and 5617, Special Collections Department, University of Pennsylvania Library.

23. For discussions of the coalitions that supported urban renewal, see Robert H. Salisbury, "Urban Politics: The New Convergence of Power," *Journal of Politics* 26, no. 4 (November 1964), 775–797; Richard M. Flanagan, "The Housing Act of 1954: The Sea Change in National Urban Policy," *Urban Affairs Review* 33, no. 2 (November 1997), 265–286.

24. Abrams to Charles C. Diggs, Jr., October 3, 1963, reel 9, AP.

25. Abrams, *Home Ownership for the Poor: A Program for Philadelphia*, rev. ed. (New York: Praeger, 1970), xiii, xvi, xviii, quote at xix. The original report Abrams submitted in late 1966 was entitled *The Negro Housing Problem: A Program for Philadelphia*. In 1970, a revised edition was published; Kolodny added a new preface and an additional chapter, but other than these emendations, the work remained unchanged. Since the revised edition is easier to obtain, the present study provides citations from it, rather than from the original report. For a draft of the latter, see reel 24, AP.

26. Abrams, *Home Ownership for the Poor*, quote at xvi.

27. Ibid., 116–117, quote at 96.

28. Ibid., 103–111, 120, quotes at 121 and 122; *Philadelphia Inquirer*, April 15, 1967, no page number given, reel 34, AP; *The Sunday Bulletin*, April 30, 1967, no page number given, reel 34, ibid.; *Philadelphia Inquirer*, no date or page number given, 1967, reel 34, ibid. Abrams explained what he meant by "move-in" condition in a letter to Robert Weaver: "It surprised me too to find that Philadelphia had houses cheap enough for the low-income Negro to buy and good enough to live in. The term " 'move-in' " means exactly what it implies, i.e. that it is ready to move into, does not require major repairs, perhaps some painting, as one might do with any house in good condition." See Abrams to Weaver, January 23, 1967, reel 12, AP.

29. Abrams, *Home Ownership for the Poor*, 124, 128. Abrams amplified his feelings in a letter to Robert Weaver: "In view of my findings, I do think that extravagant expenditure for rehabilitation on these buildings by H.A.A. [Housing Assistance Administration] would be a grave mistake, is unnecessary and would make tenants of those who would be owners." See Abrams to Weaver, January 23, 1967, reel 12, AP.

30. Abrams, *Home Ownership for the Poor*, 135, 139, quotes at xxii and 127.

31. Ibid., quote at xxiv.

32. Ibid., xv, quote at xxiii; Abrams, "Statement . . . Before the Sub-

Committee on Executive Reorganization of the Committee on Government Operations," U.S. Senate, 89th Cong., 2d sess., submitted on April 20, 1967, 5, 16, quotes at 9 and 15, reel 34, AP. Abrams likewise told Senator Abraham Ribicoff (D-CT): "My Philadelphia study emphasizes the dangers of a hierarchy of federal programs into which each city must fit its applications for assistance, irrespective of whether the federal programs suit its particular requirements." See Abrams to Ribicoff, March 13, 1967, reel 7, AP.

33. Mollenkopf, *The Contested City*, 3–4.

34. "Charles H. Percy," in *Current Biography Yearbook, 1977*, ed. Charles Moritz (New York: H. W. Wilson, 1978), 341–344; Stephen Hess and David S. Broder, *The Republican Establishment: The Present and Future of the G.O.P.* (New York: Harper, 1967), chap. 7; Martha Cleveland, *Charles Percy: Strong New Voice from Illinois* (Jacksonville, Illinois: Harris Wolfe, 1968), 163; David Murray, *Charles Percy of Illinois* (New York: Harper, 1968), 18–35; Robert E. Hartley, *Charles H. Percy: A Political Perspective* (Chicago: Rand McNally, 1975), 21.

35. *Congressional Record—Senate*, 90th Cong., 1st sess., January 27, 1967, quotes at 1524; Percy to Abrams, December 31, 1966, reel 7, AP; Johnson, "Annual Message to the Congress on the State of the Union," January 10, 1967, in *Public Papers of the Presidents of the United States: Lyndon B. Johnson, 1963–1969*, vol. 7, book 1 (Washington, D.C., 1968), 5; Cleveland, *Charles Percy*, 163. Other elected officials also contacted Abrams for information about various housing programs. See James E. Scheuer to Abrams, June 30, 1965, reel 9, AP; Jacob K. Javits to Abrams, January 18, 1966, reel 5, ibid.; Warren G. Magnuson to Abrams, May 19, 1967, reel 46, ibid.; Robert F. Kennedy to Abrams, August 17, 1967, reel 5, ibid.; Paul Simon to Abrams, September 15, 1967, reel 8, ibid.; William F. Ryan to Abrams, November 29, 1967, reel 46, ibid.; Margaret Smith to Abrams, September 20, 1968, reel 7, ibid.

36. Percy to Abrams, May 16, 1967, reel 7, AP; Abrams, "Statement by Charles Abrams . . . Before the United States Senate, Committee on Banking and Currency," 4–6, quotes at 1 and 3; Warren W. Magnuson to Abrams, May 19, 1967, reel 46, AP. On at least one occasion, Percy referred to Abrams as the "dean of America's urban scholars." See Percy, "Youth and the Challenge of Our Cities," speech, Villanova University, Villanova, Pennsylvania, February 14, 1967, 1, reel 46, AP.

37. *Congressional Record—Senate*, 90th Cong., 1st sess., April 20, 1967, 10288–10302, quotes at 10297; Percy to Abrams, May 16, 1967, reel 7, AP; "Percy Explains Home-Owner Plan," *Christian Science Monitor*, April 19, 1967, 12; Warren H. Butler, "An Approach to Low and Moderate Income Home Ownership," *Rutgers Law Review* 22 (1967–1968), 72, 75, 76, 77, 95.

38. *Congressional Record—Senate*, 90th Cong., 1st sess. April 20, 1967, Brooke's quote at 10293; *Congressional Record—House*, 90th Cong., 1st sess., April 20, 1967, Luken's quote at 10367, Bush's quote at 10376.

39. Robert C. Weaver, "Statement . . . on the Proposed National Home Ownership Foundation Act," April 21, 1967, quote at 1, reel 46, AP; Johnson, "Special Message to the Congress: America's Unfinished Business, Urban and Rural Poverty," March 14, 1967, in *Public Papers of the Presidents of the United States: Lyndon B. Johnson, 1963–1969*, vol. 7, book 1 (Washington, D.C., 1968), 341; "Democrats Seeking Alternative To Percy Plan on Homeowners," *New York Times*, July 23, 1967, 50. Percy's response to Weaver's criticisms can be found in "Factual Analysis of Statement by Robert C. Weaver . . . Issued April 21, 1967," June 20, 1967, reel 46, AP. In addition to the Percy bill, Abrams gave advice concerning two bills submitted by Senator Abraham Ribicoff. See Abrams to Ribicoff, March 13, 1967, reel 7, ibid.

40. Abrams to Percy, May 31, 1967, reel 46, AP; U.S. Senate, *Hearings Before the Subcommittee on Housing and Urban Affairs of the Committee on Banking and Currency on Proposed Housing Legislation for 1967*, 90th Cong., 1st sess., July 26, 1967, 715, quotes at 713 and 716 (hereafter *Proposed Housing Legislation for 1967*); Percy to Abrams, May 16, 1967, reel 7, AP; Warren G. Magnuson to Abrams, June 22, 1967, reel 46, ibid.; Abrams to Percy, May 31, 1967, reel 7, ibid.; Percy to Abrams, June 19, 1967, reel 7, ibid.; Percy to Abrams, June 27, 1967, reel 7, ibid.; Percy to Abrams, July 10, 1967, reel 7, ibid.; "Appendix Two: Explanatory Statement Submitted by Senator Percy on the National Homeownership Foundation Act," *Proposed Housing Legislation for 1967*, 1517–1545; "Aid to Poor Asked for Owning Homes," *NYT*, May 24, 1967, 40.

41. Percy to Abrams, November 13, 1967, reel 7, AP; John McClaughry, "The Troubled Dream: The Life and Times of Section 235 of the National Housing Act," *Loyola University Law Journal* 6, no. 1 (Winter 1975), 13, 16, 17. Other assessments of Section 235 and 236 can be found in Robert Schafer and Charles G. Field, "Section 235 of the National Housing Act: Homeownership for Low Income Families?," *Journal of Urban Law* 46, no. 3 (1969), 667–685; Anthony Downs, *Federal Housing Subsidies* (Lexington, Massachusetts: D.C. Heath & Company, 1973), 49–66.

42. The 1968 Housing Act is located at 82 Stat. 476 (National Homeownership Foundation provisions at 491–495); Johnson, "Special Message to the Congress on Urban Problems: 'The Crisis of the Cities,' " February 22, 1968, in *Public Papers of the Presidents of the United States: Lyndon B. Johnson, 1963–1969*, vol. 9, book 1 (Washington, D.C., 1970), 252; McClaughry, "The Troubled Dream," 17, 18.

43. McClaughry, "The Troubled Dream," quote at 18.

44. U.S. Senate, *Housing and Redevelopment Act of 1967*, 90th Cong., 1st sess., November 28, 1967, S. Rept. 809, quote at 71; Hartley, *Charles H. Percy*, 186.

45. McClaughry, "The Troubled Dream," 4; Michael Danielson, *The Politics of Exclusion* (New York: Columbia University Press, 1976), 81, 83, 86–87, 104, 106; Douglas S. Massey and Nancy S. Denton, *American Apartheid: Segregation and the Making of the Underclass* (Cambridge: Harvard University Press, 1993), 205.

46. Percy to Abrams, September 30, 1968, reel 7, AP; Abrams to Percy, October 15, 1968, reel 7, ibid.; Nixon, "State of the Union Message to the Congress on Community Development," March 8, 1973, in *Public Papers of the Presidents of the United States: Richard M. Nixon, 1969–1974*, vol. 5 (Washington, D.C., 1975), 175; Ford, "Statement on the Housing and Community Development Act of 1974," August 22, 1974, in *Public Papers of the Presidents of the United States: Gerald R. Ford, 1974–1977*, vol. 1 (Washington, D.C., 1975), 44; McClaughry, "The Troubled Dream," 33, 35–38; U.S. House, *Hearings Before the Committee on Banking and Currency (Interim Report on HUD Investigation of Low- and Moderate-Income Housing Programs)*, 92d Cong., 1st sess., March 31, 1971, 17; Allen J. Matusow, *The Unraveling of America: A History of American Liberalism in the 1960s* (New York: Harper, 1984), 234. The Housing and Community Development Act of 1974 is located at 88 Stat. 633 (Section 235 and 236 amendments at 671–672).

47. Danielson, *Politics of Exclusion*, 87. For the general phenomenon of "unanticipated consequences," see the landmark essay by Robert K. Merton, "The Unanticipated Consequences of Purposive Social Action," *American Sociological Review* 1, no. 6 (December 1936), 894–904.

48. President's Committee on Urban Housing, *The Report of the President's Committee on Urban Housing: A Decent Home* (Washington, D.C., 1968), 3, quote at 2.

11. "When the Grey Mist Subsides"

1. Edwin P. Uhl to Abrams, February 22, 1967, reel 1, AP; Abrams to Edwin P. Uhl, February 27, 1967, reel 1, ibid.; Don H. Grusin to Abrams, February 19, 1967, reel 1, ibid.; Abrams to Don H. Grusin, reel 1, ibid.; Alfred E. Prettyman to Abrams, February 19, 1969, reel 12, ibid.

2. "Abstract," Lawndale Community Conference, Recordings and Transcripts, State Historical Society of Wisconsin, Madison, Wisconsin (hereafter *Lawndale Transcript*). For the Kings' visit to Lawndale, see David

L. Lewis, *King: A Biography* (Chicago: University of Illinois Press, 1970), 315–316; Roger Biles, *Richard J. Daley: Politics, Race, and the Governing of Chicago* (Dekalb, Illinois: Northern Illinois University Press, 1995), 120–121.

3. For the general reaction against planners, see Robert Fishman, "The Anti-Planners," 243–252.

4. "Workshop #1, Housing for Lawndale," June 6, 1967, 19–20, *Lawndale Transcript*; "Workshop #1, Part I—Second Day," June 7, 1967, quotes at 2, ibid.

5. "Workshop #1, Housing for Lawndale," quotes at 2 and 3. For a discussion of "participatory democracy," see James Miller, *"Democracy is in the Streets": From Port Huron to the Siege of Chicago* (New York: Simon & Schuster, 1987), chap. 8.

6. "300 Protesting Columbia Students Barricade Office of College Dean," *NYT*, April 24, 1968, quote at 30; "Columbia Closes Campus after Disorders," ibid., April 25, 1968, 41; "Columbia Halting Work on Its Gym; Suspends Classes," ibid., April 26, 1968, 50. See also Charles Kaiser, *1968 in America* (New York: Weidenfeld & Nicolson, 1988), 155–156; Todd Gitlin, *The Sixties: Years of Hope, Days of Rage*, rev. ed. (New York: Bantam, 1993), 306–309; Miller, *Democracy Is in the Streets*, 290–292.

7. "300 Protesting Columbia Students," 1, 30; "Columbia Closes Campus after Disorders," 1, 41; "Faculty's Effort Fails to Resolve Columbia Dispute," *NYT*, April, 27, 1968, 1, 18.

8. Abrams to David B. Truman, April 28, 1968, reel 11, AP; Abrams, "Memorandum Re Columbia Situation" (not dated but probably April 28, 1968), quote at 1, reel 11, ibid.; "Columbia Closed as Efforts to End Dispute Continue," *NYT*, April 29, 1968, 1. The "Memorandum" contains a reference to an April 29 faculty meeting, but this is likely an error; given the context of the memo and its cover letter, the date for the faculty meeting should have been identified as April 28.

9. Abrams, "Memorandum," quotes at 1, 2, and 3.

10. Abrams to Daniel Bell, May 1, 1968, quotes at 1 and 2, reel 11, AP; Abrams, "Memorandum," 1; "1,000 Police Act to Oust Students from Five Buildings at Columbia; Move in at University's Request," *NYT*, April 30, 1968, 1, 36; Kaiser, *1968 in America*, 163.

11. Robert Kolodny, telephone interview by author, May 18, 1998. An additional problem was that the students' definition of "amnesty" was different from Abrams.' See Jerry L. Avorn et al., *Up Against the Ivy Wall: A History of the Columbia Crisis*, ed. Robert Friedman (New York: Atheneum, 1969), 174.

12. Diana Trilling, "On the Steps of Low Library: Liberalism and the

Revolution of the Young," *Commentary*, November 1968, quote at 39; Dwight Macdonald, "An Exchange on Columbia," *New York Review of Books*, July 11, 1968, quote at 42. For the representativeness of Trilling's remarks, see Bloom, *Prodigal Sons*, 345; Barbara Ehrenreich, *Fear of Falling: The Inner Life of the Middle Class* (New York: Harper, 1989), 57–60.

13. Abrams to Bayard Rustin, May 8, 1968, reel 11, AP; "Memorandum to Bayard Rustin from Charles Abrams, May 8, 1968," quote at 1, reel 11, ibid.; Abrams to David Truman, May 9, 1968, reel 11, ibid.; Abrams to Grayson Kirk, August 8, 1968, reel 11, ibid.

14. Abrams to Peter A. Carmichael, February 11, 1959, quote at 1, reel 2, AP; Abrams, lecture notes, November 26, 1968, quotes at 5, reel 12, ibid.; Abrams, *Language of Cities*, 24, 347, quotes at 23 and 346.

15. Abrams, *Language of Cities*, quotes at vii.

16. Ibid., quotes at viii; Clement E. Vose, "Political Dictionaries: A Bibliographical Essay," *American Political Science Review* 68, no. 4 (December 1974), quote at 1696.

17. Abrams, *Language of Cities*, quotes at 35, 39, and 289.

18. Ibid., quotes at 89 and 102.

19. Ibid., quote at 46–47; Vose, "Political Dictionaries," quote at 1698.

20. Abrams, *Language of Cities*, quote at 131.

21. Ibid., quote at 60.

22. "Discharge Summary," October 29, 1967, reel 54, AP; "Discharge Summary," January 6, 1968, reel 54, ibid.; "Discharge Summary," January 7, 1969, reel 54, ibid.; Henry Banks to Abrams, May 29, 1969, reel 54, ibid.; Abrams to Herman Wouk, October 8, 1969, reel 9, ibid.; Abrams to Averell Harriman, November 12, 1969, reel 4, ibid.; Lloyd Rodwin to Abrams, December 17, 1969, reel 7, ibid.

23. Abrams to Henry Goldschmidt, May 29, 1969, reel 54, AP; Abrams to Ruth Abrams, January 22, 1954, reel 54, ibid.

24. Abrams to Bill Wurster, March 27, 1969, reel 10, AP.

25. Abrams to Courtney Brown, May 20, 1969, reel 11, AP; Abrams to Otto Koenigsberger, December 30, 1969, reel 5, ibid.; Israel Stollman to Abrams, February 12, 1970, reel 11, ibid.; Hans B. C. Spiegel, letter to author, April 21, 1998.

26. "In Memoriam: Charles Abrams," *Trends in Housing* 14, no. 1 (Winter 1970), quote at 13; Gazzolo, "Charles Abrams," quote at 178; Bernard Botein, "Charles Abrams," reprinted from The Association of the Bar of the City of New York, *Memorial Book*, 1970, quote at 1, reel 1, AP; "ASPO Medal Award to Charles Abrams," no date or page numbers given, reel 11, ibid.

27. Abrams to Julia J. Pugliese, February 23, 1954, reel 7, AP.

28. Data concerning contemporary housing policies are discussed in Kevin Fox Gotham, "Blind Faith in the Free Market: Urban Poverty, Residential Segregation, and Federal Housing Retrenchment, 1970–1995," *Sociological Inquiry* 68, no. 1 (February 1998), 1–31.

29. Abrams, "Robert Moses vs. 'Robert Moses,' " quote at 1.

30. Abrams, *City is the Frontier*, 204.

Bibliography

Interviews and Personal Correspondence

Abby Abrams, letter to author, July 28, 1996 and telephone interviews by
  author, May 13 and July 10, 1998
Judy Abrams, letters to author, February 21 and August 2, 1996
Lois Dean, letters to author, April 15, April 20, and April 28, 1998
Robert Kolodny, telephone interview by author, May 18, 1998
Lloyd Rodwin, interview by author, Cambridge, Massachusetts, October 12,
  1994
Hans B. C. Spiegel, letters to author, April 19, April 21, and April 26, 1998
Walter Thabit, telephone interview by author, May 18, 1998 and letter to
  author, May 19, 1998

Manuscript Collections

Archives of American Art: Ruth Abrams Papers
Columbia University: Edith Elmer Wood Papers
Cornell University: Charles Abrams Papers and Microfilms; Warren J.
  Vinton Papers

Georgetown University: Robert F. Wagner Papers

John F. Kennedy Presidential Library: Housing and Home Finance Agency Microfilms; Lee White Files; White House Subject Files

LaGuardia and Wagner Archives, LaGuardia Community College: Fiorello H. LaGuardia Papers; New York City Housing Authority Records

Library of Congress: William O. Douglas Papers; National Association for the Advancement of Colored People Papers

New-York Historical Society: Bernard Botein Papers

New York Public Library: V. F. Calverton Papers

Oral History Collection, Columbia University, Reminiscences of: Charles Abrams; Louis Pink

Oral History Program, John F. Kennedy Presidential Library, Recorded interviews of: Burke Marshall; Norbert A. Schlei; Lee White

State Historical Society of Wisconsin: Lawndale Community Conference Recordings and Transcripts

New York State Human Rights Commission: New York State Commission Against Discrimination Records

Social Welfare History Archives, University of Minnesota: United Neighborhood Houses Papers

University of California at Berkeley: Catherine Krouse Bauer Wurster Papers

University of Pennsylvania: Lewis Mumford Papers

Yale University Library: Alvin Saunders Johnson Papers

Newspapers Consulted

Amsterdam News
Brooklyn Daily Eagle
Christian Science Monitor
New York Age
New York Herald Tribune
New York Post
New York Times

Government Publications

New York City Housing Authority. *First Houses.* New York: New York City Housing Authority, 1935.

————. *Report to His Honor Fiorello H. LaGuardia, Mayor of the City of New York, by the New York City Housing Authority, Pursuant to Article Five of the State*

Housing Law, on Its Investigation and Public Hearings on Living and Housing Conditions in the City of New York. January 25, 1937. Leg. Doc. 85.

———. *Must We Have Slums?.* New York: New York City Housing Authority, 1937.

———. *Toward the End To Be Achieved.* New York: New York City Housing Authority, 1937.

———. *Twenty-Five Years of Public Housing, 1935–1960.* New York: New York City Housing Authority, 1960.

New York Legislature. *Joint Committee of the Senate and Assembly Appointed to Investigate the Affairs of Life Insurance Companies.* 1906. A. Doc. 41.

———. *Report to the Legislature of the Temporary Commission to Examine and Revise the Tenement House Law.* February 4, 1929. Leg. Doc. 54.

———. *Report of the Sub-Committee of the Joint Legislative Committee to Recodify the Multiple Dwelling Law.* February 1, 1947. Leg. Doc. 47.

New York Legislature. Assembly. *Report of the Select Committee Appointed to Examine Into the Condition of Tenant Houses in New York and Brooklyn.* March 9, 1857. A. Doc. 205.

———. *Report of the Committee on Public Health, Medical Colleges and Societies, Relative to the Condition of Tenement Houses in the Cities of New York and Brooklyn.* March 8, 1867. A. Doc. 156.

———. *Report of the Tenement House Commission.* January 17, 1895. A. Doc. 37.

———. *Report of the Tenement-House Commission of 1900.* February 25, 1901. A. Doc. 76.

New York Legislature. Senate. *Report of the Tenement House Commission.* February 17, 1885. S. Doc. 36.

———. *Report on the Tenement-House Problem.* January 13, 1888. S. Doc. 16.

New York State Board of Housing. *Reports.* February 1928–March 1937.

New York State Commission Against Discrimination. *Reports of Progress.* 1955–1958.

New York State Tenement House Committee of 1894. *Report.* Albany: n.p., 1895.

U.S. Congress. Congressional Record. Washington, D.C.: Government Printing Office, July 1932–February 1970.

———. *Hearings Before the Temporary National Economic Committee.* 76th Cong., 1st sess., 1939.

———. Temporary National Economic Committee. *Monograph No. 8: Toward More Housing.* Washington, D.C., 1940.

———. *Hearings Before the Joint Committee on the Economic Report (Anti-Inflation Program as Recommended in the President's Message of November 17, 1947).* 80th Cong., 1st sess., 1947.

U.S. Congress. House. *Hearings Before a Subcommittee of the Committee on*

318   BIBLIOGRAPHY

Banking and Currency on H.R. 7620 (Creation of a System of Federal Home Loan Banks. 72d Cong., 1st sess., 1932.

———. *Creation of Not Less Than 8 and Not More Than 12 Federal Home Loan Banks.* 72d Cong., 1st sess., 1932. H. Rept. 1418.

———. *Loans to Home Owners.* 73d Cong., 1st sess., 1933. H. Rept. 55.

———. *Hearings Before the Committee on Banking and Currency on H.R. 9620 (National Housing Act).* 73d Cong., 2d sess., 1934.

———. *National Housing Act.* 73d Cong., 2d sess., 1934. H. Rept. 1922.

———. *General Interim Report of the House Select Committee on Lobbying Activities.* 81st Cong., 2d sess., 1950. H. Rept. 3138.

———. *Hearings Before the Select Committee on Lobbying Activities (Housing Lobby).* 81st Cong., 2d sess., 1950.

———. *U.S. Savings and Loan League.* 81st Cong., 2d sess., 1950. H. Rept. 3139.

———. *Report and Recommendations on Federal Lobbying Act.* 81st Cong. 2d sess., 1951. H. Rept. 3239.

———. *Hearing Before the Committee on Banking and Currency (Interim Report on HUD Investigation of Low- and Moderate-Income Housing Programs).* 92d Cong., 1st sess., 1971.

———. Subcommittee on Housing and Community Development of the Committee on Banking, Currency and Housing. *Evolution of Role of the Federal Government in Housing and Community Development.* 94th Cong., 1st sess., 1975. Committee Print.

U.S. Congress. Senate. *Hearings Before a Subcommittee of the Committee of Banking and Currency on S. 1317 (Home Owners' Loan Act).* 73d Cong., 1st sess., 1933.

———. *The Home Owners' Loan Corporation.* 73d Cong., 1st sess., 1933. S. Doc. 74.

———. *Hearings Before the Committee on Banking and Currency on S. 3603 (National Housing Act).* 73d Cong., 2d sess., 1934.

———. *Hearings Before the Committee on Education and Labor on S. 1685 (To Create a United States Housing Authority).* 75th Cong., 1st sess., 1937.

———. *Monograph No. 26: Economic Power and Political Pressure.* Washington, D.C., 1941.

———. *Hearings Before the Subcommittee on Housing and Urban Redevelopment of the Special Committee on Post-War Economic Policy and Planning.* 79th Cong., 1st sess., 1945.

———. *Hearings Before the Committee on Banking and Currency on S. 1592.* 79th Cong., 1st sess., 1945.

———. *Hearings Before the Committee on Banking and Currency on S. 287, S. 866, S. 701, S. 801, S. 802, S. 803, and S. 804 (Bills Pertaining to National*

Housing). 8oth Cong., 1st sess., 1947.

———. *Hearing Before the Committee on Banking and Currency on S. 2889, S. 2938, and S. 2949 (Bills to Expand and Extend Title III, Servicemen's Readjustment Act of 1944, National Housing Act, and Housing Act of 1949)*. 83d Cong., 2d sess., 1954.

———. *Hearings Before the Subcommittee on Housing and Urban Affairs of the Committee on Banking and Currency on Proposed Housing Legislation for 1967*. 90th Cong., 1st sess., 1967.

———. *Housing and Redevelopment Act of 1967*. 90th Cong., 1st sess., 1967. S. Rept. 809.

Charles Abrams: Select Publications

A complete bibliography of Abrams' works can be found in O. H. Koenigsberger, S. Groak, and B. Bernstein, eds. *The Work of Charles Abrams: Housing and Urban Renewal in the USA and the Third World* (New York: Pergamon Press, 1980), 257–264. Only Abrams' books and most important articles are listed below.

"Taxation and Land." *Real Estate News* 19, no. 3 (March 1938), 87, 102–103.

"Slum Clearance or Vacant Land Development?." *Shelter* 3, no. 7 (February 1939), 23–24.

Revolution in Land. New York: Harper & Row, 1939.

"Government and Housing." *The Nation*, October 21, 1944, 498.

"The Walls of Stuyvesant Town." *The Nation*, March 24, 1945, 328–330.

"The Subsidy and Housing." *Journal of Land & Public Utility Economics* 22, no. 2 (May 1946), 131–139.

"Homeless America: Part I. Illusions About Housing." *The Nation*, December 21, 1946, 723–725.

"Homeless America: Part II. Bailing Out the Builders." *The Nation*, December 28, 1946, 753–755.

The Future of Housing. New York: Harper & Row, 1946.

"Homeless America: Part III. A Workable Housing Program." *The Nation*, January 4, 1947, 15–16.

"Home for Aryans Only." *Commentary*, May 1947, 421–422.

"Race Bias in Housing: The Great Hypocrisy, Part I." *The Nation*, July 19, 1947, 67–69.

"Race Bias in Housing: Will Interracial Housing Work?, Part II." *The Nation*, August 2, 1947, 122–124.

"Race Bias in Housing: Our Chance for Democratic Housing, Part III." *The Nation*, August 16, 1947, 160–162.

Race Bias in Housing. New York: American Civil Liberties Union, 1947.

"The Segregation Threat in Housing." *Commentary*, February 1949, 123–131.

"Stuyvesant Town's Threat to Our Liberties." *Commentary*, November 1949, 426–433.

"Human Rights in Slum Clearance." *Survey* 86, no. 1 (January 1950), 27–28.

"The New 'Gresham's Law of Neighborhoods'–Fact or Fiction." *The Appraisal Journal* 10, no. 8 (July 1951), 324–328.

"The Time Bomb That Exploded in Cicero." *Commentary*, November 1951, 407–414.

Forbidden Neighbors: A Study of Prejudice in Housing. 1955. Reprint, Port Washington, New York: Kennikat Press, 1971.

"Rise of Intolerance over the World." *American Journal of Economics and Sociology* 18, no. 4 (July 1959), 352.

Man's Struggle for Shelter in an Urbanizing World. Cambridge: MIT Press, 1964.

The City is the Frontier. New York: Harper & Row, 1965.

"The Housing Problem and the Negro." *Daedalus* 95, no. 1 (Winter 1966), 64–76.

"Emerging Social Problems in an Urbanizing World." *Ekistics* 24, no. 145 (December 1967), 457–461.

Home Ownership for the Poor. Rev. ed. New York: Praeger, 1970.

The Language of Cities: A Glossary of Terms. New York: Viking, 1971.

Books

Alchon, Guy. *The Invisible Hand of Planning: Capitalism, Social Science, and the State in the 1920s.* Princeton: Princeton University Press, 1985.

Alfred, Helen L. *Municipal Housing.* New York: League for Industrial Democracy, 1932.

Amenta, Edwin. *Bold Relief: Institutional Politics and the Origins of Modern American Social Policy.* Princeton: Princeton University Press, 1998.

Anderson, Martin. *The Federal Bulldozer: A Critical Analysis of Urban Renewal, 1949–1962.* Cambridge: MIT Press, 1964.

Aronovici, Carol. *Housing the Masses.* New York: John Wiley & Sons, 1939.

Auerbach, Jerold S. *Unequal Justice: Lawyers and Social Change in Modern America.* New York: Oxford University Press, 1976.

Babcock, Frederick M. *The Valuation of Real Estate.* New York: McGraw-Hill, 1932.

Banfield, Edward C. *The Unheavenly City Revisited.* Boston: Little, Brown, 1974.

Barth, Ernest A. T. and L. K. Northwood. *Urban Desegregation: Negro Pioneers and Their White Neighbors.* Seattle: University of Washington Press, 1965.

Bauer, Catherine. *Modern Housing.* Boston: Houghton Mifflin, 1934.

Bauman, John F. *Public Housing, Race, and Renewal: Urban Planning in Philadelphia, 1920–1974.* Philadelphia: Temple University Press, 1987.

Bellush, Jewel and Murray Hausknecht, eds. *Urban Renewal: People, Politics, and Planning.* Garden City, New York: Doubleday, 1967.

Berle, Jr., Adolf A. and Gardiner C. Means. *The Modern Corporation and Private Property.* New York: Macmillan, 1932.

Bloom, Alexander. *Prodigal Sons: The New York Intellectuals and Their World.* New York: Oxford University Press, 1986.

Bodfish, Morton. *History of Building of Loan in the United States.* Chicago: U.S. Building and Loan League, 1931.

Bodnar, John. *The Transplanted: A History of Immigrants in Urban America.* Bloomington: Indiana University Press, 1985.

Boyer, M. Christine. *Dreaming the Rational City: The Myth of American City Planning.* Cambridge: MIT Press, 1983.

Brauer, Carl M. *John F. Kennedy and the Second Reconstruction.* New York: Columbia University Press, 1977.

Brinkley, Alan. *The End of Reform: New Deal Liberalism in Recession and War.* New York: Knopf, 1995.

Buenker, John D. *Urban Liberalism and Progressive Reform.* New York: Charles Scribner's Sons, 1973.

Bulmer, Martin. *The Chicago School of Sociology: Institutionalization, Diversity, and the Rise of Sociological Research.* Chicago: University of Chicago Press, 1984.

Burk, Robert F. *The Corporate State and the Broker State: The DuPonts and American National Politics, 1925–1940.* Cambridge: Harvard University Press, 1990.

Caro, Robert A. *The Power Broker: Robert Moses and the Fall of New York.* New York: Random House, 1974.

Cherry, Gordon E., ed. *Shaping an Urban World.* New York: St. Martin's, 1980.

Colean, Miles L. *Renewing Our Cities.* New York: Twentieth Century Fund, 1953.

———. *A Backward Glance: An Oral History.* Washington, D.C.: Mortgage Bankers Association of America, 1975.

Collins, Robert. *The Business Response to Keynes, 1929–1964.* New York: Columbia University Press, 1981.

Danielson, Michael. *The Politics of Exclusion.* New York: Columbia University Press, 1976.

Davies, Pearl Janet. *Real Estate in American History.* Washington, D.C.: Public Affairs Press, 1958.

Davies, Richard O. *Housing Reform During the Truman Administration.* Columbia, Missouri: University of Missouri Press, 1966.

Dawley, Alan. *Struggles for Justice: Social Responsibility and the Liberal State.* Cambridge: Harvard University Press, 1991.

Dean, John. *Home Ownership: Is It Sound?.* New York: Harper & Row, 1945.

DeForest, Robert W. and Lawrence Veiller, eds. *The Tenement House Problem.* 2 vols. 1903. Reprint, New York: Arno Press, 1971.

Duhl, Leonard J. ed. *The Urban Condition: People and Policy in the Metropolis.* New York: Basic Books, 1963.

Dyckman, John W. and Reginald R. Isaacs. *Capital Requirements for Urban Development and Renewal.* New York: McGraw-Hill, 1961.

Ebenstein, William. *The Law of Public Housing.* Madison: University of Wisconsin Press, 1940.

Eccles, Marriner. *Beckoning Frontiers: Public and Personal Recollections.* New York: Knopf, 1951.

Eichelberger, Clark M. *U.N.: The First Twenty Years.* New York: Harper & Row, 1965.

Evans, Peter B., Dietrich Rueschemeyer, and Theda Skocpol, eds. *Bringing the State Back In.* New York: Cambridge University Press, 1985.

Ewalt, Josephine Hedges. *A Business Reborn: The Savings and Loan Story, 1930–1960.* Chicago: American Savings and Loan Institute Press, 1962.

Fairbanks, Robert B. *Making Better Citizens: Housing Reform and the Community Development Strategy in Cincinnati, 1890–1960.* Urbana: University of Illinois Press, 1988.

Fairfield, John. *The Mysteries of the Great City: The Politics of Urban Design, 1877–1937.* Columbus: Ohio State University Press, 1993.

Fisher, Robert Moore. *Twenty Years of Public Housing.* New York: Harper & Row, 1959.

Ford, James. *Slums and Housing.* 2 vols. Cambridge: Harvard University Press, 1936.

Fraser, Steve and Gary Gerstle, eds. *The Rise and Fall of the New Deal Order, 1930–1980.* Princeton: Princeton University Press, 1989.

Freedman, Leonard. *Public Housing: The Politics of Poverty.* New York: Holt, Rinehart & Winston, 1969.

Friedman, Lawrence M. *Government and Slum Housing.* 1968. Reprint, New York: Arno Press, 1978.

Galbraith, John Kenneth. *American Capitalism: The Concept of Countervailing Power.* Boston: Houghton Mifflin, 1952.

Gelfand, Mark. *A Nation of Cities: The Federal Government and Urban America.* New York: Oxford University Press, 1975.

George, Henry. *Progress and Poverty.* New York: D. Appleton & Company, 1882.

Gordon, Colin. *New Deals: Business, Labor, and Politics in America, 1920–1935.* New York: Cambridge University Press, 1994.

Graham, Hugh Davis. *The Civil Rights Era: Origins and Development of National Policy.* New York: Oxford University Press, 1990.

Graham, Jr., Otis L. *Toward a Planned Society: From Roosevelt to Nixon.* New York: Oxford University Press, 1976.

Grebler, Leo, David M. Blank, and Louis Winnick. *Capital Formation in Residential Real Estate.* Princeton: Princeton University Press, 1956.

Greenberg, Jack. *Race Relations and American Law.* New York: Columbia University Press, 1959.

Haskell, Thomas. *The Emergence of Professional Social Science: The American Social Science Association and the Nineteenth-Century Crisis of Authority.* Chicago: University of Illinois Press, 1977.

Hawley, Ellis W. *The New Deal and the Problem of Monopoly.* Princeton: Princeton University Press, 1966.

Hays, Arthur Garfield. *City Lawyer: The Autobiography of a Law Practice.* New York: Simon & Schuster, 1942.

Hays, R. Allen. *The Federal Government and Urban Housing: Ideology and Change in Public Policy.* Albany: SUNY Press, 1985.

Helper, Rose. *Racial Policies and Practices of Real Estate Brokers.* Minneapolis: University of Minnesota Press, 1969.

Higbee, Jay Anders. *Development and Administration of the New York State Law Against Discrimination.* University, Alabama: University of Alabama Press, 1966.

Hirsch, Arnold. *Making the Second Ghetto: Race and Housing in Chicago, 1940–1960.* New York: Cambridge University Press, 1983.

Howe, Irving. *World of Our Fathers: The Journey of the East European Jews to America and the Life They Found and Made.* New York: Simon & Schuster, 1976.

Huthmacher, J. Joseph. *Senator Robert F. Wagner and the Rise of Urban Liberalism.* New York: Atheneum, 1968.

Ickes, Harold L. *Back to Work: The Story of PWA.* New York: Macmillan, 1935.

Ingalls, Robert. *Herbert H. Lehman and New York's Little New Deal.* New York: New York University Press, 1975.

Jackson, Anthony. *A Place Called Home: A History of Low-Cost Housing in Manhattan.* Cambridge: MIT Press, 1976.

Jackson, Kenneth T. *Crabgrass Frontier: The Suburbanization of the United States.* New York: Oxford University Press, 1985.

Jacobs, Jane. *The Death and Life of Great American Cities.* New York: Random House, 1961.

Jacoby, Russell. *The Last Intellectuals: American Culture in the Age of Academe.* New York: Basic Books, 1987.

James, Marquis. *Metropolitan Life: A Study in Business Growth.* New York: Viking, 1947.

Karl, Barry D. *Executive Reorganization and Reform in the New Deal: The Genesis of Administrative Management, 1900–1939.* Cambridge: Harvard University Press, 1963.

———. *Charles E. Merriam and the Study of Politics.* Chicago: University of Chicago Press, 1974.

Keith, Nathaniel S. *Politics and the Housing Crisis Since 1930.* New York: Universe Books, 1973.

Kessner, Thomas. *Fiorello H. LaGuardia and the Making of Modern New York.* New York: Penguin, 1989.

Keynes, John Maynard. *General Theory of Employment, Interest and Money.* New York: Harcourt, Brace, 1936.

Kingdon, John W. *Agendas, Alternatives, and Public Policies.* Boston: Little, Brown, 1984.

Kloppenberg, James T. *Uncertain Victory: Social Democracy and Progressivism in European and American Thought, 1870–1920.* New York: Oxford University Press, 1988.

Koolhaas, Rem, and Bruce Mau. *Small, Medium, Large, Extra-Large: Office for Metropolitan Architecture, Rem Koolhaas and Bruce Mau.* Edited by Jennifer Sigler. New York: Monacelli Press, 1995.

Krueckeberg, Donald A., ed. *The American Planner: Biographies and Recollections.* New York: Methuen, 1983.

Lubove, Roy. *The Progressives and the Slums: Tenement House Reform in New York City, 1890–1917.* Pittsburgh: University of Pittsburgh Press, 1962.

Marvell, Thomas B. *The Federal Home Loan Bank Board.* New York: Praeger, 1969.

Massey, Douglas S. and Nancy S. Denton. *American Apartheid: Segregation and the Making of the Underclass.* Cambridge: Harvard University Press, 1993.

McQuaid, Kim. *Uneasy Partners: Big Business in American Politics, 1945–1990.* Baltimore: Johns Hopkins University Press, 1994.

Meyerson, Martin and Edward C. Banfield. *Politics, Planning, and the Public Interest: The Case of Public Housing in Chicago.* New York: Free Press, 1955.

Miller, Donald. *Lewis Mumford: A Life.* New York: Weidenfeld & Nicolson, 1989.

Mitchell, Jerry, ed. *Public Authorities and Public Policy: The Business of Government.* New York: Greenwood Press, 1992.

Mollenkopf, John H. *The Contested City.* Princeton: Princeton University Press, 1983.

Moses, Robert. *Public Works: A Dangerous Trade*. New York: McGraw-Hill, 1970.

Mumford, Lewis. *The Culture of Cities*. New York: Harcourt, Brace, 1938.

———. *Sketches from Life: The Autobiography of Lewis Mumford*. New York: Dial Press, 1982.

Park, Robert, Ernest W. Burgess, and Roderick D. McKenzic. *The City*. Chicago: University of Chicago Press, 1925.

Peterson, Paul E. *City Limits*. Chicago: University of Chicago Press, 1981.

Philpott, Thomas Lee. *The Slum and the Ghetto: Neighborhood Deterioration and Middle-Class Reform, Chicago, 1880–1930*. New York: Oxford University Press, 1978.

Pink, Louis H. *The New Day in Housing*. New York: John Day, 1928.

Plunz, Richard. *A History of Housing in New York City: Dwelling Type and Social Change in the American Metropolis*. New York: Columbia University Press, 1990.

Post, Langdon W. *The Challenge of Housing*. New York: Farrar & Rinehart, 1938.

Rabkin, Jeremy. *Judicial Compulsions: How Public Law Distorts Public Policy*. New York: Basic Books, 1987.

Radford, Gail. *Modern Housing for America: Policy Struggles in the New Deal Era*. Chicago: Chicago University Press, 1996.

Riis, Jacob A. *The Battle With the Slum*. 1902. Reprint, Montclair, New Jersey: Patterson Smith, 1969.

Rodgers, Daniel T. *Atlantic Crossings: Social Politics in a Progressive Age*. Cambridge: Harvard University Press, 1998.

Rutkoff, Peter M. and William B. Scott. *New School: A History of the New School for Social Research*. New York: Free Press, 1986.

Saltman, Juliet. *Open Housing: Dynamics of a Social Movement*. New York: Praeger, 1978.

Schaffter, Dorothy. *State Housing Agencies*. New York: Columbia University Press, 1942.

Schon, Donald A. *The Reflective Practitioner: How Professionals Think in Action*. New York: Basic Books, 1983.

Schultz, Stanley K. *Constructing Urban Culture: American Cities and City Planning, 1800–1920*. Philadelphia: Temple University Press, 1989.

Schwartz, Joel. *The New York Approach: Robert Moses, Urban Liberals, and Redevelopment of the Inner City*. Columbus: Ohio State University Press, 1993.

Schwarz, Jordan A. *The New Dealers: Power Politics in the Age of Roosevelt*. New York: Knopf, 1993.

Simkhovitch, Mary Kingsbury. *Here Is God's Plenty: Reflections on American Social Advance*. New York: Harper & Row, 1949.

Simon, Arthur. *Stuyvesant Town, U.S.A.: Pattern for Two Americas.* New York: New York University Press, 1970.

Skowronek, Stephen. *Building a New American State: The Expansion of National Administrative Capacities, 1877–1922.* New York: Cambridge University Press, 1982.

Stein, Maurice. *The Eclipse of Community: An Interpretation of American Studies.* 2d ed. Princeton University Press, 1972.

Straus, Nathan. *The Seven Myths of Housing.* New York: Knopf, 1944.

Teaford, Jon C. *The Rough Road to Renaissance: Urban Revitalization in America, 1940–1985.* Baltimore: Johns Hopkins University Press, 1990.

Vose, Clement. *Caucasians Only: The Supreme Court, the NAACP, and the Restrictive Covenant Cases.* Berkeley and Los Angeles: University of California Press, 1959.

Walker, Mabel. *Urban Blight and Slums.* Cambridge: Harvard University Press, 1938.

Ware, Caroline. *Greenwich Village, 1920–1930.* 1935. Reprint, New York: Harper & Row, 1965.

Weir, Margaret, Ann Shola Orloff, and Theda Skocpol, eds. *The Politics of Social Policy in the United States.* Princeton: Princeton University Press, 1988.

Weiss, Marc A. *The Rise of the Community Builders: The American Real Estate Industry and Urban Land Planning.* New York: Columbia University Press, 1987.

Wilson, James Q. ed. *Urban Renewal: The Record and the Controversy.* Cambridge: MIT Press, 1966.

Wilson, William H. *The City Beautiful Movement.* Baltimore: Johns Hopkins University Press, 1989.

Wood, Edith Elmer. *Slums and Blighted Areas in the United States.* 1934. Reprint, College Park, Maryland: McGrath Publishing, 1969.

Wright, Gwendolyn. *Building the American Dream: A Social History of Housing in America.* Cambridge, Massachusetts: MIT Press, 1981.

Articles

Anderson, Martin. "Fiasco of Urban Renewal." *Harvard Business Review* 43, no. 1 (January–February 1965), 6–21.

Ascher, Charles S. "The Puzzle of Public Housing." *Survey* 70, no. 8 (August 1934), 243–248.

Babcock, Frederick M. "Influence of the Federal Housing Administration on Mortgage Lending Policy." *Journal of Land & Public Utility Economics* 15, no. 1 (February 1939), 1–5.

Bauer, Catherine. "Slum Clearance or Housing." *The Nation,* December 27, 1933, 730–731.

———. "The Dreary Deadlock of Public Housing." *Architectural Forum* 106, no. 5 (May 1957), 140–142, 219, 221.

Biles, Roger. "Nathan Straus and the Failure of U.S. Public Housing, 1937–1942." *The Historian* 53, no. 1 (Autumn 1990), 37–44.

Birch, Eugenie Ladner and Deborah S. Gardner. "The Seven-Percent Solution: A Review of Philanthropic Housing, 1870–1910." *Journal of Urban History* 7, no. 4 (August 1981), 403–438.

Bodfish, Morton. "Toward an Understanding of the Federal Home Loan Bank System." *Journal of Land & Public Utility Economics* 15, no. 4 (November 1939), 416–437.

Bohn, Ernest J. "Housing As a Political Problem." *Law and Contemporary Problems* 1, no. 2 (March 1934), 176–184.

Boyd, Jr., John Taylor. "Rebuilding Blighted Districts." *Architectural Forum* 56, no. 3 (March 1932), 295–298.

Brown, Lewis H. "Using Private Business Agencies to Achieve Public Goals in the Postwar World." *American Economic Review* 33, Supplement, pt. 2 (March 1943), 71–81.

Brudno, Ezra S. "The Emigrant Jews at Home." *World's Work* 7, no. 4 (February 1904), 4471–4479.

———. "The Russian Jew Americanized." *World's Work* 7, no. 5 (March 1904), 4555–4567.

Caldwell, Lyton K. "The Role of the Technical Expert." *Annals of the American Academy of Political and Social Science* 323 (May 1959), 91–99.

Cam, Gilbert A. "United States Government Activity in Low-Cost Housing, 1932–1938." *Journal of Political Economy* 47, no. 3 (June 1939), 357–378.

Chase, Stuart. "The Case Against Home Ownership." *Survey Graphic* 27, no. 5 (May 1938), 261–267.

"Cities and the Single Girl." *Newsweek,* November 15, 1965, 120.

"City Planning: Battle of the Approach." *Fortune,* November 1943, 164–168, 222, 224, 226, 228, 230, 234.

Crane, Jacob. "Huts and Houses in the Tropics." *Unasylva* 3, no. 3 (May-June 1949), 99–105.

Dean, John P. "Only Caucasian: A Study of Race Covenants." *Journal of Land & Public Utility Economics* 23, no. 4 (November 1947), 428–432.

Desmond, Thomas C. "Blighted Areas Get a New Chance." *National Municipal Review* 30, no. 11 (November 1941), 629–632.

Downs, Anthony. "The Successes and Failures of Federal Housing Policy." *The Public Interest,* no. 34 (Winter 1974), 124–145.

"The Dreary Deadlock of Public Housing–How to Break It." *Architectural Forum* 106, no. 6 (June 1957), 218.

Dyckman, John W. "National Planning for Urban Renewal: The Paper Moon in the Cardboard Sky." *Journal of the American Institute of Planners* 26, no. 1 (February 1960), 49–59.

Ecker, Frederick H. "Own Your Own Home?." *Review of Reviews*, February 1932, 30–32.

Ely, Richard T. "Research in Land and Public Utility Economics." *Journal of Land and Public Utility Economics* 1, no. 1 (January 1925), 1–6.

Fahey, John H. "Competition and Mortgage Rates." *Journal of Land & Public Utility Economics* 15, no. 2 (May 1939), 150–154.

"Finding the Expert." *United Nations Review* 5, no. 1 (July 1958), 33–34.

Flanagan, Richard M. "The Housing Act of 1954: The Sea Change in National Urban Policy." *Urban Affairs Review* 33, no. 2 (November 1997), 265–286.

Foard Ashley A. and Hilbert Fefferman. "Federal Urban Renewal Legislation." *Law and Contemporary Problems* 25, no. 4 (Autumn 1960), 635–684.

Foley, Jr., E. H. "Legal Aspects of Low-Rent Housing in New York." *Fordham Law Review* 6, no. 1 (January 1937), 1–17.

Ford, James. "The Enforcement of Housing Legislation." *Political Science Quarterly* 42, no. 4 (December 1927), 549–560.

Fox, Annette Baker. "The Local Housing Authority and the Municipal Government." *Journal of Land and Public Utility Economics* 7, no. 3 (August 1941), 280–290.

Frank, Jerome. "Why Not a Clinical Lawyer-School?." *University of Pennsylvania Law Review* 81, no. 8 (June 1933), 907–923.

Genevro, Rosalie. "Site Selection and the New York City Housing Authority, 1934–1939." *Journal of Urban History* 12, no. 4 (August 1986), 334–352.

Gotham, Kevin Fox. "Blind Faith in the Free Market: Urban Poverty, Residential Segregation, and Federal Housing Retrenchment, 1970–1995." *Sociological Inquiry* 68, no. 1 (February 1998), 1–31.

Gould, F. H. "Special Municipal Corporations." *American Political Science Review* 14, no. 2 (May 1920), 286–291.

Graham, Hugh Davis. "The Stunted Career of Policy History: A Critique and an Agenda." *Journal of Policy History* 15, no. 2 (Spring 1993), 15–37.

Groner, Isaac N. and David M. Helfeld. "Race Discrimination in Housing." *Yale Law Journal* 57, no. 3 (January 1948), 426–458.

Hansen, Alvin H. "Urban Redevelopment." *Survey Graphic* 33, no. 4 (April 1944), 204–205.

Harris, Richard. " 'A Burp in Church': Jacob L. Crane's Vision of Aided Self-Help Housing." *Planning History Studies* 11, no. 1 (1997), 3–16.

————. "The Silence of the Experts: 'Aided Self-Help Housing,' 1939–1954." *Habitat International* 22, no. 22 (1998), 165–189.

Hartman, Chester W. "The Housing of Relocated Families." *Journal of the American Institute of Planners* 30, no. 4 (November 1964), 266–286.

Henderson, A. Scott. " 'Tarred with the Exceptional Image' ": Public Housing and Popular Discourse, 1950–1990." *American Studies* 36, no. 1 (Spring 1995), 31–52.

————. "Charles Abrams and the Problem of a Business Welfare State," *Journal of Policy History* 9, no. 2 (Summer 1997), 211–239.

"The High Cost of Slums." *Review of Reviews*, June 1934, 46–47.

Holden, Arthur C. "Facing Realities in Slum Clearance." *Architectural Record* 71, no. 2 (February 1932), 75–82.

Huchison, Janet. "Building for Babbitt: The State and Suburban Home Ideal." *Journal of Policy History* 9, no. 2 (1997), 184–210.

Jackson, Kenneth. "Race, Ethnicity, and Real Estate Appraisal: The Home Owners Loan Corporation and the Federal Housing Administration." *Journal of Urban History* 6, no. 4 (August 1980), 419–452.

Jones, Edgar L. and Burke David. "Slum Clearance at a Profit." *Atlantic Monthly*, May 1949, 35–38.

Katznelson, Ira and Bruce Pietrykowski. "Rebuilding the American State: Evidence from the 1940s." *Studies in American Political Development* 5, no. 2 (Fall 1991), 301–339.

Kettleborough, Charles. "Special Municipal Corporations." *American Political Science Review* 8, no. 4 (November 1914), 614–621.

Keyserling, Leon. "The Middle Way for America." *The Progressive*, May 1949, 5–9

Lindblom, Charles E. "The Science of 'Muddling Through.' " *Public Administration Review* 19, no. 2 (Spring 1959), 79–88.

Lowi, Theodore J. "The Public Philosophy: Interest-Group Liberalism." *American Political Science Review* 61, no. 1 (March 1967), 5–24.

Marcuse, Peter. "The Beginnings of Public Housing in New York." *Journal of Urban History* 12, no. 4 (August 1986), 353–390.

McClaughry, John. "The Troubled Dream: The Life and Times of Section 235 of the National Housing Act." *Loyola University Law Journal* 6, no. 1 (Winter 1975), 1–45.

McDougal, Myres S. and Addison A. Mueller. "Public Purpose in Public Housing: An Anachronism Reburied." *Yale Law Journal* 52, no. 1 (December 1942), 42–73.

Merriam, Charles. "The Present State of the Study of Politics." *American Political Science Review* 15, no. 2 (May 1921), 181, 184, 185.

Mitrany, David. "The International Technical Assistance Program." *Proceedings of the Academy of Political Science* 25, no. 2 (January 1953), 145–155.

Moses, Robert. "The End of Santa Claus." *Saturday Evening Post*, June 27, 1936, 23, 32, 34, 36–37.

———. "Mr. Moses Dissects the 'Long-Haired Planners.' " *New York Times Magazine*, June 23, 1944, 16–17, 38–39.

———. "Slums and City Planning." *Atlantic Monthly*, January 1945, 63–68.

Mumford, Lewis. "Prefabricated Blight." *The New Yorker*, October 30, 1948, 70–73.

———. "Stuyvesant Town Revisited." *The New Yorker*, November 27, 1948, 61–68.

Nichols, Jr., Philip. "The Meaning of Public Use in the Law of Eminent Domain." *Boston University Law Review* 20, no. 4 (November 1940), 615–641.

Post, Langdon. "My Clash with LaGuardia." *The Nation*, January 29, 1938, 125–126.

"PWA Pledges Action on Low-Cost Housing and Slum Clearance." *American City* 49, no. 9 (September 1934), 99.

Robinson, John I. and Sophie Robinson. "Equivalent Elimination Agreements in Public Housing Projects." *Boston University Law Review* 22, no. 3 (June 1942), 375–389.

Skocpol, Theda and Kenneth Finegold. "State Capacity and Economic Intervention in the Early New Deal." *Political Science Quarterly* 97, no. 2 (Summer 1982), 255–278.

Sparkes, Boyden. "Can the Cities Come Back?." *Saturday Evening Post*, November 4, 1944, 28–29, 42, 44.

Stanton, John. "Town Within a City." *New York Times Magazine*, May 11, 1941, 12, 27.

Taper, Bernard. "A Lover of Cities, I." *The New Yorker*, February 4, 1967, 39–42, 44, 47–48, 50, 55–56, 58, 61–62, 64, 69–70, 72, 75–76, 78, 83–84, 86, 89–91.

———. "A Lover of Cities, II." *The New Yorker*, February 11, 1967, 45–50, 53–54, 56, 59–60, 62, 67–68, 70, 73, 76, 78, 80, 85–86, 88, 90, 92, 95, 97–98, 103–104, 106, 109–110, 112, 115.

Trilling, Diana. "On the Steps of Low Library: Liberalism and the Revolution of the Young." *Commentary*, November 1968, 39–55.

"Urban Redevelopment." *Yale Law Journal* 54, no. 1 (December 1944), 116–140.

Veiller, Lawrence. "Housing Reform Through Legislation." *Annals of the American Academy of Political and Social Science* 51 (January 1914), 68–77.

Wallace, E. S. "Survey of Federal Legislation Affecting Private Home Financing Since 1932." *Law and Contemporary Problems* 5, no. 4 (Autumn 1938), 481–509.

Weaver, Robert C. "Housing in a Democracy." *Annals of the American Academy of Political and Social Science* 244 (March 1946), 95–105.

Weiss, Marc A. "Marketing and Financing Home Ownership: Mortgage Lending and Public Policy in the United States, 1918–1989." *Business and Economic History*, 2d ser., 18 (1989), 109–118.

————. "Richard T. Ely and the Contribution of Economic Research to National Housing Policy, 1920–1940." *Urban Studies* 26, no. 1 (February 1989), 115–126.

Wirth, Louis. "Urbanism as a Way of Life." *American Journal of Sociology* 44, no. 1 (July 1938), 1–24.

Wood, Elizabeth. "Social-Welfare Planning." *Annals of the American Academy of Political and Social Science* 352 (March 1964), 119–128.

Index

Abrams, Abby, 192
Abrams, Abraham, 9, 16–18
Abrams, Charles: on the 608 program scandals, 306*n*18; antidiscrimination ordinance for New York City Council drafted by, 135–138; on appraisal methods for real estate, 266*n*17; birth of, 8, 239*n*3; on Black Power, 221; on the Cain-Bricker Amendment, 154–155; and V. F. Calverton, 34; childhood of, 12–13, 16–18; on the Cold War, 174; on core housing, 183–184; on cremation, 225; on death, 227; on developing countries, 174, 178, 184, 186, 192; *Dorsey v. Stuyvesant Town* argued by, 140–142; on the FHLBS,

102–104; on the FHA, 109–111, 117, 148–149, 156; on Henry George, 93–94; move to Greenwich Village, 32, 33; and Arthur Garfield Hays, 27–29; deteriorating health of, 225–226; on the HOLC, 104–107, 156; on home ownership, 111, 199–200, 203, 208; hostility directed at, 294*n*50; and Housing Act of 1937, 257*n*43; on housing discrimination, 157, 288*n*23, 293*n*47; and the development of a housing movement, 87, 259*n*51; on integration and property values, 156, 287*n*21; on Jane Jacobs, 307*n*22; part-time jobs held by, 18–19; on Fiorello LaGuardia, 79; and the

Abrams, Charles *(continued)*
Lawndale Community Conference, 216–217; legal training
and career of, 26, 29; on lobbies, 113–115; marriage to Ruth
Davidson, 30; on "mixed" and
"blurred" economies, 116; on
Robert Moses, 20, 21, 229, 130;
as NCDH president, 167–171;
on the NHOA, 210; *NYCHA v.
Muller* argued by, 72–74; resignation as NYCHA's general
counsel, 79; counsel to
NYCHA's hearings on old law
tenements, 77–78; and the *New
York Post*, 130; as New York
SCAD chairman, 158–166,
288n27; and the New York State
Liberal Party, 159, 160; work on
the New York State Municipal
Housing Authorities Law,
56–58; as the New York State
Rent Administrator, 158; on the
New York State Urban Redevelopment Companies Law,
126–127; *New Yorker* "Profile" of,
8, 16, 215; oral memoir of, 8;
parties given by, 87–88; investigation of Philadelphia's housing
conditions undertaken by,
203–205, 308n28, 308n29,
309n32; on public housing, 71,
199, 200; on public speaking,
26; puns and limericks composed by, 35–36, 44, 226; on
race relations 132, 152; real
estate activities of, 38–40; as a
reflective practitioner, 41–42,
180, 182, 243n36; on restrictive
covenants, 148–151; on security
clearance procedures, 176; on

segregation, 10, 15, 133,
205–206; on self-help housing,
183, 299n27; on slum clearance,
62–63, 81, 198, 201, 304n13;
"slum-ghetto" concept formulated by, 155; on the "perversion"
of social reform, 200–201; moti-
vation as a social reformer, 22;
on "socializing" trends in American industries, 112; on squatting, 184–185; on the student
sit-in at Columbia University
(1968), 219–221; on Stuyvesant
Town, 130–135; on subsidies,
145, 283n55; teaching experiences of, 88–89, 215, 217; theatrical interests of, 34, 242n25;
UN mission to Ghana, 181–183;
UN mission to Singapore,
187–189; UN mission to Turkey,
179–180; on U.S. assistance policies, 190–191; on urban planning, 14, 73, 216, 307n19; on
urban renewal, 195, 196,
197–198; urban studies developed by, 85–87; words coined
by, 42; *see also* Business welfare
state; *The City is the Frontier;
Democracy in Crisis; Forbidden
Neighbors; The Future of Housing;
The Language of Cities; Man's
Struggle for Shelter; Revolution in
Land*
Abrams, Esther, 9
Abrams, Freda, 9, 16
Abrams, Joseph, 9, 23
Abrams, Judy, 192
Abrams, Ralph, 9, 23, 192
Abrams, Ruth Davidson, 29, 227,
240n14; artistic philosophy of,
30; bequest of funds to Grey Art